FAMILY BUSINESS

Family Business

Litigation and the Political Economies of Daily Life in Early Modern France

JULIE HARDWICK

OXFORD
UNIVERSITY PRESS

OXFORD
UNIVERSITY PRESS

Great Clarendon Street, Oxford OX2 6DP

Oxford University Press is a department of the University of Oxford.
It furthers the University's objective of excellence in research, scholarship,
and education by publishing worldwide in

Oxford New York

Auckland Cape Town Dar es Salaam Hong Kong Karachi
Kuala Lumpur Madrid Melbourne Mexico City Nairobi
New Delhi Shanghai Taipei Toronto

With offices in

Argentina Austria Brazil Chile Czech Republic France Greece
Guatemala Hungary Italy Japan Poland Portugal Singapore
South Korea Switzerland Thailand Turkey Ukraine Vietnam

Oxford is a registered trade mark of Oxford University Press
in the UK and in certain other countries

Published in the United States
by Oxford University Press Inc., New York

First published 2009

British Library Cataloguing in Publication Data
Data available

Library of Congress Cataloging in Publication Data
Hardwick, Julie, 1962–
Family business : litigation and the political economies of daily life in early
modern France / Julie Hardwick.
p. cm.
Includes bibliographical references.
ISBN 978–0–19–955807–0
1. Domestic relations courts—France—History. 2. Family—Economic aspects—
France—History. 3. Family-owned business enterprises—France—History. I. Title.
KJV939.H37 2009
330.944'033—dc22 2009013904

Typeset by Laserwords Private Limited, Chennai, India
Printed and bound in the UK
on acid-free paper by the
MPG Books Group, Bodmin and King's Lynn

ISBN 978–0–19–955807–0 (Hbk)

1 3 5 7 9 10 8 6 4 2

Contents

Acknowledgements

Twenty-first-century economies of many kinds made this book possible. The National Endowment for the Humanities provided both a Summer Stipend and a year-long Fellowship. Norman Fiering, then Director of John Carter Brown Library at Brown University, welcomed me for a semester to that collegial and stimulating early modern centre. Texas Christian University and the University of Texas at Austin provided other kinds of financial support. Alan Tully, the chair of the History Department at the University of Texas, gave me a teaching load reduction at a critical point to allow me to reach the finishing line.

Numerous friends and colleagues offered many forms of encouragement, enthusiasm, and engagement with many parts of this project over the years. I discussed aspects of it on many occasions at which I benefited from formal discussion and informal conversation. I have appreciated all their suggestions even when I did not heed them. In particular, I was fortunate to be invited to two engrossing seminars that had profound impacts on the ultimate shape of this book: 'Law, Family and the State in the early modern Atlantic World' hosted by the Institute for Legal Studies at the University of Wisconsin at Madison, and 'In the Maelstrom of the Market: women and the early modern economy' at the Folger Institute in Washington DC. I thank all the participants for the dialogues on those occasions. As I finished the manuscript, Tom Green raised a series of important questions that I valued very much.

At Oxford University Press, Rupert Cousens, Seth Cayley and Melanie Johnstone welcomed and stewarded this project with warm efficiency. I thank my readers for their thoughtfulness.

Much earlier versions of some parts of this book first appeared elsewhere, and I am grateful for permission to include material from the following pieces, often in much modified form: 'Seeking separations: gender and household economies in seventeenth-century France', *French Historical Studies* 21, 1 (Winter 1998); 'Early modern perspectives on the long history of domestic violence: the case of seventeenth-century France', *Journal of Modern History* 78 (March 2006); 'Between state and street: witnesses and the family politics of litigation in early modern France', *Family, Gender, and Law in Early Modern France*, ed. by Suzanne Desan and Jeffrey Merrick (Penn State University Press, 2009).

My writing group at the University of Texas has been a model of collegial camaraderie. Susan Dean-Smith, Martha Newman, and Cyndy Talbot have read numerous more and (usually much) less polished versions of all the pieces of this book in many different forms. I thank them for their intellectual vigour and rigour as well as for their friendship and solidarity.

I did not have any children when I made the initial foray into the archives for what became this book, and I finish it as the mother of two. I have been lucky to navigate the exhilaration as well as the exhaustion of working motherhood in the company of Erika Bsumek, Beth Hedrick, Lori Wallace, and Gretchen Webber. I also thank all the many people whose childcare made my work on this book possible.

I worked on this book through some extended difficult personal circumstances. Chris Adams, Erika Bsumek, Faulkner Fox, Beth Hedrick, Bruce Hunt, Steve Lofgren, Dirk Maxwell, Gunther Peck, Alan Shepard, Lori Wallace, Gretchen Webber, and Andy Weinberg deserve a better reward than this book, but I would not have persisted with it, nor with much else, without them.

Karin Wulf and Martha Newman are in a special gold star category on both personal and professional fronts.

This book is for my family: for Bob Olwell who knows why, and for our daughters, Grace Hardwick Olwell and Rosie Hardwick Olwell, whose company has proved to be the most extraordinary and impossible to articulate pleasure of my life.

Abbreviations

ADLA	Archives Départementales de Loire-Atlantique
ADR	Archives Départementales du Rhône
AML	Archives Municipales de Lyon
ADSA	Archives Départementales de Saône et Loire
Isambert	François Isambert, *Recueil Général des anciennes lois Françaises depuis l'an 420 jusqu'à la Révolution* (Paris, 1829–33)

Introduction: Family Business

On an eventful night in the spring of 1691, Louis Thebaudeau, a shoemaker in the city of Nantes, was asleep alone in a small room off his workshop when he was awoken by a ghost in the shape of his wife, Marie Monnier. He was so astounded that he sunk to his knees to ask forgiveness for his sins. Only after he got back into bed 'all trembling', and the ghost pulled off the blankets and boxed his ears, did he think it was in fact his wife, although she almost never came to his workshop, as they lived in an apartment a few houses away. They slept together. In the morning he presumed she must have left early for work, and thinking the events of the night meant they were 'reconciled' after much previous contestation, went to look for her. To his surprise, Monnier denied that she had been in his room at all: she declared that he must indeed have seen a ghost, so it was the devil he had had sex with, and he ought to be excommunicated for it.[1] Neighbours described this episode and other multi-faceted difficulties in court some months later when Monnier requested a separation of person and property, a step Thebaudeau opposed. The spectre of spousal discord that appears quite literally in this curious story illuminates a reality of many marriages, but the challenges the household faced haunted all pre-modern families.[2]

The *family business* of the Thebaudeau–Monnier household provides one indication of how early modern spouses, families, communities, and the state sought to manage the political economies that underpinned daily life. These economies included a broad range of tangible and intangible resources—law,

[1] ADLA B5843, 31 July 1691. All material referring to this case is drawn from depositions given on this date or depositions taken on 19 July 1691.

[2] The story itself is fascinating. Was Thebaudeau astonished and on his knees at the sight of the ghost, fearful because he had last seen Monnier alive, or grateful because her unexpected death resolved their endless battles? Why would he take such events as evidence of 'reconciliation'? Was the whole event a construct of his mental world, or was she teasing him when she said she had not been there? The depositions suggest the latter, but if so her representations were also quintessential of early modern cultural frameworks. For appearances of ghosts as expressions of social tensions in the early modern world, see, for instance, Laura Gowing, 'The haunting of Susan Lay: servants and mistresses in seventeenth-century England', *Gender and History*, 14, 2 (August 2002), 183–201, and Douglas Winiarski, '"Pale Blewish Lights" and a dead man's groan: tales of the supernatural from eighteenth-century Plymouth, Massachusetts', *William and Mary Quarterly*, 55, 4 (October 1998), 497–530.

borrowing, violence, and marital status among them—that needed to be managed, deployed, or mobilized strategically. Household members, neighbours, and authorities invested enormous energy and effort in the daily negotiation of relationships to manage resources. The business of family life involved relationships that could be intimate (family and neighbours), intermediate (litigant and judge), or distant (governing authority and subject), and the resources in question were the currency of the early modern world these people knew.[3]

This family business was important on its own terms, and because its negotiations had implications for larger processes of the seventeenth century—such as state formation and the market transitions—as matters of daily practice rather than macro-structure. In these seventeenth-century political economies of daily life, the growing use of litigation by households was central. By this process, families came into more frequent contact with the state insomuch as the court system was a part of the state (albeit a very complicated one), and resorted to the authority of the courts as one (although not the only) arbiter of their daily affairs. Courts were primary sites for interaction between spouses, between different households, and between state and subject in a wide range of affairs. These negotiations were not only related to, but in many ways constituted, key elements of the early modern state and economy. Both were in part a product of the ways in which a range of tangible and intangible resources—marriage, property, force—were managed, deployed, and mobilized.

The political economies of daily life were embedded in daily decision-making, negotiation, and conflict between spouses, between neighbours, and between communities and the state. Monnier sold fabric while Thebaudeau worked as a shoemaker, and they relied on borrowing to make ends meet. They funded bread, rent, and many other essentials through credit. Monnier participated independently in these arrangements, and sometimes admonished her lenders not to mention her borrowing to her husband. They argued and fought for years over money, over working habits, and over the location of property. She was fiercely protective of her personal property, especially linen, as well as cash, and he was intent on tracking her use of that personal property. Their decisions over these matters were complicated by a changing macro-economic climate in which market forces increasingly dominated the European economy, leaving many individuals to negotiate rising risk and uncertainty.

Marital status itself was a negotiable resource, as was the availability of the law and the authority of the state. The spouses had accused each other of drunkenness, and each cast sexual slurs on the other. They assessed the performance of each other as spouses. Both Thebaudeau and Monnier had made repeated choices about marital status: to marry their first spouses, to marry each other, and then

[3] Note that early modern meanings of economies and business were distinctive and broader than their modern counterparts. For early modern definitions of economy and business in these ways, see http://dictionary.oed.com.

she to press for separation while he resisted in favour of continuing their conjugal relationship. Their opposing stakes in the future of a marriage that was by every account unsatisfactory on modern terms indicate the significance of marital status.

Neighbours were critical players in all aspects of the economies of daily life. They had seen Thebaudeau hit and kick Monnier, and had tended to her bruises. They had seen her punch him, and draw blood too. Neighbours quizzed each about their behaviour, stepped in on occasion to reprimand or provide aid, and heard secrets that they promised not to tell the other spouse. They noticed when Thebaudeau came home drunk, or when Monnier took linen and clothes out of their apartment to another. Their neighbours—as observers, interveners, lenders, collaborators, nurses, and witnesses—formed judgements critical to the household's viability and reputation. Both spouses and neighbours participated in an economy of information. This economy underlay individual access to credit (would people lend money?), coercion (would people regard the use of force as legitimate or inappropriate?), and court (would people witness?).

Why did Monnier go to court as a solution to her problems? For early modern people, the use of the courts was usually a matter of choice rather than a requirement, but it was a choice they made increasingly to deal with all kinds of issues. Local courts could be called on at the discretion of plaintiffs to broker disputes and negotiations. What individuals and their communities hoped to gain bears examining, but their decisions also created openings for the expansion of the role of the state. The rulers of early modern states, in France and other European countries, desired to regulate family life and to emphasize the convergence of political and familial stability as ways of enhancing the power of the state; they sought to impose some regulations with uneven effect in practice. Yet subjects also increasingly invited states through local courts into family and community life, with regard to matters such as spousal strife, borrowing, or the use of force that had public and commercial as well as domestic implications. Their ability to do so again depended in part on the involvement of neighbours whose testimony was critical to success in lawsuits. Endless rounds of micro-litigation about marriage, borrowing, and the use of force not only reveal how resources were transacted but also illustrate the ways in which households, neighbourhoods, and the local courts contested expectations about how families, economies, and the state could, should, and did work.

PERSPECTIVES: THEMES AND DEBATES

This book explores the mundane but ubiquitous choices and decisions of Louis Thebaudeau and Marie Monnier and other working couples in two seventeenth-century French cities: Lyon and Nantes. The experiences and choices of these families highlight both the social history of families of this milieu, and three central, interrelated, and little-examined aspects of early modern urban life in France: popular uses of the civil legal system, the impacts of borrowing in urban households, and the dynamics of family violence. These issues in turn provide perspectives on the symbiotic relationships between micro- and macro-political economies that were central to some of the largest themes in early modern historiography: the unsteady process of state formation, changing attitudes towards dispute resolution, privacy, and uses of the law, and the emergence of a market economy. In exploring these multi-faceted questions that were at the heart of family business, this book lies at an intersection of a number of historiographies: of working families, of gender and family, of law, of state formation, and of economic history.

First, marriage, as we all know, was a central early modern institution, and from every angle, marital status was a defining feature of life for both men and women in early modern France. Marriage as an institution was experiencing transition as state, church, and communities sought to determine the nature of an appropriate conjugal union. The literature on early modern marriage is dense but fragmented, focusing, for example, on households as sites of religious reformation, political practice, economic productivity, cultural discipline, or social reproduction.[4]

Across this literature, a little examined assumption is that early modern marriages were stable, and broadly encompassed two spouses in lifelong partnership (however short the life due to high mortality rates) working in cooperation, whether side by side or in separate occupations, in a family economy to keep their household afloat. Certainly, despite the promise of the Protestant Reformation to support divorce, women found divorce difficult to obtain in practice in Protestant regions. Even in England, despite the famous equation of the English Reformation with Henry VIII's divorce from Katherine of Aragon, historian Martin Ingram has argued that the ultimate effect of the Reformation debate on divorce was to tighten rather than slacken the bonds of marriage.[5]

This book rather sees marital status as a negotiable resource, and marriage as a process that might be made and remade, not only by mortality but by the decisions and negotiations of either party. Despite the low rate of divorce, remarriage was common: around 25 per cent of all of early modern marriages included at least one spouse who had been married previously, and blended families of step-parents and 'his, hers and our' children were a part of everyday life. Thebaudeau's cot in his workshop illustrates how working men might occasionally or routinely have accommodation separate from their wives (as in

[4] The literature on early modern gender and family issues is now vast. For synthetic overviews that include valuable bibliographies, see Merry Wiesner, *Women and Gender in Early Modern Europe*, 2nd edn. (Cambridge, 2000), and Olwen Hufton, *The Prospect Before Her: A History of Women in Western Europe, 1500–1800* (New York, 1996).

[5] Martin Ingram, *Church Courts, Sex, and Marriage in England, 1570–1640* (Cambridge, 1987), 157.

the case of Parisian journeymen bakers who often lived apart from their wives, or men in rural areas who migrated for part of each year as seasonal workers). Within the life course of a marriage, as this book will show, spouses had many moments of opportunity to contest or renegotiate terms of their relationships. Many, perhaps most, early modern Europeans lived in families in which fluidity rather than stability must have been the keynote, and certainly had neighbours and family members for whom that was true.

Moreover, the definition of marriage itself was in transition in the seventeenth century. The French state, like other European governments, had introduced new national legislation to regulate marriage from the second half of the sixteenth century, requiring parental consent for marriage, whereas the consent of the future bride and groom had previously been the only requirement. New regulations also emphasized that marriages should be publicized rather than permitting private promises to suffice. The state, in its civil courts, gradually took jurisdiction over marriage from the church's ecclesiastical courts. The government too began to mark marriage in new ways, especially in terms of requirements for a paper-trail recorded in parish registers and in marriage contracts.[6] The relationship between these new prescriptions and the experience of marriage itself, however, remains less clear. Much of the regulation focused on the moment of the formation of first marriages or on sexuality rather than on subsequent marriages or the course of marriage itself, and these new laws co-existed with a large body of other laws—customary, Roman, or ecclesiastical—that provided sometimes contrary imperatives.[7]

Second, the symbiotic relationship between individuals, communities, legal systems, and the state in the early modern period is interrogated. We have discovered a great deal about the criminal law system in recent decades, but much less about the uses of the civil courts, although civil cases were far more numerous.[8] Going to court became a far more familiar experience for early modern people than for their ancestors, whether as plaintiffs, defendants, or

[6] Historians have focused on the question of marriage formation as being the critical measure of the impact of the changes, and as a pivot of the state–family relationship. For influential statements about marriage formation as a key indicator of the family–state nexus in France, see Sarah Hanley, 'Engendering the state: family formation and state building in early modern France', *French Historical Studies*, 16, 1 (Spring 1989), and 'Family and state in early modern France: the marriage pact', in Marilyn J. Boxer and Jean H. Quataert (eds.), *Connecting Spheres: Women in the Western World, 1500 to the Present* (Oxford, 1987). For a German example of the relationship between regulation of marriage, sexuality, and state formation, see Ulrike Strasser, *State of Virginity: Gender, Religion, and Politics in an Early Modern Catholic State* (Ann Arbor, 2004).

[7] For the difference in regulation even of subsequent marriages, see Janine Lanza, *From Wives to Widows in Early Modern Paris: Gender, Economy and the Law* (Ashgate, Aldershot, 2007). For the complex interplay of royal legislation, regional customary law, and local practice in relationships to family life and issues about the state, see Julie Hardwick, *The Practice of Patriarchy: Gender and the Politics of Household Authority in Early Modern France* (University Park, PA, 1998).

[8] An important exception is the recent rich work on early modern England which I have found invaluable for comparison, as the following chapters and notes indicate. Hervé Piant, *Une Justice Ordinaire: Justice Civille et Criminelle dans la Prévôté de Vaucouleurs sous l'Ancien Régime* (Rennes,

witnesses, and yet many matters continued to be handled outside the judicial framework. Litigation, however, involved a wide swath of the population, and people such as the urban working men and women of this book were heavy users of the civil system. When they and their peers chose to go to court, they must have expected or at least hoped their local courts would arrive at decisions they would find appropriate—or they would have not bothered to go down that path at all. They became consumers of the legal system, as Daniel Lord Smail has recently argued.[9] Going to court became a key economy to be deployed, managed, and negotiated just like other aspects of life.

This book examines how the members of working households participated in litigation communities that explicitly addressed specific aspects about the political economies of daily life in many different kinds of cases, and implicitly engaged macrocosmic implications such actions raised about a broad range of issues, including the relationship between gender and property, household and state, the proper functioning of the market, and appropriate uses of violence. Litigation communities—composed of plaintiffs, defendants and witnesses, as well as royal prosecutors and judges—coalesced around their participation in the debates about the legal processes that were ubiquitous in urban working communities. The combination of neighbourhood opinion and judges' preferences, as well as jurisdictional rules, created powerful local legal cultures.[10]

One key theme of litigation communities was family politics, a matter that also had implications for community governance and state formation. Households were key sites where political, economic, and cultural patterns and changes were negotiated within families, between families, in communities, and between families and the state. For spouses, communities, and the state in the seventeenth century, marriage as a resource had a multi-valency that encompassed economic as well as political and social roles. Contemporaries recognized these varied qualities. A seventeenth-century notarial manual defined the marriage contract as 'without doubt the most important act of all those made between men, since it serves as the foundation for civil life, for family peace and for the good of the State'. In seventeenth-century state rhetoric, the political stability, economic productivity, and cultural significance of families were recurring themes: families were, to take only three examples, the 'seminaries of the state' and 'the fecund sources from which the strength and greatness of the state derive', or 'the source and origin of civil society . . . in which the natural reverence of children towards

2006), provides a pioneering exploration of dynamics of one local provost's court in eastern France after 1670.

[9] Daniel Lord Smail, *The Consumption of Justice: Emotion, Publicity and Legal Culture in Marseille, 1284–1463* (Ithaca, 2003).

[10] I thank Jay Westbrook for suggestions about local legal cultures. See the discussions in Teresa A. Sullivan, Elizabeth Warren, and Jay Lawrence Westbrook, *As We Forgive our Debtors: Bankruptcy and Consumer Credit in America* (Oxford, 1989), and Teresa A. Sullivan, Elizabeth Warren, and Jay Lawrence Westbrook, *The Fragile Middle Class: America in Debt* (New Haven, 2001).

their parents is the link of the legitimate obedience of subjects towards their sovereign'.[11] If household stability guaranteed economic productivity as well as political order, economic disorder as well as immorality and violations of authority were very threatening. Louis XIV's edict of 1666, for example, offered tax exemptions to fathers of ten or more living children, and linked that form of productivity to political stability. Meanwhile, unpropitious second marriages (in which women disinherited children by gifting property to new husbands) not only affected the children, but 'the distress of good families that follows from such gifts besides quarrels between mothers and their children consequently diminished the strength of the public state'.[12]

These associations meant that the practices by which spouses and communities, inside and outside of the courtroom, negotiated family business had significant implications for the process of state formation. In recent decades, historians have re-thought the dynamics of early modern state formation in efforts to explore what actually happened in the wavering progression of early modern governance whose on-the-ground limitations stood in such stark contrast to the extraordinarily ambitious claims of its rhetoric. From William Beik's nobles in Languedoc working out taxation with Louis XIV, to Steve Hindle's vestrymen administering Elizabethan Poor Laws across the counties of England, to Ulrika Strasser's burghers in Munich regulating sexuality under Emperor Maximilian, this revisionism has transformed our understanding of how states worked.[13] The traditional concept of the state as a matter of institutions or ministers or bureaucrats has been re-made by these elaborations of the complex, multi-tiered, diversely peopled apparatus of early modern states, by the focus on governance and authority as process, and by the recognition that the early modern state was a claim to authority as much as a concrete reality.[14]

[11] 'Recueil de traitez sur le droit public . . . faite par order de Monsieur Colbert,' quoted in Alain Lottin, 'Vie et mort du couple: difficultés conjugales et divorces dans le nord de la France aux dix-septième et dix-huitième siecles', *Dix-Septième Siècle*, **102–103** (1974). Isambert, *Recueil Général*, **18**, 90; Claude Joseph de Ferrière, *La Science Parfaite des notaires ou le parfait notaire* (Paris, 1682; revised edn., Paris, 1741), 251.

[12] Isambert, *Recueil Général*, **16**, 520; The Edict on Second Marriages quoted in Lanza, *From Wives to Widows*; Isambert (ed.), *Recueil Général*, **18**, 90.

[13] William Beik, *Absolutism and Society in Seventeenth-Century France: State Power and Provincial Aristocracy in Languedoc* (Cambridge, 1985); Steve Hindle, *The State and Social Change in Early Modern England* (London, 2001); Strasser, *State of Virginity*.

[14] For a particularly insightful discussion, see Hindle, *State and Social Change*, 17–38. Recent efforts to rethink state-making have emphasized not only the collaborative quality, but the extent to which participation included many social layers from elites downward. See, for instance, Beik, *Society and Absolutism*; Hanley, 'Engendering the state' and 'The family, the state, and the law in seventeenth- and eighteenth-century France: the political ideology of male right versus an early theory of natural rights', *Journal of Modern History*, **78**, 2 (June 2006), 289–332. I have found the formulations in Hindle, *State and Social Change*, Giovanni Levi, *Inheriting Power: The Story of an Exorcist* (Chicago, 1988), and Leslie Pierce, *Morality Tales: Law and Gender in the Ottoman Court of Aintab* (Berkeley, 2003), especially helpful in thinking about the significance of the agency of middling people or lower in shaping large political patterns.

Relationships within households, between households in communities, and between communities and states in the early modern period were constantly negotiated and renegotiated in a process in which law played a vital role. Certainly rulers and theorists of early modern states imagined the role of the state expansively. They sought to appropriate familial governance in part because it was all inclusive as well as for its potency as a broadly disseminated cultural vocabulary. The early modern family became an important subject of scrutiny in both legislation and rhetoric because families were regarded as integral to the economic as well as political strength of the state. But given the limited practical resources of early modern states, however grandiose the rhetoric, authorities wanted to encourage as well as compel families to align themselves with the state. Historians have recently explored the ways in which litigation politicized family life and familiarized politics and could offer litigants—male and female—a powerful tool for critiquing state as well as marital arrangements.[15] Beyond that, however, litigation communities participated in a grassroots debate about families and politics through which assumptions about marriage and the power relations it embodied, both for the couple and as a way of imagining other kinds of relations, were contested and asserted. In repeated and numerous lawsuits in local courts of first instance, local understandings of authority in urban working neighbourhoods were articulated in detail. Individual, family, and neighbourhood decisions about when to choose to invite the state in were important.

These choices made the realities of negotiating the various economies which were critical to family business central in the production of a complex conceptualization of state as well as household authority. While families, communities, and the state had common interests (whether political in households that were stable, economic in households that were productive, or cultural in households that were morally upright), their perspectives on what stability, productivity, or morality involved did not necessarily align perfectly. For spouses, their neighbours, and the state, inherent and potentially evolving tensions existed between these goals. They might not agree on what stability entailed, on how productivity might best be achieved, or what really mattered in terms of morality.

Consequently, the politics of daily life were integral to the early modern state-building process. Men's and women's decisions about choosing to use the legal system, and thereby associating themselves with the authority of the state, depended in part on local courts' willingness to authorize local opinion which encouraged communities to continue using courts for dispute resolution. This symbiotic relationship was fragile in the seventeenth century, as indicated by

[15] On the politics of family litigation of various kinds, see Suzanne Desan, *The Family on Trial in Revolutionary France* (Berkeley, 2004); Sarah Hanley, 'Engendering the state', and 'Social sites of political practice: lawsuits, civil rights, and the separation of powers in domestic and state government, 1500–1800', *American Historical Review*, **102**, 1 (1997), 27–52; and Sarah Maza, *Private Lives and Public Affairs: The Causes Célèbres of Prerevolutionary France* (Berkeley, 1993).

the innumerable riots and rebellions during which working people declined to use institutional means to remedy their grievances. The success or failure of state-making depended in part on the choices of members of working families as well as elites.

Third, the risks and choices that working spouses and their communities faced are essential in our understanding of early modern economic processes. While much of the debate about the timing and nature of that evolution has been associated with macro factors or with elite merchants and entrepreneurs, the real-life decisions made repeatedly every day about issues such as what goods to stock, when to extend credit, under what conditions to borrow money, about when to repay, and about when to go to court to demand repayment, were vital to economic transformation. Without the benefits of hindsight, precariousness and uncertainty characterized working people's experience of economic transformation. Yet despite an extraordinarily vigorous debate about the early modern economy, whether as an intensification of market practices or as transition to capitalism, we know little about the experiences of the people whose daily choices were integral to the patterns that emerged, especially in the French case.[16] Their often perilous paths are critical subjects for enquiry because, as historian Scott Sandage has observed, 'failure pervades the cultural history of capitalism'.[17]

This book focuses in particular on borrowing as an essential factor in domestic and market economies. For working families, commercial and personal survival depended on the creation of credit and resolution of debt. French historians have made elaborate reconstructions of family budgets which almost entirely disregard the role of credit, even while the reality of widespread indebtedness is well known. As Steven Kaplan has pointed out, while historians have learned much about credit on macro levels, we 'have uncovered much less about how it engulfed daily life'.[18] Nothing was more important, however. The management of borrowing

16 For a synthesis of the debates and by omission the relative lack of attention to lived experience, see Robert Duplessis, *Transitions to Capitalism in Early Modern Europe* (Cambridge, 1997), 1–12. A rich literature has looked at the relationships between guilds and a changing economy. See, for instance, two very important statements in Natalie Davis, 'Strikes and salvation in Lyon' in her *Society and Culture in Early Modern France* (Palo Alto, 1975), and James R. Farr, 'On the shop floor: guilds, artisans, and the early modern economy, 1350–1750', *Journal of Early Modern History*, 1, 1 (February 1997). I have found work on economic change in rural areas especially helpful in terms of thinking about the role of individual decision making as well as larger structures. See in particular, Phillip Hoffman, *Growth in a Traditional Society: the French Countryside, 1450–1815* (Princeton, 1996), and Sheilagh Levine, *A Bitter Living: Women, Markets, and Social Capital in Early Modern Germany* (Oxford, 2003).

17 Scott A. Sandage, *Born Losers: A History of Failure in America* (Cambridge, Harvard University Press, 2005), 10.

18 For a typical example of budget calculations that ignore credit/debt, see Daniel Roche, *A History of Everyday Things: The Birth of Consumption in France, 1600–1800* (Cambridge, 2000), 62–72. Kaplan's own work on Parisian bakers in the eighteenth century is very suggestive about the role of debt. See Steven Laurence Kaplan, *The Bakers of Paris and the Bread Question, 1700–1775* (Durham, 1996), esp. 137–51 and 377–99. For early modern England, see Craig Muldrew, *The*

required constant attention, especially in the shifting terrain of the seventeenth century when litigation over debt was the single largest category in court case loads, bankruptcy had become a capital offence, and loans were ubiquitous. This book interrogates the reliance on borrowing and the cultural work that attached positive and negative meanings of borrowing. It explores both day-to-day money management in which loans were essential, and the energetic debates played out in neighbourhoods and courts about expectations and meanings attached to borrowing. Litigation communities negotiated these matters, and the outcomes had large implications, such as whether market forces, as represented by the rights of creditors, flowed or were checked in neighbourhood opinion and court judgement.

Law-making was a key means for the rulers of early modern states to assert themselves, but legal process provided an essential and reciprocal link between families and states. Neighbourhoods of working families could seek to utilize the authority of the state in many different ways as part of their strategies to manage their own resources. They might pay notaries to make public records of private transactions, for instance, or ask a local court to intervene in a dispute. They might use legal resources to manage borrowing (whether to document loans or sue for unpaid debts), clarify marital status (in marriage contracts or in petitions for separation), enforce the boundaries of the acceptable use of force (in asking notaries to record statements about what happened for future use, or ask courts to discipline family or community members who used inappropriate force). How they understood appropriate authority, however, rested in their own experiences in the laboratory of marriage; their choices suggest that the perceptions of authority and power they brought to the larger polity were much more heterogeneous than monolithic.

CONTEXTS: SETTING THE SCENE

This book explores family business in two French cities, Nantes and Lyon, in the long seventeenth century. Urban working families in these two cities at this time are at the core of this project. Their lived experiences of key aspects of early modern political, economic, and cultural transitions are especially compelling for demographic, chronological, and geographical reasons.

Demographically, urban working families like these straddled the integrally intertwined borders of economic and political uncertainty. They were a key group in terms of exposure to the rising vulnerabilities of the market. They depended on trading labour or goods for income. They almost always rented their primary residences, and rarely had any real estate except for perhaps a rural

Economy of Obligation: The Culture of Credit and Social Relations in Early Modern England (London, 1998).

smallholding. More than either peasants or elites, they were entirely dependent on movables; and all movables could be distrained for debt, whereas immovables (that is, real estate) could not. They were reliant on the market with all of its risk, opportunity, and precariousness.[19] They aspired to be what in France were termed '*gens de biens*', but they were in danger of becoming 'gens de néant'. To be a part of the '*gens de biens*'—a person of both good standing ('*bien*') and property ('*biens*')—was to be a part of the community who maintained order, and whose opinion mattered. But to be associated with the '*gens de néant*' (of no standing and without property) was to be someone who was alienated from local governance and associated with disorder.[20]

Questions of early modern social definition that were naturalized for contemporaries have become a science and a puzzle for historians. The families who dominated litigation in local urban courts were generally from households that were squarely among the ranks of skilled artisans and small shopkeepers such as bakers and tailors, as the 1,100–1,200-*livre* median value of their dowries indicated; but their witnesses also included many semi-skilled workers or day labourers; that is, men who were manual labourers, such as porters or boatmen, and women who were servants or secondhand vendors.[21]

Such working families had much in common in terms of their more or less but always precarious grip on security, as well as many aspects of the lives they shared in densely packed urban neighbourhoods. Historians have traditionally framed guildsmen, whether master artisans or journeymen, as having cultures that were distinct from those of manual workers such as porters, but most workers were not members of guilds, and not all masters (not to mention journeymen) were equally financially successful or influential. By the seventeenth century, many journeymen spent their adult married lives as employees rather than follow the traditional path by which they would eventually became masters of their own shops. They may have had as much in common with their semi-skilled or unskilled neighbours as with their masters. Most of the working people whose evidence as witnesses was critical to community discussion and to the legal process represented the parts of the urban workforce who were not part of the guild elite. Whether male or female, whether surgeons, shoemakers, journeymen, small shopkeepers, apprentices or servants, porters, boatmen, secondhand vendors, or stall sellers, they shared many experiences and outlooks with their neighbours. Even when successful skilled men who were probably near the top of the

19 I thank Martha Howell for this observation.

20 For discussion of the usages of '*gens de bien*' and '*gens de néant*' as markers of what he calls the 'frontier of order', see James B. Collins, *Classes, Estates, and Orders in Early Modern Brittany* (Cambridge, 1994), 17–18.

21 The urban poor and peasants from the urban hinterlands rarely used these courts as litigants, although they did speak as witnesses. Nor did peasants use the rural seigneurial courts in their own communities for these kinds of cases. Such families, whether urban or rural, perhaps lacked the financial wherewithal to go to court, and may have resolved their differences by other means, such as simply abandoning their spouses.

guild ladder testified, I have found it impossible to distinguish between their views and those of witnesses drawn from other ranks of working men and women.[22]

The attitudes and experiences of elite families are suggestive about the importance of rank. The circumstances of groups who might legitimately be called elites in early modern France varied widely depending on whether they were, for instance, part of the urban bourgeoisie, petty nobility, or aristocracy. I have with some admitted arbitrariness regarded families as members of one of these elites if their dowry, title, or husbands' occupations (if the men were professional, such as barristers or wealthy merchants) indicated that they were clearly part of a higher social milieu than working families. The small number of elite cases does not indicate that their family dynamics were smoother, but that wives whose families had large resources and reputations may have preferred options other than using local courts of first instance. Many such families had the right to take their cases immediately to the regional *parlements*, although they do not usually appear to have done so; or they may have (as we will see) preferred to pursue private remedies.

Chronologically, a long seventeenth century provides the parameters for the experiences examined here. Many key issues in terms of managing the economies of everyday life were shifting, and great uncertainty characterized the lives of families who lived through these transitions. The decisions they made helped usher in new patterns that were to become clear by the middle third of the following century.

Geographically, Nantes and Lyon are on opposite sides of France, but they shared important similarities as well as illuminating differences. They were both bustling, large cities by early modern standards. As quintessential sites of economic change they were in the front wave—albeit on different trajectories—of the intensification of market practices that transformed the early modern economy. Although neither was the seat of a *parlement*, they were important judicial centres that hosted a variety of courts and jurisdictions at a time when courts had substantial administrative as well as judicial roles. The overlapping legal patchwork of both cities was common to all of France as well as much of early modern Europe. Like all early modern cities, their residents included wealthy elites, a middling sector of what would later be called the bourgeoisie, and an increasing group of the indigent poor. The working families who are the subjects of this book, aspiring to join the middling ranks but often only a few steps from indigence, were the largest element in the populations. Lyonnais and Nantais families, like all early modern households, were subject to the recurring great crises of early modern life, whether disease or food shortage. Local parish registers

[22] I do not mean, of course, that no hierarchies or tensions also shaped close-knit neighbourhood relations, but that common ground was important too.

and other records clearly show the spikes in mortality and falls in marriage and birth rates that took place across all of France in, for instance, the late 1590s, the mid 1630s, the middle of the seventeenth century, and the early 1690s.[23]

Nantes, on the west coast of France, was in the sixteenth century a typical (if such existed) early modern city with many guilds and many unincorporated trades in a diverse craft economy. In the seventeenth century the city's population was about 25,000. As the Atlantic trade grew, from the middle of the seventeenth century, so too did the city's role in it as its quays along the Loire River, just a few miles inland from the ocean, filled with warehouses and as its merchants built the mansions whose famous African-headed sculpted facades still attest to the role of slave trading in the transformation of the city's economic fortunes. Nantes was subject to that royal legislation that proliferated in the early modern period, but those initiatives co-existed, not always smoothly, with the region's customary law, and local practice.[24]

Lyon, on the eastern side of France, at the confluence of the Rhône and Saône rivers, had been an important commercial crossroads since the Roman era. With a population that grew (largely by immigration—Lyon was known for being full of 'strangers') from perhaps 35,000 in 1600 to 75,000 by the end of the seventeenth century, most residents lived in the tightly packed and very densely inhabited streets that survive largely intact today between the Saône River and a steep hillside. Early modern Lyon—a pivot of late medieval trade, with its great fairs—remained an important centre for printing, for long-distance trade, and for the banking on which those exchanges depended. From the seventeenth century, silk production became increasingly important, and in the eighteenth century, silk dominated the city's economy with towards a third of the city's population—men and women, married and single—involved in its production. The manufacture of silk was organized into one giant guild, the *fabrique*, which dominated much of economic life in the city by the eighteenth century.[25] While Lyon shared with Nantes royal jurisdiction, its local legal practices were shaped by Roman law, and the jurisdictional variations common to all of France meant that cases heard in one kind of court in Nantes were heard under the auspices of a different court in Lyon.

[23] The causes and consequences of these demographic crises have been much studied by historians. Françoise Bayard, *Vivre A Lyon sous L'Ancien Régime* (Paris, 1997), 110 and 199–206, details the particulars of these dynamics for Lyon.

[24] Alain Croix, *La Bretagne aux Seizième et Dix-septième Siècles: la Vie, la Mort, la Foi* (Paris, 1981); Croix, *Nantes et le Pays Nantais au Seizième Siècle: Etude Démographique* (Paris, 1974); Hardwick, *Practice of Patriarchy*.

[25] The history of seventeenth-century Lyon falls between two majestic monographs on the previous and subsequent centuries: Richard Gascon, *Grand Commerce et Vie Urbaine au XVIe Siècle: Lyon et ses Marchands (Environs de 1520–Environs de 1580)* (Paris, 1971); and Maurice Garden, *Lyon et les Lyonais au XVIIIe Siècle* (Paris, 1970). An excellent synthetic history of the city for the whole early modern period is Bayard, *Vivre A Lyon*, esp. 94–115 for the economy and population.

READING THE ARCHIVES: SOURCES

This book explores the economies of family business from the perspectives of practice and process, primarily through an extraordinary range of archival material from the cities of Lyon and Nantes. The records of civil actions in local courts provide a huge and much underutilized set of materials, through which the agency and negotiation of the members of working families can be explored, and, of course, in which the role of litigation is drawn into sharp focus.

Local courts of first instance had jurisdiction over many matters, but I have concentrated on cases in which violence, borrowing, and negotiations over marital status were at stake. These included suits in which any one of these was the specific subject of the action, as well as a core of almost 1,000 cases of marital separation in which more than one or more of these issues was at stake. I have also consulted the records of the cities' merchants' courts that include many disputes about debt. In particular, the archives of Lyon merchants' court (the *cour de conservation*) comprise an unparalleled series of family papers as well as the court's own documents.[26] These include account books, receipts, letters, records of litigation, and often examples of the items which household members made or sold.

My analytical approach to this material is primarily qualitative. While the large number of cases might seem to lend itself to a quantitative analysis, the material is fragmentary. The majority of the surviving cases date from the second half of the seventeenth century. Sometimes the initial petitions survive, sometimes the depositions, sometimes royal prosecutors' recommendations, sometimes the sentences, and sometimes more than one of these pieces for particular cases. In fact, counting anything more than the most basic patterns would provide a misleading impression of the coherence of the data.[27]

Moreover, my emphasis is on practices from the actors' perspective: that is, I am interested in the processes and decision-making that the material reveals, rather than the judicial results *per se*. First, as many studies have shown, people entered litigation for varied reasons, and the pursuit of a judicial remedy was often a minority consideration. Second, the records themselves reveal as much or more about the daily circumstances surrounding the event technically in question.[28]

[26] When a court started to investigate household affairs to determine whether their financial difficulties were the result of misfortune and should be classified as a simple failure (*faillité*), or were attributable to fraudulent behaviour and merited prosecution for bankruptcy—a capital crime—relevant papers of all kinds were deposited. For this process, see Kaplan, *Bakers of Paris*, 400–3. Amelia Kassler's recent work on the Paris merchants' court offers some useful perspective on the jurisdiction: see Amelia Kassler, *A Revolution in Commerce: the Parisian Merchant Court and the Rise of Commercial Society in Eighteenth-Century France* (New Haven, 2007).

[27] Likewise, see Piant's observations about the shortcomings of quantitative interpretations of very heterogeneous surviving materials. Piant, *Une Justice Ordinaire*, 12.

[28] See the observation of Edward Muir and Guido Ruggiero that criminal court records are less valuable for what they say about a particular crime than for what 'they reveal about otherwise

I want to retain a sense of process that includes actors as well as actions with the goals of locating key structures and practices of early modern communities. This emphasis on practice is particularly important in thinking about the choices working people had to manage available resources, whether about law, violence, borrowing, marital status or other issues, as well as the constraints of the structures they faced.[29]

I have approached the archival material with this same sense of process in mind. The material used here ranges widely, from very diverse family papers deposited as part of court proceedings to plaintiffs' initial petitions, witnesses' depositions, the recommendations of prosecutors, and judges' sentences. Each of these had their own conventions, of which I have sought to take account. In recent years, historians have explored the problematics of using legal materials at length.[30] Were the documents formulaic, dominated by the perspectives of elite authorities, dictated by lawyers, framed by narrative tropes, or representative of the sentiments of the men and women whose speech was recorded? Certainly such material is multi-layered but, with due careful consideration to the richly textured cultural production represented, it nevertheless offers an unparalleled avenue by which to examine working peoples' debates and decisions about meeting the challenges they faced.[31] The stories of the lived experiences of working families are critically important to our understanding of the long historical backdrop to the complex web of relations among families, economies, and state.

POLITICAL ECONOMIES OF DAILY LIFE

When Marie Monnier and Louis Thebaudeau and their neighbours discussed their marital conflict in court, they not only provided a documentary record of the

invisible or opaque realms of human experience'—a perspective applicable to civil cases too. Edward Muir and Guido Ruggiero, 'Introduction: The crime of history', in Muir and Ruggiero, *History From Crime* (Baltimore, 1994), vii.

[29] My approach has been influenced by work that has interrogated practice as an analytical category. See in particular, Pierre Bourdieu, *Outline of a Theory of Practice* (Cambridge, 1977); Michel de Certeau, *The Practice of Everyday Life* (Berkeley, 1984); Frank Munger, 'Law, change, and litigation: a critical examination of an empirical research tradition', *Law and Society Review*, 22, 1 (1988), 57–101, and Frank Munger, 'Afterword: Studying litigation and social change', *Law and Society Review*, 24, 2 (1990), 595–615.

[30] Those I have found most helpful include Natalie Zemon Davis, *Fiction in the Archives: Pardon Tales and their Tellers in Sixteenth-Century France* (Palo Alto, 1987); Malcolm Gaskill, *Crime and Mentalities in Early Modern England* (Cambridge, 2000), 24–7; Laura Gowing, *Domestic Dangers: Women, Words, and Sex in Early Modern London* (Oxford, 1996); and Tim Stretton, *Women Waging the Law in Elizabethan England* (Cambridge, 1998).

[31] For very helpful discussions of how considering the conditions of cultural production informs readings of archival documents, see in particular Kathryn J. Burns, 'Notaries, truth and consequences', *American Historical Review*, **100**, 2 (April 2005), 350–79, and Cornelia Hughes Dayton, 'Rethinking agency, recovering voices', *American Historical Review*, **99**, 3 (June 2004), 827–43.

struggles of working families in the seventeenth century, but revealed a process through which spouses, communities, and the state navigated the deployment of resources in ways that shaped the largest as well as smallest politics of a formative century. In the hundreds of similar legal records examined here, and the thousands upon thousands of similar actions that took place not only in Lyon and Nantes, but across France, working families both revealed the constraints under which they struggled, and illustrated the strategies by which they sought to manage the resources available to them. This book explores these political economies through five chapters and an epilogue.

The first chapter, *Economies of Marriage*, interrogates marital status as a critical resource. We are often inclined to think of marriages of the past as stable, lifelong affairs that stand in stark contrast to the patterns of twenty-first century partnerships. In fact, however, high mortality rates as well as economic pressures and personal preferences combined to create many varieties of married life in the seventeenth century. This chapter explores the decision to seek legal separation as one choice, in a spectrum of options that men and women made about managing marital status. Separation was a possibility open primarily to wives, as men had other means to resolve marital grievances: they could discipline their wives, abandon their families, or put their wives into convents. Early modern French women could seek either a separation of property (*séparation de biens*) or a separation of person and property (*séparation de personne et de biens*). Separate property meant that the spouses would continue to live together, although the wife would gain control of a proportion of the property she had brought to the marriage, and of property she might inherit or money she might earn after the separation. After a wife secured a separation of property and person, the spouses lived separately. They could not, however, remarry, as the sacramental bond of marriage remained.

Separations offered antidotes for households that were the antithesis of orderly. Legally, petitioners for separations were required to demonstrate that their households were disorderly. To secure separate property, a wife had to show that her husband's mismanagement of their revenues endangered her dowry. To secure a separation of person and property, a wife had to show that her husband's violence endangered her life. In practice, wives, neighbours who provided testimony, and judges applied these principles more creatively, but as a matter of possibility as well as legal principle, separation cases rested on wives' ability to demonstrate disorder of many kinds: economic (especially with regard to household budget management), moral (especially with regard to marital sexuality, gambling, and drinking), and political (especially with regard to behaviour, whether physical abuse or otherwise, that undermined household stability). If there was a consensus about the desirability of stable households, separations indicate the room for negotiation, correction, and remaking of marital status more clearly than the high rates of marriage and the impossibility of divorce. Seeking separations was only the tip of the iceberg in this regard, albeit an unusually well documented one.

The spectrum of possibilities explored in *Economies of Marriage*, however, also indicates that the project of negotiating what marriage meant, in other senses, was ongoing. Spouses, neighbours, and the state had to work out where the common ground lay in terms of what constituted a valid marriage, and it is clear that multiple versions of marriage continued to exist. Did it mean cohabitation, publicity, having the right papers, or sharing in a joint endeavour? This variety of opinion and indeed practices was worked out between partners and in neighbourhoods in ways that are invisible to us now, but it was also worked out in court. If the state's vision of itself, as represented in familial rhetoric and marital legislation, was monolithic and expansive, working families' experience of, and perception of, authority and power suggested that a heterogeneous state fitted their reality.[32]

The second chapter, *Economies of Justice*, examines going to court as a popular resource. Early modern people were highly litigious, as litigation rates across Europe rocketed from the mid-sixteenth century. This chapter demonstrates that despite the undoubted complexities and shortcomings of the early modern legal system, local courts were a key element in the popular economy in two ways: large numbers of people used local courts for many different purposes, among them management of marital status as well as borrowing and violence, and working people rather than elites were the main users of this level of the judicial system.

Economies of Family Politics, the third chapter, explores the ways in which discussions about marriage and gendered authority in families, among neighbours, and in court, staged a public debate with broad implications. The litigation communities who debated these issues served important functions. They asserted particular sets of expectations, not only about spousal relations but about the basis of authority. They emphasized the secular and contingent nature of authority as well as the intertwined economic and moral attributes that husbands as well as wives had to meet to secure what members of local working communities recognized as household 'order'. The process shaped political economies large and small in defining the usual power relations in and between households. Litigation communities did not challenge the concept of male authority, but the judicial process around lower courts repeatedly and consistently redefined and refined conjugal and paternal power. In a century of state-building and economic transition, plaintiffs, witnesses and judges were emphatic that authority was a practice contingent on the fulfilment of obligations rather than a sacred right,

[32] For discussion of the need to problematize the varied rather than monolithic nature of French institutions, see for example, for courts, Jonathan Dewald, Review of John Hurt, *Louis XIV and the Parlements: The Assertion of Royal Authority* (Manchester and New York, 2002), for *H-France*, 2, 84 (August 2002); and for guilds, Claire Haru Crowston, *Fabricating Women: The Seamstresses of Old Regime France, 1675–1791* (Durham, 2001).

and that the preservation of families was an important priority over the rigour of a developing market.

The fourth chapter, *Economies of Markets*, explores borrowing as an essential component of the economy and a key flashpoint for crisis for families, communities and the state. It explores both the circulation of loans in working families, and the shifting attitudes towards borrowing that marked some loans as good credit and others as bad debts. Nothing was as critical to working families' survival as access to credit, and nothing except death more potentially threatening to their households' existence than debts. Urban working families needed to borrow money to fund every part of their lives. Maintaining access to it was an important skill for both spouses, and if either husband or wife endangered that supply, disaster could quickly overtake a family. Yet they also had to negotiate with lenders at a time when practices were shifting as a market economy intensified. How was a family to know when a lender would accept long delays in paying off debts, and when that lender would insist on timely repayment? How would they know when a form of in-kind payment that had always worked was to become unacceptable? How did gender shape experiences of borrowing and assessments of creditworthiness or indebtedness? How did a good borrower become a bad debtor? Laws in part structured these challenges, but legal action also provided families and communities with a way to seek to have their perspectives endorsed.

Economies of Violence, the fifth chapter, examines the use of force as a resource in which families, communities and states were all invested. The use of force was an early modern fact of life, as mundane as the use of borrowing. Yet just as some kinds of borrowing were coded as credit and a source of high status while others were coded as debts which undermined status, the use of force was subject to interpretation, negotiation, and contestation by those involved, by the neighbours who observed it, and by the state in and out of court. This chapter explores the boundaries between the privilege, and, indeed, obligation, of household discipline and the abuse of family members. The definitions of appropriate or excessive treatment depended both on the behaviour of the subject and above all on the gender, rank, and role of the aggressor. Thus men's battery of their wives was assessed differently than women's battery of husbands, or parents of children, and elite women were situated differently from working women. Shifting attitudes towards violence and towards privacy affected experiences of domestic violence.

Finally, in the epilogue, *Family Business on the Cusp of the Modern World*, I suggest some of the ways in which new political economies of daily life slowly emerged by the middle decades of the eighteenth century. Although economic insecurity and family violence continued to pervade the lives of working families they began to face different options and to make different choices. New emotional grids for family life developed, litigation rates declined, the meanings and practices that underlay borrowing were redefined, and attitudes to violence were reformed.

These and other shifts reshaped the political economies of family business for households, communities, and states as the early modern world gave way to the modern.

In exploring this range of tangible and intangible resources critical to political economies of daily life, this book analyses the negotiations, conflicts, and compromises, and the power relations that were inherent in them within and between households and communities. It emphasizes grassroots practice as a critical influence in major early modern transitions, such as state formation, the intensification of market practices, and the remaking of marriage to emphasize grassroots practice as a critical influence.[33] Common themes underlay all the economies examined here. Gender was critical in the politics of daily life that wove from household to neighbourhood to state, but its impact was kaleidoscopic rather than black and white, so men's and women's experiences of using the courts, of borrowing, or of marriage, overlapped in significant measure as well as being distinguished in key ways. An economy of information was integral to judgements about marriage, borrowing, and force, as well as to the use of the courts in which witnesses would frequently offer information based on 'people say . . . ' as well as on their own experience. Neighbours provided oversight, mediation, loans, emergency help, witnesses for court cases, and myriad other tasks.

In this process, litigation communities, constituted by laws, neighbourhood values, and urban courts, were vitally important in mediating the relationships between individual behaviour, local expectations, and state goals. The judgement of neighbours was an essential factor in court cases and by extension in the authorization of local opinion in court and in the legitimatization of the use of courts in neighbourhoods. Throughout, communities of working families contributed to and responded to the transitions through which marriage, the economy, and the state were being remade. For Louis Thebaudeau and Marie Monnier, as well as their peers in working families in other towns and cities, decisions about the tangible and intangible resources that lay at the heart of their daily existence, repeated over and over again, made them unwitting but potent participants in the social, economic, and political dynamics of a precarious century.

33 I do not, of course, mean to deny the role of other factors.

1

Economies of Marriage: Managing Marital Status

Marye Oger married Jean Renault, a miller, not long after her first husband died. The two were soon at odds. Neighbours saw them argue, intervened when Renault hit Oger, and sheltered her when she ran out of their apartment at night to avoid him. They listened to her fears that he would kill her, and his threats that he would not kill her but would beat her so severely that she would die from the beatings. Oger and Renault fought repeatedly over a mutual donation of property that he wanted them to make to each other, but to which she insisted she 'would never' agree. Oger petitioned the Nantais provost's court for a separation of person and property from Renault, and her request was granted. It allowed her to live apart from her husband and to manage her own property.

Marye Lechou married Jan Mesney, a buttonmaker, gave him 200 *livres* as her dowry, and believed him to be a capable householder (*homme mesnager*). Instead, she claimed, he abused her daily, sold her property, engaged in debts with all kinds of people when he was drunk, and reduced her to 'the last resort'. She asked her local court for a separation of property, and the royal prosecutor recommended that her petition be granted because 'he is debauched instead of busying himself with his work to support his family'.[1] Thus while the couple continued to live together, she was allowed to administer her own property.

Judic Sallic married François Gardinet, a barber, but later left and told neighbours and a parish priest that she no longer wished to live with him. She took various personal, household, and barbershop supplies with her. He admitted that there had been 'bad husbandry' (*mal mesnage*) between them, due, he claimed, to her failure to pay the costs of his setting up shop as a barber, but he asked her to return. She stubbornly refused because she was unhappy. She told several acquaintances that although she had been trapped by a good-for-nothing man, in the end she had trapped him because while she had not given him anything, she had taken everything he had of any value. She never sought to

[1] ADLA B5810, 6 November 1637; ADLA B6133, 7 November 1636; ADLA B6149, 5 June 1674.

legalize their *de facto* separation, but continued to live alone, making do as best she could. She remarried quickly after Gardinet's death.[2]

For these three couples, like all their peers, marital status was a critical resource with tangible and intangible benefits and costs. The impossibility of divorce, in France before the Revolution, gives a false sense of the stability of early modern family life. Judicial separations of persons and property (*séparations de corps et de biens*) or simply of property (*séparations de biens*) offered means of dissolving some of the temporal bonds of marriage in early modern France, just as they did in some other European countries.[3] Separations, moreover, illuminate one facet of a spectrum of negotiations about marital status of which some parts, like Judic Sallic's, are difficult to recover because they did not create a legal paper-trail. Despite the sacramental nature of marriage, many spouses sought to negotiate and renegotiate the terms of their household relationships through a variety of formal and informal means, sometimes mutual but often unilateral.[4]

[2] ADLA B5852, 29 April 1717.

[3] For accounts of early modern family breakdown in various forms across Europe, see Joanne Ferraro, *Marriage Wars in Late Renaissance Venice* (Oxford, 2001); Roderick Phillips, *Putting Asunder: a History of Divorce in Western Societies* (Oxford, 1988); Lawrence Stone, *Road to Divorce: England, 1530–1987* (New York, 1990); Thomas Safley, *Let No Man Put Asunder: The Control of Marriage in the German Southwest: a Comparative Study, 1550–1600* (Kirksville, MO, 1986); and Jeffrey Watt, *The Making of Modern Marriage: Matrimonial Control and the Rise of Sentiment in Neuchatel, 1550–1800* (Ithaca, 1992). Work on separations of either kind in early modern France has been very limited. For separations of person and property, see Giacomo Francini, 'Divorce and separations in eighteenth-century France: an outline for a social history of law', *The History of the Family*, **2**, 1; Wendy Gibson, *Women in Seventeenth Century France* (London, 1989), 85–6; Sarah Hanley, 'Engendering the state: family formation and state building in early modern France', *French Historical Studies*, **16**, 1 (Spring 1989), 13–14, 18–19 and 24, and 'Social sites of political practice: lawsuits, civil rights, and the separation of powers in domestic and state government, 1500–1800', *American Historical Review*, **102**, 1 (1997); Alain Lottin, 'Vie et mort du couple: difficultés conjugales et divorces dans le nord de la France aux XVIIe et XVIIIe siècles', *XVIIe Siècle* **102–103** (1974); and Lottin *et al.*, *La Désunion du Couple sous l'Ancien Régime: l'Exemple du Nord* (Paris, 1975); James Traer, *Marriage and the Family in Eighteenth-Century France* (Ithaca, 1980). Two works on divorce in the French Revolution also briefly examine separations of person and property in the decade before 1789: Dominique Dessertine, *Divorcer à Lyon sous la Révolution et l'Empire* (Lyon, 1981); and Roderick Phillips, *Family Breakdown in Late Eighteenth-Century France: Divorces in Rouen, 1792–1803* (Oxford, 1980). Historians have largely left aside the issue of property separations. Dessertine, Hanley, Lottin, Phillips, and Traer concentrate only on separations of person and property. Likewise, the studies by Safley and Watt, that both compare Catholic and Protestant regions, make no mention of petitions for separate property in their analyses of aspects of marriage breakdowns. Francini, 'Divorce and Separations'; Wendy Gibson, *Women in Seventeenth Century France* (New York, 1989), 85; Daryl Hafter, *Women at Work in Preindustrial France* (University Park, 2007), 76–9; Zoe Schneider, 'Women before the bench: female litigants in early modern Normandy', *French Historical Studies*, **23**, 1 (Winter 2000), 20–1, look very briefly at property separations. Separation patterns very similar to those found in Nantes and Lyon are used as evidence in a recent study of a court of first instance in a much smaller town in eastern France; see Herve Piant, *Une Justice Ordinaire: Justice Civille et Criminelle dans le Prévôte Royale de Vaucouleurs sous l'Ancien Régime* (Rennes, 2006), 159–64.

[4] Although this chapter focuses on variations of spousal status and the overwhelming majority of early modern working people who were married, some individuals, of course, managed marital status by choosing not to marry. For the significance of the practice of single life in the eighteenth century, see Claire Crowston, *Fabricating Women: The Seamstresses of Old Régime France, 1675–1791* (Durham, 2001).

This chapter explores the strategy of separation in the broad context of individual, community, and state management of the economies of marriage. Early modern women and men navigated among the legal, economic, social, and cultural imperatives that sought to create stable households as the basis of neighbourhood and national well-being to improve, remake, or even escape from unsatisfactory unions. The French elite, like other European authorities, embarked on a well-explored, decades-long project to transform marriage from the mid-sixteenth century. The vision of marriage as defined in the state legislation of the later sixteenth and seventeenth centuries was quite specific: a marriage entered into with parental consent, regularized with a notarized contract and celebrated with a public ceremony, created a hierarchical and large father-headed family that was obedient, loyal, and reliable as a foundation stone for the state. This secular oversight in itself marked a shift from traditional ecclesiastical jurisdiction over marriage, as did the emphasis on publicity, parental consent, and the very specific equation of familial and state interests.[5] Certain aspects of this ideal marriage were subject to elaborate legislative attention, whether in terms of regulations (for example, about parental consent), incentives (for example, the 1666 scheme to provide tax exemption for fathers of ten children), or deterrents (for example, the crime of *rapt*—either abduction or elopement—became a capital offence).

Yet while this royal legislation is eye-catching and thought-provoking, it is not only unclear how much of it was enforced, but is clear that many other aspects of marriage received virtually no legislative scrutiny. Arrangements for second marriages, which were very common, were often quite different than those for first marriages.[6] Meanwhile, events during the course of marriage itself received almost no attention whatsoever. Longstanding regional law practices continued to provide the framework for separations, and local judges had broad discretion about how the specifics were put into play. What local communities made of the new expectations remains largely unclear. Notaries and priests acted as guarantors for the state of the 'new' marriage by requiring proof of consent and publicity, but once the first marriage ceremony was over, subsequent expectations and boundaries were subject to local as well as legal and royal input.

Marriage itself was a risk, fraught with uncertainty, with negotiation, and with the prospect of failure as well as success. Marriage as an institution, a lived experience, and an economy was in transition: under pressure from the desire of ruling authorities to remake marriage, from economic changes, from increasing use of courts as a strategy and as a remedy, and from the emergence

[5] For the series of legislative acts that defined these imperatives, see Hanley, 'Engendering the state', and 'Family and state in early modern France: the marriage pact', in Marilyn J. Boxer and Jean H. Quataert (eds.), *Connecting Spheres: Women in the Western World, 1500 to the Present* (Oxford, 1987).

[6] For the differences in the arrangements for second marriages, see Janine Lanza, *From Wives to Widows in Early Modern Paris: Gender, Economy, and Law* (Ashgate, 2007).

of new expectations about privacy and violence. These are themes that run throughout this book, as are the stakes each spouse as well as neighbours and local judges (the arbiters in state courts) had in family business. This chapter interrogates the specific issues surrounding separations as well as other means of resolving spousal difficulties. The choices of spouses as well as the responses of their families, neighbours, and local officials suggest that while stable households were of paramount concern to almost everyone, in reality marriages faced many challenges, and perhaps, in fact, part of the rhetorical energy that surrounded marriage lay in this recognition. They were more subject to spousal and neighbourhood correction as well as to alternative formations than hindsight or history often seem to suggest. As Marye Oger and Jean Renault or Marye Lechou and Jan Mesnay or Judic Sallic and François Gardinet and their neighbours knew all too well, the agreement to marry and the ceremony were only the start of an often rocky road.

LEGAL PARAMETERS

Despite all the legislative attention to the formation of marriages, royal ordinances said little about their partial dissolution. The only interest the early modern state expressed in separations was in terms of promoting the economy. Edicts in 1629, 1647, and 1673 whose primary goal was the protection of commerce insisted that separation agreements had no legal force until they had been publicized to safeguard the interests of creditors.[7] Secular courts gradually extended their jurisdiction to include most marriage matters, including separations, from ecclesiastical courts in the sixteenth century.[8] However, local legal regimes, whether in customary law areas like Nantes or in Roman law regions such as Lyon, continued to provide the primary guidelines as to separations, and local judges had great discretion about the implementation of those codes.

The legal grounds for separation of property and person were very specific: severe ill-treatment, aggravated adultery, a husband's conviction of attempted wife murder, or his deadly hatred of her. They were intended to respond to very clear and very extreme kinds of wrongdoing by the husband. As one commentator pointed out: 'Separations of person must only be granted for grave causes: thus the different temperaments & even the little altercations which can arise between husband and wife are not sufficient cause.'[9] If granted,

[7] Isambert, *Recueil Général*, **16**, 267, **17**, 64, **19**, 102.

[8] Only the diocese of Cambrai (the region of Lottin's study of separations of person and property) retained control over separations, probably because Cambrai did not become part of France until 1677. Lottin, 'Vie et mort du couple'.

[9] The grounds for separations of person and property are discussed in Roderick Phillips, *Family Breakdown in Late Eighteenth-Century France: Divorces in Rouen 1792–1803* (Oxford, 1980), 4–6; James Traer, *Marriage and the Family*, 39–40. Quote, with list of causes for separation of person,

women were able to live apart from their husbands. (Husbands were not thought to need such a resort, no doubt because they had other options such as abandonment or, as one commentator noted, putting intractable or violent wives into convents.)

Both customary and Roman law regimes allowed women to demand separate property under broadly similar conditions: women who were granted separate property were not permitted to establish independent households, but were allowed to administer (although not alienate) their own property. An eighteenth-century jurist, Robert Joseph Pothier, observed that women in customary law regions could ask for separate property for the same reasons as women under Roman law; that is, that the dowry was 'in peril' because of the disorder of the husbands' affairs. A synthesis in Diderot's famous *Encyclopedia* project from the same period offered some general parameters: 'The separation of property can only be requested by the wife in the case of dissipations by her husband. She is not however obliged to wait until the husband has squandered [*dissipé*] all his property and still less the dowry of his wife [because] the separation would then be a useless remedy; it is sufficient that the husband is [a] spendthrift [*dissipateur*] and . . . the dowry is in peril.'[10]

Customary law regimes offered loose sets of criteria about the nature of appropriate or inadequate husbandly behaviour. Burgundian customary law, for example, noted that while a husband had full control over his wife's property, if he committed a wrong (*délit*) she had the right to ask for separate property. A late seventeenth-century commentator noted that 'the husband must only be deemed the Master of the Community [property] when he makes good use of it', and that in Burgundy, as in other customary law régimes, failure to manage property properly opened the door to a petition for separate property. Breton customary law offered a clearer definition of a husband's property rights and its limits: 'Property is at the disposition of the husband, and he can do with it what he wants, maintaining his wife appropriately during their marriage, until the husband is found making ill use of his property.'[11]

Generally separate property provisions entitled wives to reclaim the portion of their dowry assigned as lineage property, and their trousseaus (usually household goods which often included a bed, cooking pots, and household linens), along with the dower rights which were designated to support widows. Regardless of regional legal variations, wives were in principle able to demarcate what was always a substantial part of household resources as their own property, although the specific proportions and types of property that wives could claim varied

under the article 'Séparation' in *Encyclopedie ou Dictionnaire Raisonne des Sciences des Arts et Métiers*, 35 vols. (1765; reprinted Stuttgart, 1967), 15, 60.

[10] Robert Joseph Pothier, *Oeuvres Complètes de Pothier* (Paris, 1835), 128; *Encyclopedie*, 15:59.

[11] *Coutûme Générale des Pays et Duché de Bourgogne avec le Commentaire de Monsieur Taisand* (Dijon, 1698), 70–5; *Coustumes Générales des Pays et Duché de Bretagne*, 2nd edn. (Rennes, 1680), article 424.

according to local jurisdictions, as the differences between Nantais and Lyonnais guidelines illustrate. When, for example, the Nantaise Claude Pelletier petitioned for separate property from her husband François Arlais, a 'merchant', in 1692, after ten years of marriage, she claimed the 800 *livres* designated as her lineage property in her 1,200-*livres* dowry, along with the 'customary' dower and the value of her trousseau, which she gave as 24 *livres* for a bed and its covers plus nine *livres* for a dozen women's shirts. Her claim neatly portrayed in practice the local customary law allowance that defined wives' separate property as the portion of their dowry assigned as lineage property (an amount arranged in marriage contracts, but usually worth between one half and two thirds of the dowry), their dower settlement (also usually defined in marriage contracts) and trousseau, together with any gifts which husbands promised in marriage contracts. In Lyon, Roman law allowed women to claim their whole dowries (the distinction between lineage and community marital property was rare in Roman law regimes) and trousseau, plus the dower (called, in this region, the *augment*, for which the amount was negotiable but often half the value of the dowry) together with any spousal gifts. Thus when Marguerite Chastenay sought to separate her property from that of her tailor husband seven years into their marriage, she claimed her whole dowry of 1,000 *livres* plus a dower of 500 *livres* and the clothing and jewels her husband had promised to give her 'appropriate for their status'. On occasion the dower could be less, as when Gasparde Cheneut received only 200 *livres* from Mathieu Duplex on a dowry of 1,400 *livres*.[12]

In working households, the value as well as practical importance of the trousseau made that part of a woman's claim very significant, especially since the latter was usually in cash and immediately used, whereas trousseau items usually remained intact if they had not been seized by creditors or pawned. When, for instance, Anne Brun secured separate property from Jean Thondeau in 1677, after eight years of marriage, her dowry of 1,300 *livres* (almost exactly the median for Lyonnais separations) was complemented by a trousseau valued at 1,000 *livres* that included a bed, its red curtains and covers, and a dozen sheets.[13]

Husbands whose wives secured separations of person and property were also sometimes ordered to pay small 'pensions' (called provisions) above and beyond wives' claims to the return of their dowries and trousseau. Isabeau Dendeau, for instance, who noted that her income was not sufficient to support her and her children, was awarded a pension of 50 *livres* a year as part of her separate property settlement, although she later complained that Horace Mallet, her husband, failed to pay this amount. Estimiette Gravier, who said she was staying with her father and had a nine-month old child at a wet nurse, secured a pension of 60 *livres*.[14]

In comparison to most other early modern European societies, in principle the prospect of separations of either kind offered French women a potentially valuable

[12] ADR BP3984, 17 December 1675 and 5 July 1681.

[13] ADR BP3984, 18 June 1677.

[14] ADR BP3985, no date but in folder for 1652; ADR BP4045, 26 April 1710.

recourse in which the legal construct of lineage property was key. In England, common law strictures gave husbands control over wives' property, and William Strahan, an eighteenth-century jurist, noted that in comparison to France there was 'no such' separation of goods in England. Even in other customary law regions, such as the German territories, separate property provisions were often refused to women.[15] Protestant regions, including England, Switzerland, and some German territories, introduced divorce in principle in the sixteenth century, but in practice women had great difficulty in securing decisions in their favour. In Venice, where church courts retained jurisdiction over separations of person and property, either spouse could seek such actions, and people of all social classes seem to have had some prospect of using them successfully to remedy their marital woes.[16]

SEEKING SEPARATIONS

Spouses who found their marriages unsatisfactory could choose several paths: they could tolerate their predicament, use family, neighbours, priests, and court officials to mediate their situation, agree to separate voluntarily, abandon the marital household, or seek a legal separation. The decision to seek a legal separation was only one possibility, albeit by far the best documented. Wives throughout the seventeenth century were always more apt, and increasingly sought, to petition for separate property rather than for separations of person and property. Wives in urban working families were far more likely to go to court than other social groups. While wives made that decision at many different moments in the marriage cycle, certain points seem to have been especially likely to push women to seek a legal remedy for their difficulties. These patterns suggest that while conjugal negotiations were ubiquitous, the economies of marriage were of course in part rank specific.

Spouses could simply separate without seeking legal ratification of their choices. Some couples certainly chose this path, although their numbers are impossible to

[15] On the lack of separation of goods in England, see Jean Domat, *The Civil Law in Its Natural Order*, translated by William Strahan, 2 vols. (London, 1737), 1, 173. On separate property provisions in other continental regions as well as England, see Laurence Fontaine, 'Women's economic spheres and credit in pre-industrial Europe', in Beverly Lemire *et al.* (eds.), *Women and Credit: Researching the Past, Refiguring the Future* (New York and Oxford), 16–18. Jacques Lelièvre argued nearly fifty years ago that a Parisian wife in the late eighteenth century 'in face of the juridical omnipotence of the husband [with regard to her property], was protected quite efficiently' by a balancing system of rights that included the ability to seek separate property and to renounce the marital community. Jacques Lelièvre, *La Practique des Contracts de Mariage chez les Notaires au Chatelet de Paris de 1789 à 1804* (Paris, 1959), 148–56.

[16] For the difficulty of divorce in practice in Protestant countries, see, for example, Safley, *Let No Man Put Asunder*; Stone, *Road to Divorce*; and Watt, *Making of Modern Marriage*. For Venice, see Ferraro, *Marriage Wars*.

determine. On occasion, one spouse simply abandoned the other. The resonance of the Martin Guerre story, the most famous early modern French marriage crisis, may in fact have lain as much in its commonplace starting point (everyone knew a spouse whose partner had disappeared) as well as in its astonishing denouement.[17] Marie Jamy and Claude Choppin, for example, had a notary record their agreement to live apart. This degree of formality that may have been unusual for extra-legal separations, but its frequency as a practice is impossible to estimate quantitatively.[18]

These kinds of informal separations, whether voluntary or involuntary, saved the expense and publicity of lawsuits, but had some other costs, both for men whose head of household status was undermined by the absence of wives, and for women who could find their financial circumstances, legal standing, and reputation left vulnerable. A royal prosecutor responded to a husband's request, for example, that his wife be required to move back into his household with the comment that it was 'scandalous to see a woman who lives apart'. When Yves Regnaudin asked the court to investigate his wife's departure from their household in 1650, his concerns showed that such divisions affected men's reputations too. He asked the court to intervene because 'his honour' as well as his property was at stake.[19]

If wives alone could not show that they had their husbands' permission or the legal right to act without his permission, their legal ability to manage their property or income was circumscribed, and they remained vulnerable to their husbands' whims. Charlotte Bonnefoy and Jan Delagarde, a surgeon, mutually agreed to separate, and he promised to pay her a 'provision' to support her. Their families were aware of the decision which was also recorded in writing. Yet Delagarde did not pay what he had promised, leaving Bonnefoy without any money and forcing her to become a servant to support herself because her parents could not afford to have her at home with them indefinitely. Even then she could not maintain an independent life, because Delagarde wrote letters, filled with 'scandalous and false' charges about her behaviour, to her employer, so that she was dismissed.[20] In search of some legal and economic security, Bonnefoy came to court to seek to clarify her marital status.

Wives who chose to use the courts as a way to manage their marital status were far more likely to seek separate property than separations of person and property, and apparently increasingly more likely to choose the former rather than the

[17] For the most famous modern retelling of the Guerre saga, see Natalie Zemon Davis, *The Return of Martin Guerre* (Cambridge, MA, 1983). It was extremely unusual, however, for wives to ask for separations on the grounds that their husbands had absconded years earlier. Other spouses mutually agreed to pursue separate paths.

[18] ADR BP3984, 4 November 1683. Despite extensive searches I have not found any other such agreements in notarial and court archives.

[19] ADR BP419, 20 November 1630; ADLA B6666, 31 October 1650.

[20] ADLA B5815, no date, but in the *liasse* for 1647.

Table 1.1. Extant separation cases in Nantes, 1598–1750.

Dates	Nature of cases: Property alone	Person and property	Unknown	Total
1598–1610	1	0	2	3
1611–1620	8	1	3	12
1621–1630	2	2	4	8
1631–1640	12	8	9	29
1641–1650	18	9	9	36
1651–1660	5	7	3	16
Date unknown but before 1660	1	1	4	6
1661–1670	39	10	1	50
1671–1680	33	13	15	61
1681–1690	74	15	7	96
1691–1700	71	8	4	83
1701–1710	27	1	10	38
1711–1720	29	5	0	34
1721–1730	22	1	3	26
1731–1740	24	2	4	30
1741–1750	15	1	0	16
Total	381	84	78	544

Note: five additional cases were initiated by husbands.

latter course. Petitions for separate property outnumbered those for separations of property and person by at least four to one in the seventeenth century, and by wider margins as requests for separations of person and property became more infrequent in the early decades of the eighteenth century. (See Table 1.) These petitions accounted for almost two thirds of all those made between 1600 and 1660 (in which the nature of the requested separation is clear), more then three quarters in the 1670s, and for all but one in the decade between 1700 and 1710.[21] Moreover, pleas for separations of property were almost always granted.

Meanwhile, requests for separation of persons were not only less frequent and decreased over time, but were less successful. While before 1660 a third of wives' petitions asked for separations of person as well as property, they fell to less than a quarter of the total in the 1670s, and almost disappeared from the first decade of the eighteenth century. Judges granted about two out of three of such requests; when they denied a request, they often granted a separation of property instead, but insisted that wives remain with their husbands in the conjugal households.

[21] I have used the separations from Nantes alone for this table, as I have identified all surviving separations material. In Lyon, the huge size of the surviving civil records make it impossible to complete a systematic search of a kind that would lend itself to a credible table, but the evidence of more then four hundred Lyonnais cases does suggest a similar pattern.

These patterns indicate (despite the need for some caution due to the variation from decade to decade in the number of surviving petitions) that fewer than a fifth of early modern women who sought a legal remedy were able to secure separate households.[22] Many wives who used the court may not have wanted to secure separate households *per se* in any case, because women might deploy going to court as a resource for various reasons (as we will see), but property separation offered wives a flexible and usable alternative.

Indeed, the pattern of frequent, proliferating, and easily procurable petitions for separate property, in contrast to the increasingly sporadic use of separations of property and persons, seems to have been widespread throughout the early modern French world. Patterns in Lyon were similar to those in Nantes. In Vaucouleurs, requests for property separations far outnumbered those for separation of person and property, and similarly were highly successful in terms of the percentage of successful suits. In Normandy, cases of separations of property grew steadily in the early eighteenth century. Both contemporary commentators and subsequent historians have asserted that separations of property were widespread and easily available in eighteenth-century Paris. In the colony of New France, settlers pursued four times as many suits for separate property alone as for separations of person and property.[23] Even if systematic evidence remains scarce, property separations seem to have been relatively common and, given the material difficulties that almost all working households faced, relatively easy to obtain.

Wives who chose to manage marital status by resort to the courts for separations were primarily members of urban working families and, as in managing other kinds of resources, the decision to use courts was often related to rank-specific concerns. Their households, as we have seen, were overwhelmingly from urban commercial milieus: husbands were artisans of every variety, tradesmen who ran their own shops, or manual workers. These families were on the front line of the uncertainty of the early modern economy and dependent on liquid assets, and they may have had more familiarity with using the courts as an everyday economy than people in rural areas. Elite families may have taken their cases directly to a

[22] The rarity of petitions for separations of property and person has led historians, searching only this issue, to conclude that judicial separations (or divorces in Protestant regions that permitted them) were of little import in early modern society. See, for instance, the conclusions of Phillips and Watt.

[23] For Vaucoulers (for which Piant notes—as in the far larger cities of Nantes and Lyon—that petitions for separate property were so successful that 'it seems it was enough to ask for it to get it'), see Piant, *Une Justice Ordinaire*, 159–64; for Normandy, see John A. Dickinson, 'L'activité judiciare d'après la procédure civile: le bailliage de Falaise 1668–1790', *Revue d'Histoire Economique et Sociale*, 54, 2 (1976), 163–4; for Paris (from the Châtelet jurisdiction for the years 1750, 1752, and 1785), see Francini, 'Divorce and separations', 106; for the perception of widespread separation usage in Paris in the eighteenth century, see Steven Kaplan, *The Bakers of Paris and the Bread Question, 1700–1775* (Durham, 1996), 328–9; for separation patterns in New France, see Peter Moogk, *La Nouvelle France: The Making of French Canada: A Cultural History* (East Lansing, 2000), 229–32.

higher court, as they were legally entitled to, or probably more often resolved their differences privately out of concern for potential damage to their reputations. The urban working poor and peasants rarely sought to use this particular form of remedy for spousal difficulties, perhaps because their assets were too small and the costs of the court too high to make the option attractive. Moreover, the records of seigneurial courts outside Lyon that served as courts of first instance include no separations cases of any kind. In 1673, however, Benoiste Barollier—a wet nurse with two very young children aged 1 and 2—asked the Lyon *sénéchaussée* for separate property from Antoine Mausset, a peasant, although her dowry was only 25 *livres*.[24] Why this one peasant household sought to use the nearly urban court for a separation is a mystery. Like Bertrande de Rols and Martin Guerre, who lived in a small village in southern France, wives and especially husbands in rural areas and families of the urban poor may simply have chosen abandonment over legal separation.

Wives' previous marital history seemed to have little relevance in their decisions to seek separations. The women who went to court varied from newly-weds to those who had been married for decades. Women who had been widowed in earlier marriages often compared their current husbands very unfavourably to their former ones, but widows were not represented at a higher rate than they were in the general population.

Two periods in marriages did seem more likely to trigger requests for separations than others, either within a year or around ten years. In just under 15 per cent of cases, marriages had lasted less than one year. In these cases, wives were probably taking quick action to avoid the erosion of whatever assets they had brought to a household. Claudine Burel, for example, noted that six months earlier she had promised her husband-to-be, Guillaume Berenger, who ran a bar, a dowry of 1,000 *livres*: 200 *livres* inherited from her parents, 200 more from her employer (a half in cash and a half in the form of a bed and its covers), clothes and household goods worth 200 *livres,* plus 400 more that her employer owed her. Her careful detailing no doubt reflected her effort to gather a dowry. Many of these quick separation requests specifically requested that no marital property community should be formed, and wives might still have had substantial assets to protect, relative, of course, to the status of the family.[25] After between eight and ten years of marriage, many families had experienced repeated interruptions of wives' labour through pregnancies, and had perhaps several very small children who were too young to contribute labour or income to households but still had to be maintained, even simply at wet nurses. At such times, a working family's

[24] ADR BP3985, 11 February 1673.

[25] Thirty-six of 251 cases in which the length of marriage is certain. ADR BP3985, 1 July 1685. Moreover, in Nantes the proportion of a dowry identified as community rather than lineage property in marriage contracts did not take effect until after a year and a day of marriage, so a wife who asked for separate property within a year could seek to avoid any of her dowry being identified as community property, and could reclaim it in its entirety.

always fragile grip on subsistence might be especially likely to slip, leading wives to resort to the remedy of legal separation to protect their core store of household property from husbands or creditors.

Women's goals, when they requested separations, were diverse and complex, not only because of the quite different outcomes that were possible, but because wives used the legal option to seek separations in a variety of ways depending on their circumstances. Most obviously, reasons for requests of separate property that would leave spouses living in the same households were less clear cut than those for separations of property and person that brought with them the prospect of separate households. In fact, women used these petitions as threats and as calculated levers in contests over household political economies, as a means to ward off creditors, and as desperate last resorts.

Wives, like all early modern litigants, often viewed going to court as a negotiating tactic rather than a remedy. Women could use the threat of legal action or even start the initial complaint as a way to try to pressure their husbands into different patterns of behaviour, often in combination with the intervention of a wide variety of other acquaintances of the couple. Charlotte Bonnefoy, for example, noted that she had frequently warned her husband, Jean Delagarde, a surgeon, that if he did not start to treat her better she would take him to court. She claimed that she had often warned him that if he continued to abuse her he would make it impossible for her to live with him, and she would be forced to complain to her kin and to 'Justice'.[26] In 1640, Martin Gasnier consented to a separation of property with his wife, Jeanne Lancelot, as a compromise by which she withdrew her intention to seek a separation of property and person. The spouses reached this resolution after negotiations involving both her mother and his father.[27]

The prospect of legal remedy was thus an element of ongoing processes of conflict, negotiation, and compromise within as well as between households, one that made the possibility of seeking separations valuable for many more women than those who ultimately went to court. The constant manoeuvering that characterized many marriages was occasionally revealed in rare cases in which women explicitly repeated threats they had made to go to court, or where records of withdrawn petitions were presented as part of later actions. By such means, women could elicit promises from husbands to behave in ways that they found more satisfactory.

For some women, petitions for separation were definitive steps to pursue legal solutions to situations they found to be intolerable for a variety of reasons. Women who soon after marriage discovered shortcomings in their spouses, for

[26] ADLA B5815, no date, but in *liasse* for 1647.

[27] ADLA B6135, 18 August 1640. A case between Gasnier and his mother-in-law did reach the provost's court, as they continued to disagree over how much Gasnier was to pay to support his wife's mother.

example, could act quickly to correct part of their error. Pierrette Saupin, for example, successfully sought a property separation from her husband Nicolas Davy in 1634, after explaining that she had married him nine months earlier 'believing that he was a man capable of running a household and trading goods'. She found 'on the contrary' that he spent all his time in *cabarets*, made 'bad deals' on which he sustained heavy losses, and had already squandered 300 of her *livres* gambling. The judge agreed that they would not have any community property and that she should have her 300 *livres* back.[28] Other women's petitions similarly claimed that they had discovered that their new husbands were less than they bargained for—because of previous debts and/or incompetence—and they sought to remove themselves from entering into liabilities which they had not anticipated.

In other cases, women endured years of abuse, sloth and debt before they decided to file for separations, although the catalysts that led to their seeking legal recourse are usually not clear. Sometimes, women in long marriages pointed to a particular incident or set thereof as spurs for their actions. Jullienne Jamet complained in 1676, for example, that her husband, a tailor, had not only taken the 500 *livres* he received from their marriage contract and lost it gambling instead of 'using it profitably', but that he had engaged in a lawsuit against the tailors' guild that he had insisted on taking to the Breton *parlement*, presumably at far greater expense than they could afford. A different kind of workplace difficulty motivated Christine Josse in 1674. Her husband, a surgeon, had been taken to court by a patient he treated, and the court had fined him 600 *livres* as well as ordering him to close his shop and to not work as a surgeon for a year. Josse noted that as they already were over a year behind with their rent, and the wronged patient was seeking a court order to secure payment, she, 'seeing the loss and total ruin of her husband', requested separate property.[29]

PRESERVING HOUSEHOLDS

Women's choices were only one part of marriage negotiation, a process that was itself an important element of larger efforts to define the parameters of gender and authority in local communities. Neighbours and friends were important resources for women. Women complained to their contemporaries about their spouses on all sorts of grounds. The corroboration of members of the local community as to crucial issues, such as men's financial ineptitude, debauchery, or violence without cause, was vital if women hoped to bring petitions successfully. By gossip and action, people in the community could express disapproval of men's behaviour, and hope for informal regulation of it.

[28] ADLA B6131, 17 January 1634.
[29] ADLA B6150, 16 November 1676; ADLA B6149, 11 June 1674.

Yet local people seem often to have preferred to reconcile spouses rather than to justify a permanent household breakdown. Thereze Massoneau and Pierre Laporte ran a bar called the 'Royal Sword'. When Massoneau appeared at the bedside of her neighbours and said she needed help, neighbours said she could stay but only for one night. They went to tell Laporte she had left him, negotiated between the couple, and refused to hold the money and cutlery she had taken when she fled.[30] Neighbours were apparently willing to reprimand husbands recognized to be poor husbanders, but were unwilling to exacerbate marital tensions or to facilitate long-term hostility, suggesting that they were reluctant to be party to the break-up of households.

Judges expressed their preference for solutions other than the creation of separate households in several ways. They were more cautious about the validity of suits for separations of property and person than separate property, and willing to use separate property cases to address varying kinds of behaviour. Other aspects of their interventions also indicated their inclination to find solutions by which households were maintained. Judges could act to discourage the possibility of separate households long before any judgement was rendered. In the dispute between Massoneau and Laporte, for instance, Laporte went to the judge with his lawyer. He said that his wife had been drinking heavily for over a year and, in a drunken state, had left him and gone to stay with others, taking with her money, cutlery, and clothes. The judge accompanied Laporte to the house where Massoneau was staying, but she denied taking anything and said her husband had threatened to kill her. The judge recorded the statements of both parties, but drew no conclusions. He added that 'as it was 9:45 at night and Laporte and his wife seemed very antagonistic towards each other and exchanged harsh words', she should remain for the night in the house, but 'return to her husband in the morning with whatever, if anything, she had removed'. He also enjoined her husband to treat her 'humanely and maritally and she to obey her husband as the duty of a wife requires', and forbade the couple who had sheltered her to take her in again.[31]

Judges in fact seem to have preferred to discipline husbands for a variety of misdemeanors without allowing marital hostilities to result in separate households. Judges who turned down petitions for separations of person and property, or accorded only separate property, often included injunctions not only to women to live with their husbands but to husbands to treat their wives 'maritally and humanely', thereby implicitly recognizing the previous exercise of undue force.[32] Moreover, when women enumerated domestic abuse among their complaints

[30] ADLA B5829, 19 March 1676.

[31] The judge's efforts to repair the household were futile in this case, as, after depositions on behalf of both parties, he granted Massoneau a separation of property and person three weeks later. ADLA B5829, 16 March 1676; ADLA B6150, 1 April 1676.

[32] According to Pothier, 'maritally' meant 'to provide her with all that is necessary for the necessities of life, according to his abilities and status'. Pothier, *Oeuvres Complètes*, 82.

in petitions for separate property, although legally these were quite irrelevant as grounds, judges again often acknowledged that more than 'inadequate maintenance' or poor husbandry of property was involved by urging men to treat their wives better. Judges were aware of the costs of allowing separate households to be established when separate property might be just as effective a remedy for what ailed spouses. As one judge explained, a separation of person and property deprived a husband of a wife's work, revenue, and mutual help, whereas separate property meant only financial disgrace.[33]

The attitudes of all parties involved in these cases may suggest that while from a legal standpoint the two kinds of separations seemed very distinct, in practice these differences often blurred in terms of the strategies involved in their implementation as options in daily life. The attitudes of neighbours and judges may in part explain wives' greater (and growing) use of separate property petitions, rather than petitions for separations of property and person, to resolve diverse spousal grievances. No easy explanation, such as new legislation, exists for the apparent greater utilization of property separations that occurred in the later seventeenth century, and this trend was accompanied by an apparent increase in husbands' stated opposition. Women could pursue the solution of settling for separate property as a remedy for an array of marital grievances much wider than its legal parameters alone might suggest.

MATERIAL REALITIES

Women who successfully sought separations faced the challenge of making a reality of the new possibilities that their legal successes had given them. The financial circumstances they faced were often fraught with difficulty for at least two reasons. Most households in which wives sought separations had run down what were usually limited resources even before court actions began. Consequently, wives' prospects for collecting what they were technically entitled to were often very problematic. Moreover, these realities also meant that husbands whose wives had secured separate property faced high, and perhaps insuperable, financial obligations. Men's frequent opposition to separations of either kind was no doubt rooted in large part in the monetary constraints they imposed.

What can we say about the actual situation of households when women sought separate property? Clearly a range of circumstances existed, depending in part on the original resources of the spouses as well as the subsequent experiences of their households. When Anne Brisson sought to secure separate property in 1649, she revealed that only 100 *livres* of lineage property was at stake, and she and her shoemaker husband had probably never had many possessions of any kind,

33 ADR BP3984, 14 February 1680.

much less significant liquid assets. In contrast, Gratienne Papin sought to protect 6,200 *livres* as the lineage portion of an 8,700-*livres* dowry her husband, a silk merchant, had received. [34] Such a couple most likely had substantial property of various sorts.

Overwhelmingly, however, women who litigated for separate property came, as we have seen, from working households, and their stories provide more evidence about the gritty and mean struggle of daily urban life for most families than of efforts to protect significant assets from creditors. Despite legal commentators' suggestions that for separate property to have meaning it had to precede disaster, pictures of households whose modest resources were always stretched so thin as to be near breaking point emerged in Nantes and Lyon. Although women had vested interests in stressing the run-down condition of their households to justify the legal protection of separate property, anecdotal evidence from women's own accounts, and concrete evidence from household inventories taken after separations were granted as preludes to the division of property, indicate that financial dire straits were the rule in the families of female litigators.

Women often noted that sales of their household assets had already taken place, that they did not have enough money for basic provisions, and that most of their dowries or other assets had already gone, so at most they sought to protect what a typical complainant described as 'what little property remains'. At worst, as one petitioner pointed out, just the costs of a sale would entirely consume the property they had left.[35] Over the course of the seventeenth century, similar accounts of sparse and desperate circumstances were repeated. In 1617, Mathurine Priou said that after several sales of household goods, her family were left with only a table and two or three old straw mattresses. In 1662, Charlotte Cerisier explained how the sale of her husband's shop and most of their furniture four months earlier had left them with only a table and small chest. In 1698, Perrine Chevillard noted that she had already sold almost everything, having only a bed and its covers left.[36]

Inventories taken as part of separation settlements confirm that households had very few resources before wives applied for separate property. When the household of Perrine Arondel and Pierre Coquelin, a 'merchant', was inventoried in the spring of 1704, three months after the judgement for separate property, its total value of 240 *livres* just about covered the 200 *livres* she was claiming as her lineage property. After Marguerite Sumur secured separate property from her husband, Henry Lohier, 'everything that was found in their residence' was assessed at only 107 *livres*. The list, like those of other households, suggests the scarcely imaginable paucity of material possessions with which many working families managed. The couple had one poster bed worth 32 *livres*—again by far

[34] ADLA B6138, 19 December 1649; ADLA B6163, 11 November 1699.
[35] ADR BP419, 22 July 1630.
[36] ADLA B5802, 10 May 1617; ADLA B5819, 21 January 1662; ADLA B5846, 5 August 1698.

the most valuable object in their possession—two small trundle beds, two tables, seven chairs, two armoires, two andirons and an iron cooking hook, a chest, twenty pounds of pewter, sundry linens, three cooking pots, and six men's shirts. The only items that went beyond absolute necessities were a small mirror and three paintings—one of Christ, one of the assumption of the Virgin, and one of the Holy Family.[37]

The items categorized as a woman's trousseau in separation settlements suggest what kinds of minimal assets separate property protected in practice. Guillemette Grelier, for instance, was assigned a trousseau valued at 276 *livres* a week after her court decision. The bed and its supplies alone—mattress, quilt, covers, and valence—was worth almost half of that sum, in a pattern common in non-elite households in which beds and bedding usually represented a high proportion of household wealth. The other belongings assigned to her included a table, a chest on a stand, some bed and table linen, a dozen women's shirts, four skirts, and a coat. Her *greffier* husband protested the inventory as he had opposed her petition, perhaps because it left him with little to call his own. Other trousseau assignments were similar. Renée Mesnard, for example, was assigned a trousseau valued at 165 *livres*. Her husband, François Fleurieu, had been the *consul des marchandes*, but her trousseau was still very modest. It included a bed and covers with various linens, an armoire, two cheap tables, and six silver knives and forks, along with some clothing and cooking pots. In some households, even these basic essentials were already gone before inventory. Jeanne Merlin, for example, noted that her shoemaker husband had pawned some of the cooking pots that should have been part of her trousseau, and asked that those pots be returned to her as part of the settlement.[38]

The circumstances of the households suggest the gap between the apparent generosity of the legal provisions for separate property and the material reality of separate property. What wives with separations were able to protect from creditors were the barest essentials and any future income or revenue rather than substantial assets. In fact, in many cases they may have tried to protect those possibilities from their husbands more than from their creditors. Many wives not only argued with their husbands endlessly over the allocation of household financial resources, but themselves worked to support the families. Their own earnings, from the myriad petty occupations that early modern urban women pursued, became clearly theirs to use as they wished once they had separate property. For instance, Jeanne Monnousseau, who sold fish to support herself and her children, saw separate property as a means to protect her income and

[37] ADLA B6165, 2 March 1704; ADLA B5834, 9 April 1682.

[38] ADLA B6153, 28 January 1683; ADLA B6160, 20 August 1693; ADR BP3984, 4 February 1675. For the importance of bedding as a proportion of wealth in non-elite households, see Julie Hardwick, *Practice of Patriarch: Gender and Politics of Household Authority in Early Modern France* (University Park, 1998), 81, and Annick Pardailhé-Galabrun, *La Naissance de l'Intime: 3,000 Foyers Parisiens, Dix-Septième–Dix-Huitième Siècles* (Paris, 1988), 282–3.

their subsistence in the face of a bargeman husband who had virtually no earnings and drank away hers after beating her to get his hands on it.[39]

Surely in most cases, wives had little real hope of obtaining the full value of the lineage portion of their dowries or even their trousseau goods. Husbands had little hope of raising the money to make good on the legal promise of separate property. In most working households, the lineage portion of the dowry was a cash payment that would have been spent immediately after marriage, and spouses had little prospect of restoring that liquidity. Action for separate property was very much like shutting the stable door after the horse has bolted: the dowries were already gone. What wives' petitions for separate property could achieve, however, was the ability to protect any future revenues, whether earned or inherited, as well as to preserve household goods such as beds, pots and pans, or linen that they had brought as part of their dowries.

THE OTHER SPOUSE

Men very rarely sought separations in their own right, and the recourse was not designed for them, but they often and sometimes aggressively opposed their wives' suits. The material realities of the circumstances of households in which women sought separations, especially separate property, illustrate the financial burden that separate property created for men who had to meet the legal obligations to cede management of household goods and dowry rights to wives. Many men either could not possibly pay or would not pay because to do so would leave them with virtually nothing. These realities raise important issues about why men so often opposed separations, about women's ability to collect what the court had endorsed as their legal rights, and about the broad financial implications of separations for men, for women, and for extended kin.

Wives' petitions for separate property did not necessarily indicate an antagonistic climate between spouses, as they could use it as a collaborative device to seek shelter of part of their household assets from creditors. This use of a different kind of separate property later became common among Anglo-American elites.[40]

[39] ADLA B5848, 17 June 1702.

[40] Early modern Anglo-American historians have closely examined the issue of separate settlements, although they are different in some important ways from French petitions for separate property. Contradictory arguments exist about the possible meanings of the evolving practice of separate estates for married women that elite Anglo-American families utilized from the late sixteenth century, and a broader group in those societies from the late eighteenth century. Was separate property a sign of the increasingly egalitarian nature of spousal relationships, a family strategy to protect at least part of the household property from creditors, or a reaffirmation of patriarchy that sought to ensure women who were abused by their husbands did not become disruptive public charges? See the respective arguments of Lawrence Stone, *Family, Sex and Marriage in England 1500–1800* (New York, 1977); Marylynn Salmon, *Women and the Law of Property in Early America* (Chapel Hill, 1986); and Susan Staves, *Married Women's Separate Property in England, 1660–1833* (Cambridge, MA, 1990).

Some spouses mutually agreed to seek separate property. Etienne Bonnefont, for example, admitted that what he called 'the continual vexations of surgeons and their general animosity' gave his wife subject to seek separate property after she showed the court evidence that the surgeons' guild had secured a court order to seize their assets for non-payment of a debt of 902 *livres*. In 1670 a creditor of Marie Lecoq and Guillaume Hore, a notary, asked that 'her alleged action for separation' be denied, and creditors were not uncommon opponents of petitions for separate property. The opposition that creditors expressed to requests for separations affirms the potential of the strategy as a spousal means to protect part of their household patrimony, as may the occasional explicit assent of a husband to a separation with the admission that his wife was right about their indebtedness.[41]

Yet in practice the strategy of spouses using separate property as a mutual household strategy seems to have been infrequent, and there is little evidence to suggest that spouses routinely used separate property to defraud creditors. Creditors very rarely, and judges never, raised the prospect of fraud; in fact, on the rare occasions when creditors intervened in separate property petitions to allege fraud, judges quickly brushed aside their charges as baseless, even while they acknowledged that if collusion had been involved then it would indeed be a serious matter. Moreover, wives' requests for separations of either kind often infuriated husbands. Spouses had alternative means to relieve pressure from creditors. They could defer that pressure quite successfully by seeking to come to terms with their creditors, and arrange a repayment schedule that promised reimbursement of some portion of the debt over a certain period of time. Many couples did choose this strategy—sometimes while the husband was temporarily absent—to avoid harassment.[42] Almost any woman in this position could have successfully sought a separation of some kind, but chose not to. Why would a woman whose husband had left town while she sorted out a debt disaster, or in other circumstances, avoid separate property? Legal recourse necessitated costs, publicity, and witnesses, and involved an identification of separate spousal interests. Any one of these requirements might have been sufficient for spouses to try something else.

In fact, many separation proceedings of both kinds indubitably had adversarial characters.[43] In 1631, for example, Yves Leblond acknowledged financial difficulties but opposed Jeanne Brossart's petition for a separation of person and

[41] ADR BP3985, 11 February 1673; ADLA B6148, 14 July 1670; ADLA B6169, 19 December 1711.

[42] See Chapter 4 for a full explanation of the issues raised briefly here.

[43] Historians have paid little attention to separate property suits in practice, and tended to take at face value the claims of jurists about the frequency of collusion. For the tendency to read jurists' claims as evidence of practice of collusion, see, for example, Schneider, 'Women before the bench', 20–1, and Hafter, *Women at Work*, 76–9. For a reading based on a sampling of separate property suits in eighteenth-century Paris that identifies spousal conflict as key, see Kaplan, *The Bakers of Paris*, 335.

property because, 'the losses and poor husbandry for which he was blamed had only been made by accident and the losses he had made on his trades were like those other merchants had experienced'. Forty years later, René Grassineau described his wife's behaviour as 'chicanery' in asking that she be required to return to live with him, whereupon he would 'treat her maritally as he always had done'.[44] Even when wives sought separate property alone, their actions were more often (and perhaps increasingly) the outcome of women's assertion of their ability to protect themselves as of spousal collaboration against creditors.

For some men, requests for separation merely exposed their financial precariousness rather than protect their household from creditors, or at least rumours thereof, and threatened to ruin their reputation—a key asset in access to credit—as well as material circumstances. When Perrine Ripocheau requested a separation in 1624, for example, on the grounds of her husband Sebastien Jarnigan's poor husbandry and mistreatment of her, he argued that her claims were slanderous, and not only opposed the petition but asked that she have to pay him compensatory damages.[45] Husbands might hope to use their opposition in such cases to defend their reputations. In 1647, for example, François Rousseau, a merchant, offered a robust response to the allegations of his wife Barbe de Chailles following her request for separate property. Five witnesses attested to his excellent qualities as head of household: that they had never seen him and his wife quarrelling, that he was a 'good husbander', that he was always assiduous in his shop, and that nobody (except his wife) had anything bad to say about him.[46]

In all cases, in the aftermath of successful petitions, the news of the separations was publicized in the couples' localities, as the royal edicts of the seventeenth-century strove to ensure. A court clerk announced the decision both at the main market and at the end of Sunday mass in the home parish of the couple concerned, and tried to ensure that news of the change of circumstances was as widely circulated as possible in the neighbourhood by pinning up placards on a post in the market square and on the main door of the parish church.[47] The public character of such declarations, although legally designated as safeguards for creditors, also must have had a chastening effect on the men whose reputations were thus diminished.

Husbands increasingly and actively opposed wives' petitions, as they sought to have their household power and financial standing preserved without qualification. Husbands opposed at least 20 per cent of the petitions made between 1600

[44] ADLA B6130 *bis*, 11 February 1631; ADLA B6148, 20 June 1671.

[45] ADLA B6127, 2 March 1624. A similar claim was made by the butcher Mathurin Galtier in opposition to Julliene Angebaud's request for separate property in 1636; ADLA B6133, 6 May 1636.

[46] ADLA B5815, 16 September 1647.

[47] See, for instance, ADLA B6137, 4 November 1644; ADLA B6139, 28 August 1647; ADLA B6179, 29 December 1729; ADLA B6179, 30–31 August 1732; ADLA B6179, 26 January 1732.

and 1660, at least 30 per cent in the 1670s, and at least 44 per cent in the first decade of the eighteenth century.[48] Just as women's goals in petitioning for separations were varied, so men's reasons for stating their opposition in court could result from different agendas. In a few cases, husbands' opposition may have been part of a rhetorical legal strategy to ensure the success of the petitions. Usually, however, their stands were adversarial, and suggest the threat that women's petitions for separations posed to their spouses' financial stability and cultural authority as heads of households.

Although formal spousal opposition to separation petitions became increasingly common, judges appear to have taken little notice. Spousal opposition did not stop even a single petition for separate property, although it seems to have played a more important role in undermining petitions for separate person and property. Husbands were also universally condemned to pay the costs of petitions for separate property. This outcome was apparently so widely anticipated that one spouse, who complained in 1705 that he did not have the 'means' to oppose his wife's request, did ask—unsuccessfully—that she at least be required to pay the costs.[49] Often, husbands' opposition was merely noted, or husbands simply denied that their wives' complaints had any basis. In 1637, for example, Jullien Dorleans opposed his wife Jeanne Poullain's petition for a property separation on the grounds that her claims lacked any validity.[50]

Husbands' explanations for their opposition (like their wives') undoubtedly highlighted some issues over others, and raised factors as problems that were usually elided in wives' accounts, especially with regard to the actions of kin from outside the conjugal family, and wives' property management. What husbands saw as inappropriate interference of members of wives' families in spousal relationships was frequently mentioned as a cause of disturbance within conjugal households. Some claimed, for instance, that wives' parents or siblings had encouraged them by offering places to stay or helping remove property. When Pierre Becot successfully opposed his wife Marguerite Bardon's request for a separation of person and property only four months after their marriage in 1673, his grievances were focused on her father who, he said, still owed him 300 *livres* he had promised to pay besides the dowry 'in favour' of the marriage, and who should be forbidden from stopping his daughter coming back to live with her husband.[51]

Women's removal of property from households was another common cause of husbandly grievance, and one in which family or neighbours were also often

[48] The rider 'at least' is used here because only cases where the husband's opposition was clearly identified were counted. It is possible that more oppositions occurred—perhaps in cases in which no mention was made of the husband's position, and certainly in the cases for which few details of either side were recorded.

[49] ADLA B6166, 31 January 1705.

[50] ADLA B6134, 15 January 1637. Dorleans' protests were ignored.

[51] ADLA B6149, 1 July 1673. For other objections by husbands on the grounds that kin had meddled in their households, see, for example, ADLA B6127, 12 and 30 April 1625; ADLA B6131, 19 December 1634.

implicated. René Grassineau, for example, not only opposed his wife's petition for a separation of property and person in 1671, but asked that she have to report the property she had already taken from their household and be forbidden to do so in the future. Françoise Ouairy had left her household almost fifty years earlier, and asked for a separation of property and person after detailing her husband's physical abuse. He, however, complained of the property she and her father had removed, and successfully requested not only that her petition be denied but that her father be ordered to stop encouraging her to leave or to remove property again.[52]

Husbands who contested their wives' petitions, but admitted using violence, often cited their wives' removal of property or what they regarded as moral shortcomings in their wives as justifying their behaviour. Pierre Laporte opposed his wife's suit for a separation of person and property on several grounds. He alleged that she drank and had made a pact with the devil. Neighbours said his wife had removed various monies, cutlery and clothes from their household. As one recalled, when Laporte heard that his wife told neighbours that he had looked for a knife with which to kill her, he said that 'it was a matter for a knife that his wife was a whore', and that he had beaten her and would beat her again. From Laporte's perspective, apparently, his own actions were justified by his right and need to govern a household made intolerable by his wife's actions.[53]

Husbands' opposition to wives' petitions not only gave full expression to the hostile climate between spouses, but implicitly asserted the right of household heads to manage their own households, and acknowledged the threat their wives' claims to separate property entailed.[54] The complaints about the interference of kin suggest a contestation within this community over the relative power and distinctness of the conjugal household in a society in which kin were given considerable discretion to oversee and supervise the patrimonial affairs of households.

For many husbands, separate property involved the relinquishing of control over the few assets and small monies to which the household had access, as well as the creation of perhaps insurmountable legal obligations on future income to repay dowries. This financial reality was surely critical in husbands' opposition. Husbands who opposed their wives' efforts to establish separate residences probably had very practical motives besides their denial of the alleged grievances. A husband who had to repay his wife's dowry faced a significant financial burden—one so proportionately large, in fact, that their prospects for

[52] ADLA B6148, 20 June 1671; ADLA B5806, 16 January 1626.

[53] ADLA B5829, 16 and 19 March 1676.

[54] In discussing husbands' opposition to petitions for separations of property and person heard before the *Parlement* of Paris, Sarah Hanley notes that 'the division of capital that occurred if a wife legally withdrew her dowry spelled disaster for the household'. However, husbands in those cases opposed the petitions on the basis of their wives' alleged adultery. Hanley, 'Engendering the state', 24.

paying it back seemed slim. Moreover, a husband also faced the loss of his wife's labour and earnings, both indispensable to successful working households. Pierre Joubert voiced a rarely articulated acknowledgement of this reality when his wife, Guillaumette Michou, sought to leave him. It was, he said, 'true that there had been differences between he and his wife on different occasions that had obliged him to treat her badly'. Yet, he went on, 'for the good of their business and to more easily be able to feed and raise the children of their marriage, [he] asked the court to let them continue to live together on condition of the promises he makes to live peacefully with his wife and without using any violence'. Claude Lespere, a stockingmaker in Nantes, voiced a similar perspective, saying simply that he 'did not have sufficient means for the separation', and besides, he was not a squanderer, he was able to pay his debts, and his problems were due simply to the 'difficulties of the times'.[55] Men whose wives received separate property found themselves humiliated by the public announcement of their households' difficulties, faced with the loss of control over household property that was an integral privilege of married men, and often in very practical dire straits. Although wives with separate property were supposed to support their husbands and families with whatever income they had, many men must have sharply felt the precariousness of their situation. As one man who opposed his wife's petition said plaintively, he had 'no means in the world of living' without the work and money of his wife.[56]

Husbands often articulated their hostility to their wives' legal actions directly through violence or appropriation of household property, as well as, or instead of, in court. Sometimes, wives came back to court to complain that their husbands were outraged by their successful separation suits and had beaten them in the wake of separate property decisions. The tension that lay behind such violence was articulated in the complaint of a wife who said that her husband was so angry when he discovered that she had successfully secured separate property that he beat her severely and threatened to beat her to death, telling her 'then you'll have your separation'. Catherine Arthaud said, in 1683, that after she 'had been obliged' to obtain separate property, her husband Etienne Descouleur, 'out of hatred for the separation had beaten her on several occasions'.[57] Other men sought to seize household assets, presumably to preserve them for their own use, by more or less confrontational means. Isabel Petit, for example, who worked as a secondhand goods seller, complained to the court that while she was at the river doing the family wash, her husband stole 30 *livres* that she had saved from her earnings to settle a debt.[58]

Husbands could continue to express their opposition and to raise obstacles to the implementation of court decisions in myriad ways. Women complained

[55] ADSL B1669, 23 February 6177; ADLA B6177, 7 July 1727.
[56] ADSL B6128, 30 January 1604.
[57] ADR BP3984, 11 June 1683.
[58] ADR BP3985, 20 July 1656.

not only that their husbands' frustrations with their wives' court decisions led to violence, but that husbands refused to allow inventories which preceded settlements to go ahead, or that they refused to pay when the settlements amounts had been decided.[59] Men could themselves use the court system to harass their wives. Antoinette Clerc complained that Pierre Berthaud's 'hatred' of her separate property status led him, 'hoping to ruin her finances and reputation', to start 'unfounded' legal actions against her over money he claimed she had received earlier in their marriage. Leonard Rang complained to the court that his stepfather had alleged that his mother had stolen household property simply 'to vex' his mother after she started a separation action against him.[60]

Spouses frequently also had disputes, whether genuine or fabricated by one party, over which goods belonged to whom. Henry Lagoute, for instance, who had opposed his wife's suit, refused to allow sergeants to inventory the household items in his room because, he said, all the goods he and his wife had had been auctioned before their separation to pay their debts, and the few items he had now belonged to his landlord. Julienne Hamon produced seventeen witnesses who had seen her buy, or had sold to her, all manner of household basics to counter her husband's assertions that they belonged to him and were not part of her trousseau.[61]

Clearly, wives to whom the courts had awarded separations of either kind often, and perhaps usually, faced significant challenges in collecting what they had gained on paper. If husbands refused to (or could not) meet the financial obligations of the settlement, wives faced decisions about whether to use the courts to pursue collection. The costs of going to court alone, while not excessive by many measures, still presented significant burdens for families whose grip on financial subsistence was already eroded. Elizabeth Franchon, a Lyonnais wife, admitted as much in 1700. She said that her efforts to obtain her property had consumed the little money she had, money that she had borrowed, all to no avail. In the meanwhile, she and her husband fought about money so much, and he had been beaten her so badly as a reiteration of his opposition to her legal action, that now she wanted separation of person too.[62] Even without overt husbandly opposition, lack of resources presented a simple and sometimes insurmountable obstacle to wives' ability to transform their legal success into the collection of what they were in principle owed. While cases that came to court were certainly among the most contentious, they illuminate what must have been common problems. Pernette Rondet noted that her husband's liquid assets were simply not enough to cover what he owed her, so

[59] See, for example, ADR BP3984, 9 January 1674; ADR BP4052, 10 July 1700; ADLA B6184, 29 November 1742.

[60] ADR BP3985, 29 April 1663; ADR BP2865, 24 January 1680.

[61] ADLA B5854, 30 July 1627; ADLA B5858, 6 December 1737.

[62] ADR BP4045, 3 September 1700.

she asked the court to accept her offer to take a rural smallholding parcel he had inherited.[63]

Women whose husbands could not pay often had another resort if, as commonly happened, their husbands' kin had guaranteed repayment of the dowry in marriage contracts. These kin guarantees meant that wives' separate property rights also entailed obligations for siblings or parents as well as husbands, and claims on this basis could also be the source of intense intra-familial conflict. In 1672, for example, nine years after Magdalene Tarvier secured separate property from Jacques Daguin, he finally paid her 1,700 of the 2,000 *livres* he owed her. She asked her parents-in-law to pay her the balance because they were the guarantors of her lineage property in the marriage contract. When they resisted, she took them to court. Anne Tisseur sued her brothers-in-law as heirs of her father-in-law for her dowry after her husband failed to pay, and despite their declaration that they wanted to reduce her rights to a 'just' amount, the court found for her and they were required to pay the amount she requested.[64]

A wife with a separation might also seek other kinds of financial support from her husband's kin in the wake of his failure to pay. Courts found kin of wives with separate property liable to pay for the maintenance of women and their children if husbands did not or could not pay. Marie Chapellier, for example, successfully pursued her mother-in-law Pierette Quercy for a yearly pension of 60 *livres* to supplement the income she had after her separate property agreement with her husband. Quercy claimed in turn that her own remarriage had led to the loss of the property she had inherited from her first husband, Chapellier's father-in-law, losses that she blamed on her new husband, from whom she too had sought separate property, and which she said had left her in such straits that 'without the assistance of her kin she would have been reduced to begging'. Françoise Gastineau, who secured separate property from Jacques Caillaud in 1607, successfully sought support for four of their children from his kin in 1610.[65]

Wives' difficulty in collecting the property to which they were legally entitled may explain why some seem to have started to remove property before starting legal action, or while the court proceedings were going on. Although some husbands' complaints on this score were probably motivated by a desire to harass, husbands so frequently asserted that wives had removed property prior to the granting of separations that some wives seem certainly to have explored such pre-emptive actions. Anne Levesque started separation proceedings against Guillaume Pichou, for example, on the grounds of his threats and abuse as well as his maintenance of a 'girl of ill repute' in their house. Pichou contested Levesque's claims, and added that as soon as she started the court case she had

63 ADR B4052, 10 March 1698.
64 ADR BP3984, 14 September 1677; ADR BP3984, 2 May 1681.
65 ADLA B6118, 22 December 1610; ADR BP785, 30 August 1670.

removed her goods and broken into an armoire to take the money inside. Three years later, Pichou complained to the court that Levesque had taken goods worth 20 *livres* from his shop, and the court ordered her to repay.[66] In both cases, Levesque's strategy was rooted in her expectation and experience of the difficulty of translating legal victory into a meaningful access to resources. Pierre Amballeur alleged that before and since his wife had left him, complaining of battery with no grounds as far as he was concerned, she had removed property that included a bed with its mattress and covers, all their linen, and her jewellery. She also took their two older girls with her, but left him with a younger child and a baby at a wet nurse. These actions, Amballeur claimed, 'reduced her husband to such indigence that he and the two children could not survive' even before legal action started.[67] What Amballeur's wife had removed amounted roughly to what she had probably brought to the household as her trousseau.

The financial implications were not only one-sided either, as although many wives may have had trouble collecting their legal entitlements, separate property awards enjoined wives with the responsibility to support their family with their revenues, creating obligations for them too which could be difficult to meet. Husbands sometimes complained that their wives had not used their revenue they had to support them. Rudolph Coize finally went to court, for example, to persuade Marie Perrin to pay him the 300 *livres* a year she had been directed to provide him in her separate property decisions five years earlier, and which he claimed she had never paid.[68]

SEPARATE LIVES

The what next question, that is, what happened after wives secured separations of either kind, is very difficult to answer, because couples usually disappeared from court records. While historians have argued that elsewhere separations of property and person often formally recognized already existing situations, this pattern does not seem to have held true in early modern France. It certainly was not the case in the vast majority of cases in which separations spoke to issues of property only. Couples in those cases usually continued to maintain common households, and might have more children. Separations of either kind did not allow spouses to live completely independent lives, and the ongoing intertwining of spousal interests and resources created many complicated situations. In 1703, for instance, Michelle Delaville promised to co-sign a loan of more than 2,000 *livres* for Estienne Grilleau so that he could be freed from jail, where he was imprisoned for debt, and he gave her a power of attorney to make the necessary arrangements, although her promise was conditional on the recognition that this

[66] ADLA B6139, 6 February 1647.
[67] ADR BP3984, 13 May 1682.
[68] ADR BP3984, 8 April 1680.

arrangement 'in no way nullified or prejudiced the separation between them'.[69] Women's experiences of post-separation lives depended not only on which type of separation they had been granted, but on their financial situation, their economic opportunities, and their rank. Separations remade marriages, but in widely diverse forms.

Wives were permitted to live apart from husbands during the legal proceedings, and sometimes judges recognized the potential for tension that such court actions caused when they designated cooling-off periods in their judgements. It is difficult to establish what proportion of wives chose to leave while their cases were being conducted, but clearly many did—perhaps virtually all women who sought separations of person and property, and a significant proportion even of wives who requested separate property alone. Judges who gave women six months before they had to return to their conjugal households tacitly acknowledged that the daily task of remaking marriages in the wake of legal decisions was challenging, even aside from the inherent financial pressures and complications. Even with cooling-off periods and certainly without, the re-establishment of households, whether after separate property requests succeeded or separation of person requests failed, was often fraught with difficulties.

Wives who secured separations of property and person embarked on significant turning points, although finances and family concerns shaped their options. Sometimes their movement to different residences could entail joining another household rather than living on their own terms. The judgements typically required them generally to 'live respectably according to their status', or more rarely, specifically to return to their birth families. Wives with separations of person and property who moved in with their birth families or took up residence in convents were primarily very young or from wealthier families. Wives from more affluent families were much more likely to go to convents or even to live with kin, perhaps because their reputations as well as financial resources were involved. Women from families with substantial property who secured separations of person and property often found that their lives continued to be closely regulated by the courts and/or their families. For example, Magdelaine de Montouard secured, in 1675, a separation of property and person that included a substantial yearly pension of 4,000 *livres*, indicating that her circumstances were far superior to those of most women who sought separations in courts of first instance. After an apparently extensive conflict about where she would reside, in 1678 the court ordered her to live in Lyon for two years, and permitted her husband to visit her.[70] Wives who were young, or who had worked with their husbands, may have lacked the most basic financial wherewithal to live alone. For women in these kinds of circumstances, renewed dependence on kin was the price of their day-to-day release from intolerable married life.

[69] ADLA B6165, 19 June 1703.

[70] ADR BP3984, 8 October 1680.

Separated wives who lived independently may have been able to do so in part because of social status and in part because of their ability to support themselves. Wives who were able to follow the kinds of independent occupations open to women were better positioned to try to maintain independent households after they secured separations of person and property. Isabel Petit, for example, supported 'her little family' of herself and six small children as a reseller of 'cheese, soap, groceries, cabbages, oil and other little items', continuing the trade she had engaged in beforehand. Thereze Massoneau left the bar she had run with her husband, to run another bar in a nearby street.[71]

Separations did not, of course, always end spousal conflicts. Sometimes they exacerbated them, as we have seen, and judges often anticipated the possibility of ongoing conflict when they attached the early modern equivalent of restraining orders to judgements for separations of property and person. These usually included an explicit threat that a man should not threaten or harm his newly separated wife with words or actions, on pain of judicial penalty. Nevertheless, the prospects for any real punishment of men who continued to harass their wives seems to have been slim, in part because of the treatment of marital problems as a civil matter.

Certainly, on occasion the types of behaviour that had led women to seek legal action continued afterwards, despite the warnings that judges gave husbands. Marguerite Pinel, for example, came back to the court almost a year after she had secured a separation of property and person, to complain about her husband François Bernardeau. She explained that 'he won't stop' coming to where she lived, and that he 'breaks the furniture, takes her merchandise, linen, and money', did not even leave her bread to live on, and battered her on a daily basis 'so that there is not a place on her body that he has not bruised with his blows'.[72] In a legal system in which criminal penalties for domestic violence short of murder were virtually unknown, plaintiffs' ability to use the civil system to combat battery could not thwart obstinate persistence. Pinel and Bernardeau continued to have a very contentious relationship for years, although their affairs remained tightly intermingled. Later, for example, she complained that some grain she had bought from her husband had turned out to be of such poor quality that she could not resell it. Four bakers consulted by the court agreed that the grain was too poor to be used to make bread for human consumption, and the judge ruled that the grain should be dumped in the river and that Bernardeau should pay back half of what his wife had paid him.[73]

Wives with separate property alone had to continue (or to resume, if they happened to live elsewhere during the court proceedings) to co-habit with their spouses. How issues of control over property or other matters were determined in such cases is elusive. Subsequent household life no doubt depended in large

[71] ADR BP3984, 20 July 1656; ADLA B5831, 26 June 1677.
[72] ADR B6676, 21 July 1683. [73] ADR B5838, 13 and 27 July 1686.

part on whether the petitions had been mutual goals or antagonistic, on the degree of contention about the financial implications of separate property, and on the extent to which men were inclined to accept the rebuke they had received, whether about their property administration, the broader disorder of their household, or their use of force against their wives.

The tensions and hostilities were often great, not least because of the practical difficulties in working out how households were to function under separate property arrangements. Wives were charged with using their incomes to support their families, but what might this obligation really involve? Spouses could disagree about what household costs a *femme separée de biens* was responsible for, about what remained part of a husband's responsibilities, and about what separate property would mean for the management of their domestic lives. Renée Bretineau, for example, secured a property separation from Julien Jouneaux in 1652, but subsequently left to stay with her mother-in-law when she and Jouneaux argued about the financial implications of her action. He insisted that her complaints as to his failure to support her were ill-founded. She was, he said, 'the mistress of her own property and revenues', and could support herself. She claimed that he had a continued obligation to maintain her, pointing out that 'if he took a servant he would have to feed her'. Jouneaux seemed to think that having secured separate property it was only fair that she should cover a share of household costs and could not expect continued maintenance, whereas Bretineau continued to assert her entitlement to his support. Yet despite their bickering, after a three-and-a-half-year break either side of their dispute, the three children they had had between 1647 and 1650 were joined by seven more from 1653 onwards.[74]

Although separate property legally required that the conjugal household should continue, some wives seem to have taken separate property awards as a lever or tacit permission to establish separate residences. For example, François Chabret, a silk worker, said that after Anne Pillard's separate property suit she had taken all his property 'without wanting to give [him] the least help', and left their home 'with the design of keeping all their goods without giving even a piece of bread' to Chabret. He asked the court to order her to return to their marital household.[75]

Separate property was far from a guarantee of future security for wives. Hellayne Laplaine, for example, was owed 600 *livres* for her dowry by her husband Antoine Pinet, but to avoid his debts Pinet departed town and left 'very little property which was not sufficient to pay'. By the spring of 1666, Laplaine was more than six months behind with her rent and owed 200 *livres* to her landlord, who obtained a court order to sell her goods. Laplaine's father, a

[74] ADLA 4E2/1480, 28 January 1652; ADLA J sous série 25j, Registres Freslon under entries for 'Jouneaux'.

[75] ADR BP3984, 8 January 1682.

saddler, stepped in, offering to pay the 200 *livres* rather than see the sale proceed because, as he noted, her goods would not cover the debt.[76]

Although many early modern families fell behind with their rents, Laplaine's difficulties were only one of many reminders that separated women often found themselves in very precarious circumstances. Their specific situations varied widely, but the remaking of their marriages, in whatever form, offered challenges of every kind—logistical, social, and cultural, as well as financial. The particulars of their endeavours are often impossible to reconstruct, but the cases that reveal wives' experiences in longer timeframes indicate the treacherous waters that women faced when they sought to remake their marriages.

Spouses who had secured separations of person and property moved into a kind of marital *demi monde* where earthly bonds of property and household were dissolved, but in which sacramental ties that prevented either from remarrying were upheld. Judges who granted such separations sometimes sought to clarify what the subsequent status of separated wives would be by ordering them to live with their birth families or in convents. Moreover, many such women probably faced financial constraints that required them to live with family members. Yet some such wives did subsequently maintain their own households in ways that defined liminal in early modern terms: neither dependent nor independent, whether legally or financially.

Separate property alone muddied the categories of husband and wife, along with the rights, privileges, and reputations they bestowed. Separate property came with a price for both spouses. Men lost the right to manage household property, and saw news of their financial difficulties publicized in their parish and marketplace. Wives' separate property eroded a defining pillar of adult masculinity, and effectively emasculated married men for whom the link between property and potency was severed, as well as damaging their credit. Moreover, while honourable failure could happen to anyone, separate property carried the slap of mismanagement, and not just bad luck or hard times. As we will see in Chapter 4, this association with wrongdoing rather than misfortune was a serious matter. Wives with separate property were, rhetorically, radically repositioned as the first creditors of their householders and as the supporters of their families, but their material circumstances were often precarious, and public property management could be perilous to women's reputations. Women with access to property were in incongruous positions that made them potentially vulnerable to scurrilous slander, whether as wives with separate property, widows, or, at risk to more than their good names, alleged witches. Catherine Cornet and Pierre Carcanac, for instance, complained to the court about the damage done to their honour and businesses when, in the wake of her securing separate property, customers called her a 'bitch and a whore' and alleged that Carcanac

[76] ADR BP3985, 17 May 1666.

defrauded his creditors.[77] Remaking the terms of marriage could come with a price.

NEGOTIATING MARITAL STATUS

The significance of marital status as a negotiable resource for spouses, communities and the courts, is highlighted particularly clearly at moments when uncertainty about marital status led to interrogations of it. Two such moments indicate some of the varied, if often elusive, ways in which marriages could be remade. These stories of early modern marriages not only illuminate the life course of less conventional marriage possibilities, but are richly suggestive about aspects of married life and of representations of marital status. The meanings of marital status involved complex calculations in a multi-dimensional grid. The categories of girl, wife, and widow were not absolutes but encompassed a range of possibilities, good and bad. Thinking about marriage as a critical category was not only a matter of politics or ideology. The desire to stabilize marital status was more than a historiographical construct or prescriptive or ideological device. The energy that spouses, communities, and officers of the state invested in stabilizing the varied components of the marriage matrix indicate the deeply rooted perception that the stakes were high. Paper and publicity were key elements in the negotiation and interpretation of marital status, as was an economy of information.

'The widow Arnaud' rented a single room in Nantes, and had so few possessions that she took her meals with her landlord. Her room lacked a bed or table, and contained only an armoire in which she kept some bed linen, her clothes, and a little box with some silver cutlery. She gave music lessons to support herself, and although she quickly fell behind with the 10 *livres* a month that she owed for rent and board, and still needed to borrow money from her landlord, she lived respectably and paid her local poll tax. After having toothache for several days, she dressed carefully in a brown and white dress with a cherry petticoat, bedecked herself with a watch, a diamond ring and gold earrings, and set off to find a surgeon to help her. During her treatment the house caught fire, and in a panic she jumped from the third floor window and died of a broken neck. Everything in her room except the armoire, jewellery and silver was subsequently sold to a secondhand vendor for the pitiful sum of 12 *livres* and 5 *sous*—two thirds of which went to pay for her funeral and the remainder for legal fees.[78]

[77] ADR 8B729-6, 7 October 1707. For suspicion about property-managing widows, see Julie Hardwick, 'Widowhood and patriarchy in seventeenth-century France', *Journal of Social History*, **26**, 1 (September 1992). For the role of access to property in witchcraft allegations, see Carol Karlsen, *The Devil in the Shape of a Woman: Witchcraft in Colonial New England* (New York, 1987).

[78] It is unclear what happened to the bed coverings and a rug that were inventoried in August 1724 as Renault's claim began to be processed and were then valued at 100 *livres*. They were not

Neighbours no doubt sighed or shrugged over the pathetic ending of a mundane life, until three months later, when the widow Arnaud's good reputation was posthumously blown by the arrival of her husband. Her efforts to represent herself as a respectable widow came to naught, as her death left her husband, Nicolas Regnault, a lawyer (*procureur*) in the appeals court (*presidial*) at Rouen, with the field clear to characterize her as an uppity, runaway wife. His self-positioning as the wronged spouse was not entirely persuasive (he remembered, for instance, being married in Paris when in fact they had married in Rouen), but without anyone to oppose him he successfully secured his right to her property. The widow Arnaud, it turned out, was in fact Jeanne Bonhumeau, who had married at 20, lived to regret it, and finally, nine months before her death, had left her husband and Rouen and taken her bed linen, clothes, jewellery, some pewter dishes, and some silver cutlery, to start a new life in Nantes. All but the pewter were in her armoire or on her body when she died.[79]

Although Jeanne's reputation was sullied after her death, she was more successful in creating a stable self-representation during her life than were some of her contemporaries. Like Jeanne, Françoise Gastier arrived in Nantes without a husband and rented a single room. Yet within months, some of her neighbours complained to the city's provost about her. Françoise, they said, 'sometimes calls herself girl and sometimes widow and without wanting to say which [and] she invites all kinds of people' to her room.[80] Even with the judge and his clerk in her room, Françoise said 'she did not want to give her name and wasn't obliged to'. When they continued to press her for her name, her place of birth, and about whether she was married, she finally gave her name and said she was 'married but is not obliged to say the name of her husband, being separated from him and not knowing where he is'.

The judge disliked Françoise's response so much that he quickly made an inventory of the room (where, unlike Jeanne, she at least had a bed and table), locked and sealed the door, and took Françoise, with a small child of 4 or 5 years of age 'who she said was hers', downstairs to take her to the poorhouse (*hospital générale*) while he investigated her 'conduct'. Faced with confinement, Françoise admitted that her husband was a journeyman called Jullien Robin who then worked for a weaver in town. Nevertheless, the judge took her to the poorhouse and continued on to find the absent husband, who proved equally reluctant to acknowledge his status. As the judge investigated, the spouses told him complex

mentioned in the list of property handed over to Renault in March 1725 when he took the silver, and sold the jewellery for 44 *livres* and the remainder of the clothes and goods for 12 *livres*. The armoire was not mentioned in either list, and probably belonged to the landlord.

[79] ADLA B6176, 20 April 1724 (capitation); 29 April 1724 (judge's enquiry into death); 17 July 1724 (husband's complaint); 12 August 1724 (inventory of room); 5 March 1725 (sentence in favour of Arnaud, and sale of property).

[80] ADLA B6679, 25 February 1689. The complaint summarized the neighbours as saying that she 'se disant quelques fois fille & quelques fois veuve & sans voulloir dire dont'.

and conflicting stories of marital conflict, but they agreed that a court in the nearby town of Vannes had granted a separation of person and property. To the judge's frustration, neither seemed to have any papers of any kind to attest to any stage of their relationship.

In these stories, publicity and paperwork provided the battlegrounds for both individuals and local officials in determining marital status; that is, the key prerequisites of how the early modern state wanted to envision marriage became markers that officials looked for, and markers that working people recognized but could also manipulate for their own purposes. The French state marked marital status primarily through publicity about the ceremony and through a paper-trail, whether by parish records and/or marriage contracts. Working people were also usually careful to safeguard marriage contracts, for instance, in acknowledgement of the property as well as personal and legal commitments which they guaranteed. Françoise Gastier and Jullien Robin, however, claimed to have neither the papers that marked their movement from single to spouse, or from conjugal entity to separate spouses. The local judge called in by neighbours to investigate their status resolved this matter to his satisfaction when he created a new paper-trail to replace their missing papers, and reconstructed a paper record of their marriage in which each publicly acknowledged their spousal relationship, however hostile.

Yet working people, recognizing the importance of publicity and the paper-trail, could also use those tools to reconstruct their own marital identity. When Gastier and Robin claimed to have 'lost' all their papers, they may also have sought to lose a marital status with which neither was satisfied and which neither any longer desired. Jeanne Bonhumeau similarly sought to manage the paper-trail and neighbourhood opinion to secure her new status as a widow. Prescriptive practices about naming were an important part of the marital matrix. A woman was virtually always identified by marital status as 'wife of. . .', but did not take her husband's name. If Arnaud du Tihl (the imposter in the Martin Guerre case) could pretend to be a husband, wives as well as men could pretend not to be. She not only represented herself as a widow, but chose a new name, neither her birth family's nor her husband's. She had successfully solidified her new standing at the time of her death, when not only her neighbours identified her as 'the widow Arnaud', but even her tax receipt from the city formalized her self-chosen marital status in that way. In claiming a new identity for herself in neighbourhood opinion and on her tax receipt, she effectively used publicity and built a new paper-trail to corroborate it.

The mesh of marriage could be pulled tight or loosened in these ways. For Françoise, the designation of wife seems to have been the detritus of a failed marriage—one that had no meaning for her (or whose meaning she sought to ignore) as she continued with her life. She sought to elide it whether in paper or publicity as she demurred to clarify whether she was girl or widow in response to neighbours' questions. But her neighbours tied uncertainty about marital status to immorality, and the local judge was so bent on stabilizing her status that he sought to force her to accept her wifedom by confinement and by reconstructing it through his own interrogations. With the fact of her marital status confirmed, the judge released Françoise from the poorhouse, but felt it appropriate to deal with the confusion clearly created by a wife with separate property, who refused to identify herself, by immediately transferring her for detention in the city's home for wayward girls (*refuge des filles penitentes*). Françoise was certainly not a girl, nor was there any demonstrated need for her to repent for the usual reason: immorality of the sexual kind. In fact, the judge's investigation of her conduct had focused on the clarification of her marital status, not on the matter of her visitors. Yet like other unconventional wives, she too found herself, literally in this case, in the realm of whoredom.

In these cases, spouses engaged in elaborate self-fashioning of marital status for the consumption of others, and sought to manage paper and publicity to represent their marital status in particular ways. Jeanne Bonhumeau's efforts to locate herself as a respectable widow, for example, involved continuous assertions of her standing. Despite the varied evidence of penurious circumstances that emerged after her death, she wore all her jewellery to go to have her tooth fixed on what turned out to be her last journey. In this way and others she determinedly conveyed to the watching community an image of economic well-being that could hardly have contrasted more starkly with her actual financial circumstances. In fact, the intensity of construction of a public self may have been in inverse correlation to the reality being hidden.

The persuasiveness of this self-fashioning, however, was tied not only to the capacity of the producers of self, but to what the community would allow. Neighbours' willingness to be persuaded by such representations or concerns was rooted in economic as well as moral concerns. In neighbourhoods, clarity of marital status was tied to financial as well as moral security. Elaborate networks of credit linked individuals and households, and the consequence of these debt practices was that community decisions about marital representations were tied to economic as well as legal and cultural issues. A woman—whether with separate property, separation of property and person, or living alone but still legally married—met less contestation about her status if her situation was financially as well as in other terms stable. Jeanne Bonhumeau's efforts to demonstrate economic wellbeing were so successful that she was assessed in the capitation for 4 *livres*. This figure was far above the poverty line, and represented her situation as being far more secure than her real circumstances indicated.[81] Her management of the economy of marriage was integral to her ability to manage the other economies of daily life such as borrowing and information.

[81] Thanks are due to Nancy Locklin for the significance of a capitation assessment of this size.

THE ECONOMIES OF MARRIAGE

If for kings of France, early modern marriages were 'the colonies of his state and the seminaries of his subjects', as an official of Louis XIV's chief minister, Colbert, wrote in 1670, what were the political and personal implications of a marital matrix that was rooted in such a multidimensional grid?[82] While marriage was a primary legal, economic, and cultural category, spouses, communities, and the state negotiated the meaning of marital status. Spouses made elaborate efforts to fashion a particular marital status for public consumption, and neighbours and judges were deeply invested in stabilizing representations of marital status. Yet none of these practices and concerns undermined the centrality of marriage. On the contrary, the intensity of energy around questions of spousal behaviour and marital status indicates how marriage was regarded as fundamental in early modern life.

Despite the lack of divorce, disgruntled spouses had many judicial and extrajudicial options to remake their marriages. For early modern French women who sought to reorder their marriages, property separations emerged as an option that was more viable than separations of property and person. The relative ease with which property separations were granted provided married women with a valuable lever, whether in the form of just threatening or actually petitioning, to counter the legal privileges which their husbands had over marital property, and to use as a pressure point in terms of kinds of behaviour other than the narrow management of property. Yet property separations also maintained the conjugal household, and, at least in principle, the ultimate authority of the husband, without whose consent wives could still not alienate their property, and to whom they still owed obedience and respect. As a compromise, women's access to separations gave them more manoeuvring space, but within a context in which judges and community ensured that the basic structure of conjugal households was maintained.[83]

The success of property separations highlights the importance of women's own property in its various forms in early modern French marriage dynamics. As wives'

[82] 'Recueil de traitez sur le droit public . . . faite par order de Monsieur Colbert', quoted in Alain Lottin, 'Vie et mort du couple: difficultés conjugales et divorces dans le nord de la France aux dix-septième et dix-huitième siecles', *Dix-Septième Siècle*, **102–103** (1974).

[83] A lively debate over the relationship between litigation in a variety of marital areas and court actions took place in early modern German historiography. Safley and Watt argued that courts formed a positive alliance with women that benefited feminine power, while Lyndal Roper argued that courts' protection of wives came at the price of perpetuating their status as weak dependants whose defence depended on their continued submissiveness. The case of separations examined here suggests a middle course between these two positions; that is, there were limits to the ways in which women could expect the courts to protect them, although their ability to seek resolution, and the terms on which they did so, placed them as negotiating partners. For a summary of this debate, see Safley, *Making of Modern Marriage*, 57–120.

own assertions testify, their capital (from dowries and inherited property) and labour were critical pillars of a successful household economy, and essential safety-nets worth protecting from creditors in an unsuccessful economy. Moreover, the presence of lineage property in the patrimony of households was a critical issue in causing tension between birth families and spouses as well as between spouses. A comparison to early modern England highlights the importance of the legal category of lineage property in shaping the French situation. In England, where there was no lineage property, there was also no common-law right to separate property, nor any separate property agreement until the nineteenth century. Furthermore, separate domicile was easier for women to obtain than separate property.[84]

While women were the usual subjects of enormous legislation and litigation as the bearers of disorder in early modern society, in these cases men's behaviour was also identified as disruptive. Husbands' competence was questioned rather than assumed. Indeed, some of the women in these cases seemed almost to be marrying 'on spec', and were able to use separation petitions to reshape the political economies of their households in ways more protective of their own interests if on closer inspection their husbands proved inadequate.

As the negotiations and contests over separations showed, however, the state, the local community and the extended family were all parties in the process. For the state as represented by its judges, and for the local community and for kin anxious to protect their lineage property interests, separations were a means of disciplining and regulating households. All three, however, shared an impulse to seek to limit the disruption by tending to try to reconcile the parties, and to favour property separations as checks on the internal problems of households, rather than to support the disintegration of conjugal households that separations of property and person entailed. For these groups, property separations offered numerous advantages as solutions to various types of marital strife besides the narrowly patrimonial. They ensured that a wife and children would have some means of subsistence, and relieved family, neighbours or parish of the need to support them. They bounded a husband's exercise of power, whether over property or person, by making public and implicitly censuring his wrongdoing.

Conceptualizing marriage as a work in process and as a negotiable resource complicates our notion of the impact of early modern reformations on marriage. While Protestants in theory permitted divorce, in practice not only was divorce very difficult in Protestant regions, as many studies have shown, but the option of separation with its origins in Catholicism was lost. Even in Catholic areas such as France, however, marriage became a matter of secular jurisdiction. Alain Lottin argued that ecclesiastical courts offered women better options than civil courts. While it does seem true from the single surviving region where ecclesiastical jurisdiction survived in France, and from Venice, that women were more likely

[84] I thank Carol Shammas for this point.

to obtain separations of property and person in church courts, French civil courts, as we have seen, offered the remedy of separate property quite flexibly to fit a wide range of marital woes. Women might not have had the right to divorce, but they sought to remake their marriages in a variety of ways in court and out of it.

The process of seeking separations illuminates marriage as a key political economy of urban households. The day-to-day negotiations that maintained the hierarchical relationships between gender and authority at the heart of early modern society, were pervasive but not rigid. Petitions for separation in either form illustrate the ways that women sought to employ, rather than evade, the apparatus of the state. They could appeal to their families and community, and through their local judicial system, the state, to intervene on their behalf into their households against their husbands, or utilize the possibility of separations (with the tacit support of their spouses) to protect their households against the interventions of creditors. Thus the activities of women seeking separations in many ways countered the political and rhetorical energies that are often more evident in early modern society.

The negotiations that surrounded marital status suggest that what early modern French men and women learnt about authority and power in the seminary of marriage was a sense of a heterogeneous state.[85] Spouses and communities used the legal process of seeking separations as a means to debate the parameters of marital responsibilities and obligations. The tensions and strategies involved in these accounts suggest that while royal rhetoric and decrees over marriage formation increasingly emphasized paternal and conjugal power in early modern France, an ongoing debate about the underpinning of gendered authority continued on a day-to-day level in urban communities. As spouses and as subaltern subjects, prescription and practice taught them that political economies rested on contingencies that required elaborate efforts at maintenance and left considerable room for assertion. The management of marital status was only one of the many ways in which crown, community, and subject engaged in endless rounds of complex interactions through which authority was constructed and circumscribed. The economies of marriage were integrally intertwined with other essential quotidian political economies: of justice, of litigation, of borrowing, and of violence. The individual decision-making, neighbourhood debate, and possibility of legal intervention that were embedded in marriage-making were critical elements in these other economies too.

[85] For perspectives that emphasize the varied rather than monolithic nature of various French institutions, see Jonathan Dewald, Review of John Hurt, *Louis XIV and the Parlements: The Assertion of Royal Authority* (Manchester and New York, 2002), in *H-France*, 2, 81 (August 2002); and Crowston, *Fabricating Women*.

2

Economies of Justice: The Possibilities of a People's Court

In early November 1639, Ysabel List walked along her neighbourhood streets to the Nantais court house in the centre of town just a few hundred yards from the cathedral. She joined the bustle of people who were in the court house that day, whether as plaintiffs, defendants, lawyers, legal workers from judges to bailiffs, or witnesses, all seeking their own ends in the many different kinds of cases heard in a building that housed the provost's, the *sénéchaussée* and the *presidial* courts. She told her story to court officials in making a request for a *séparation de biens* from her husband, Jan Bernier, a merchant, and the royal prosecutor found her story persuasive enough to give her permission to go forward with an investigation within a couple of days. The prosecutor noted the name of the lawyer who would act for her, and with him she selected three witnesses and produced a list of questions they should be asked. Bailiffs delivered notices to appear to the witnesses, and they in turn walked to the court house to provide evidence on her behalf. By the second week of January 1640, two months after List's first complaint, the judge ruled in a sentence that gave her, as she had sought, control over her own property.[1]

Like List, early modern men and women flocked to courts of first instance, whether as plaintiffs, defendants, or witnesses. Moreover, to accuse someone of enjoying, unnecessarily starting, or prolonging lawsuits became a popular insult. For example, Nicolas Bachaud, a shoemaker, described his neighbour Simon Grangeot as a 'perpetual plaintiff [*processif*]' who 'starts many ill advised cases in which he loses'.[2] Although being 'litigious' in these ways was a negative and carried the connotation of 'bad neighbour', the willingness and skill to use legal avenues judiciously were invaluable resources for List and her peers.[3] For members of working families, readiness or reluctance to go to court was critical in the management of household lives. Moreover, legal process became a key

[1] ADLA B5810, 7 November 1639; ADLA B6135, 10 January 1640.

[2] ADLA B5841, 10 November 1689.

[3] Dictionary definition as well as popular usage framed a *processif* as a 'bad neighbour' as well as a promiscuous litigator: see the 1694 first edition of the *Dictionaire de l'Académie Française* at http://colet.uchicago.edu/cgibin/dico1look.pl?strippedhw=processif.

element in negotiations within communities and in interactions between state and subject.

List's use of the court, like that of so many of her early modern contemporaries, raises many questions about the civil system in practice rather than principle, and in lower rather than elite courts. Literally millions of French men and women participated in civil proceedings, whether as plaintiffs, defendants, or witnesses. Hundreds of thousands of civil suits fill the archives throughout France as part of a distinctive early modern pattern that has been documented across Europe: the levels of litigation rose dramatically in the sixteenth century, and remained high throughout the seventeenth century before declining in the eighteenth century.[4]

Yet List's experience and these popular perceptions of going to court were in many ways at odds with the prescriptions of seventeenth-century political rhetoric and literature which consistently conjured up images of a litigation system that was onerous, expensive, inefficient and inaccessible. Calls for reform of the civil system were at the forefront of the demands made at the meeting of the 1614 Estates-General. The preface to Louis XIV's famous Civil Ordinance of 1667, designed to reform the litigation process, noted the shortcomings that caused 'the ruin of families': different courts following different practices, costs of proceedings, long delays, variations in sentences, and so on. In 1669, Racine's play *Les Plaideurs* satirized the civil system with its description of cases over such minor matters as efforts to recover damages for two bales of hay that lasted fifteen to twenty years and cost 5,000–6,000 *livres*.[5] Certainly, early modern Europeans were highly litigious, and perhaps far more so than today. Indeed, our contemporary rhetoric about frivolous lawsuits bogging down courts, damaging our economy, and indicating some kind of pathological breakdown of society

[4] Historians are divided as to the reasons for this increase. For this debate and the high levels of early modern litigation and the eighteenth-century decline, see the essays in John Bossy (ed.), *Disputes and Settlements: Law and Human Relations in the West* (Cambridge, 1983). For Spain, Richard Kagan, *Lawsuits and Litigants in Castile, 1500–1700*; for Germany, Christian Wollschlager, 'Civil litigation and modernization: the work of the municipal courts of Bremen, Germany in five centuries, 1549–1984', *Law and Society Review*, 24, 2 (1990); for France, John A. Dickenson, 'L'activité judiciare d'après la procedure civile: la bailliage de Falaise', *Revue d'Histoire Economique et Sociale*, 54, 2 (1976); Colin Kaiser, 'The deflation in the volume of litigation at Paris in the eighteenth century and the waning of the old judicial order', *European Studies Review*, **10**, 3 (July 1980), 309–36; Zoe Schneider, 'The Village and the State: Justice and the Local Courts in Normandy, 1670–1740', 3 vols., Ph.D. thesis, Georgetown University, 1997; and especially Herve Piant, *Une Justice Ordinaire: Justice Civille et Criminelle dans le Prévôte Royale de Vaucouleurs sous l'Ancien Régime* (Presses Universitaires de Rennes, 2006). Work on civil matters has been particularly rich on early modern England. See, in particular, the pioneering work of C.W. Brooks, *Pettyfoggers and Vipers of the Commonwealth: The Lower Branch of the Legal Profession in Early Modern England* (Cambridge, 1986), and Craig Muldrew, *The Economy of Obligation: The Culture of Credit and Social Relations in Early Modern England* (Basingstoke, 1998).

[5] Jeffrey K. Sawyer, 'Judicial corruption and legal reform in early seventeenth-century France', *Law and History Review*, **6**, 1 (Spring 1988), 102–8; Isambert, *Recueil Général*, **18**, 104–5; Racine, quoted in John Carey, *Judicial Reform in France before the Revolution of 1789* (Cambridge, MA, 1981), 11.

echoes early modern complaints about the consequences of what a 1554 royal decree in France termed the 'disease' of litigation.

Traditionally, historians have largely accepted the characterizations of early modern commentators, and concurred in highlighting the corruption, nepotism and costliness of the legal process. They have noted the fortunes made by lawyers and judges, and patrimonies lost by hapless litigants trapped in endless cycles of cases that could be appealed and re-appealed, that demanded never-ending payments of fees and bribes to multitudes of court officials, and that could be moved from court to court in the myriad overlapping jurisdictions that constituted the early modern French legal system.[6] Historians have also, by and large, considered litigation as a man's world, noting the legal disabilities of married women or minor daughters.[7]

Some thoughtful qualifications have revised the usual wisdom about litigation. Phillip Benedict has observed that litigation provided employment for a whole host of people whose work was directly or indirectly linked to the provision of legal services. Richard Kagan has noted that many criticisms were based on unrealistic idealism about what early modern judicial systems could be like.[8] A dense emerging literature on many aspects of popular experiences of civil litigation as well as criminal procedure in early modern England has challenged many aspects of traditional views of its legal system, and provides a useful point of comparison.[9] Historians have also explored other ways of resolving disputes through varied means of informal dispute resolution, termed in France as '*infrajustice*', to argue that this was an alternative to, and perhaps more effective than, using the institutional justice system.[10]

Yet for France, we know very little about the practice of litigation in courts of first instance that was the most common judicial experience in the lives of working people. Most people who brought civil suits did so in local courts of first instance, and not in the elite courts that have received far more of historians' attention. Most people who were in court were involved in civil rather than criminal cases, although the latter have dominated historiography, and even then primarily for the decades leading to the Revolution rather than earlier.[11] We

[6] See, for instance, Sawyer, 'Judicial Corruption', and Carey, *Judicial Reform*, 11–20.

[7] Richard Kagan, *Lawsuits and Litigants in Castile, 1500–1700* (Chapel Hill, 1981), 10.

[8] Phillip Benedict, 'More than market and manufacturing: the cities of early modern France', *French Historical Studies*, **20**, 3 (Summer 1997), 521–2; Kagan, *Lawsuits and Litigants*.

[9] Examples include Brooks, *Pettyfoggers and Vipers*; Laura Gowing, *Domestic Dangers*; Muldrew, *Economy of Obligation*; Tim Stretton, *Women Waging Law in Elizabethan England* (Cambridge, 1998); Steve Hindle, *The State and Social Change in Early Modern England* (Basingstoke, 2001).

[10] In France, Benoît Garnot and Alfred Soman have pursued the significance of 'infrajustice' in a wide variety of articles. For a succinct review of their work and broader patterns in French legal historiography, see Piant, *Une Justice Ordinaire*, 10–13. For explorations of the variety of forms of dispute resolution in many times and places, see the essays in Bossy, *Disputes and Settlements*.

[11] Piant calls attention to the huge but 'forgotten' world of civil litigation in lower courts; see Piant, *Une Justice Ordinaire*, 9–10. Tim Stretton's observation about England that 'historians have only scratched the surface on the subject of local litigation' is even more trenchant for France.

know very little about the people who used the civil process. If we focus on the varied experiences of participants in the litigation process, as witnesses as well as defendants and plaintiffs, rather than on institutional patterns, the possibilities of litigation emerge. When we observe the mundanity of litigation, its perils and contagion recede, and its political, social, and economic centrality in early modern society emerge.

This chapter explores the legal lives of working families in the seventeenth century. It uses marital litigation as a case study to investigate the practical impact of institutional complexity by exploring how people dealt with similar problems in different jurisdictions, and examines similarities and differences in men and women's options, experiences, and uses of the courts. Litigation was indisputably a popular phenomenon in two key senses: not only did enormous and increasing numbers of people experience court proceedings whether as plaintiffs, defendants, or witnesses, but participants in litigation in courts of first instance were all far more likely to be from the ranks of working families, broadly defined, than from elites. Their practice with legal process provided a key resource for early modern urban families to use in managing many aspects of their lives. Going to court was an accessible and indispensable element of family business.

ACCESS TO LITIGATION IN COURTS OF FIRST INSTANCE

What kind of access did working people have to litigation in courts of first instance? Various measures can be taken as indicators: the socio-economic circumstances of people who went to court, as well as the costs they faced and the length of time their suits occupied, were all important factors in determining potential barriers to use of the courts. In practice, all these pointers suggest that the bar for using civil suits as a viable resource was quite low. The practical popularity of litigation supports this reality despite the doom-ridden rhetoric about it. Exploring some basic issues about who had access to urban courts of first instance, what their experiences of litigation were like, and what impact the institutional context had (that is, in which type of court the case was heard)

Stretton, *Women Waging Law*, 6. Studies of criminality in the sixteenth and seventeenth centuries include Christiane Plessix-Buisset, *Le Criminal devant ses Juges en Bretagne aux 16e et 17e Siècles* (Paris, 1988); James R. Farr, *A Tale of Two Murders* (Durham, 2005); Malcolm Greengrass, *An Economy of Violence in Early Modern France: Crime and Justice in the Haute Auvergne, 1587–1664* (University Park, 1994). Work on the eighteenth century is far more extensive, and includes, among others, Richard Mowery Andrews, *Law, Magistracy, and Crime in Old Régime Paris, 1735–1789* (New York and Cambridge, 1994); Nicole Castan, *Justice et Repression en Languedoc à l'Epoque des Lumières* (Paris, 1980); Yves Castan, *Honnêtété et Relations Sociales en Languedoc (1715–1780)* (Paris, 1980); Steven G. Reinhardt, *Justice in the Sarladais, 1770–1790* (Baton Rouge, 1991); Julius Ruff, *Crime, Justice and Public Order in Old Régime France: The Sénéchaussées of Liborne and Bazas, 1696–1789* (London, 1984).

highlights the relative significance and attractiveness of these courts for working families.

Early modern men and women lived under a dazzling array of overlaid jurisdictions with multiple and sometimes conflicting legal regimes whose reach depended both on the subject of conflict and the social rank of the parties. A modern dictionary of the Ancien Régime characterized its legal system as one of 'unbelievable complexity'.[12] Like other European countries, France was divided into a patchwork of overlapping and competing jurisdictions in which multiple local legal regimes (customary and Roman) operated alongside the national decrees issued by the crown, and canon law (although the latter had declined in importance by the seventeenth century), as well as the *arrêts* of the relevant sovereign courts.

So, for instance, a Nantais might find himself or herself in the provost's court, in the *sénéchaussée*, in the *presidial* (an appeals court), in an ecclesiastical court, in the *consul* (a merchants' court), or in front of the city council. He or she was subject to regional customary law as well as national decrees, to court judgements known as *arrêts*, to canon law, and to municipal regulations. A variety of other courts had subject-specific jurisdiction that might apply on occasion, such as the *cour des monnaies* that was responsible for regulating the country's money supply. A Lyonnais resident faced similar but not identical choices, as while both cities were, of course, under the jurisdiction of the monarchy, some sharp differences in their formal legal systems existed. Nantes was in a customary law region, while Lyon observed Roman law. The same kinds of cases could be heard in different courts. Separation cases, for example, were heard in a *sénéchaussée* court in Lyon, but in a provost's court in Nantes, even though Nantes also had a *sénéchaussée*. This kind of complexity, unbelievable or not, was common in many parts of early modern Europe.

In principle, the early modern equivalent of a zip-code lottery, in terms of jurisdiction, might seem to have been important for a person's prospects in pursing a particular kind of case, such as a separation. A provost's court's jurisdiction was strictly limited in terms of both types of action and status of plaintiffs, whereas a *sénéchaussée* dealt with a broader range of cases and people. A *sénéchaussée* (a level of court also known as a *bailliage* in some regions) could deal with all kinds of cases, civil and criminal, and all kinds of people, except for those specifically reserved for other jurisdictions. (Nobles always had the right to be heard by *parlements* if they chose.) A provost's court (also variously known as *vicomtes*, *vigueries*, and *chatellenies*, depending on the area) had jurisdiction over people who might be characterized as 'floaters'; that is, people who were marginal and/or transitory residents of a particular area, such as vagabonds, the homeless, or soldiers. After 1670 the matters before them were not to exceed 300 *livres* in

[12] Lucien Bely, *Dictionnaire de l'Ancien Régime: Royaume de France XVIe–XVIIIe Siècle* (Paris, 1996), 1016.

value. Its charge was integrally linked to the maintenance of public order and management of disorder.[13]

Traditionally, historians have concurred on the significance of these prescriptive differences to characterize provosts' courts as providers of summary justice (on the spot, and without formal proceedings) to outsiders, in contrast to the judicial process of the *sénéchaussées,* which provided legal gateways and a rule of law for established families.[14] Geoffrey Parker and Bruce Lenman, for example, described them as 'two separate networks' that handled two categories of offenders 'with their own clients and their own codes of punishment'. They cite Olwen Hufton's contrast: 'beggars, vagrants, and poor thieves commanded a monopoly of attention [in the provosts' courts]. To be brought before such a court was almost proof that one belonged to the down and outs, amongst those whose word could not be trusted . . . the justice of the *bailliage* or *sénéchaussée* is about compensation; that of the *prévôté* about punishment. *Prevotal* justice is the justice of the harsh example.'[15]

Yet Herve Piant has recently pointed out that such arguments rest on very unusual cases, and a broader view of the practice in lower courts challenges many such assumptions about legal process in the seventeenth century.[16] Specific evidence about the global numbers of civil actions in local courts is very limited, despite the rich anecdotal evidence about the ubiquity of legal actions. Samplings of Norman courts in the later seventeenth and early eighteenth century show that civil cases outnumbered criminal cases by more than four to one, and an exhaustive review of actions in a provost's court in France in the same period show an even more striking ratio of 20 or 25 to one. Indications from many parts of Europe suggest that while criminal prosecution rates were low throughout the early modern period, civil litigation rates soared. Craig Muldrew's study of the town of King's Lynn in eastern England, one of the most ambitious studies of a

[13] For these distinctions, see Isambert, *Recueil Général,* 15, 372–6. Varieties of court names in different regions, and the abolition of the provost's courts, are summarized briefly in Bely, *Dictionnaire,* 1015. The *sénéchaussée* courts also had some public order charge. See Marcel Marion, *Dictionnaire des Institutions de la France aux XVIIe et XVIIIe Siècles* (Paris, 1923; reprinted New York, 1968), 441.

[14] For conclusions of this kind, see the essays by Nicole Castan, 'Summary justice', and André Zysberg, 'Galley rowers in the eighteenth century', in Robert Forster and Orest Ranum (eds.), *Deviants and the Abandoned in French Society: Selections from the Annales: Economies, Sociétés, Civilisations* (Baltimore, 1978).

[15] Bruce Lenman and Geoffrey Parker, 'State, community and criminal law', in V. A. C. Gatrell, Bruce Lenman, and Geoffrey Parker (eds.), *Crime and the Law: The Social History of Crime in Western Europe since 1500* (London, 1982), 28.

[16] Piant notes that such observations about provosts' courts have relied primarily on analysis of the very small fraction of cases—generally very unusual—that were appealed to higher courts. He argues that these appealed cases, although they may appear to support such interpretations, were entirely unrepresentative of the handling of the overall caseload. Piant, *Une Justice Ordinaire,* 276–83.

local early modern court, documented extraordinarily high levels at court of first instance activity.[17]

The demographics of the Nantais and Lyonnais local courts of first instance were resolutely popular, but in both courts, members of established rather than marginal families were the primary instigators of litigation. Plaintiffs were drawn overwhelmingly from the ranks of working families, and they were mostly of modest or very modest means, but not indigent (although some clearly were in circumstances that left them in danger of slipping from respectability, however precarious, to poverty). Occupations and dowry sizes offer two measures of the broad social access to courts of first instance. In these cases the husbands were usually craftsmen, or were described as the loosely defined 'merchant', meaning that they ran their own shops trading a range of goods. Very few elite families used these courts of first instance, and very few households who would be characterized as poor by the standards of the old regime. The median value of dowries was only 1,400 *livres*—far less than even the bourgeoisie, and much less than elites would provide for their daughters.[18] The social profiles of families who litigated separation cases in both the Nantais provost's court and the Lyonnais *sénéchaussée* were very similar. The dowries of Lyonnais wives (a median of 1,425 *livres*) were only a couple of hundred *livres* larger than those of Nantais spouses (a median of 1,200 *livres*), and in either case the dowry level attested to the modest quality of the parties. People of similarly modest background seem to have dominated civil actions in courts of first instance in other parts of France and other parts of Europe.[19]

Most cases seem to have been settled quickly by any standard. The time elapsed from the plaintiff's initial petition to have the case heard to the court's judgement was in most cases under three months. Few cases lasted longer than a year, and none lasted longer than two years. Petitions for property separations were handled very expeditiously, with more than 90% being settled in less than three months. Requests for separations of person and property were usually settled within six months. The courts seem to have handled the cases efficiently, without any obvious sign of corruption or nepotism. Little evidence of delaying tactics of any kind was apparent. It seems that only one defendant asked for a case to be moved to a different court, arguing that a family connection between his wife and a judge made it impossible for him to obtain a fair hearing.

[17] Dickinson, 'L'Activité Judiciare'; Schneider, 'The Village and the State', **1**, 9–17, and **3**, 606–8; Piant, *Une Justice Ordinaire*, 133; Lenman and Parker, 'State, community, and criminal law'; Muldrew, *Economy of Obligation*, 199–271.

[18] Dowry size was specified in 234 petitions for separate property.

[19] For similar patterns of court users elsewhere in France, see Piant, *Une Justice Ordinaire*, 108–11, for the provost's court in Vaucouleurs; and Schneider, 'The Village and the State', **3**, for courts in Normandy. For England, see the evidence summarized in Stretton, *Women Waging Law*, 95 and 239.

I have not been able to find any indication of cases being appealed, so the decisions of the courts of first instance seem to have been routinely accepted as final.[20]

The costs of suits seem to have been relatively modest, to gauge by the example of separations, although we know remarkably little about court costs in general. The totals for costs of cases are elusive, and so any estimates of costs are highly speculative. The costs, based on various fragments of evidence, usually seem to have amounted to one to two weeks' wages. About 10% of sentences noted costs, with the average being 16 *livres*—the equivalent of what many master artisans could expect to earn in two to four days in the mid-seventeenth century.[21] These figures probably represent the cost of court fees alone, with other possible additional costs, including payments to the legal representatives of the parties, and perhaps payments to cover the expenses of witnesses. Plaintiffs and defendants in these kinds of cases almost always hired lawyers (*procureurs*) and avoided the notoriously expensive barristers (*avocats*). Witness fees (a matter we will examine later) rarely ran over 5 *livres* in the seventeenth century, or over 20 *livres* in the first half of the eighteenth century.

One surviving bill for a Lyonnais separation of property and person in 1637 provides some basis for speculation about total costs.[22] It concerned a case that was unusual in many regards, giving every reason to believe that its fees were exceptionally high. It was by far the most highly documented extant case in the Lyonnais records, with more than eighty pages of documents surviving, and the spouses were very wealthy. Moreover, separations of person and property took longer to process, as we have seen, and so may have been more expensive. Nevertheless, this case provides a useful indication of the variety of fees. Rather than simply note the total charge as judges usually did, the president of the court made an itemized list of 'costs and fees' that totalled 114 *livres*. The itemized charges comprised 30 *livres* for the court (including fees for the wife's initial complaint, for four days of inventorying her property, and for verification of the documents provided); nine *livres* for the depositions gathered by the court; 24 *livres* for the royal prosecutor; 18 *livres* for the plaintiff's lawyer (a *procureur*); 18 *livres* for the court clerk; and 15 *livres* for the bailiff. If the first itemized amount (30 *livres* for the court) represents the figure usually listed on sentences for costs, the fees in this exceptional case were almost double the average of 16 *livres*, which, in view of the complexities of the case, is not surprising. If the other fees were also approximately double, the total costs for more mundane cases for separation of property and person might have run to 50 or 60 *livres*, and the far more common cases for separate property a little less than that.

[20] ADR BP3984, 8 October 1680. Likewise, there were very few appeals of decisions in the provost's court at Vaucouleurs. Piant, *Une Justice Ordinaire*, 276–83.

[21] For sample daily wages for artisans, see Farr, *Hands of Honor*, 107.

[22] ADR BP3985, 28 February 1637.

Costs in the range of 50 *livres* would have represented a couple of weeks' earnings for a master artisan, a sizeable but not enormous expense. The significance of this level of obligation should not be underestimated for working households whose financial stability was always precarious, but it suggests that cases like these were certainly not ruinous in themselves, and it counteracts the rhetoric of extortionate litigation.[23] Moreover, the common practice of initiating a case as a negotiating strategy (and then not pursuing a judicial remedy) meant that many plaintiffs incurred few costs because few court fees were involved in the initial complaint that secured permission to proceed.

Finally, the procedures of the Nantais provost's court, from the initial petition to the gathering of evidence from witnesses, to the royal prosecutors' recommendation, and the sentence, closely resembled *sénéchaussée* practice. While provosts' courts could exercise summary justice, the Nantais court never did so in any separation case. There is no evidence of either court being only the first step in a long series of appeals upwards, and when judgements were made they usually ended the legal proceedings at this level. Judges ruled in similar ways on similar matters, whether in *sénéchaussée* or provost's court. Both courts were very responsive to requests for separate property, and both were more cautious about petitions for separations of person and property.[24]

Analysis of the practice of litigation in courts of first instance, from the perspective of what it was like to be a party in one of these courts rather than at the institutional arrangements, suggests that traditional characterizations of sharp differences between the *sénéchaussée* and provost court systems are erroneous, at least in civil matters. Civil cases in local courts were relatively affordable, offered timely resolution of suits, and highlighted how women as well as men could utilize the civil process for their own ends. Moreover, the same was true for Nantais and Lyonnais residents, although their cases were heard in two different courts of first instance in cities where two different legal regimes prevailed. The demographics of court users, and the time and costs associated with their going to court, were similar. This corner of the legal system functioned well for a wide range of working people.

WHAT DIFFERENCE DID JURISDICTION MAKE?

In these regards, the striking correspondence between courts raises the question of whether the patchwork geography of France's legal system made any difference to people's experience of, and options with, litigation. Yet while similarities

[23] For modest costs in England, and the difficulty of calculating total costs as opposed to specific legal fees, see Stretton, *Women Waging Law*, 83–4.

[24] For similar patterns of rare appeals and consistent procedure in the provost's court in Vaucouleurs, see Piant, *Une Justice Ordinaire*, 275–7.

included process, social profile, costs, time and outcome, one difference between the courts is striking: litigants tended to emphasize different kinds of evidence in the two different courts while seeking the same ends. These patterns suggest that local legal cultures, informed by judges' preferences and neighbourhood opinion as well as jurisdictional patterns, shaped the kind of evidence presented.

Jurisdiction over cases varied in towns across France, and it was therefore not exceptional that different courts had authority over actions for separations in Lyon and in Nantes. In terms of separations, for example, secular courts had, by the seventeenth century, taken over jurisdiction from church courts through almost all of France, although different secular courts handled the cases in different areas.[25] In Normandy, wives in Falaise, which had an active *vicomte* (the equivalent of a provost's court), went to the *sénéchaussée*. In Macon, not far from Lyon, both *bailliage* (the peer of a *sénéchausséé*) and provostal courts heard separations cases. Social status seems to have determined who went where, as elite women took their cases to the *bailliage*, and working women to the provost's court. For instance, Claude Augustin, the wife of a barkeeper, took her case for separate property to the provost, whereas Claude de Civay, the wife of the nobleman Hugues de Mazelles, sued for separate property in the *bailliage*.[26]

Judicial inconsistencies of this kind were rife in early modern legal systems, and were usually rooted in earlier conflicts between courts over jurisdiction. They created a jurisdictional geography, within and between towns, that involved many kinds of legal actions beyond separations. In Dijon, for instance, one such dispute between the *bailliage* and the municipal court over who had the right to apply seals on household property in preparation for post mortem inventories, led to the decision that one court had jurisdiction after the death of the first spouse, and the other after the death of the second.[27] Due to the legacies of these jurisdictional disputes, court authority could vary not only from town to town (as in the case of separations in Lyon and Nantes), but sometimes from house to house (as in the case of separations in Macon), or even from spouse to spouse (as in the case of Dijonnais inheritance matters).

These inconsistencies were, in fact, one of the main concerns of jurists and legal commentators, but litigants seem to have had little problem with them

[25] The exception was the diocese of Cambrai in north-eastern France. For the church courts' handling of separations in that diocese, see Alain Lottin, 'Vie et Mort du Couple: difficultés conjugales et divorces dans le nord de la France aux XVIIe et XVIIIe siècles', *XVIIe Siècle Revue*, **102–103** (1974), 59–78.

[26] For Falaise, see Dickinson, 'L'Activité Judiciare'. A small sample of thirty cases from Macon suggests that social status determined which court the plaintiffs used. ADSL B930, 13 February 1598, and ADSL B1631/1, 30 June 1610.

[27] For details of this dispute, and the phrase 'jurisdictional geography', I thank Professor Christopher Corley; see Corley, '*Justice Gracieuse*: Municipal Magistrates and the State in Early Modern Dijon', paper presented at the Annual Meeting of the Society for French Historical Studies, Scottsdale, March 2000.

in the seventeenth century. Reformers feared that the variations opened up potential abuses in terms of discrepancies in decisions, and cases brought in several jurisdictions. Yet no concrete indications survive of litigants who engaged in what legal historians call forum shopping, the practice of moving their cases from court to court in pursuit of the most favourable result. By the seventeenth century, the chronic conflicts over jurisdictional precedence of the previous century had been largely resolved, so that, for example, the court that had jurisdiction over separations varied, but the validity of that jurisdiction had been clearly established.[28]

From the litigants' perspectives, the main discernible impact of jurisdictional variety came not in terms of outcome, social profile, costs or time, but of the type of evidence each court preferred. In Nantes, wives who pursued separations of either kind presented a broad range of evidence of disorders of many kinds, and largely disregarded the legal technicalities that separate property required proof that the husband's financial mismanagement was threatening a wife's dowry while separation of person and property required proof of real danger to a wife's life. They focused on broad indications of what they often called '*mal mesnagement*' (literally, 'bad husbandry' or 'bad householding'), pointing out how their husbands spent too much money on gambling, or drank too much, or did not work hard enough at their occupations. They often linked this disarray to other kinds of household disorder, and especially to men's violence. When Perrine Couillard sought separate property from her street porter husband Jan Priou in 1617, she and her witnesses emphasized a list of spousal shortcomings that were common in many cases. Priou was a 'bad householder' who drank too much, 'never moved from bars', argued with all and sundry, used violence to force his wife to find money for him, and caused a 'tumult day and night'.[29] Like Couillard and Ysabel List (cited at the beginning of this chapter), Nantais wives and their witnesses portrayed households in which men's behaviour undermined orderliness on several fronts, even when the remedy they sought was separate property alone.

The cases of Lyonnais wives, on the other hand, observed the legal conventions of separations more closely. They highlighted domestic violence in suits for separation of person and property, and usually focused on very specific types of financial threat in petitions for separate property alone. Lyonnais wives who requested separate property usually cited immediate dangers to their household's financial standing, and thus to their own dowries, by offering proof that creditors had taken legal action to start to seize and sell the family's assets to cover unpaid debts. They frequently highlighted actions from specific creditors who were owed particular amounts of money. When, for instance, Marguerite Chaine sought

[28] For resolution of jurisdictional conflicts, and very little evidence of cases being shaped by them in Normandy, see Dickinson, 'L'Activité Judiciare', 14–16.

[29] ADLA B5802, 10 May 1617.

separate property from her husband Pierre Rozic, a butcher, in 1677, she noted the 400-*livres* dowry she had brought to their marriage nine years earlier, claimed they had 'diverse debts', and noted that another butcher, Germain Chenas, had procured a court order to secure their household goods (a *saisi*) in preparation for a sale to cover what they owed him. In the same year, Claudine Dumas filed a separate property suit against her husband, a master silkworker, with a very similar laying out of evidence. They had married in 1654, when she had a dowry of 600 *livres*, they had had various debts which had led to *saisis*, and she provided proof of one particular action for repayment, started by a silk dyer, for 181 *livres*.[30] Elaborations on their husbands' work ethic, debauchery, or capacity for abuse were much rarer in separate property suits in Lyon.

Local legal cultures, rooted both in the institutional charges of the courts and in the preferences of judges in various localities, reveal these differences of presentation of evidence. Since the provost's court was in principle primarily concerned with maintaining public order, that focus may have shaped the presentation of Nantais separation cases that often prioritized evidence of household disorder of all kinds. Yet local judicial practice resulted from the particular dynamics of the region as well as institutional parameters. Judges had wide discretion to interpret, in practice, the legal requirements that a wife's dowry was imperiled in the case of separations of property, or that her life was threatened by violence in the case of separations of person and property.

Even amongst the legal elite, opinions could vary on the kind of evidence necessary in a particular type of case in a particular jurisdiction. The 1628 edition of Claude de la Rochette's handbook of judicial practice was published in Lyon and dedicated to the chief judge of the city's *sénéchaussée*. It addressed, among many other matters, the issue of 'why a separation can be pursued'. The handbook explained that it 'happens when the husband lives prodigally' and the wife is 'ready to fall into evident indigence'. The author noted that exceptions would be made if the husband was impoverished or indigent at the time of marriage, or if the dowry had been lost without the husband being at fault.[31] Rochette's guidelines suggested that the kind of broad evidence that Nantais women usually provided was appropriate, yet in practice the indications of household disorder on many fronts that characterized Nantais petitions were rarely articulated in Lyonnais suits. Instead, Lyonnais *sénéchaussée* judges focused on specific, narrow kinds of evidence. Proof of creditors' actions dominated the evidence, and Lyonnais royal prosecutors, assessing cases for the courts' judges, bluntly noted that this was what mattered in their court. Mathurin Galliot, a royal prosecutor in the 1670s, repeatedly made the link between creditors'

[30] ADR BP3984, 4 September 1677; ADR BP3984, 7 December 1677.

[31] Claude LeBrun de la Rochette, *Les Proces Civil et Criminel contenants la Methodique Liaison du Droict, et de la Practique Judiciare* (Lyon, 1628), 302–3.

initiation of legal action to secure repayment by way of having the debtors' goods sold (the first step was known as a *saisi*, by which the creditor obtained a court order to have the debtor's property secured prior to its sale), and separate property. In a case in 1673, for example, he wrote that 'usually' separations were not agreed 'unless the household goods were secured [*saisi*]'.[32] Such legal actions indicated some degree of financial constraint, but of a kind that was common in many working families.[33] It did not necessarily indicate a husband's prodigal behaviour, nor was it proof of the imminent indigence of the wife. Neither did it provide any indication of the husband's standing at marriage, nor whether financial difficulties were or were not his fault.

This narrow interpretation of what constituted proof of an imperilled dowry had the advantage of offering the Lyon *sénéchaussée* court a clear-cut and expedient means of handling separate property claims. As one Lyonnais prosecutor succinctly expressed it: 'The disorder of the husband's affairs has been established by the *saisi* that has been made'.[34] A low-key debate took place over whether any *saisi* would in fact suffice. In a Lyonnais case in 1690, for instance, a creditor complained that the *saisi* the plaintiff cited was 'too modest' to justify separate property, but the royal prosecutor said it was big enough 'given the rank' of the spouses. In practice, however, there is no indication that judges used the size of a *saisi* as a measure of whether or not separate property should be assigned.[35]

Such variations in local legal cultures, expressed in the kind of evidence presented, probably proliferated across jurisdictions. Women who requested separate property in the early seventeenth century in Macon—a smaller city not far from Lyon—whether in the *bailliage* or provost's court, framed their requests in a pattern that was midway between those in Nantes and Lyon. They usually complained that their husbands dissipated household property, that creditors had pursued them, and that they were reduced, or about to be reduced, to poverty. Maconnais plaintiffs often also mentioned their small children, ubiquitous members of households who were almost never mentioned in Lyonnais or Nantais suits, and sometimes raised the issue of domestic violence. Janne Noblet, for example, argued that the 'disorder' of her husband's affairs was due to his 'propensity to guarantee the loans of his neighbours and friends', that their household property was about to be auctioned to meet a debt which he had incurred as guarantor, that she had a 'number of small children', and that 'she feared falling into begging and poverty'. Jehanne Cochet said that her innkeeper husband 'does what he wants to without wanting to take the trouble to work with [her] to earn their living', that they had many creditors, and that

[32] ADR BP3984, 18 April 1673. For similar statements by other royal prosecutors, see, for example, ADR BP3984, 24 November 1676; ADR BP3984, 9 September 1676.

[33] For more on the implications of debt practices in these households, see Chapter 4, *Economies of Markets*.

[34] ADR BP3985, 15 July 1672.

[35] ADR BP802, 26 April 1690.

he had already sold most of the jewellery she brought, along with a 500-*livres* dowry, to their marriage. She wanted to protect 'her children', and noted how her husband 'threatened and insulted' her. Meanwhile, a husband who opposed his wife's petition said it was not his 'bad husbandry', as she had alleged, that caused their difficulties and threatened their children, but genuine market losses and the costs of illness, so his wife's request should be denied.[36] These kinds of justification for or against separate property requests closely resembled those that De la Rochette advocated in his judicial handbook dedicated to the Lyonnais *sénéchaussée*.

The plight of children, although not alluded to at all in the legal guidelines, was another variable in evidence rooted in local legal cultures. Women in Lyon almost never mentioned their children, wives in Nantes, over the course of the seventeenth century, slowly began more often to raise their obligation to support their children, and from early in the seventeenth century Maconnais wives frequently mentioned children. Nantais wives hardly mentioned children until the 1670s, much less justified the request for a special public status separation implied on the basis of their responsibilities as mothers. From then, however, the presence of minor children began to arise as an issue in petitions for separate property. In 1671, for instance, Anne Marguignon explained that her husband's debts, gambling, and lack of attention to his job or householding motivated her to try to protect her own property 'to avoid being reduced to last resorts, poverty and beggary with the two children she has in her arms'. When Jeanne Mesnard sought to establish separate property from her husband, a candlemaker, three years later, she complained not only that he had paid his many debts with her money and that he abused her to coerce her into co-signing for more loans, but that he 'had reduced her and her children to beggary'.[37] Children's situation was legally irrelevant, but their presence may be another indicator of how local legal cultures shaped the evidence presented.

In the eighteenth century the patterns of the Nantais and Lyonnais courts came more closely in line, although the number of separations cases declined just as the general volume of litigation declined. Nantais wives who sought separate property seem to have begun to focus more closely on the issue of specific debts as threats to the financial standing of their households. From the 1720s, references to specific creditors' actions in the local commercial court became much more common, and claims about more general disorder or domestic violence were left

[36] ADSL B930, 18 June 1598; ADSL B6132, 23 October 1613; ADSL B1628, 30 January 1604.

[37] ADLA B6148, 3 July 1671, and ADLA B6149, 5 June 1674. See also, for example, ADLA B6149, 6 July 1673; ADLA B6149, 25 October 1674; ADLA B5828, 17 January 1675; ADLA B6150, 25 June 1675; ADLA B5830, 17 December 1677. Lottin noted the absence of children as an issue continued in the church court that handled separations in Cambrai in the eighteenth century in another interesting illustration of regional variation in local legal practice. Lottin, 'Vie et mort du couple', 68–74.

aside. The explanations for this convergence remain speculative, but a number of factors may be involved. Legal reform efforts, such as the Civil Code of 1667, had little obvious short-term effect, but may have fostered greater consistency in judicial practice over several decades. Wives began to use other means to deal with complaints of domestic violence, such as emerging local police organizations, just as the entire population increasingly used means other than litigation for solutions to their difficulties.[38]

If these regional variations suggest that local legal culture, popular as well as judicial, shaped what constituted appropriate evidence of endangerment to person or property, it is an open question whether or how these differences affected who could persuade a particular court to grant petitions. The social profiles of households in which wives used this resource in either city seem so similar in terms of resources and occupations that perhaps these local patterns simply led plaintiffs to choose to emphasize one kind of evidence over another. Many Nantais wives could have provided evidence of creditor pressure if they had needed to, and many Lyonnais wives could have complained fulsomely about their husbands' shortcomings. Many wives could have cited the plight of their children if it seemed helpful. The patterns of decision in separations cases seem to have been very similar, regardless of court. So, neither access to legal process nor results in terms of legal remedy seem to have been measurably affected.

For working people who wanted to use litigation as a resource, the issue of jurisdiction seemed less important in practice than historians' traditional highlighting of the institutional patchwork of France's legal system has suggested. The particularities of local jurisdictional differences may have been relatively unimportant for participants, but important questions remain about when and why they chose that option. Local legal knowledge provided potential litigants with a wealth of information about where and how to present their cases.

LEGAL LIVES

For working people's legal lives, the particularity of jurisdiction may have been less important than the ubiquity of legal process. Law was intertwined with the everyday in many ways. Working people used notaries, as well as the judicial

[38] For the concern of legal reform initiatives to standardize judicial practice see, for example, the 1667 Code Civil. Women in Paris in the eighteenth century used a variety of means to combat domestic violence, including securing *letters de cachet* and filing complaints with the recently established Parisian police. Isambert, *Recueil Général*, **18**, 105–6; Arlette Farge and Michel Foucault, *Le Désordre des Familles: Lettres de cachet des Archives de la Bastille au XVIIIe Siècle* (Paris, 1982); Alan Williams, 'Patterns of conflict in eighteenth-century Parisian families', *Journal of Family History*, **16**, 1 (1993).

system, to make public legal records of many of their personal transactions.[39] Like the other economies of daily life explored in this book, manifestations of legalities were matters of daily observation, frequent participation, and manageable resources for working people. Even neighbours who were not plaintiffs or witnesses must certainly have been spectators and no doubt producers and consumers of an economy of information that was central to family business, whether in terms of litigation, marriage, borrowing, violence or any other matter. Indeed, frequency of observation of, and discussion about, legal process, as well as participation, helped create the popular expertise about use of law that shaped decisions about whether or not to choose a judicial strategy.[40]

In the many steps and among the many parties involved, litigation as a practice materialized discursively and spatially in many sites beyond the courtroom. The language of the law pervaded daily life in a variety of ways. Wives threatened their husbands with 'going to justice' in the midst of domestic disputes at home. Family members and neighbours made similar threats in reprimanding husbands whose behaviour they found unacceptable. Insults rooted in legal status—calling someone a 'bankrupt' (which by the seventeenth century was legally fraud, and not simply the inability to pay debts, as we will see) or a 'perpetual plaintiff'—were part of the vocabulary of shame that loomed large in early modern interactions. Working people could appropriate legalese in their own interactions with each other as well as the courts. When Anne Collaud negotiated with her landlord over her rent arrears, for instance, she appropriated legal language in describing these events: she said she wanted to carry out herself (*s'executer*) the landlord's demand (presumably as opposed to having a bailiff carry it out on his behalf), and gave him a bundle of household linen as 'security' (using a word '*gage*' which had a double entendre as fee for a legal official).[41]

Legal process was not only reserved for court houses or even lawyers' or notaries' offices. The role of legal officials was expansive spatially as well as judicially. While some judges in higher courts might never have seen the people on whose cases they ruled as they worked from written evidence, judges in

[39] For early moderns the centrality of law in the everyday was observed long ago by Phillipe Ariès (who also argued—debatably but provocatively—that it was one of the factors separating modern from early modern life). See Ariès, *L'Homme Devant la Mort* (Paris, 1977), 1. For the use of notaries, see Julie Hardwick, *The Practice of Patriarchy: Gender and the Politics of Household Authority in Early Modern France* (University Park, PA, 1998).

[40] If early modern historians have become increasingly convinced of popular legalism in the sense that early modern people knew a great deal about legal process and could use it to their advantage, it has been less clear how they might have acquired that expertise. Natalie Davis argues that even in the case of quite exceptional legal actions—petitions for pardons for murder—ordinary people were sufficiently informed to present their cases persuasively (even while she also acknowledges the role of notaries and lawyers). Sarah Hanley has emphasized the role of 'judicial publicity', that is the publishing of legal writing of various kinds. See Hindle, *State and Social Change*, and Natalie Zemon Davis, *Fiction in the Archives*; Hanley, 'Jurisprudence of the arrêts'.

[41] ADLA B6681, 21 March 1691.

lower courts often came out to the community. Because of their broad charge to oversee public order they were often called to sites of disorder, whether caused by brawls, unexpected deaths, abandoned babies—or spousal quarrels. On such occasions, in disputes spousal and otherwise, the judges on the spot, in the street or in the household, and often in front of a crowd of onlookers, questioned participants and witnesses, proffered mediation, or propelled court action as we see throughout this book. These interventions might be a preliminary to court action, but sometimes these kinds of informal judicial actions deflected formal court proceedings.[42]

The myriad minor court workers, such as bailiffs and sergeants, whose work was indispensable to legal process, were also highly visible in neighbourhoods. They delivered notifications to defendants or orders to appear to witnesses. They announced judgements such as separations in market-places on Saturdays, and outside churches as masses finished on Sundays. They oversaw the seizures and sales of household goods to cover unpaid debts that were commonplace in a world where borrowing was endemic.

Witnesses too were crucial players in litigation, and their roles were likewise not contained by the court house. Between the bailiff's delivery of the court notice to give evidence to a witness in his or her residence and the post-testimony walk home from the court house, there were many moments of discussion and decision. Witnessing was a public and neighbourhood matter. Although French witnesses usually gave their depositions at the court house and did not tell their stories in front of listening neighbours, as in English jury boxes or taverns, their testimony was often not secret. Although judges and their clerks were supposed to hear each witness privately, witnesses often referred to what earlier witnesses had said.[43] Discussion outside the courtroom between plaintiffs or defendants and witnesses, and between neighbours who were potential witnesses, was probably routine. For example, Marie Lebreton and Marie-Angelique Masson, each of whom had previously worked for the same family, conferred about their possible participation in a case. Masson told Lebreton that the husband 'wanted to call her to depose, [and] that if she was summoned it would not be to the advantage of' the wife because of what she knew. She then told what she knew—a story about the wife, a male visitor, and suspiciously rumpled bed sheets that Lebreton duly repeated in court. Toussaint Jouanat, an apprentice panmaker, took part in another kind of predeposition consultation. As a 'good friend' of candlemaker Nicolas Guischard and his wife, Marguerite Cousturier, he was one of a group who had proposed to the spouses, a few days before depositions were taken, 'that they should resolve their differences to avoid spending their money going to

42 Nor was this 'judge on the streets' role unique to Nantes or Lyon. For similar behaviour by judges in Vaucouleurs, see Piant, *Une Justice Ordinaire*, 45–6. Piant summarizes this practice as 'justice was everywhere'.

43 Isambert, *Recueil Général*, **18**, 145.

court against each other'.[44] As witnesses were called to testify, or walked to and from the court house, they brought neighbourhood values to litigation and took court experiences and information home.

STRATEGIC LITIGATORS

Embedded in a world of legal practice, early modern men and women used courts for a variety of purposes, not simply to resolve conflicts, but to negotiate, and for administrative as well as judicial purposes. Their goals therefore were not always to 'win the case'. Although studies of early modern litigation emphasize that this recourse was only one among many available for dispute resolution, historians have often seen going to court as the last resort, that is to seek an institutional, formal path to dispute resolution rather than utilize one of the more longstanding informal forms of community mediation. Much of this analysis has been based on the study of criminal procedures, and is epitomized by Bruce Lenman and Geoffrey Parker's assessment of early modern people as 'reluctant prosecutors'.[45] Looking closely at the ways people used local courts of first instance in civil procedures, however, suggests that early modern men and women were strategic rather than reluctant legal actors—at least in civil cases—for whom the decision to go to court was one element in the complex set of strategies needed to manage daily life. Litigation was integral to these economies rather than an alternative to them.

Although court records provide a snapshot of a particular household's involvement at a particular moment, the rare instances in which the legal lives of working households can be even partially reconstructed over time suggest that most households had many different kinds of contacts with the civil process in many different capacities. They made personal decisions and disputes public in a host of ways. They used notaries to draw up public instruments recording wills, marriage contracts, leases, and loans, served as witnesses or made complaints to a court, or were primary parties as plaintiffs or defendants, most often in cases about debt or in family litigation such as inheritance disputes, or in the many other kinds of issues such as insults, property disputes, or separations that could be pursued in part through judicial process.

Certainly many forms of dispute resolution were concurrent. The decision whether or not to litigate was shaped by many factors, and people might try myriad options. For example, in separations cases, as surely in many other kinds of dispute, the possibilities for mediation seemed almost endless. Men and

44 ADLA B5840, 3 December 1688, and B5839, 11 December 1687.

45 Parker and Lenman, 'State, community, and criminal law', quote on 15 *et passim*, for a succinct account of an interpretative attitude found in much of the historiography on criminal law.

women consulted, argued and negotiated over how to manage the difficulties they faced with numerous different peers. Family members were important facilitators, as were neighbours. Parish priests seem frequently to have extended their pastoral responsibilities quite far in seeking to reconcile warring parishioners. Other clusters of people offered more specific advice and expertise, such as the neighbourhood elite women who intervened in domestic violence (as we will see). People were in and out of court.

The conflict between the spouses Catherine Huet and Jan Dugast indicates some of the multiple strategies, legal and extra-legal, that working people deployed to their efforts to effect resolutions. Huet was unhappy with her husband because she thought he was engaged in an affair with their neighbour, Anne Priou. In September 1685, while she was away at their rural smallholding to gather in the harvest and to crush grapes, Priou visited their room every day, 'which caused a big scandal among their neighbours', and Priou 'was obliged' (presumably by a court order) to go to the city's home for wayward girls (*refuge des filles penitents*). In Huet's account, as soon as Priou returned home she lured Dugast back into their immorality, even making an opening in the wall between their two attics, and her behaviour forced Huet to go to stay with her brother. Huet was pregnant, and she went to find her husband when her labour started; but Priou spat at her, ripped off the handkerchief covering her neck, and kicked and punched her. The child was born dead several days later. Even while she was in labour, her husband and Priou 'had several rendezvous'. All of this had led her to complain to the court during Carnival in the spring of 1686. She withdrew that complaint when Dugast and their kin put Priou in a convent 'against her will'. Yet no sooner was Priou out of the convent than she and Dugast resumed their affair. Huet said she could not tolerate it any more and complained to the court again, although the remedy she sought was unspecified, and perhaps unclear even to her.[46] Huet tried strategies that she thought might work.

Family, friends, neighbours, priests or local elites commonly engaged in informal mediation, not simply as an alternative to judicial process, but as an interwoven and integral part of court cases. Many women noted that they had previously resisted making formal complaints to the court or withdrew actions after negotiations with these informal mediators. Louise Desvignes, for example, was in and out of court over a period of fifteen years, during which time neighbours, family members, a doctor, a marquise, 'several ladies of high rank', and her parish priest all at different moments tried to settle spousal differences.[47] As with all kinds of litigation, threatening to going to court, or starting a case, was often as much about negotiating strategies as it was an effort to seek an explicitly judicial remedy to a problem.

[46] ADLA B6678, 25 June 1686.

[47] ADR BP3984, folder 1682, 22 September 1682 and 9 January 1683.

People could use going to court as one of their negotiating strategies in many different kinds of dispute. Many cases were dropped before the sentence stage, and this proportion may have been as as high as 15:1. In these kinds of situation, the court option was a manoeuvring tool, whether meant as a lever or as a threat. In separations cases, women often either said that they had told their husbands that they would go to court if their spouses did not change their way, or withdrew their suits when husbands promised to do better in the future. In many disputes over the repayment of loans (and debt cases dominated the civil case load), creditors took the first legal step to obtain court orders demanding seizures of debtors' assets as preludes to sales of whatever was necessary to cover the debts, but went no further down the legal road. Many households had repeatedly been the subject of such actions (*saisis*), most of which had not proceeded to legal closure with the actual sale. Creditors no doubt had different ideas about when to step up the pressure to use the *saisi* strategy, with some being quicker than others, and deciding too on the basis of many other factors such as personal knowledge of the creditors, pressure they themselves felt from their own creditors, and so on. This kind of negotiating did not involve either an abandonment of informal mediation nor a commitment to judicial remedy.

People also made choices about the type of legal action to deploy to manage a particular situation, as well as about whether or not to litigate. In the case of debt difficulties, for instance, couples could choose to negotiate repayment plans with their creditors, wives could seek separate property, or households could allow or fail to prevent one or repeated sales of their assets until they had nothing left. Many couples chose to organize repayment schemes, by agreeing, if they could not hope to clear the whole debt, to pay a proportion off in a set period of time. When the merchant Louis Pelleteau and his wife found themselves overwhelmed by debts, for example, they met with creditors at their house and, saying they wanted to continue their trade, offered to pay off their creditors at a discount of 50 per cent over the next four years. René Dugast and Marie Chauveneau asked for seven years to pay off their creditors, but were given only five.[48] Yet in other cases, wives chose to pursue separate property claims (a strategy that positioned them as the first creditor of their household and ahead of all other creditors) or couples allowed repeated sales of their goods to cover unpaid debts without seeking a legal brake on proceedings.

Working people were strategic litigators who used litigation as a flexible resource that was inextricably intertwined with informal means of dispute resolution. Many factors shaped decisions about which course to pursue when faced with the challenges of daily life. Diverse strategic calculations, financial as well as otherwise, were intrinsic in choices about if, when, or how to litigate. Moreover, each household's web of financial, logistical, psychological and affective threads shaped decision-making, and the law was only one of

[48] ADLA B5599, 14 December 1716; ADLA B6161, 14 September 1695.

the resources available. Informal mediation, while important and ubiquitous, was not a separate track from the court system. Neighbourhood negotiations of various kinds were key in many disputes in which legal action was taken, and actual or threatened legal action was a central part of much informal mediation. The same neighbors who might participate in extra-legal efforts to resolve conflicts also served as witnesses when those disputes went to court. Many initial steps, such as making a complaint and being given permission to proceed to collect evidence, involved very little expense, and many cases did not go further in the judicial process, although perhaps they would not have been resolved without it.[49]

THE GENDERING OF LEGAL LIVES

Gender shaped legal lives and experiences of litigation as a popular and flexible economy. The example of marital litigation offers a very specific window into men's and women's encounters with the legal system, but it illustrates some general issues too. The legal process offered men and women different and unequal kinds of resources, and could require them to use varying strategies in this regard as with others. Yet the ways in which men and women used the legal system to resolve marital difficulties demonstrates not only their differing legal rights and constraints, but significant similarities in men's and women's strategic use of litigation. Legal options shaped the avenues that men and women used, but husbands and wives deployed the legal means available to them for very similar ends, whether as threats or to resolve their household problems. Men and women each used the legal system creatively as well as narrowly to threaten or discipline their spouses and to establish household arrangements in particular forms.

Looking broadly across all kinds of civil action, women were active though not equal participants in the litigation process, but gendered experiences of litigation varied from region to region, from court to court, and from one type of action to another. If men were overall more likely to be plaintiffs or defendants than were women, women were still common users of the legal system. Although our knowledge of French patterns is very limited thus far, women were either plaintiffs or defendants in almost a quarter of all civil proceedings in lower courts in Normandy, and constituted 13 per cent of plaintiffs in Vaucouleurs. Women dominated particular kinds of litigation, bringing suit in over 95 per cent of separations cases, for example. These patterns match those found in regions of the early modern world where legal patterns have been more closely studied. In English courts, for example, the proportion of female principal parties ranged

[49] Piant found 'inseparable' and 'complementary' modes of resolving disputes in Vaucouleurs in the eighteenth century. See Piant, *Une Justice Ordinaire*, 211.

from single digits to 75 per cent or more, depending on the region, type of court, and type of case.[50] Women monopolized certain actions elsewhere too, such as slander suits in London, or played prominent roles in particular kinds of cases, such as those for debt in Connecticut.[51] This range in the gendering of legal action suggests that women's domination of separations suits in France was not anomalous, but rather represented one element of a typically diverse range of litigation experiences.

Men and women became principal parties in lawsuits, including legal, economic, and cultural factors with different frequencies for a variety of reasons. Married women's legal standing was limited, and although the specifics differed from region to region, essentially wives could not act in courts independently, but only with the authorization of their husbands. This disability could be mitigated if a woman established her legal status as a female trader (*femme marchande*), which enabled her to undertake any actions, or on a case-by-case basis through a court's permission. Judges routinely noted that they had authorized a married woman to act, either with no explanation or 'after the refusal of her husband'. Economic activity took place at many levels, much of which escaped formal regulation or oversight. Debt cases, for example, were the most common civil suits in court dockets, and although women were engaged as borrowers and lenders in many kinds of debts (as we will see) they were very often involved in informal exchanges of the kind that were difficult to pursue in court.[52]

In the specific case of separations, legal standing was quite strictly gendered. The right to seek separations, whether of property or of property and person, was basically a legal facility for women. Men rarely sought separations of either kind, and most men who wanted to leave their wives probably did so without seeking legal affirmation. Men's use of separate property to protect themselves against their wives' creditors, a practice that became common in Anglo-American regions by the eighteenth century, did not materialize in France. Men's efforts

[50] For women's activity in French lower courts, for Normandy, see Zoe A. Schneider, 'Women before the bench: female litigants in early modern Normandy', *French Historical Studies*, **23**, 1 (Winter 2000), 3–4 and 16–19; and for Vaucouleurs, see Piant, *Une Justice Ordinaire*, 104–6. No doubt women also appeared on their own behalf or acted for their families in other cases and jurisdictions. See, for example, the role of women in appeals heard by the Chambre de l'Edit, established within the Paris Parlement to hear appeals of cases involving Catholics and Protestants, in Diane Margolf, *Religion and Royal Justice in Early Modern France* (Kirskville, 2003), 104–47. Gender patterns in several English courts are reviewed in Stretton, *Women Waging Law*, 38–41.

[51] Laura Gowing, 'Language, power and the law: women's slander litigation in early modern London', in Jennifer Kermode and Garthine Walker (eds.), *Women, Crime and the Courts in Early Modern England* (Chapel Hill, 1994), 26–47, and Cornelia Hughes Dayton, *Women Before the Bar: Gender, Law and Society in Connecticut, 1639–1789* (Chapel Hill, 1995), 69–104.

[52] For women's involvement in borrowing, see Chapter 4, *Economies of Markets*. Cornelia Dayton's study of seventeenth-century Connecticut notes that women were often active in debt cases in the seventeenth century when informal debts prevailed, but dropped out of debt litigation in the eighteenth century as more formalized debts became the norm. Dayton, *Women Before the Bar*, 69–104.

to use separations of property and person were rare, and usually did not succeed. Generally, men had little to gain from legal separations rather than simple desertion, and would in fact incur the expense of obligation to provide for their wives in a minimal manner if they sought to legalize authority for their abandonment of their spousal responsibilities.

Men might seek to use separations when property as much as residence was in dispute. For example, Pierre Sauget, an ironmonger, asked the court to allow himself and his wife to 'live in separate houses' after a long contentious dispute between the spouses and her parents over property that Sauget claimed they had taken from him. The judge agreed that Sauget 'could establish [a] separate residence' from his wife provided he pay her a pension of 30 *livres* a year and return 100 *livres* he had received as part of her dowry. If Sauget sought to use the case to recover his contested property as well as to be rid of his unsatisfactory wife, however, he was disappointed: the judge concluded that what Sauget claimed his wife and in-laws had made off with was worth about the same as they claimed he owed them, so neither side had to pay the other anything.[53]

Nevertheless, judges probably recognized that there was little they could do when men were determined to leave their wives, even if the request to the court had no legal merits. Jan Caraveau, for instance, asked for a separation and said that he wanted 'to repudiate his wife' Janne Henry because of her 'dishonest' life which had left her with 'venereal disease', as surgeons would attest. She countered that he had abandoned her, and asked for the return of the 300 *livres* assigned in her marriage contract and for 'a pension to support her in her future needs'. The court ruled that Caraveau had not proved his claims, and ordered him to pay the expenses of 30 *livres*, thereby denying his request for a separation. Yet the judge added that because of Caraveau's declared repudiation of Henry, he should pay her a pension of 6 *livres* (although it was not specified how often it should be paid), and the judge also prohibited Caraveau from mistreating Henry in any way.[54] Presumably, the judge thought that despite the failure of the legal case, Caraveau was unlikely to re-establish his conjugal household, and attached this addendum to deter Caraveau from simply abandoning his wife without any financial support.

Men also pursued other kinds of marital litigation that gave them advantages not provided by separations, although they might desire the same ends; that is, to use legal means to threaten their spouses with the goal of trying to change their behaviour, or to discipline them for what they found to be unsatisfactory behaviour. For instance, Jean Baptiste Gerard, a master fabric worker, and Antoinette Gat, his wife, were embroiled in a no doubt contentious marital dispute. Gerard complained to the court that when he noticed that his wife's jewellery was missing and asked her where it was, she told him it was none of his business. Then, the previous Sunday, while Gerard was out having supper

[53] ADLA B6161, 30 April 1695. [54] ADLA B6130, 6 February 1629.

at a friend's house, his wife 'stole' a variety of household goods including a roll of fabric, a wardrobe filled with linen and 150 *livres* in cash, a table with two benches, a chest 'filled with dirty linen', and a cooking pot. Two days later, a court clerk went with Gerard to a fourth-floor garret where Gat's widowed mother lived, and found some of his bed linen. They also learnt that Gat herself was downstairs, and found her with the missing items, 'working making buttons'. The clerk made an inventory of the property, gave the keys to the chest, the wardrobe and the room to 'Marie Baum wife of Jacob Nepeu the nearest neighbour', and left. Later that same evening, a lawyer for both spouses came to court to say that now the goods had been found safely, the spouses 'had worked out their differences' and wanted the property returned to them.[55] Gerard's tactic here in accusing his wife of theft echoed an allegation often made by wives who asked for separate property: that their husbands had taken money or property from the household and had mysteriously disposed of it. In both cases, the same principle of clarification of control over household property was at stake in the different legal processes spouses initiated.

Men could also use the courts to obtain early modern versions of custody orders over their wives, usually with one of two opposing goals: either to have their spouses committed to the city poorhouse as a form of discipline, primarily for alleged sexual immorality, or to require their absent wives to return home to their husbands. On occasion, men used court orders to punish and reform their spouses for what they claimed was sexual immorality. Charles Etienne Beday, for example, complained to the court about his wife's 'licentious and unruly life', and asked to 'have her shut up'. Pierre Handemont told court officials that Françoise Fromartin, his wife of nine months, indulged in all kinds of vices, 'letting all kinds of people sleep with her and a girlfriend of hers'. Yet when he 'remonstrated with her' she threatened to kill him! So he wanted her 'shut up in the poorhouse'. The royal prosecutor and a couple of clerks went with him to their residence, and interviewed the wife and the girlfriend. Both denied any wrongdoing. They said they had slept two nights in the same bed 'without committing any sin', but that no soldiers or any other men had spent the night with them. Nevertheless, the court officials accused both of them of prostitution, told Fromartin that her work as a prostitute was 'without the will and consent of her husband' (an assertion that raises the question of whether it would have been acceptable with his permission), put the wife in their carriage, and took her to the poorhouse 'to do penitence for a month'. Ten days later, Handemont came back to tell the provost that 'as his wife had promised him to behave better in the future, he asks for an order to return her to him'.[56] Men could use these kinds of action in response to other spousal infractions too, but they rarely did so, perhaps because the courts might not agree that other kinds of alleged wifely unruliness presented the threats to households, and to

[55] ADR BP2865, 27 January 1680. [56] ADLA B6159, 25 April 1692.

the community at large, that they perceived the spectre of female adultery to represent.

Husbands' use of the institutions of the court and the poorhouse to discipline their wives again echoes a female strategy of women using separation threats or petitions to elicit better behaviour from their spouses, but men's ability to use the courts to secure personal institutional confinements was sharply different from women's. Husbands were able to initiate private court action to confine wives whose behaviour they personally found aggravating. Although, in theory, women could apparently seek the same recourse, they did not seem to choose this option, whether because they felt the courts would be unsympathetic, or for other reasons. Moreover, husbands were not required to provide evidence of the alleged behaviour in the form of witnesses, and any wife could therefore find herself threatened with this possibility, whereas witnesses able to corroborate wives' allegations were essential to separations cases.

There is little evidence that seventeenth-century working wives or husbands had access to the means of household discipline that circumvented the court system of the kind that were common among elites or became prevalent in some regions in the eighteenth century. Elite men may have preferred to commit their wives to convents where their rank and reputation might be better safeguarded, but this option was expensive. For working men, municipal institutions such as the poorhouse were more attractive. In eighteenth-century Paris, working women used the extrajudicial means of royal orders (*lettres de cachet*) to have their husbands imprisoned, but such usage seems to have been rare in Paris before the 1720s, and it is unclear how widespread, geographically or socially, these types of instructions were outside of Paris after that point.[57]

Men also used the courts to force wives to live with them in a kind of legally coerced reconciliation that had the goal opposite to women's requests for separations of person and property. Sometimes, husbands made these requests in response to their wives' petitions as part of their opposition to the suits.

[57] Catharina Lis and Hugo Soly have studied such actions, which they term 'private confinements', among eighteenth-century urban families in the Netherlands, and found women as well as men using them; but this does not seem to have been the case in France in the seventeenth and early eighteenth century. They suggest that in the eighteenth century, there was an increase in such individual use of the courts to secure orders to detain unruly relatives of all kinds in various local institutions of correction. For the use of *lettres de cachet* in eighteenth-century Paris for the purpose of spousal confinement and for other familial problems, see Farge and Foucault, *Le Désordre des Familles*; Lis and Soly, *Disordered Lives: Eighteenth-Century Families and their Unruly Relatives* (Cambridge, MA, 1998). The only evidence of the use of these orders that I have found is for a family in the mid-eighteenth century. In 1743, two barristers in the Breton *parlement* obtained—apparently with the collusion of their sister-in-law—a 'king's order' to imprison their brother, who had 'squandered much of his property and fallen into disorders that dishonoured them', in a citadel on the Breton island of Belle Isle. In the same month, they asked the Nantais provost's court to appoint them as guardian of his daughter if her mother died, and the court agreed. Two years later, the barristers assumed the guardianship of their niece—their brother presumably still incarcerated. ADLA B6184, 17 January 1743.

Wives who were granted permission to go forward with separation of person and property suits were often also allowed to live separately from their husbands while their cases worked their way through the courts. Husbands who opposed the suits as unfounded might also explicitly ask that their wives return to live with them. Yves Leblond, for instance, contested Janne Brossart's request for a separation of person and property on the grounds that what she claimed was his mismanagement was no more than the accidental losses other merchants experienced, and asked that 'she return to live with him'. The butcher Mathurin Gaultier asked that Jullienne Angebaud's petition be denied, and that she be 'required to return to live with him and to compensate him for the lying accusations she made'. Michel Texier asked that his wife be required to return to him, and to be 'forbidden to leave him again in the future'.[58] In these and other similar responses, husbands countered their wives' suits with very express demands that the court re-establish their conjugal households.

Husbands could also ask for court orders to force wives who were absent, without the permission of either their spouses or the courts, to return to live with them. François Mocet, for instance, asked the court to 'achieve [the] reconciliation of husband and wife in order to have them live in peace in their old age'. He attributed their conflict to 'difficulty with [their] kin, especially' her oldest son (from an earlier marriage) 'who does all he can to remove his mother from the power of her husband'. This son, Claude Garnier, had left Mocet, he claimed, 'without the means to see or communicate' with his wife. Claudine Vaucher, Mocet's wife, said they had had a dispute about money which Garnier said was because Mocet and their son (his half-brother) ran the household in ways that were going to cause his 'ruin'. Mocet said he would agree to whatever adjudication kin made about the property matters, as 'he wants to do anything he can to have peace and enjoyment from his marriage'. This conflict was obviously very complicated, and extended beyond the spouses. The court, however, agreed to Mocet's request, and ordered Vaucher to 'reconcile herself to living with her husband and to serve and honour him as a wife must do to her husband'.[59]

Husbands who turned to the courts to re-establish their conjugal households may have done so in part because of the absence of property and labour as well as the persons of their wives. Pierre Barat asked the court to assist him in re-establishing a household with his wife, Jeanne Peuble, who had left him five months earlier. She had taken their bed, linen and some cash, and her absence, he said, had left him in 'necessity' and unable to support the two young children who were still with him. The royal prosecutor agreed to call her in to

[58] ADLA B6130 *bis*, 11 February 1631; ADLA B6133, 6 May 1636; ADLA B6135, 4 May 1639.

[59] ADLA B6671, 14 March 1667.

answer his allegations.[60] Other husbands might have been left with more, but still complained that their wives had removed significant quantities of goods of all kinds, often while they were out of town for a few days tending to rural smallholdings or on business. Louis Blanc, for instance, complained that during the twelve years of his marriage to Guyonne Guy she had often sold wine without telling him, but while he was at their smallholding during the previous week, she had not only sold wine 'very cheaply' but removed linens (including his shirts), papers, cash, cutlery and a bed. Two female witnesses testified that they had seen Guy loading goods onto a wagon while Blanc was out of town. Blanc asked the court to verify the property she had removed, and to require her to come back to him.[61] Although one husband claimed that his reputation was threatened by the absence of his wife, petitioning husbands, such as Barat and Blanc, usually emphasized the material absences that accompanied their wives' illicit departures.

The court's effective rather than rhetorical powers, however, seemed limited in this regard, as husbands sometimes found to their frustration. Just as judges could do little about men determined to leave their wives, they had little ultimate leverage over women who had decided to live elsewhere. Jean Rozeras, a merchant, had secured a court order that required his wife Perette Durand to live with her husband 'and start to do her duty' in March 1691. Durand, he said, returned 'with a grimace' and 'maliciously invented' all kinds of lies about how he treated her, using these as a pretext to leave him again on three occasions, on each of which he brought her back to their residence. Finally, on 5 April, only ten days after the sentence, she left twice on the same day, and he spent the day trying to get her back. He went back to court the next day, saying her actions did not allow him 'to do the least bit of work nor live in peace with her', and so he wanted the court to investigate again and require her to act as a wife should.[62] The financial implications for women who chose *de facto* separations, and who would be left without any property other than what they carried with them in such circumstances, were far more serious than for men, but no doubt some pursued that course regardless. Perhaps some of the women who chose this course may have thought that they lacked the grounds or supportive witnesses for judicial separations, and so chose an extralegal strategy.

On occasion, the court admitted the limits of judicial power and appropriated religious sanctions, suggesting that judges too recognized the ultimate inefficacy of courts' coercive powers by civil means over recalcitrant spouses. Take the example of Marye Galliot and Yves Jourdanot, a lawyer, who married in December 1621. Their marriage was soon unhappy, and Galliot repeatedly left her husband, who tried a variety of remedies to procure her return. In January 1623, the provost's

[60] ADSL B936, 17 July 1600; ADR BP3984, 13 May 1682.

[61] ADR BP3985, 26 March 1669.

[62] ADR BP4045, 6 April 1691.

court ordered her 'to go to live with her husband as she was obliged by the Law of God and of nature on threat of excommunication'. A week later the Bishop of Nantes issued an order that reiterated the same threat, and urged the 'rector and priests' of their parish, St Denys, to withhold communion until she complied. Two other court orders later in the same year ordered Galliot's parents not to take her from Jourdanot's household. In April 1625, Galliot herself asked the court for a legal separation of property and person which Jourdanot successfully contested. Yet again, the court ordered her to go back to Jourdanot 'to live and household with him as she was obliged as his wife'.[63]

Men and women might therefore both find that the court's willingness or ability to resolve their domestic struggles by legal means was limited. If a spouse were determined enough to leave, no judicial action could provide the necessary glue to effect reconciliation. Just as wives might find that they did not have the justification to seek either kind of separation, husbands might find that even a court order was not enough. A Lyonnais wigmaker, Antoine Vial, asked the court to investigate the behaviour of his wife who stole various items from their household 'daily', and to send her to live with family members or in a convent while the investigation proceeded. Four days later, Vial complained plaintively to court officers that not only had his wife, Antoinette Trastoit, refused to leave according to the court's order, but that she continued to remove property and insult him. Vial asked the court to reissue the order requiring her to leave, and offered to pay her a pension in advance if she would do so. Finally, he asked that if she continued to refuse, the court should allow him to 'forcibly put her out of his house' until the court ordered otherwise. The Lyonnais judges agreed to send Trastoit an order to this effect the next day.[64]

Moreover, access to effective use of the civil courts was limited by social status as well as gender. When Pierre Handemont sought to confine his wife, for example, her girlfriend said she was not a prostitute but was 24, and orphaned for a dozen years, during which time she had worked as a servant in many households. She said that five months earlier she had been raped by a lawyer in his office and was pregnant, and currently lived with a widow who worked as a fruitseller. At first glance such a marginal young woman evidently involved in illicit sexuality would seem just the type to attract the attention of the authorities, as many historians of criminality have argued. Yet the provostal officials had no interest in her besides 'admonishing her', despite the various kinds of disorder her situation represented.[65] Yet she had little prospect of using the courts on her behalf to secure formal redress, as prosecution rates for rape were very low. As we saw earlier, the primary users of the civil system in courts of first instance

[63] ADLA B6127, 12 April and 30 April 1625.

[64] ADR BP1643, 12 April 1707.

[65] ADLA B6159, 25 April 1692. For the selective prosecution of 'marginal' individuals see, for example, the argument in Ulrinka Rublack, *The Crimes of Women in Early Modern Germany* (Oxford, 1999).

were working households and middling families with a few elites, with very little participation by the poor.

Men's and women's legal abilities varied, but they shared approaches as strategic litigators who saw going to court as an option that could be exercised in diverse ways and for myriad reasons. Men and women often had different kinds of legal options, and men had important legal abilities that women did not have. The differentials in rights, in coercive power, and in the capacity for autonomous legal action without the support of witnesses, were part of the kaleidoscope of ways in which men were advantaged and women disadvantaged in early modern society. Nevertheless, wives seem to have been as skilled and as willing as husbands to utilize judicial process, where and when they could to negotiate, pressure, and resolve the dilemmas they faced.[66]

A PEOPLE'S COURT

Early modern working families had expansive legal lives. Working men and women went to the court house as witnesses as well as plaintiffs or defendants, and watched court officials visit the homes in their neighbourhood for many purposes. They used varied judicial and non-judicial means to negotiate disputes, and incorporated legal idioms into their own exchanges court. They also paid notaries to draw up a wide variety of legal instruments. In all these ways, they made choices about the use of legal process that provided one of the essential resources which they had available to manage the challenges of their lives.

Courts of first instance, whether provostal or *sénéchaussée*, were, of course, far from equal opportunity legal sites, but they were indubitably popular. They were open to a wide, although not unlimited, range of people, to men and women, although not equally and not in the same ways, and they processed huge numbers of infinitely varied legal actions of all kinds. Local urban courts offered both men and women a certainly imperfect, but nonetheless viable, efficient, and valuable opportunity and tool with which to help manage many aspects of the endless challenges involved in maintaining daily life for working families.[67]

The social world of civil process, dominated by established working households, was in many ways the opposite of that of criminal procedures, in which people on the margins (whether by virtue of gender, age, lack of ties in the community, and so on) were by far the most likely to be prosecuted.[68] Litigation in courts

[66] For a different kind of example of women's ability to use the gendered assumptions of the law to their advantage, see Julie Hardwick, 'Women "working" the law: gender, authority and legal process in early modern France', *Journal of Women's History*, **9**, 3 (October 1997).

[67] So little is known about the dynamics of the seigneurial courts which served as first instance sites in rural areas in the seventeenth and early eighteenth century, that judgement about them should still be reserved.

[68] For the social profiles of those prosecuted for criminal activities see, for example, Rublack, *The Crimes of Women*, 16–42.

of first instance was the province of working families, a particular social group with specific lower bounds and also a clear if porous upper divider. Few elites used courts of first instance. Members of the floating, indigent, poor were rarely involved, even in provosts' courts. Some of the reasons for these patterns are clear: the need to be able to pay costs, and the prominence of property disputes of various kinds in civil process, both of which ruled out most of the poor.

Moreover, working people's practice of litigation suggests that the institutional chaos that characterized French courts of first instance for jurists and political commentators was much less of a factor in practice. Whether the separation suit was heard in one kind of court or another made relatively little difference to the feasibility of the legal option. The households of litigants had very similar characteristics, whether their suits were heard in a provost's court or in a *sénéchaussée*. Their cases took about the same amounts of time, and the costs in both courts were comparable. The legal procedures from first petition to evidence gathering via depositions to the patterns of sentences were very much alike.

Working men and women were strategic litigators who quite dexterously used economies of justice as a resource integrally intertwined with other economies of daily life to negotiate and navigate the opportunities and risks they faced. Much more was at stake for working people in participation in litigation than the narrow and specific outcome of judicial remedy. Active involvement in litigation could be, and perhaps most often was, a strategy rather than an end.

How can the popularity of civil actions among working families in the seventeenth and early eighteenth century be reconciled with the pervasive maligning of litigation in legal and political rhetoric? A variety of factors contribute to the apparent disjuncture. While some cases certainly were endlessly appealed at prohibitive cost, and served as notorious mascots of the legal reform calls, the view from practice in the lower courts rather than the appeal courts suggests that in fact lengthy, much appealed, and vastly expensive cases may have been much the exceptions to the rule. Richard Kagan, in a path-breaking study of Castilian litigation published more than twenty years ago, observed that emphasis was the key, in that if there was much that was problematic about early modern justice, much worked quite well too. It may be that a partial explanation is the variability that social rank introduced into the different kinds of cases and courts that elite and working families used. Elites were also very litigious, and may have had resources, motivation, and leisure to devote to extended, expensive litigation as well as to making complaints about the system.[69]

The significance of the legal lives of witnesses and spectators, for neighbourhoods and for governing authorities, as well as plaintiffs, defendants, and court officials, could go far beyond the confines of a particular case. These participatory local legal cultures were key in shaping the politics of litigation. As we will see

[69] Piant, *Une Justice Ordinaire*, 276–83; Kagan, *Lawsuits and Litigants*, 77–8. For elite litigation, see Stuart Carroll, *Blood and Violence in Early Modern France* (Oxford, 2006), 185–213.

in the next chapter, in repeatedly and increasingly choosing to invite the state into their lives through the use of litigation, working families both borrowed the state's authority as a way to deal with their challenges, and contributed to increasing the authority of the state by making its courts a central element of managing daily life.

3

Economies of Family Politics: Litigation Communities, Subject, and State

Anne Douard and Jean Gobin ran a bakery in a Nantais neighbourhood in the parish of St Croix. He did the baking; she did the selling. Over the space of six years, Douard asked her local court on three occasions to grant her a separation. At first she requested a separation of person and property on the grounds of her husband's mistreatment of her, and of his dissipation and debauchery. Within weeks she was back in court to complain that as soon as she started the action, Gobin had begun to behave worse than ever, and had sold his work tools. The judge, Charles Valleton, accompanied her to their residence, where he questioned Gobin, who said he was 'very surprised' at his wife's allegations because he 'had always had all possible respect for her', although he admitted to a little dispute over the keys to a cabinet where they kept money. Soon Douard's aunt and second cousin joined the judge and his clerk. The judge waited in the bakery while the kin went into a back room, and when they came out they said that the spouses were reconciled. The spouses promised the judge that they would live 'conjugally'. Gobin promised to work hard and not to play billiards, and Douard promised to 'obey her husband in all reasonable ways'. With informal mediation by judge and kin, Douard withdrew her complaint.

Their compromise apparently did not hold. Three years later, Douard asked for and secured separate property despite Gobin's opposition. After another three years, Douard went back to the court again to repeat the request for a separation of person, and Gobin, still working as a baker, again denied her accusations. Douard was pregnant, and focused her allegations on battery. The outcome of her petition is unknown, and she may again have dropped the formal legal action as she did the first time in a pattern that frequently occurred in all forms of litigation.[1]

The business of managing family economies in and out of court was a community project. Besides the spouses, the judge and court officials, 28 people participated as witnesses in the Douard and Gobin conflict, and Douard's

[1] ADLA B6167, 16 March 1706; ADLA B5850, 20 September 1709; ADLA B6168, 11 November 1709; ADLA B5851, 20 and 28 July 1712. No evidence (if any) survives as to the eventual outcome of the 1712 case, and it may have been withdrawn.

aunt, second cousin, sister, and mother were all mentioned at various times as informal mediators. The witnesses were a microcosm of the local community. All lived in the city, and 21 lived in the same little neighbourhood. Fifteen were women. Three sets of spouses testified. Four members of one household who testified were the druggist Siphorien Doreau, his wife Marie Rolland, an apprentice, and a servant. Rolland, in fact, gave testimony twice, and both Douard and Gobin called Janne Lamoureux, the wife of a spurmaker. The witnesses' circumstances represented the range of possibilities in working households. They were guildsmen whose skill brought status (such as the surgeon), and workers whose jobs were unskilled and unincorporated (such as the boatman). They were masters, journeymen, apprentices and manual workers. They were married and single. Some women like Douard worked together with their husbands in family workshops, while others followed their own occupations, like Janne Poulain who sold wine while her husband worked on the river. They were young and old (the youngest was a teenager and the oldest in her sixties). They were literate and illiterate (sixteen could sign their names).

When disputes such as that between Douard and Gobin were played out in legal process, the spouses, their kin, their neighbours, their witnesses, and legal officials assessed their relationship in ways that explored individual spousal difficulties in the context of the local community's and court officials' expectations about appropriate behaviour in marriage. When was gambling or socializing or use of force a problem? What did it mean for a wife to promise to obey her husband 'in all reasonable ways', and did it mean the same for the wife, the husband, and the judge who supervised the promise? What did 'living conjugally' imply for the spouses, their neighbours, and the court officials? What did it mean to move a personal dispute between spouses into the community judgement of the neighbourhood and into the public and institutional forum of a court? The attitudes of Douard and Gobin, as well as the judge, the witnesses, and the kin, raise fundamental questions not only about household dynamics but also about the broad relationship of gender and authority.

Working people's legal lives made them key participants in the grassroots forums that I term as *litigation communities*, where many kinds of challenges were negotiated. If we expand our thinking about litigation past plaintiffs' complaints and judges' sentences to focus on unpacking a legal process in which many purposes and parties were involved, we find a commonplace and effective interstitial forum in which an unusually broad range of voices could make themselves heard. This process through which working people worked out, sometimes in consensus and sometimes in conflict, a set of common beliefs in households, on the streets, and in courts is what I mean by community.[2]

[2] For a very stimulating review of the various meanings of, and debates over, 'community', see Alexandra Sheppard and Phil Withington, 'Introduction: Communities in early modern England', Sheppard and Withington (eds.), *Communities in Early Modern England* (Manchester, 2000). The

Working men and women asserted their opinions in a variety of settings, and in a variety of ways, whether as litigants, witnesses, informal mediators, or casual observers.

In all these ways, the varied parties in litigation communities engaged in a public dialogue, in court and outside of it, about matters that were of critical importance to households, neighbourhoods, and the state.[3] The possibility of litigation as well as participation in the process offered an expansive and very open forum in which working people debated key issues. The judicial system promised a potential means through which an early modern government could hope to exert some authority over its subjects, whether in promoting particular values or managing strife, but the practice of litigation offered the prospect of participation for a wide range of people in negotiating the parameters of a wide range of issues.

This chapter explores one focus of litigation communities: the family politics writ small and large in which debates about marriage were embedded. If early modern communities were notoriously litigious, and early modern lawsuits provided critical sites for political contestation (two historiographical givens at this point), litigation provided a locus for dialogues about questions that were intensely politicized.[4] Moreover, it offered a site of repeated encounters between subjects and early modern governments through their judicial representatives.

Litigation communities' discussions about marriage engaged in a debate about the appropriate constituents and parameters of gendered authority whose political implications were manifest in early modern society. Mundane cases about commonplace spousal difficulties had varied implications and were inherently political. Participants discussed power relations in the social context of the family, and they participated in judicial institutions that have often been

focus on community as a process in which conflict and negotiation were inherent (rather than in the teleological *Gemeinschaft* to *Gesellschaft* pattern, for instance) is also usefully discussed, for example, in Christopher Marsh, 'Common prayer: the view from the pew', *Past and Present*, **171**, 1 (May 2001), 71–2; Anthony Cohen, *The Symbolic Construction of Community* (London, 1985, reprinted 1993); and David Sabean, *Power in the Blood* (Cambridge, 1984), 28–30.

[3] My emphasis here is on exploring a different side of the relationship between legal process, politics, and the state, than on the rich work that has highlighted the roles of jurists, lawyers and elites in those relationships, so stimulatingly explored by David Bell, Michael Breen, and Sarah Hanley, among others. See David Bell, *Lawyers and Citizens: the Making of a Political Elite in Old Régime France* (Oxford, 1994); Michael Breen, *Law, City, and King: Legal Culture, Municipal Politics, and State Formation in Early Modern Dijon* (Rochester, 2007); and Sarah Hanley, 'The jurisprudence of the arrêts: marital union, civil society, and state formation in France, 1550–1650', *Law and History Review*, **21**, 1 (Spring 2003). See also Hanley, 'The family, the state, and the law in seventeenth- and eighteenth-century France: the political ideology of male right versus an early theory of natural rights', *Journal of Modern History*, **78**, 2 (June 2006), 289–332, which explores the implications of the extraordinary litigation over inheritance between members of an enormously wealthy aristocratic family.

[4] A variety of early modern French historians have emphasized the significance of politics by lawsuits. See, for example, William Beik, *Absolutism and Society in Seventeenth-Century France: State Power and Provincial Aristocracy in Languedoc* (Cambridge, 1985).

regarded as the local embodiment of the French state. Moreover, they helped define the parameters of authority from the ground up, because they not only negotiated what kinds of spousal behaviour were considered desirable in working neighbourhoods, but also joined, wittingly or unwittingly, in a broader debate about family life that was at the centre of early modern governance. As historians have shown, the early modern family was an important subject of legislation, rhetoric, and litigation from the sixteenth century to the Revolution, because families were regarded as integral to the strength of the state. Domestic language and life became politicized, and provided resources for political contestation as well as authorization.[5]

The negotiations of litigation communities about family politics positioned working men, women, and young people as legitimate actors in a public debate about issues of gender and power that were fundamental to understandings of who had authority, and why, at every level from husband and wife to monarch and subject.[6] Plaintiffs and witnesses came from groups who were usually excluded from institutionalized politics (as opposed to popular actions such as street protests and riots), and yet they were integral to the negotiations with lawyers and judges in litigation communities. Dialogue about the appropriate characteristics and parameters of gendered authority as a family business took place in and out of court. They could publicize personal conflicts for their own ends, and make public rebukes that transferred communal judgement into legal sites as well as speak to the details of the specific case. Their expectations about spousal relations combined prescriptive and pragmatic notions of authority, and they articulated their understandings of family in a state-sponsored legal process that authorized local standards and practices.

This chapter explores how litigation communities provided an often overlooked form of political participation in which working people as plaintiffs and witnesses as well as legal officials, whether royal prosecutors or judges, sought to clarify the terms of gendered authority in marriage. Witnesses, plaintiffs, prosecutors, and judges came from different judicial and social perspectives to attend to the issues of how familial and political authority was constructed and justified. Their interventions in litigation communities showed how the

[5] Work exploring the politicization of family life includes Suzanne Desan, *The Family on Trial in Revolutionary France* (Berkeley, 2004); Sarah Hanley, 'Engendering the state: family formation and state building in early modern France', *French Historical Studies*, **16**, 1 (Spring 1989), and 'Social sites of political practice: lawsuits, civil rights, and the separation of powers in domestic and state government, 1500–1800', *American Historical Review*, **102**, 1 (1997); Sarah Maza, *Private Lives and Public Affairs: The Causes Célèbres of Prerevolutionary France* (Berkeley, 1993); Jeffrey Merrick, 'The cardinal and the queen: sexual and political disorders in the Mazarinades', *French Historical Studies*, **18**, 3 (1994), 667–99.

[6] For the political character of witness testimony, see Thomas Cohen and Elizabeth Cohen, *Words and Deeds in Renaissance Rome: Trials before the Papal Magistrates* (Toronto, 1993), 19; and Gowing, *Domestic Dangers: Women, Words, and Sex in Early Modern London* (Oxford, 1996), esp. 232–62.

formulations that flourished at the grassroots level, whether from the side of the court officials or from local people, differed in important ways from those associated with French elites in rhetoric and institutions. A core of consensus about the relationships between gender and authority, as well as some contestation, emerged in these dialogues. Although the model of a powerful household patriarch was unchallenged, the discussions about gender and authority showed diverse understandings of the critical elements of that role, and illustrated how working people were especially likely to emphasize the contingency of gendered authority and root it in day-to-day practice.

The negotiations of litigation communities about such issues mattered in building cohesion and consensus, or in feeding discontent, not only within and between households, but between households, communities, and the state. As court decisions endorsed the neighbourhood perspectives articulated by witnesses, litigation provided a bridge with two-way traffic between state and subject as street opinion as well as state-legislated prescription shaped models of family politics. Interrogating the understandings of the basis of the correlation between gender and authority that were worked through requires us to rethink our understanding of the relationships between popular, legal, and elite constructions of authority, familial and royal, and of the interactions of law, state, and family.

THE POLITICS OF PLAINTIFFS

Wives who petitioned the courts for permission to initiate actions against their husbands laid out their grievances to justify their requests. They sought to demonstrate that the proper ordering of life had been overturned, and to use the legal process to affirm a particular set of expectations about marriage. They sought to legitimize their cases by telling stories, like other petitioners, and very explicitly framed their understanding of gender and authority, occasionally in quite overt political terms.

Whether female petitioners had already consulted lawyers before they came to court is unclear, but certainly wives would know much about what they needed to demonstrate from the experience and expertise of their own legal lives and from those of their kin and neighbours, as we have seen.[7] It seems impossible to know how often or why court official rejected initial complaints, an important matter because such decisions effectively threw out cases before they started. All

[7] For other examples of the wide extent of popular knowledge about what kinds of evidence worked in particular kinds of court cases, see Davis, *Fiction in the Archives* (for seekers of pardons for capital crimes), and Gowing, *Domestic Dangers* (for slander suits). Both also emphasize the way in which tropes of storytelling as well as popular expertise, and lawyers if consulted, shaped what people chose to say in court.

the extant separation petitions include permission to proceed, although some must have been denied.[8] If the royal prosecutor gave permission to proceed, a decision usually taken within two or three days of the complaint, he noted the name of the lawyer who would handle the paperwork at that moment, without clarifying whether the lawyer had already participated in the complaint. At any rate, the lawyers that wives hired were paper-shuffling *procureurs* rather than the more highly paid brief-shaping, argument-making barristers (*avocats*). Although we know little about the lowly *procureurs*, historians have usually regarded them as paper-trail guardians rather than legal experts.[9]

Marguerite Cottin told the court her story when she petitioned for relief (without specifying which kind of separation she was seeking) in 1690. She had married Jean Marin, a scalemaker, eight years earlier, and brought him 'a lot of goods' and 'done all she could to meet the basic needs of their household', while he 'didn't do much'. She made 'some profit' from her work as a midwife, and 'gave him what she made from deliveries'. Although she had always 'behaved appropriately and without reproaching him', he had begun battering her only three weeks after they married, and she had endured his treatment 'without complaining'. She then listed various incidents of battery, including one when she was pregnant, and one where her eye was damaged. She ended by noting that she was five months pregnant, and detailed beatings the day before yesterday (five or six slaps) and even on the very day of her complaint (six slaps and several kicks which had left her all bruised). These last had 'finally constrained her recourse to justice'.[10]

Cottin's story had many of the central qualities in wives' narratives, which usually adopted a predictable pattern, whatever their specific grievances. They laid out long periods of manly malfeasance that rose to a dramatic crescendo. Like hers, they often began at the moment of marriage, either commenting that married life had initially been smooth, or that their difficulties began immediately. Wives emphasized the long history of their discontents, seeking to demonstrate some fundamental shortcomings in their husbands rather than one-off displays

[8] For an instance where the prosecutor did turn down a petition—a decision revealed only by subsequent court proceedings—see the Blanchard–Chevallier case discussed in the last section of this chapter. The extant first petitions are disproportionately from Lyon (74 of 79). Nantais sentences frequently summarized key aspects of the wives' initial complaints, but the petitions themselves rarely survive. 70% of the extant petitions are for separations of person and property, although these represented only 20% of the total number of separations suits (56 of 79).

[9] Plaintiffs in these courts virtually never engaged the much more expensive services of *avocats* whose expertise was legal, whereas the expertise of *procureurs* was procedural. Bell notes, in his work on the Parisian bar, that very little is known about the early modern history of *procureurs*; but see his succinct categorization of eighteenth-century *avocats* as lawyers who took care of 'everything requiring legal knowledge and reasoning', and *procureurs* as guardians of the 'minutiae' of legal procedure (filing motions, collecting evidence, and so on). See Bell, *Lawyers and Citizens*, 38–40, and Lisa Silverman, *Tortured Subjects: Pain, Truth, and the Body in Early Modern France* (Chicago, 2001), 52–4.

[10] ADR BP4045, 30 June 1690.

of bad judgement. They often gave very specific details about the date, place, and time on which incidents had occurred, whether of abuse, drunkenness, or debt. They contrasted their own model wife attributes (patience, forbearance, and sometimes pious acceptance) with their husbands' aberrant behaviour (financial mismanagement, debauchery of various kinds, and violence). Their stories stressed how neighbours and others had been drawn in in various ways (whether offering financial help, aid during or after battery, or mediation) to the household drama.

These dramatic recountings served several purposes, besides conveying key information so that the courts would find the requests had merit. Laura Gowing has argued that even the public telling of a story in court could give an early modern woman a voice and sense of self that was significant. Storytelling was such a central form of popular expression, as Natalie Davis has noted, that it could seem a natural way to petition.[11] Certainly, women told marital histories that spotlighted key legal facts (serious and even life-threatening abuse, and/or dowry-imperiling financial disarray) in dramatic and moralistic ways that deployed cultural tropes to accentuate the urgency, even imperative, of court action. Certainly, they were inherently selective, and gave a one-sided account of events (sometimes countered forcefully by husbands). In their tellings, the unusualness of their current situations justified the unusual remedies (judicial intervention) that they sought.

Yet much more than the power of narrative was in play in these petitions, as women worked hard to naturalize happy marriages in particular forms, thereby laying the groundwork for the contrasting specifics of their own situations. Wives' petitions spun a powerfully specific version of the good marriage to which they claimed to aspire: financial stability secured by mutual hard work and cooperation. Women always nodded to a wife's obligation to be deferential and long-suffering, but strongly articulated a version of married life based on mutuality and reciprocity. Spouses, they said, should 'live in union' or 'in civility'. Marguerite Molande, after proudly noting that she had brought a dowry of 500 *livres* that she had earned herself, lamented that 'the marriage where she expected to find some succour has been the source of her misfortune'. Marguerite Barry, the wife of a master saddler, contrasted the first ten years of her marriage when the spouses had 'lived in a harmonious union . . . and had nine children, four of whom survive' with the subsequent four years of unhappiness.[12]

Wives constantly emphasized hard work as the essential spousal attribute. They highlighted their own labour, and often contrasted their expectations of their husbands with the reality of their lack of diligent application, whether due to slothfulness or too much time spent drinking, gambling, or being otherwise

[11] Gowing, *Domestic Dangers*; and Davis, *Fiction in the Archives*.

[12] ADR BP3984, 23 December 1682; ADR BP3985, 20 April 1673; ADR BP3984, 25 November 1683; ADR BP3985, 17 August 1656.

distracted. They made no secret of the role of material interest in shaping their decision-making. Suzanne Paillard observed bluntly that when her silk-worker husband proposed to her 'he seemed to have quite significant property and had the reputation of being a hard worker, so [she] had reason to hope he would easily earn something to live on and the marriage was contracted'. Laurence Morineau, contrasted how 'she has tried on her side to earn their living by her work selling fish' with, 'on his side', her husband Pierre Mahu, a grain-carrier, who 'instead of contributing to their food and bringing some revenue to their household' spent all his earnings in bars. His behaviour, she thought, was 'without consideration for the continuation of their marriage'.[13] In these petitions, hard work was the key to financial stability and respectful mutuality as the heart of successful marriages.

Throughout wives' narratives of marriage, uncertainty and risk were keys. Women often portrayed themselves as unlucky, or the subjects of deception. Marguerite Vaubert, married to a haberdasher, said, like many women, that she had had the 'bad luck' to marry such an unsatisfactory husband. Alleged deceptions might include occupation, wealth or background. Anne Mace said she 'had been deceived by the latter [her husband] in all kinds of ways', as he had said he was a 'master hatter when he was only a simple worker'. Jeanne Terasse said that her husband had told her he was a surgeon from a nearby town, but she later learnt that he came from far away, and had never been a surgeon.[14]

Wives' stories frequently involved sexuality, often in relation to risk and deception. Many referred to their own pregnancies when abuse occurred. This legitimate expression of sexuality contrasted with husbands' errors in the same regard. Most women claimed that their husbands had insulted their reputations by calling them whores or bitches, and wives quite often also made specific allegations about their husbands' sexual misconduct. Some women, like Françoise Laradiere, complained that their husbands had fathered illegitimate children.[15] By far the majority of wives' complaints in this regard, however, were about husbands' illicit relations with bad girls of various kinds that often resulted in repeated bouts of venereal disease.

The repetition of themes of disease and deception, although legally irrelevant, reframed the realities of household governance. While early modern authorities often seemed preoccupied with women's sexuality, these petitions made men's sexuality an issue. The emphasis on disease foregrounded material consequences rather than moral concerns, by which women were often blamed for inappropriate sexuality, or legal consequences where married men's adultery was of little importance.

13 ADR BP3984, 6 February 1679; ADLA B6670, no date, but in folder for 1666.

14 ADR BP4045, 31 August 1720; ADR BP3985, 26 May 1671.

15 ADR BP3984, 22 June 1683.

These wifely emphases illustrated the central dynamics of the economies of marriage. The motif of deception, so common in early modern popular culture, played on the threat of the uncertain in a face-to-face culture. It put into relief the tension between the contractual obligations of marriage and the daily importance of having to rely on others, whether in terms of lending money or in commercial matters. Moreover, the emphasis on hard work and cooperation spoke directly to the precarious environment that working families faced. Hard work seemed like one way to manage risk, and also affected (as we will see) individual ability to secure continual access to borrowing, despite financial difficulty, because it was a principle measure in the economy of information that was critical to local judgements about lending. Wives' language articulated a sense that while a good marriage could hope to reduce uncertainty, a bad marriage exaggerated the perils that households faced.

Wives' interventions used the legal process to articulate a version of authority rooted in specific expectations, with implicit and, on occasion, explicit political connotations. As one aggrieved wife said, her husband's actions 'had not met the standards for marital authority'.[16] Occasionally, women employed more specifically political language, going beyond the realm of domestic shortcomings to position their spouses within a broader spectrum of exploitation. They accused their husbands of being 'tyrants' or of making their wives 'slaves'. One spouse had 'abused the authority and power of the husband', and exercised 'a continual tyranny', while another had been 'unlucky to be married or rather sacrificed' to her spouse, to whom she was 'in fact a slave rather than a wife'.[17]

While such explicitly political language was rare, its mobilization by working wives suggests how broadly the implicit link between marital and royal governance was understood. Women's versions of their marital histories represented a subjectivity that spoke powerfully about how marital power and authority, and by implication monarchical, should work. Female petitioners aimed to demonstrate that their spouses' behaviour had undermined the rights of husbands to deal with their own households, and created the openings for judicial intervention in marriage. Wives used the courts to legitimize as normative a version of familial authority that cast it as conditional rather than assured.

FROM STREET CORNER TO STATE COURT: NEIGHBOURS AND WITNESSES

Witnesses served, as a jurist wrote in a handbook for lawyers published in 1627, as 'the first judges of the trial, since they prove and decide the question of

[16] ADSL B930, 13 February 1598.

[17] ADR BP3985, 21 December 1641; ADR BP4045, 22 February 1691. Anne Simond, the wife of a bookseller, used the same kind of language a year earlier: ADR BP4045, 19 January 1690.

evidence'.[18] Yet despite witnesses' pivotal role, we know little about who they were, about the process of becoming of a witness, or about the politics of witnesses.[19] Witnesses were key actors in litigation communities in terms of sheer numbers, of their characteristics, and of their role in the process. Each of the thousands of cases litigated annually involved multiple witnesses as well as plaintiffs, defendants, and members of an industry of court officials, from judges to lawyers to bailiffs, who facilitated the mechanics of litigation. Witnesses were critical to the success of cases. Royal prosecutors' reviews of depositions showed that cases could succeed only if witnesses provided compelling evidence. Plaintiffs' choices about whom to call and what questions to ask, as well as legal and cultural parameters that defined who could offer credible testimony, shaped who served as witnesses. Their choices also suggest that what they sought to demonstrate was a violation of local and even rank-specific standards. When a witness received a summons to testify, he or she in turn faced choices about how to respond, what to say, and whether to claim compensation. Witnesses' own experiences and preferences illustrate some of the ways in which they had their own stakes in participating in litigation communities. They were chosen from the local community, and brought their neighbourhood perspective to the task of testifying.

Plaintiffs had wide discretion in their choice of witnesses, because French law allowed virtually anyone to be a witness in civil cases. The prominent seventeenth-century jurist Jean Domat noted that 'all persons of both sexes may be witnesses', with very few exceptions: 'children and madmen' or people 'whose reputation has received some blemish' through court sentences.[20] This inclusiveness contrasted with the broad exclusion of most early modern people from the majority of legal and public roles. Married women, for instance, were subject to many well-known legal disabilities, and young people could not marry without parental permission until they were in their mid-twenties, but either could, and frequently did, serve as witnesses.

[18] Antoine Favre, *Abrege de la Practique Judiciare et Civile* (Geneva, 1627), 54–5.

[19] Very little historiography exists about witnesses. Exceptions include, for early modern England, Laura Gowing, *Domestic Dangers*; and Clive Holmes, 'Women: witnesses and witches', *Past and Present*, **140**, 1 (1993), 45–78; and for late medieval France, Daniel Lord Smail, 'Telling tales in Angevin courts', *French Historical Studies*, **20**, 2 (1997), 183–215, and *The Consumption of Justice: Emotions, Publicity, and Legal Culture in Marseille, 1264–1423* (Ithaca, 2003). In a brief survey of witnesses in Vaucouleurs, Piant notes that they were critical to the case, not only for evidence but because they permitted the participation of what he calls 'public opinion' in the case. See Piant, *Une Justice Ordinaire*, 252–6. Benoit Garnot (ed.), *Les Témoins devant la Justice. Une Histoire des Statuts et des Comportements* (Rennes, 2003) focuses primarily on the eighteenth century or later, but includes a comparison of witnesses in Lyon criminal cases in 1688 and 1788 in Françoise Bayard, 'Témoins et témoignages aux XVIIe et XVIIIe siècles. Le cas Lyonnais', 197–208.

[20] Jean Domat, *Civil Law in its Natural Order together with the Public Law*, trans. William Strahan, 2 vols., **1** (London, 1737), 125. For factors in the disqualification of witnesses, see Bernard Schnapper, 'Testes inhabiles: les témoins reprochables dans l'ancien droit pénal', *Tijdschrift voor rechtsgeschiedenis*, **33**, 4 (1965), 575–616; and Christiane Plessix-Buisset, *Le Criminel devant ses Juges en Bretagne aux 16e et 17e Siècles* (Paris, 1998), 279–344.

Plaintiffs' choices were broad in practice as well as principle because the credibility of witnesses was rarely challenged, at least in civil cases in courts of first instance, whether on the basis of honesty or rank. Popular understanding of the obligations of witnesses certainly may have shaped depositions in ways that are difficult to recover. One woman recalled that a priest told her that witnesses did not have to repeat what they had been told in secret. Yet prosecutors and parties to the case only occasionally sought to undermine the credibility of witnesses. While one prosecutor suggested that a witness appeared to have been 'well taught and practiced although the others do not seem to have been coached in the same way', and another claimed that he 'did not have great regard' for the statements of 'dubious' witnesses because of their 'low life' or because they were relatives or servants or debtors, these reservations were very unusual.[21] Although some eighteenth-century jurists regarded rich witnesses as more credible than others in criminal cases, there is no indication that either socio-economic rank or gender shaped perceptions of the reliability of witnesses in seventeenth-century civil cases.[22]

With this broad discretion, plaintiffs in separation cases, as in other kinds of litigation, solicited witnesses strategically, calling people they hoped would provide reliable and persuasive testimony. The legal criteria for the two types of separation in part structured their choices. Neighbours, often female, were usually best informed about battery, while men who had bar or commercial contacts with husbands, as well as neighbours, could speak to financial disarray or debauchery. Wives who sued for separation of person and property called an average of seven witnesses, and preferred women (often neighbours or servants) by a margin of almost two to one, while wives who sought separate property alone generally provided four witnesses, and were slightly more likely to ask men to testify than women. In either case, they usually chose people who could attest to a litany of repeated problems.

Witness demographics diversified litigation communities in terms of sex, marital status, age, and literacy.[23] Witnesses were almost evenly divided between men and women. Whereas widows usually enjoyed distinctive legal and public capacities among early modern women, never-married women and wives often acted as witnesses, and widows were no more likely to be deposed than their number in the population at large would suggest.[24] Witnesses came from every

[21] ADLA B5853, 24 January 1719; and ADR BP4046, (no day or month) 1636.

[22] For the eighteenth-century claims, see Julius Ruff, *Crime, Justice, and Public Order in Old Régime France: The Sénéchausées of Liborne and Bazas, 1696–1789* (London, 1984), 13.

[23] What follows is based on a database of 150 surviving Nantais *enquêtes* in which 670 witnesses gave depositions.

[24] 315 of 670 (47%) witnesses were women, including 97 (31%) single women, 155 (48%) wives, and 63 (20%) widows. By way of comparison, Holmes ('Women: witnesses and witches') found that 10–22% of witnesses in English assize cases were female—a proportion much lower than the 43% that Gowing found in London church courts, although she notes that these courts seem to have been unusual in multiple ways.

age group, from teenagers to people in their eighties. About half the witnesses could sign their names, and men were about twice as likely as women to have that capability. Social status was an even more important variable than gender in literacy rates. More than half the men who were not given any honorary title could not write their names; neither could more than 80% of women in that category. By contrast, virtually all the men and more than three-quarters of the women who were given any title at all, even the most modest, knew how to sign. In all these regards, the mixed cast of characters who served as witnesses contrasted with the all-male, educated, elite ranks of judges and lawyers with whom they participated in the legal process.

Although plaintiffs chose witnesses who were diverse in many senses, they selected a geographically and socially homogeneous group in a strategy which suggests that they hoped to present in court a strong sense of broad-based neighbourhood endorsement that their complaints were legitimate. If overall levels of litigation were very high and working people were very knowledgeable about legal practice, litigation of particular kinds was highly localized. As we have seen, separation suits were concentrated in the parishes where working families lived. More than two-thirds of witnesses may have been neighbours or servants of plaintiffs, and even more were from the same parish or, if they lived in a different parish, from a couple of streets away.[25] Witnesses were overwhelmingly people of modest circumstances. The single most common occupation was servant, and most witnesses were from the less affluent craft households (twenty-two tailors to one goldsmith) or from the families of the working poor, in which men had jobs such as street porters and women worked in occupations such as secondhand vendors.[26] Nor were these patterns specific to separations cases, as witness demographics in other kinds of suit, both in Lyon and in other regions, seem (from admittedly fragmentary evidence thus far) to have been very similar.[27]

The spatial and socio-economic clustering of witnesses suggests that for couples, communities, and courts, the violation of neighbourhood mores was the critical measure in early modern litigation. Daniel Lord Smail has argued

[25] Almost 40% of witnesses identified themselves as neighbours, and nearly 10% more as current or former household members such as servants, apprentices, or lodgers. Many of the further 20% who had observed multiple difficulties on several occasions may also have been neighbours.

[26] The occupations of 318 male witnesses were clearly identified. 175 (55%) were craftsmen and labourers who, in addition to the goldsmiths and tailors, included ten shoemakers and eleven street porters. 56 (18%) were 'merchants', whose depositions suggested they were petty traders, although the category of 'merchant' covered diverse activities and incomes. 46 (14%) were petty legal officials. The remainder included thirteen surgeons, apothecaries and druggists, nine drapers, six servants, four barristers, four priests, three peasants, and one doctor.

[27] See, for example, the very similar demographic composition of witnesses found in Lyonnais criminal cases in samples from 1688 and 1788, in Bayard, 'Témoins et témoignages', 197–208. See also Steven Ozment, *The Burgermeister's Daughter: Scandal in a Sixteenth-Century German Town* (New York, 1996), 170; and Gowing, *Domestic Dangers*, 48–9.

that medieval plaintiffs chose witnesses from a wide range of socio-economic and geographical backgrounds to produce credible indications that their complaints were public knowledge and not just neighbourhood frays. By the seventeenth century, however, plaintiffs chose neighbours whose diversity lay far more in their age and gender than in their rank or residence. Plaintiffs sought to choose witnesses who could demonstrate that rank-specific standards of their socio-economically homogeneous neighbourhoods had been violated.[28]

To act as a witness involved a significant commitment in terms of time and the potential for conflict. Witnesses were summoned to appear, and were legally required to do so, but they could choose to say a lot or a little. Witnessing took time, because each deposition involved two steps. A witness first gave a statement in the courthouse, responding to a list of questions that the plaintiff and her lawyer had composed, and then usually returned later to verify the written version by signing or having the clerk record assent if the witness was illiterate. In a 1690 case, for example, in which four witnesses were called, the clerk recorded depositions over two days, summarizing statements made over several days. The first witness gave her testimony 'today'. 'When it was read to her', she 'affirmed it to be true [and] declared that she wanted to stick to it without adding or taking away any'. The next day, two witnesses confirmed depositions given 'yesterday', and a fourth witness confirmed a statement given four days earlier.[29]

Varying opinions about the legitimacy of a particular suit (spousal grievances in this case), the validity of litigation, and the wisdom of testifying about a particular situation, could cause tension between witnesses, between witnesses and spouses, and between witnesses and other neighbours or kin who did not testify. Witnesses took public stands that endorsed certain standards of behaviour and marked others as unacceptable, and this public taking of sides could involve costs. In 1647, four members of the same family, all living on the same street, gave testimony in a suit that illustrates possible differences of opinion about the significance of spousal conflicts. Bonnaventure Lizardiere (a 37-year-old merchant), his wife Mathurine Cosson (38), and his sister Françoise (a 28-year-old widow) testified for Barbe Dechaille, but their brother Pierre (a 30-year-old merchant) was deposed for her 'merchant' husband François Rousseau. Their versions of the marriage were remarkably different. The first three said that they had heard Dechaille's screams for help, seen various injuries that she said her husband had caused, and observed him punch her. Their brother, however,

[28] For the diverse composition of witness groups in medieval Marseilles, and the possible implications of that plaintiff strategy, see Smail, *Consumption of Justice*, esp. 226–41. For court officials' discussions about the role of rank in assessing behaviour, see, for example, ADR BP3985, 10 February 1654, and Alain Lottin, 'Vie et mort du couple: difficultés conjugales et divorces dans le nord de la France aux XVIIe et XVIIIe siècles', *XVII Siècle*, **102–103** (1974), 75–7.

[29] ADLA B5842, 31 May 1690.

claimed that Rousseau worked hard, and that he had never seen him 'do anything bad' or heard 'any gossip or scandal' about him. According to Pierre, Rousseau lived with his wife without any conflict, and treated her well, even after she initiated the separation suit and slandered him.[30]

Witnesses might also have cause to ponder the implications of giving evidence in terms of other potential consequences. If they testified against someone who was well known to be violent, that person might seek retribution. Their testimony could contribute towards a judicial penalty which they might or might not think appropriate in the circumstances. The latter issue might be less of a concern in a civil case, in which the penalty would be financial, than in a criminal case, in which the physical penalty could extend to death.[31] Nevertheless, their testimony could still have serious repercussions. If, for example, it publicized and exacerbated the financial difficulties of someone already in debt, a household might be rendered totally destitute, or they or their neighbours might never be paid.

Even so, serving as a witness also had its attractions, not least for women and working men, who gained political voices that they lacked in the rest of their lives. Men of all ages, single and married, skilled and manual labourers, gave evidence in court proceedings. Men who cut little weight in any other early modern institution, since they did not belong to guilds, militia companies, town assemblies, or parish vestries, seemed to have been regarded (like women) as witnesses no less valuable than men with more public standing. In fact, men who worked as porters or petty traders, as many witnesses did, often had very significant knowledge about which spouses had bought or sold what, whether for cash or on credit, and who took what chests or bags of goods where and when. Women, young or old, single, married, or widowed, had a virtual parity with male witnesses. Women were called nearly as often as men, and their word seems to have carried as much weight. Local court officials made no effort to give more weight to men's testimony, for instance by recording men's depositions before women's, although it was common practice in other legal documents, such as marriage contracts, to express gender hierarchies by systematically arranging men's signatures above women's signatures.[32]

Discretionary fees were allowed to cover witnesses' expenses and lost earnings, but judges and witnesses had different stakes in this matter.[33] The usual practice

[30] ADLA B5815, 2 and 16 September 1647.

[31] For an example of witness reluctance to testify in criminal cases, see Farr, *A Tale of Two Murders*.

[32] For the creation of these kinds of hierarchies in other legal documents, see Julie Hardwick, *The Practice of Patriarchy: Gender and the Politics of Household Authority in Early Modern France* (University Park, PA, 1998), 166–7.

[33] Witnesses could not elect to receive discretionary fees in other countries. In England, costs of witnesses were private matters with no judicial regulation. In Rome, witnesses received fees, but their payments were closely regulated. Thanks are due to Brian Levack and Laurie Nussdorfer for communications about these points.

of judges was to ask each witness 'if the fee is required'.[34] Judges considered the usual gender and status hierarchies rather than receipts when they assigned witness costs. They usually observed these hierarchies consistently, with only rare examples of judicial arbitrariness. In one case, Nantais Provost Valleton, for example, gave 8 *sous* each to four married women, including two shoemakers' wives, but 12 *sous* to a 15-year-old shoemaker's daughter who still lived with her parents—perhaps a pretty girl![35] Payments in the seventeenth century usually ranged between six and 15 *sous*. Women received about a third less than men, a gap that resembled gender differences in pay. In a 1674 case, for example, a weaver was paid 12 *sous*, while five women (a servant, three 'wives', and an unmarried secondhand vendor) were paid 8 *sous* each.[36] Fees increased in the eighteenth century, perhaps as part of a broader economic recovery after the well-known travails of the long seventeenth century. Payments of 20–40 *sous* or more became common, and the gender gap became wider in absolute although not in relative terms.

Witnesses' preferences in the matter of fees, on the other hand, indicate the importance they placed on their role in the negotiation of neighbourhood values through the regulation of disputes, and the differences associated with rank and gender suggest that witnesses connected the experience with their own standing.[37] A narrow majority of all witnesses declined to ask for any fee. Witnesses may have refused compensation for a variety of reasons. Given the time depositions took, witnesses probably did lose work time, so their refusals may have been rooted in other considerations. Did they feel that their word might have more weight if they were not compensated? Did they decline as a favour to the plaintiff, who had to pay the fees, although they could be recovered from the defendant if the case was won?

Witnesses may have seen their court statements as one more expression of the patterns of neighbourhood oversight and regulation essential to early modern communities.[38] The election of, or refusal of, fees fell into specific patterns that illuminate witness priorities more clearly. The few witnesses who lived out of town almost always took fees. They may have wanted to cover their travel costs, and/or did not feel any responsibility as part of the neighbourhood group involved

[34] The 1667 Civil Code noted that judges were to ask each witness 'if he claims a fee', and, if it was requested, to decide the amount based on the 'rank, amount of travel, and length of stay'of the witness. Isambert, *Recueil Général*, **18**, 145. See also Plessix-Buisset, *Criminel devant ses Juges*, 441.

[35] ADLA B5838, 30 January 1686.

[36] ADLA B5828, 20 April 1674.

[37] There is no literature on the role of these fees in French cases. For this neglect, see Herve Piant, 'Le prix de la vérité: témoignage, argent, et vérité dans la justice française d'Ancien Régime. Une analyse de la "taxe" des témoins', Garnot, *Témoins devant la Justice*, 209–20.

[38] Neighbours' roles in regulating each others' lives took many forms. Important statements about neighbourhood management of violence include James R. Farr, *Hands of Honor: Artisans and Their World in Dijon, 1550–1650* (Ithaca, 1988), esp. 150–95; and David Garrioch, *Neighbourhood and Community in Paris, 1740–1790* (Cambridge, 1986), esp. 31–55.

in informal mediation and judicial witnessing. The vast majority of witnesses, however, only had lost earnings to consider. Witnesses who were members of elites, regardless of sex, almost never asked for fees. Men who worked in the legal industry were much the most likely occupational group to ask for compensation, presumably because they were accustomed to being paid for their work with court fees of all kinds. Working men rarely took fees, although apprentices and men in manual occupations, such as porters, were more likely to do so than men in skilled occupations. Working women were the most likely of all witnesses to request fees.

Skilled men (whether in guild trades or unincorporated work) who declined to accept fees may have been keen to assert their rank as well as to claim and fulfil public responsibility. Like elites who routinely declined fees, skilled men may have seen witnessing not only as an obligation but also as an opportunity to demonstrate status. Testifying in court offered the opportunity to frame local standards and to discipline peers whose behaviour challenged those standards. Most male witnesses were of a rank in which official public roles of any kind were rare, although they may have played important informal roles in neighbourhood regulation and arbitration. For apprentices or unskilled workers, financial pressures might have been so acute that they could not afford to refuse even small amounts of cash, and they may have had less cultural capital to worry about or rank to defend.[39]

Why were working women more likely than their husbands to take fees? Cultural and economic considerations may have encouraged women and men to view the process of giving testimony and taking fees in different ways. Female witnesses, like their male peers, had little opportunity, outside the courthouse, to have their voices heard in institutional settings. Judges usually noted the fees without comment, but a reference to payment to a witness 'for her wages' highlights the equation of fees with paid work. Early modern women were invested in their work identity as well as familial. Just as female witnesses often chose to begin their depositions with declarations of personal identity that privileged their work rather than their marital status, they may have found the assignment of public value for their work through fees compelling. In a typical example, Janne Luzeau, identified by the clerk only as Jan Baudouin's wife, started her deposition by foregrounding her occupation: midwife.[40] Moreover,

[39] Direct evidence of how witnesses perceived fees is elusive. However, in 1747 the Controller General wrote that witnesses who were able (in an 'état') to cover their own costs would find it 'below them' to request fees, suggesting that for men the refusal of the fee was an expression of status and honour. Jean-Baptiste Machault d'Arnouville to Barberic de Saint-Contest de La Chataigneraye, 4 December 1747, Archives Nationales, VI 643, f. 233. I thank Al Hamscher for this reference.

[40] The significance of work identity for working women has become increasingly clear. See, for instance, Claire Haru Crowston, *Fabricating Women: the Seamstresses of Old Régime France, 1675–1791* (Durham, 2001), and Gayle Brunelle, 'Policing the monopolizing women of early modern Nantes', *Journal of Women's History*, **19**, 2 (Summer 2007), 10–35.

perhaps women's absences from home caused different kinds of disruption of the family economy than did their husbands' absences if, as many early modern historians have suggested, wives were far more willing to cover for their husbands than husbands were to do 'women's work'.

When witnesses arrived at the courthouse to give their depositions and fulfil their roles as regulators of neighbourhood values, clerks framed the records of the testimony with formulas that indicate how early modern communities conceptualized and weighed dependencies in a variety of sometimes contradictory ways. The testimony of a witness in 1680 was preceded by a formulaic template that was used on almost every such occasion:

> Izabelle Hardouin wife of Leonard Lapoterye master cake baker living in the rue de la poulaillerie parish of St Croix age 35 years or thereabouts, witness [who] swore yesterday in the hearing room following the record of this deed has promised to tell the truth purged of advice or solicitation. Examined and questioned has said not to be kin of or obligated to the parties.[41]

These formulas expressed conflicting notions of dependence. The social description privileged gender, while the oaths that guaranteed witnesses' qualifications privileged kinship and finances.

Gender played a predictably important role in the court clerks' efforts to position each witness in terms of social topography. Clerks used five coordinates in addition to name: title (if any) appropriate to social status, occupation or household status, age, street, and parish. They assigned four of these signifiers in almost all cases, but described women differently from men in one important way. Clerks almost always characterized men by occupation (such as 'Louis Jouanneau, shoemaker'), but usually defined women by household status, as in the case of Izabelle Hardouin above or 'Renée Perraud, servant living in the household of Sieur Marin'.[42] Clerks, in fact, made household status virtually inescapable for women, even if they had independent legal standing in principle. Widows' dead husbands (and both husbands if they had remarried) were identified, as were the fathers of unmarried women who lived alone. In 1694, for example, Marguerite Guihard, age 35, was identified as 'daughter of the deceased Thomas Guihard'.[43] In these ways, even legally independent women were rhetorically positioned with the households of dead men.[44] Clerks who

[41] ADLA B5833, 13 September 1680.

[42] For women's definition by household relationship rather than occupation in other legal contexts, see Carol Loats, 'Gender, guilds, and work identity: perspectives from sixteenth-century Paris', *French Historical Studies*, **20**, 1 (Winter 1997), 15–30, on apprenticeship contracts; and Gowing, *Domestic Dangers*, on English church court cases.

[43] ADLA B5844, 23 June and 7 July 1694.

[44] The occupations of female witnesses became a more significant element of clerical social description in the eighteenth century. While most women continued to be defined only by household status, their work became a common, if not usual, form of identification, and clerical social description in these matters sometimes became quite detailed. For example, in a case in 1745

drew these social maps followed other early modern authorities (including the judges who weighed up what fees were appropriate for witnesses), who often used social inscriptions as one of the many ways in which they sought to stabilize and naturalize hierarchical relations in general, and household relations in particular, through repeated reiterations of the authority of men and the dependence of women.

The same formulas, however, defined lack of independence in different terms in the oaths in which familial or financial rather than gender considerations were paramount, and these dependencies, rather than gender, were thought to entail an inability to make truthful, objective accounts of proceedings.[45] Witnesses had to swear that they were not related to the parties, because an extensive and specific set of kinship ties disqualified witnesses, extending from spouses, blood relatives, and in-laws to children of second cousins.[46] Very infrequently, court officials or defendants challenged the admissibility of testimony on the grounds that witnesses were in fact relatives. Jan Mallot objected to some of his wife's witnesses, although the relations he identified were so distant that they seemed well beyond the usual familial grounds for disqualification. One, according to him, was the grandson of the second marriage of a woman who by her third marriage was the great aunt of his wife.[47] While kinship ties disqualified witnesses, other quasi-kinship relations, including godparenthood or co-householding as servant, apprentice, or lodger, did not exclude people from testifying. Witnesses did declare ties of spiritual kinship with litigants, acknowledging that these relationships were potential dependencies, as in the case of Jacquette Seche, a tailor's wife, who said she was not related to the parties 'except that' the plaintiff was the godmother of one of her children.[48] Although a few witnesses declared that they were not servants in clarifications that indicate concern about the credibility of depositions by household members, numerous current or former household members did testify. The familial relations established through godparenthood or co-householding potentially undermined credible testimony, but did not inevitably disqualify witnesses.

Witnesses who promised that they were not 'obliged' to the parties meant that they were neither debtors nor creditors of the litigants, and potential for

with twelve female witnesses, the clerk used household definition alone for six, but described the others by their work too, as a 'female trader', a female cook, a ladies' maid, a stocking repairer, a widow 'working in linen', and a servant 'currently unemployed': ADLA B5863, 19 February 1745.

45 The 1667 Civil Code repeated the terms of a 1579 ordinance that required officials to ask witnesses if they were related to, or servants of, any of the parties. Isambert, *Recueil Général*, **14**, 429, and **18**, 145.

46 For the exclusion of kin as witnesses, see Isambert, *Recueil Général*, **18**, 144. In other kinds of cases, such as guardianship hearings, distant kin ties were frequently invoked as sources of obligation. See Hardwick, *Practice of Patriarchy*, 120–9.

47 ADLA B5814, 15 July 1651.

48 ADLA B5843, 5 September 1692.

disqualification on these grounds was interpreted narrowly. If witnesses thought any doubt existed about their capacity, they could clarify their relationship to the parties. Françoise Bree noted that she was not obliged to the litigants except that 'she and her husband [a shoemaker] sublet their residence from the parties', and a baker said the litigants owed him 'ten to eleven *livres* for bread'.[49] Judges did not disqualify witnesses who admitted these kinds of ties, which suggests that they were concerned about large loans rather than petty debts such as shop tabs. Given the webs of small-scale loans that criss-crossed early modern neighbourhoods, many litigants might have been hard pressed to find witnesses if any debt led to disqualification.

Serving as a witness must have been a common early modern experience for men and women, for the young and old, for the successful and struggling. Aside from going to church, few if any other formal, public activities included such a range of participants. Witnessing provided a rare opportunity for many people to appear in public forums in independent roles. The clerical description and witness oaths included in depositions pointed to the varied possible markers of dependence that created this opening. Within the legal system, as well as without, prerogatives and disabilities were deployed selectively rather than universally. When plaintiffs called witnesses whom they thought would verify violations of neighbourhood standards, they moved daily discussions into institutional settings and made the personal explicitly public. Witnesses took their knowledge of, and expectations about, household dynamics among their peers, literally on their street, into court proceedings that were sites of political debates as well as legal conflicts in early modern neighbourhoods.

THE POLITICS OF WITNESSES

Witnesses articulated the expectations about appropriate behaviour for both spouses that were current in their working family neighbourhoods. Their understanding of the privileges and pitfalls that husbands faced, as well as the obligations and options that wives navigated, illuminate in detailed and specific ways how working people gave daily meaning to the household model of authority drawn in broad strokes in much of the contemporary prescriptive literature, in royal edicts, and in law. Male and female witnesses expressed broadly similar assumptions about the contingency of the authority of male heads of households, and similar expectations about husbands' and wives' behaviour, in terms of financial management, sociability, speech, and sexuality.[50]

[49] ADLA B5843, 20 August 1691 and 8 August 1692.

[50] In these cases, witnesses devoted much less time to defining appropriate behaviour for women than they did for men. As wives initiated nearly all separation cases, male and female witnesses

Witnesses used their appearance in court not only to speak to the case, but also to articulate personal grievances, to make public rebukes about particular kinds of behaviour, and to assert neighbourhood critiques of matters that went beyond the legal parameters of the cases. Their priorities for orderly family life often overlapped with those of the state, but in some important ways their concerns differed from those often associated with elites or prescriptive sources.

Although witnesses did not make simple statements of fact and their depositions had complex characteristics, they were able to shape their testimonies in identifiable ways. Depositions were composites rather than self-authored accounts, framed by the questions submitted by plaintiffs and their lawyers and by clerks who transformed the questions and answers into narratives. Witnesses emphasized factors that were legally pertinent, and they employed standard narrative tropes. Depositions involved multiple layers of oral and literate culture produced through interactions over a number of days.[51] Yet witnesses were able to disrupt, in telling ways, the imperatives of the generic scripts which these circumstances might suggest. Occasionally, for example, a witness did not respond to the legal summons, and came forward only in response to a follow-up ecclesiastical order (*monitoire*) directing potential witnesses to appear. Some came to court but denied knowing anything about the matter at hand, while others did not restrict their testimony to immediately pertinent matters. Witnesses sometimes made statements that were damaging to the party who had called them. Three of the four witnesses called by Judic de Soulier, for instance, said they did not know anything about her allegations, but knew that her spouse Olivier Chevallier was a good man who worked hard—not the kind of testimony she must have hoped to elicit.[52] A witness might say that he or she had seen a man hit his wife, and then add that the spouses had quarrelled first or that the wife had also hit her husband. In these kinds of ways, witnesses expressed their own perspectives within the framework of giving depositions.

Witnesses' discussions of household roles consistently neglected the legal and religious underpinnings of patriarchal power that early modern authorities of all kinds stressed, and that have since seemed so striking to observers. Not a single witness referred to the law or to God as sources of husbandly authority, whereas royal prosecutors' discussions of the same cases were filled with references to laws

focused much more attention on how husbands should and should not act than on how wives should act. Even when husbands gathered testimony as part of their opposition to their wives' suits, their witnesses primarily focused on rebutting critiques of male behaviour, whether made by wives or witnesses, rather than exploring female behaviour.

[51] Insightful assessments of the possibilities and problems of using court records include Davis, *Fiction in the Archives*; Gowing, *Domestic Dangers*; and Tim Stretton, *Women Waging the Law in Elizabethan England* (Cambridge, 1998).

[52] ADLA B5840, 21 February 1688.

divine and human.[53] While law and religion certainly contributed powerfully to patriarchal power as an ideological construct, the quotidian cultural practices in the daily lives of urban communities linked gender and authority in other ways. Witnesses' discourse about marriage during litigation was secular, and the open and repeated discussions of marriage in these secular terms created an important alternative to prescriptive discourses that asserted divine or legal naturalization of spousal hierarchies and often explicitly or implicitly extended that concept to monarchical right.[54]

Male and female witnesses assumed that husbands and fathers should usually provide the leadership in the households, but both emphasized that household leadership was worked out through actions rather than simply dictated by law or nature. Witnesses occasionally reported men's efforts to assume gender privilege. Pierre Leroy, a buttonmaker, recalled hearing his neighbour, the hatter Louis Thebaudeau, tell his wife bluntly that he 'wanted to be the master'. Leroy, however, noted that Thebaudeau's wife, Marie Monnier, slapped her husband's face in response, in what could hardly have been a clearer expression of her perception that his behaviour had undermined any such claim to authority.[55] Men as well as women usually located the basis of husbandly authority in hard work, good providing, and careful management of resources. For them, male leadership rested on an understanding of masculinity that tied continued privileges to the fulfilment of daily obligations, rather than universal assumptions. Men as well as women found fault with husbands whose shortcomings caused household disorder, whether in their personal interactions with their wives or in their habits, especially slothfulness, the inability to control their tempers, or spending.

Witnesses indicated that a complex repertoire of practices of masculinity existed in non-elite urban communities. One important model, highlighted starkly by the imperatives of the court cases, was that of a man whose success as a *bon mesnager*—literally, a householder and husbander—was based on hard work, astuteness, and purposeful cooperation with his wife. A 35-year-old journeyman butcher, who had known the butcher Jullien Bretaigne and his wife Marguerite Delamotte 'for a long time', reported that he abused her, got drunk 'instead of working at his trade to earn his living and that of his children, he is debauched', and did not let his wife earn her living either.[56] Bretaigne's shortcomings contrasted with reputable men's behaviour—a distinction often

[53] For royal prosecutors' discussions of separation cases in these courts, in terms that naturalized men's authority, see, for example, ADR BP5985, 30 January 1653; ADR BP3985, 10 February 1654; ADR BP3985, 29 September 1656; and ADR BP3984, 14 February 1682.

[54] For the prescriptive tendency to naturalize marital and royal authority, see, for instance, Sarah Hanley, 'The monarchic state in early modern France: marital régime government and male right', in Adrianna Bakos (ed.), *Politics, Ideology, and Law in Early Modern Europe* (Rochester, 1994), 110–12; and 'Social sites of political practice', 110.

[55] ADLA B5843, 31 July 1691.

[56] ADLA B5814, 2 December 1651.

made explicitly through use of the adjectives 'civil' and 'uncivil'. Bretaigne found himself measured and criticized against a standard set by men who earned authority and acted as worthy patriarchs.

This template for men's behaviour in the household co-existed with another that emphasized sociability beyond the household. Men valued, and women at least acknowledged the legitimacy of, forms of sociability in which largesse, generosity, and fraternity were expressed through buying drinks for others, lending money, and gambling. The codes of largesse that were central to men's sociability served many valuable purposes besides entertainment. They provided cohesion in networks that could generate credit, information about work, and roles in neighbourhood regulation. That is to say that working men's reputations rested on their ability to exercise good judgement about sociability as well as household matters.

Working men and women who judged when male sociability became dangerous and contradicted good husbandry asserted that excesses and ineptitudes that endangered household order endangered the privileges of manhood. The activities themselves did not constitute a problem, but lack of appropriate parameters and boundaries did. Three 'merchants', for example, did not complain that their neighbour Jan Bernier gambled because it was after all a pastime that many working men valued. Instead their criticsm was that he gambled with men 'who were not of his status', that he 'kept on playing when he lost', and that when he 'went home after he lost, he beat his wife'.[57] Similarly, men did not criticize their peers for buying rounds of drinks or lending each other money, but for doing so for people whom they did not know or without written promises to repay. It was not gambling *per se* that mattered, but losing; not borrowing or lending money, but failing to manage debts wisely; not drinking, but drunkenness; not using force for household discipline, but exercising excessive force that constituted battery. Whether the property involved was cash, credit, or the labour and lineage property of women's bodies, witnesses tied men's authority to their management of it.

While men and women valued sociability in appropriate forms, and criticized it when men's indulgences seemed excessive, some gender difference in attitudes toward such extra-household activities may have existed. Recall Anne Douard's witnesses with whose assessments of her husband this chapter began. Whereas a male apprentice and neighbour portrayed Gobin as a convivial companion whose drinking and gambling were nothing to worry about, Douard and the neighbour's wife thought the time and money involved had crossed the boundary of the acceptable. Women were perhaps more likely than men to feel that the costs of customary sociability, whether in money, time lost, or drunken violence, outweighed the benefits.

[57] ADLA B5810, 7 November 1639.

Witnesses did not simply correlate these multifaceted masculinities to narrow social rank, although broader social divisions certainly affected expectations.[58] Skilled craftsmen and manual workers alike appreciated the value of diligence, accountability, and conjugal cooperation, but relished the rugged extra-household sociability of bar, militia, and parish characterized by drinking, gambling and reciprocity of various kinds. Working men of all ranks could enhance their reputation and household authority by managing their participation successfully, or endanger their standing with their wives and neighbours if they failed to exercise the judgements and the caution regarded as appropriate. Likewise, their judicious participation in the social world of the neighbourhood, where they might play cards with men from whom they could borrow money, or learn about work opportunities, as well as enjoy camaraderie, contributed to their public standing. This repertoire of masculinity undoubtedly had broad social parameters among working people, but there was little sign of the valorizing of conspicuous consumption and channeled violence that characterized masculinity for the nobility.[59]

Witnesses defined key areas of behaviour as critical for both men and women, with finances, speech, and sexuality as areas of common concern. Witnesses expected wives, like husbands, to endeavour to secure the financial stability of their households. They extolled hard work and astute money management in both sexes. Although married women could not legally borrow money without their husbands' consent unless they had the legal status of a female trader, witnesses commended wives for managing complex webs of debts. As we will see in the next chapter, working people seemed to find wives' legally unauthorized borrowing problematic only when it caused difficulties, no doubt in acknowledgement that debt juggling was an essential and ubiquitous element of most household economies for men and women.[60]

Witnesses were also concerned about respectful spousal speech. Neighbours as well as spouses, and women as well as men, made an issue of what husbands and wives said to each other and how they said it. Witnesses who seemed skeptical of wives' claims, or who spoke on the husbands' behalf, often commented that the spouses were 'always arguing' or that wives had insulted their husbands. They also frowned on men's disrespectful speech, and noted if a husband swore,

[58] Historians have tended to emphasize divisions among working men in discussions of masculinity. See Merry Wiesner, '*Wandervogels* and women: journeymen's concepts of masculinity in early modern Germany', *Journal of Social History*, 24, 4 (Summer 1991), 767–82; and Alexandra Shepard, 'Manhood, credit and patriarchy in early modern England', *Past and Present*, **167**, 1 (May 2000), 75–106.

[59] For consumption and channelled violence as central to elite masculinity, see, for instance, Robert Forster, *The House of Saulx-Tavannes: Versailles and Burgundy, 1700–1830* (Baltimore, 1971); and Jeffrey Merrick, 'Masculinity and effeminacy in the *Mémoires secrets*', in Jeremy Popkin and Bernadette Fort (eds.), *The Mémoires secrets and the Culture of Publicity in Eighteenth-Century France* (Oxford, 1998), 135–8.

[60] For debt practices and their implications, see Chapter 4.

blasphemed, or defamed his wife. Many historians have observed that early modern people vigorously used insults and defended their reputations against insults, but witnesses' comments suggest that speech between spouses was as coded as that between members of communities.

Witnesses may have thought that disrespectful male and female speech had different consequences. They seemed to think that wives' injurious speech undermined their right to protest their husbands' behaviour and to regard women's verbal lack of deference as legitimate provocation for men's use of force. Husbands who insulted their wives certainly damaged their own reputations as well as those of their wives, no small matter, but such speech alone did not provide grounds for any action.

The clearest gender distinction that male and female witnesses made was in the level of concern they articulated about husbands' extramarital sexuality and overly expensive sociability, whereas they seemed to have little concern about wives' sexual immorality or costly spending habits. Certainly the legal structure of separation cases may have been in part responsible for the highlighting of men's conduct in these regards. Nevertheless, as witnesses frequently raised issues that were not legally pertinent, these indications suggest that gender and rank, as well as marital status, were important factors in shaping concerns about male and female sexuality. For these witnesses from working families, the inappropriate sexuality of wives was not a high-priority concern, perhaps because in practice few married women had the time, energy, or opportunity to engage in adulterous liaisons. Even husbands who opposed their wives' claims rarely cited wifely immorality, and usually focused instead on why their wives' allegations about their behaviour had no basis. Working men rarely mobilized anxiety about wives' sexuality in other contexts. When husbands from this *milieu* justified their use of force against their wives, they claimed overwhelmingly that women's inappropriate speech had been the subject of their 'discipline'. By contrast, when elite men sought to explain why their wives needed discipline, they almost always raised the issue of sexual immorality.[61] Never-married or widowed women may certainly have been subject to different assumptions. Both male and female witnesses were inclined to frame the sexuality of single women as threatening when they did not perceive the sexual activity to be coerced, as indicated by their references to bad girls of various kinds who consorted with married men.

Witnessing frequently allowed men and women to criticize the practices and mores of those whose social and/or gender status usually trumped theirs. In a reversal of the familiar hierarchies of early modern society, servants, apprentices or journeymen, and porters spoke against their employers or neighbours. In a particularly striking example, when Dame Marianne Luzeau sought separate property from her husband Louis Belot (whose courtesy epithet of 'noble

[61] For discussion of the economies of family violence, see Chapter 5.

man' implied notable status although not legal nobility), her six witnesses were neighbourhood working women whose rank as well as gender indicated sharp inferiority to Belot.[62] A shoemaker's wife, a teenage servant, a married servant, a fruitseller, a schoolmaster's wife, and the couple's 'closest neighbour' all spoke in ways that undermined the reputation of a man who far outranked them. Their own emphasis on effective household management as a key marker of masculine authority was evident in their mocking disparagement of Belot for wasting money on 'useless things' such as flower bulbs and large numbers of oranges. The world-turned-upside-down quality of these legal testimonies illustrates the inversions common in many aspects of early modern popular culture, and indicates how assumptions about the contingency of household authority provided room for criticism when performance proved inadequate.

Witnesses' testimony that criticized people who were usually ranked above them in early modern hierarchies transformed personal differences of opinion into open rebukes, and publicly endorsed some forms of gendered authority as legitimate and others as illegitimate. The suit between Louise Testadoyais and her husband Michel Texier, a master tin-worker, exemplified processes of this kind that were repeated in many cases. Three of Texier's workshop employees testified against their master.[63] All three workers had seen arguments between the spouses escalate into violence. Two journeymen had stepped in, on occasion, to stop Texier from abusing his wife. Their decisions to intervene demonstrated that they perceived men's household authority to be limited. The journeymen were legally subject to Texier's discipline as much as was his wife. Their testimonies took their challenge to his authority beyond the household, and made the parameters of men's use of violence a public issue.

The female witnesses in the Texier–Testadoyais case provided testimony that highlighted the opportunity such litigation provided to accommodate personal politics, as well as to engage larger debates about gender and power. Yvonne Desauz, the workshop employee, a wet-nurse who worked for the family, and two neighbourhood widows, were deposed. Desauz, an 18-year-old servant in another household, worked for Texier one day a week. She testified that she had seen him abuse his wife, and had 'put herself between them' to stop another beating. Like the journeymen, Desauz not only made a personal statement about the acceptability of household violence, but also made that judgement a public matter through her testimony. By their speech as well as actions, all three asserted that men's right to use force to discipline their wives was contingent, like other forms of household authority.

Desauz also used the occasion to publicize personal grievances for which she otherwise had little recourse. She alleged that Texier had tried to coerce her to provide sexual services for him. He had repeatedly pressured her into having sex

[62] ADLA B5838, 30 January 1686. [63] ADLA B5810, 10 February 1639.

with him, promising among other things to give her an expensive dress in return. Finally, he attempted to rape her. This testimony certainly did not enhance Desauz's prospects for legal recourse, as prosecution for rape was very rare in early modern societies, but she delivered a public rebuke of his behaviour that may have given her some satisfaction.

Witnesses could make public critiques in political sites of particular kinds of behaviour that went far beyond the legal imperatives of the case, whether excesses of sociability or, as in the Texier–Testadoyais case, of married men's extramarital sexuality. The wet-nurse testified that he had propositioned her for sex, too. The two widows recalled occasions when Texier had approached each of them individually to find a place for his servant to deliver a baby he had fathered. None of these factors was legally relevant to Testadoyais's case, but the women's testimony, elicited by her, highlighted a husbands' inappropriate sexuality as sources of neighbourhood as well as household disorder.

Judgements of this kind about married men's sexual conduct complicate the patterns that historians have usually discerned in early modern society. Criminal prosecutions suggest that women's illicit sexual activities were taken far more seriously than men's, but in civil cases female witnesses publicly articulated an alternative view of the source of threatening sexuality that suggests that working people saw particular forms of male as well as female sexuality as disruptive.[64] Separation suits gave female witnesses (and plaintiffs) an opportunity for agency in articulating appropriate standards in institutional sites where favourable judgements offered official endorsement as well as neighbourhood approval of particular patterns of behaviour.

In the legal, public, and political forums of litigation, male and female witnesses articulated grassroots understanding about how and when power might be exercised legitimately. Through strategic participation in marital dramas, they provided accounts of the relations of gender and authority in sites that authorized particular expressions of power. For spouses and witnesses, courts were sites of authority that could endorse local expectations about behaviour. They did not challenge men's authority *per se*, but they did persistently and powerfully frame it in very specific and contingent ways. Although male and female witnesses differed in some ways, they shared a broad understanding of the obligations of wives and husbands, and they tied fulfilment of spousal responsibilities to neighbourhood reputation as well as household authority. Their expectations largely cut across differences in gender and rank in working households.

[64] For elite concern with the regulation of female sexuality, see, for example, James R. Farr, *Authority and Sexuality in Early Modern Burgundy* (Oxford, 1996). A study of masculinity in early modern England also highlights the centrality of men's sexuality in determining their reputations, albeit with a focus on male potency and the ability to control female sexuality, rather than on extramarital affairs. See Elizabeth Foyster, *Manhood in Early Modern England* (London, 1999).

THE POLITICS OF ROYAL PROSECUTORS

In litigation communities, plaintiffs' petitions and witness interventions jostled alongside those of royal prosecutors (*procureurs du roi*) and those of judges themselves. At the start of cases, prosecutors noted permission to proceed on the initial petitions without comment, but their recommendations to judges, as cases came to conclusions about how to rule on the basis of the witnesses' evidence, sometimes included extended explanations. Of all the participants in local litigation communities, they mused most explicitly, at least in writing, about the nature of authority. Their formulations resonated alternately both with much contemporary prescriptive literature, hewing to a version of authority that was far more naturalized than plaintiffs or witnesses allowed, and with the expansive jurist-driven legal print culture that explored the contradictions and limits of authority in family and state.[65]

Prosecutors often explicitly referred to the ancient religious and legal foundations of male power as key aspects of marriage relationships. Roman commentators loomed large in their writing, as did what the prosecutors perceived to be Christian frameworks, whether provided by a broadly referenced 'divine law' or by particular biblical and canon law prescriptions. One prosecutor, for instance, managed, in the space of three manuscript pages, to describe marriage as 'a sacrament' and 'a contract above all others' whose terms were defined by St Thomas, Cicero, and Jacques Cujas (a prominent sixteenth-century Roman law expert) among others, and regulated by 'human laws', 'civil laws', 'canon law', and the law of 'the Emperor' as well as 'divine law'.[66]

Prosecutors explicitly drew out the relationships between marriage and larger political arrangements as they frequently employed a political vocabulary similar to that which emerged occasionally in wives' petitions. One used a Christian creation trope to point out that 'a wife was a companion, not a slave' because 'the wife was not made from the foot of the man but from one of his ribs'. Another highlighted models of marriage that spoke to issues of national as well as individual identities. He compared French marriages favourably to those of Moscovites, 'whose wives believed themselves scorned and unloved if their husbands did not beat them', and Persians, 'who only want their wives to be

[65] Although we know very little about *procureurs du roi* in local courts, as with other officials in these jurisdictions, they may well have been participants—at least as readers—in the seventeenth-century debates about law and authority, family and state in which many elite lawyers were involved. For the contours of this debate in legal print culture, see Breen, *Law, City, and King*; and Hanley, 'The jurisprudence of the arrêts'. For the prescriptive literature in France, see Jeffrey Merrick, 'Fathers and kings: patriarchalism and absolutism in eighteenth-century French politics', *Studies on Voltaire and the Eighteenth Century*, 308 (1993).

[66] ADR BP5985, 30 January 1653.

servants'.[67] These kinds of allusions to despotic and alien regimes foreshadowed the synchronicity of marital and political regimes that Montesquieu was to adopt 70 years later and implicitly contrasted those with the already much in vogue prescriptions for the benefits of the right ordering of family and monarchy in France.

Although prosecutors tended to base their gender and authority modelling in law and religion, they shared the emphasis of plaintiffs and witnesses on mutuality. Prosecutors saw reciprocity as an important feature in the microcosmic polities represented by French marriages. For them, wifely submission 'does not permit violence which must have no place in a sacrament instituted for mutual comfort'. Marriage was a 'civil society' in which 'conjugal love and moderation one towards the other' were 'particularly required between husband and wife'.[68] One described 'all the help' a husband could find in his wife's 'labour and the revenues of her property', and noted the 'mutual aid that the wife and he [the husband] reciprocally owe each other in their times of misfortune and adversity'.[69]

Equally importantly, prosecutors and witnesses agreed on the varieties of authority that were appropriate within households and on the possibility that daily inadequacies could undermine authority. A prosecutor clarified the difference between spouses and other household members in criticizing a husband who 'employed mistreatment and extraordinary cruelty such as he could use on a valet or servant'. For them, wives seem to have merited superior treatment, and were worthy of a kind of protection that children, apprentices or servants might not expect.

Prosecutors' explanations of their recommendations suggest that they focused closely, if sometimes creatively, on the prescriptive issues surrounding the case, and suggest that despite the state's assertion of lay control, Catholicism still shaped judicial considerations. The suit between Marguerite de May and Louis Bolliaud in 1634, for example, demonstrated how a royal prosecutor wrestled to reconcile various prescriptive imperatives. De May requested a separation of person and property on several grounds: lack of parental consent (her widowed mother signed the marriage contract when her guardian should have done so); lack of publicity; abduction; lack of consent of spouses (she was forced into it by battery and threats from her mother); deception (her husband seemed to be a 'good Catholic' but 'reverted' to Protestantism soon after their marriage). The first three grounds all engaged the spate of late sixteenth-century royal legislation about marriage

[67] ADR BP3985, 10 February 1654; ADR BP3985, 30 January 1653.

[68] Lawyers frequently began to use the language of 'civil society' in the seventeenth century. See Sarah Hanley, 'The jurisprudence of the arrêts: marital union, civil society, and state formation in France, 1550–1650', *Law and History Review*, 21, 1 (2003), 1–40.

[69] ADR BP5985, 30 January 1653; ADR BP3985, 29 September 1656; ADR BP3984, 14 February 1682.

formation which had required parental consent, outlawed clandestine marriage, and criminalized abduction or elopement (*rapt*). None of these, however, was legally pertinent in separations. The fourth, lack of spousal consent, engaged Catholic doctrine, reinforced at the Council of Trent but rejected by the French government, that continued to make the free will of spouses the key to legal marriage. The fifth, deception, was a common claim of unhappy wives, but again had no legal standing, and introduced the question of religion which was also in principle legally irrelevant.[70] The prosecutor cast his assessment of the evidence both in terms of royal legislation and divine authority. He rejected the first four grounds, saying that the witnesses did not prove her claims. He noted that 'no remedy' existed in canon or Roman law 'for her mistake' in marrying a man who turned out to be not what he seemed.

This prosecutor, like others, invoked both secular and religious principles in making his recommendation as to sentence, but his concern about heresy led him to continue to strategize rather than simply to recommend to the judge that De May's petition be turned down because she had no case. It was true, he went on, that the Church allowed separations (although not divorce) for adultery, and also if one spouse 'committed the type of adultery that the Church calls spiritual'. Nevertheless, De May still had two obstacles (or perhaps the prosecutor himself did) in that 'the holy decrees' advised such a spouse to stay in order to lead the other 'to the path of True religion', and that since Protestants enjoyed 'freedom of conscience' in France, to 'grant a separation of person and property every time a Catholic became a Huguenot would elude the Intention of my King and contravene the Ordinances'. All these indications still seemed to point to the prosecutor's recommendation that the judge should rule against De May's request.

Yet the prosecutor continued to try to reconcile Catholic and royal imperatives. He went on to argue that the King did not mean that Protestants could 'worry and harass Catholics', and that it had 'never been the Intention of my King to allow those infected with heresy to spoil and corrupt the good subjects'. De May had shown that her husband 'wanted to threaten and force her' to abandon 'the true religion', so if her physical being was not in peril (a threat to her life being technically the requirement for a separation of person and property), her soul would be 'in great danger'. This life-endangering potential meant that even though she had not 'shown grounds that the marriage was not legally contracted', the prosecutor recommended the separation be granted.

This extraordinary discussion shows not only how prosecutors' assumptions about the centrality of prescriptive legal and religious issues could be sharply different from those of witnesses and plaintiffs, but how they too acknowledged that inappropriate behaviour could undermine the rights of husbands and fathers. In many more mundane cases they demonstrated their awareness both of the

[70] ADR BP4046, (no date or month) 1634.

national discourses about household authority and local practices. In their own way, they too sought to fill in and shade the possible meanings of familial authority as practice rather than rhetoric. They were sensitive to the nuances of authority, shaped for them by social rank and dependent status. With their recommendations in hand, judges moved to the centre of the process to rule on the case. Judges, even more than the prosecutors, were sharply positioned between state and street.

THE POLITICS OF JUDGES

Judges were the ultimate arbiters in litigation communities. While they exercised some caution about granting women the separations of property and person that dissolved households, the readiness with which they granted the far more commonly requested separations of property alone raises into sharp focus the issue of how they understood the basis of patriarchal power. Judges' motives are difficult to deduce because they did not have to provide written explanations, but their decisions suggest that they, like plaintiffs and witnesses, preferred a more flexible practice-based approach to questions about gender, property, and authority. Their decisions raise two interrelated questions: about their views on gender and authority in the family, and about their relationship to the state.

Judges in lower courts remain largely unknown to historians, far from what Herve Piant recently termed the much studied judicial 'aristocracy' *parlements*, but their attitudes suggest a proclivity to base their judicial practice on action rather than learning. The many handbooks of judicial process published in the seventeenth century, no doubt intended for judges, lawyers, and any other interested parties, were dominated by practical explanations about procedure and relevant matters in different kinds of cases, rather than judicial philosophy. Judges (perhaps especially in provostal courts) frequently took investigations out into the community (as we have seen), and they supervised depositions. This hands-on emphasis co-existed with a rich legal literature in which discussions of cases provided precedents. However, the extent to which lower-court judges observed this literature in practice remains unclear.[71]

[71] For legal guidebooks that emphasize practice, see, for example, Claude LeBrun de la Rochette, *Les Proces Civil et Criminel contentants la methodique liaison du droict, et de la Practique Judiciare* (Lyon, 1628); Francois Laye, *La Nouvelle Practique Civile, Criminelle et beneficiale ou Le Nouveau Practice Francois* (Paris, 1694); Vincent Tagereau, *Le Vray et Nouveau Practicien Francois* (dernière edition, Lyon 1666).

Since work on judges has concentrated on lawyers working in the higher echelons of the legal process, historians are divided about to what extent lower-court judges might have shared the qualities and perspectives of their peers in superior courts. Generally, historians who have worked specifically on lower courts are inclined to emphasize the differences. See, for example, for the distance between

Judges' decision-making draws into sharp focus questions about the nature of early modern institutions and the ability of the state to use judicial institutions to shape family practice. William Beik's powerful formulation of an early modern state whose effectiveness rested on its ability to secure the collaboration of elites who could make its authority real has for almost twenty years provided a compelling conceptualization of how an early modern state could work. Sarah Hanley has argued, in a series of stimulating articles, for the creation of a compact between state and judiciary that symbiotically fed royal and paternal/conjugal power, and for the emergence of a national jurisprudence.[72] The family–state compact, moreover, demonstrates a basis for alliance beyond the factors suggested by Beik.

Yet the early modern legal system, like other early modern institutions, was not monolithic, and we have yet to determine how, or if, this collaborative model of state agency reached the myriad lower courts.[73] Even in the *parlements*, judges were as often in conflict with the monarchy as they were collaborating with it. We still have little sense of how much currency the patterns of *parlementaire* jurisprudence had in practice in lower courts, and the connections of the personnel of an early modern court of first instance to the state seem at best tenuous.[74] Nor were the varied legal officials necessarily monolithic in their opinions. One study has suggested that royal prosecutors were much more closely tied to the king than were judges, and that this difference in orientation caused conflicts between the groups.[75] Certainly, in separations cases, judges did not always concur with

high-court judges and their court of first instance peers, Piant, *Une Justice Ordinaire*, 55–100. For a characterization of *sénéchaussée* judges as 'men of action rather than men of learning', see Silverman, *Tortured Bodies*, 52. This view is also evident in the attitudes of lower-court judges involved with the enforcement of monetary policy. See Jotham Parsons, 'Governing sixteenth-century France: the monetary reforms of 1577', *French Historical Studies*, **26**, 1 (Winter 2003), 22. For a characterization of lower-court judges in Normandy as educated and competent, see Zoe Schneider, *The Village and the State: Justice and the Local Courts in Normandy, 1670–1740*, 3 vols., Ph.D. thesis, Georgetown University, 1997, **2**, 345–55. For studies of the social characteristics of lower-court justice, see also Pierre Goubert, 'Les officiers royaux des presidiaux, bailliages et élections', *17e Siècle* (1959), 42–43, and Maurice Graesset, *Les Gens de Justice à Besançon de la conquête par Louis XIV à la Révolution Française (1674–1789)*, 2 vols. (Paris, 1978).

[72] See, for example, Hanley, 'Engendering the state', and 'The jurisprudence of the arrêts'.

[73] Calls to problematize the varied rather than monolithic nature of French institutions include, for courts, Jonathan Dewald, Review of John Hurt, *Louis XIV and the Parlements: The Assertion of Royal Authority* (Manchester and New York, 2002), for *H-France* (August 2002); and for guilds, Crowston, *Fabricating Women*.

[74] For scepticism of the correlation between *parlementaire* patterns and those of lower courts, see the literature reviewed in V. A. C. Gatrell, Bruce Lenman, and Geoffrey Parker 'Introduction', in Gatrell, Lenman, and Parker (eds.), *Crime and the Law: The Social History of Crime in Western Europe since 1500* (London, 1982), 3. An emerging wave of new work on the lower courts in France reinforces this perspective. See, for instance, Piant, *Une Justice Ordinaire*, 55–100, and Séverine Debordes-Lissillour, *Les Sénéchaussées Royales de Bretagne: La Monarchie d'Ancien Régime et ses Juridictions Ordinaires (1532–1790)* (Rennes, 2006), 103–207. The latter argues that over the early modern period, local court judges became more distant from the state and more embedded in their local communities.

[75] Gresset, *Gens de Justice*.

the recommendations of royal prosecutors. In fact, prosecutors were more likely than judges to be sympathetic to requests for separation of person and property; prosecutors frequently recommended these petitions be granted, whereas judges, in their sentences, agreed to separate property alone.

Moreover, although much about the workings of lower courts in civil matters remains to be explored, the French state did not apparently exercise the kind of close control over its lower-court judges and their decision-making that was evident elsewhere. Ulinka Rublack, for example, has recently analysed judicial process in early modern German territories where high levels of oversight made the state's control 'extraordinarily tight' and the influence of judges 'very limited', whereas Zoe Schneider argued that lower courts in Normandy 'showed a high degree of independence from royal direction'.[76] Lower-court judges in France, like most other court officials, secured their position by purchase rather than appointment, and the crown's preference of the sale of such offices (to raise revenue) rather than appointment has long been considered a key source of official independence from the crown.

In fact, in hundreds of courts of first instance all over France, important administrative as well as judicial sites, the judiciary's links to the state were elastic, but their roots in local communities were much more obvious. Lower-court judges were positioned, in fact, like witnesses, between state and street, or perhaps more accurately between metropole and locality. They were technically royal officials who worked in royal courts (rather than in municipal or ecclesiastical courts). Yet no national edicts legislated separations (or, for that matter, much of the other litigation that came before their courts), unlike some other family issues such as marriage formation. Regional customary laws governed separations cases, and offered so little instruction that judges had broad discretion. Moreover, customary law provisions affected family property management more broadly in many ways. In this area as in others, customary law and daily realities could be at odds with royal legislation that enhanced paternal and conjugal power. Judges exercised their function as investigators and mediators who, on the streets and in households, as well as in court, engaged directly with the members of the community as they sought to fulfil their charge and maintain public order.[77]

Lower-court judges were amenable to assigning married women separate property, granting these petitions virtually universally and in large numbers. They were more skeptical about requests for separations of property and person, although only about one fifth of separation requests fell into this category. Judges turned down about a third of these suits, but often chose to grant separate property

[76] See Ulinka Rublack, *The Crimes of Women in Early Modern Germany* (Oxford, 1999), 52; Zoe A. Schneider, *The Village and the State*, 1, 7.

[77] They did so across a variety of areas of governance. See Jotham Parsons' recent assessment of such judges as intermediaries between crown and subjects, based on their activities in monetary policy: Parsons, 'Governing sixteenth-century France', esp. 21–7.

even in those cases.[78] To allow married women to leave conjugal households and establish separate residences promised obvious potential disruptions both socially and economically, and judges probably wanted to avoid either masterless women or the possibility of single mothers becoming public charges.

Nonetheless, allowing married women to manage their own property, in a period when control over household property was among the most significant privileges of adult married men, had very wide-reaching implications. When judges agreed to assign separate property to married women, they privileged particular values. Judges who assigned wives separate property dramatically and publicly repositioned married women, not only as the legal managers of their own property and as the first creditors of their households, but also as the designated providers for their families. Judges' sentences occasionally made this revolution in circumstances clear with brief but explicit injunctions to wives 'to use their revenue to support their families'. Moreover, with these decisions, judges favoured lineage property over the contractual rights of creditors in a market economy. They favoured the economic survival of households over the legal and cultural privileges of husbands. They favoured recognizing wives' labour and capital contributions (in cash and kind via dowries) over reiterating the household hierarchies in which the very idea that wives brought dowries that their husbands would control was enmeshed.

The discursive realignment of gender and authority correlations, in which power over property was critical, was dramatic, even if the reality of the circumstances of families in which wives were given separate property certainly may have left them with little practical property of any kind. In contrast to the concern of upper courts to make paternal power over property paramount, the judges in these lower courts seemed to value the preservation of family property over market imperatives or conjugal authority. Their decisions suggest that for them too, men had to earn a gendered authority from which wives were not excluded.

In many ways, judges' granting of separate property requests represented a ratification of local opinion rather than monarchical preference, and another demonstration of how local legal cultures coalesced. The French monarchy had pursued high-profile intervention, via law-making, of certain aspects of family life such as paternal control over marriage, but in practice not a single such case survives in the extensive records of either the Nantais or Lyonnais courts of first instance. Regional law codes, meanwhile, continued to provide the pertinent and often, as in the case of separations, quite loose guidelines for much of what families actually litigated in local courts. Lower-court judges seemed as strongly

[78] More than 80 per cent of petitions were for separate property alone. In cases where the outcome is known, all but one was granted, whereas one in three requests for separations of property and person with known outcome was denied. These numbers demand some methodological caution, but the overall pattern remains striking.

rooted in their communities as they were to the state as its representatives. They shared, in significant measure, the emphasis of plaintiffs and witnesses on a practice-based model of gendered authority, rather than the ideological prescriptions of extensive paternal and conjugal right often associated with elites. Their practice was to endorse the standards that witnesses demonstrated were significant in neighbourhoods rather than attempt to impose externally constructed expectations.

PROCESS AND PRACTICE: ECONOMIES OF FAMILY POLITICS IN ACTION

A conflict between spouses Nicole Blanchard and Jehan Chevallier, a boatman, reveals in microcosm how, in the process and practice of litigation, witnesses' expectations about spousal behaviour could play a crucial role in securing a court's authorization of forms of family life.[79] Their case demonstrates how the opinions of neighbours and witnesses, as well as plaintiffs and court officers, influenced the outcome of litigation. As they articulated expectations about marriage, and about the parameters of household authority, spouses, their relatives, neighbours, and court officials used legal process as a vehicle for asserting and legitimizing patterns of behaviour and understandings of authority.

Nicole Blanchard complained about her husband to a local court in hopes that if he 'was afraid of falling into the hands of justice' he would no longer batter her as he had done innumerable times. The royal prosecutor did not accept her complaint, but told her 'to be patient and make her peace with God', and said that her husband might treat her worse 'after she denounced him in a lawsuit'. Nicole went home and 'endured' her husband's abuse 'patiently' for a month, until Chevallier beat her so severely that, 'without the help of her neighbours, she was in danger of being dead in his hands'. Nicole and a female relative, Janne Blanchard, sent for a court clerk to see her bruises. Then Janne, along with her niece Imberte and 'eight or ten' female neighbours of the spouses, came to court to demand that the prosecutor accept the suit, and to suggest 'that it would not be out of order to send for Chevallier and make him understand the mistake he was making in abusing a wife whom everyone recognized to be a good and able woman'.

Their intervention persuaded the prosecutor and his clerk to find the spouses who were in the street outside a kinswoman's home where she had taken refuge. They saw Chevallier pull his wife by the arms and 'threaten to beat her if she didn't come home with him'. The prosecutor 'remonstrated' with Chevallier, saying that he should stop 'using such cruelties' against his wife, because the

[79] ADSL B6128, 23 April 1609.

court would be forced to take action if he did it again, and insisted that 'that was no way to treat a wise and virtuous wife'. Chevallier did not respond 'other than to say [that] she was his wife and he would treat her as seemed good to him, and nobody could stop him'. The prosecutor replied that 'it would be better to have a separation between the spouses than to let such rigour continue'. When asked about the source of the enmity that led him to abuse his wife, Chevallier repeated that she was his wife, and that 'it was up to him to beat her and chastise her as it suited him'. This answer led the royal prosecutor to order that 'from now, without any other procedures', Nicole was separated in person and property from Chevallier. The latter was forbidden to threaten her in any way or to force her to come home, 'on threat of being hanged and strangled'. 'For greater assurance', the prosecutor declared, 'she is put under the protection of the King, of Us, and of Justice'. Four witnesses signed the adjudication: Janne's husband, a merchant and his son, and an assistant court clerk. Nicole was to live with Janne.[80]

The Blanchard–Chevallier case illustrates different sides of the dialogues involving witnesses and other members of litigation communities about appropriate spousal behaviour and the nature of gendered authority in households. The prosecutor's initial advice to Nicole to endure and pray rather than proceed with her case and her husband's articulation of his prerogatives, indicate how prescriptive models of patriarchal household authority, rooted in religion and law, could be real imperatives for members of elites (the prosecutor) and working people (Chevallier). The prosecutor's initial refusal to let the case proceed also demonstrates the importance of court officials as legal gatekeepers who could translate prescriptive gender dependence into practical legal disability, or who could participate in authorization of community standards by endorsing them in court.

The women who went to court to try to initiate legal action on Nicole's behalf forcefully and effectively brought a different sense of spousal propriety into play. Their insistence that she was a good wife who did not merit husbandly correction challenged the prosecutor's view that she, rather than he, needed to adjust. Later, in front of a crowd that included the same women and at least five men, the prosecutor shifted position dramatically. Although he had witnessed only arm-pulling and threats, he declared that Chevallier's past and future abuse of his wife invalidated his claims about husbandly discipline and the prosecutor's own directive that wives should pray and obey. He was presumably persuaded by the intensity of opinion among the neighbours who had witnessed other occasions of violence, and was aware that his authority, as well as that of court

[80] Some aspects of this case are extraordinary. Although provosts' courts could exercise summary justice—as they did in this case—they rarely did so, and functioned procedurally much like other lower courts. Moreover, the provost himself was not involved in this case. Men were usually warned to keep away from newly separated wives under penalty of imprisonment, not death. Chevallier's attitude may have led the prosecutor to enhance the threat for rhetorical effect.

and king, would be undermined if he did not act. Judicial officials knew that their own standing rested in part on the support of families and neighbourhoods. When the court official placed Nicole under the protection of the triumvirate 'of the King, of Us, and of Justice', he not only sought to safeguard her welfare but also acknowledged the limits of household authority. The multiplicity of powers (royal, local, and judicial) invoked by the prosecutor emphasizes that the communal judgement of neighbours and witnesses, as well as royal and judicial authority, shaped legal process.

FAMILY POLITICS BETWEEN SUBJECT AND STATE

The litigation of family business made the personal political and the political personal. Historians have often seen the early modern legal system as a key tool in social discipline and state-building, arguing that the governing authorities used judicial institutions to shape family forms, sexuality, and many other aspects of social, economic, and cultural life, and that its courts resolved disputes that communities had traditionally settled through informal mediation.[81] Historians have shown how litigants and lawyers in the later eighteenth century could also use the civil system as an effective political tool.[82] The family politics of litigation, however, involved another very significant dynamic. Working people mobilized the judicial system not only to assert their own personal interests and to express grievances or conflicts, but also, in untold numbers of cases, to shape, reiterate, authorize, and legitimize local grassroots expectations about appropriate behaviour.[83] The state's judicial authority did not simply replace community mediation, at least not by the early eighteenth century, because working people used state institutions as one of many means of resolving disputes. In the seventeenth century, witnesses joined plaintiffs to bring their working neighbourhood understanding of household authority into court and, along with judges and lawyers, participated in litigation communities whose dialogues bridged state and street. If they borrowed the authority of the state through its courts to endorse particular solutions, judges whose verdicts endorsed the prevailing opinions in the local community encouraged an increasing resort to the courts which expanded the role of the state.

[81] For a synthesis of formulations of this kind, see Bruce Lenman and Geoffrey Parker, 'The state, the community, and the criminal law', in V. A. C. Gattrell *et al.* (eds.), *Crime and the Law: The Social History of Crime in Western Europe since 1500* (London, 1982), 11–48.

[82] See, for instance, Maza, *Private Lives and Public Affairs;* and Desan, *Family on Trial.*

[83] Historians working within a variety of geographical and chronological parameters have recently emphasized the agency of a variety of participants, other than judges and lawyers, in the litigation process, whether as plaintiffs, jury members, or witnesses. See, in particular, Steve Hindle, *The State and Social Change in Early Modern England* (London, 2001); and Smail, *Consumption of Justice.*

Women as well as men took neighbourhood expectations into the public and political domain of litigation as plaintiffs, but far more frequently as witnesses. While women in other countries seem to have been disadvantaged as witnesses in numerous ways, French women of every age, marital status, and rank were credible, critical members of litigation communities. The centrality of female witnesses seems to have extended beyond courts of first instance and civil matters to other more specialized courts such as the *cour des monnaies*, which heard criminal cases involving the integrity of France's money supply.[84]

Men and women articulated, in legal, public forums, their understanding about how and why power might legitimately be exercised. In separations cases in particular, their participation made court actions not only strategies in personal marital dramas, but provided repeated retellings of versions of gender and authority in a public institutional forum that authorized particular expressions of power. They did not challenge men's authority *per se*, but they did persistently and powerfully reframe it. Men and women shared a broad understanding of appropriate earning and exercise of that power that cut across gender and rank among working households.[85] (Although in practice, plenty of room for conflict over the relative weight and extent of these factors existed, as demonstrated by specific discussions of men's use of violence explored in the next chapter.) Women mobilized the legal system to defend themselves in individual situations, and to publicize issues that criminal prosecutions seemed to leave to one side. Most prominently, women participants in litigation communities made men's inappropriate sexuality a central theme in definitions of authority and the exercise of power.

What kinds of marriage did witnesses from working neighbourhoods consider suitable building blocks for the greatness of France with which they were continually linked in royal rhetoric and legislation? The French state and working people both wanted strong families, and the legal system offered opportunities to uphold particular forms of marriage that were critical to sustainable and secure everyday life and to strong states. Yet aspects of what made for strong families were contested. While royal edicts and judges' decisions in higher courts over matters related to first marriage seem to have endorsed and extended paternal power, judges also readily awarded separate property in decisions that circumscribed husbands' legal rights and eroded their local reputations. This pattern suggests that neighbourhood judgement could prevail in the lower reaches of the legal system.

[84] For England and Italy, see Gowing, *Domestic Dangers*; and Tommaso Astarita, *Village Justice: Community, Family, and Popular Culture in Early Modern Italy* (Baltimore, 1999), 161. Thanks are due to Jotham Parsons for information on the *cour des monnaies*.

[85] This broad common ground contrasts, for example, with Laura Gowing's argument that men and women in English church courts presented gender-specific visions of married life. See Gowing, *Domestic Dangers*.

If the legal system, essentially by means of criminal prosecutions, offered elites and the state a tool for social discipline, plaintiffs and their witnesses from the working ranks used the far more numerous civil cases for the same purpose—social discipline—but in different ways. Elites and the state envisioned strong families, as represented in legislation and criminal prosecutions, built around paternal and conjugal power, with women's sexuality and legal capacities strictly managed. Law and religion provided the basis for, and reinforcements of, these versions of family life. Working people in urban neighbourhoods defined strong families, in civil cases, as secular partnerships in which men earned the privileges of head of the household by supporting their families, maintaining broader connections through sociability, and fulfilling public responsibilities such as witnessing. In these grassroots versions of family life, women's labour, property, and money management were as critical as men's. Men's authority was earned rather than assumed, and wives, kin, and neighbours conscientiously demarcated its parameters. Men's fecklessness, whether in spending or sexuality or violence, constituted as great a threat, or an even greater threat, than that of their wives.[86]

The economies of marriage, information, and justice came together as local communities, whether as contending spouses or neighbours and witnesses, mobilized to articulate and reinforce expectations about the behaviour of husbands and wives in and out of court. They observed, commented on, and acted upon behaviour as it happened, as mediators and as witnesses. Early modern historians, focusing on criminal prosecutions, have traditionally argued that men's honour was tied to economic matters and women's to sexual propriety, but articulations of communal expectations in civil cases suggest that far more common ground existed.[87] Men and women earned respect and reputation by demonstrating many of the same qualities: diligent work, astute money management, and exclusively marital sexual activity. Witnesses, often drawn from groups who had no other official public roles, mobilized the legal system to assert expectations about the responsibilities on which male authority depended, and to establish men's inappropriate sexual activity as a central theme in definitions of authority and the exercise of power.

[86] I do not mean to assert that a clear consensus existed within either elite or popular ranks about the parameters of authority. Some working men had pretensions of extensive mastery, as we have seen, and some elites, even in the seventeenth century, were committed to limited monarchical authority along constitutionalist lines. Nevertheless, general tendencies are clear. For an insightful exploration of the diverse views of provincial lawyers on the grounds for monarchical authority in the seventeenth century, see Breen, *Law, City, and King*.

[87] Some recent work has started to construct men's and women's identities in more complex ways, especially for early modern England. See, for instance, Gowing, *Domestic Dangers*; and Foyster, *Manhood*. For a similar project in late eighteenth-century France, see Claire Haru Crowston, 'The Queen and Her "Minister of Fashion": gender, credit, and politics in pre-Revolutionary France', *Gender and History*, 14 (2002), 92–116.

The family politics of litigation communities had important consequences for the understanding of how authority ought to work in a century of state-building. Plaintiffs, witnesses, and judges were emphatic about the contingency of authority and its fundamental reliance on practice. No religious prescription or fundamental constitution could compensate for actual shortcomings. These grassroots litigation communities pursued a social contract that valorized a patrimonial perpetuation that protected future heirs from the depredations of the past. The right of men to be safekeepers of that property was inherent but not automatic, so they had to earn their gender privileges by exhibiting behaviour that showed them to be appropriate guardians of their familial heritages. If they could not meet that challenge, their privileges would be revoked.

The decisions that working men and women made about and through litigation, whether as plaintiffs, defendants, or witnesses, made them the architects of conceptions of household relations, that had powerful implications for broad structures of political authority and economic activity. The plaintiffs, witnesses, prosecutors, and judges who shaped the family politics of litigation were active participants in the state-building process, rather than opponents or resisters or subjects. State-building was an everyday project, and not just a top-down process.[88] The French state had firmly asserted lay jurisdiction over marriage, and introduced dense legislation about various aspects of marriage formation. Yet jurisdiction over many other areas of family life, such as separations which been subject to virtually no legislation (as we have seen), was no less clearly rooted in local jurisdictions and the communities who used them. Witnesses challenged the immediate authority of husbands who erred, but in doing so they wove elaborate versions of how household authority could and should work legitimately. They successfully called on judges and the legal system to establish their versions as standard in local judicial as well as popular practice. In doing so, they advocated a model of contingent familial authority that could be extended to expectations about rule in states as well as households. Witnesses were emphatic about the contingency of authority and its fundamental reliance on practice. No religious prescription or fundamental law could compensate for actual shortcomings. The rights of men were inherent but not automatic, so they earned their gender privileges by demonstrating that they were appropriate guardians of their familial heritages. If they could not meet that challenge, their privileges would be revoked. In the grassroots politics of the economies of litigation, authority was secular and contingent, albeit firmly gendered, and the preservation of family property trumped the free operation of market relations.

[88] For the role of the 'private' as a key element of the construction of public authority in the early modern state, see Giorgio Chittolini, 'The "Private", the "Public", the "State"', *Journal of Modern History*, 67, suppl. (1995), S34–61.

The dynamics of litigation communities around family politics was played out in other subjects and in other kinds of court cases. Negotiations over the management of borrowing, which was essential for both commercial activity and to household survival, illustrate the ways in which family business was critical to economic, as well as political, developments.

4

Economies of Markets: Borrowing, Customary Practices, and Emerging Markets

Pierre Carcanac and Catherine Cornet worked in a house on a square in Lyon, where she sold haberdashery from a room close to where he and a partner traded in gold leaf. For well over a decade, individually and together, they borrowed money from many people in many forms to fund domestic and commercial activities. Cornet bought many items on credit, often from other women, to build her inventory, and sold items to her customers on credit. They purchased all kinds of food on tabs, and also secured services from barbers, apothecaries, and wet nurses on credit. They borrowed many small amounts of cash from neighbours in undocumented transactions, and a few large amounts in legally recorded contracts. Cornet sent meat from a butcher to a landlord as part payment for late rent. Carcanac gave clothes and other items to a secondhand seller to raise money. When Carcanac's trading partnership dissolved, Cornet's dowry made her the largest creditor listed. They were often in arrears with rent, and moved frequently, taking smaller and cheaper apartments as they went. Over the years, creditors repeatedly threatened or started legal action to sell their property to cover unpaid debts, and some sales occurred. Occasionally, the spouses started legal actions against their own debtors. They had many disputes with borrowers and lenders over who had paid what, and when. Cornet secured a separation of property. With both spouses finding trading difficult, they turned to running a café, where they sold drinks on credit and lent money to customers, and continued to use borrowing in various forms to meet their own household's needs.

The couple's reliance on borrowing, and their difficulties with creditors, were common to working families, but neighbourhood opinion was important. When bar customers called Carcanac a 'bankrupt' during a dispute about gambling rules, he found the insult 'so offensive to his honour and dangerous to his business' that he took the men to court. Carcanac explained that although it was true that he had trouble paying back his lenders, and that Cornet had secured separate property, she had opened the café with his permission, the café was so beyond criticism that they had never had any complaints from the police, he had settled with his creditors, and his financial failure was 'honourable'.[1] Carcanac's determination to distinguish his honourable failure from charges of dishonourable bankruptcy highlights the cultural and legal as well as economic stakes of borrowing for working families.

Like other Lyonnais and Nantais families, Cornet and Carcanac lived in a quintessential early modern commercial centre during a time of great insecurity as a market economy came to dominate Europe. Their experiences and attitudes highlight interlinked themes: the ways in which working households relied on borrowing as a key household strategy, and the community debate about how to manage ubiquitous borrowings in a period of changing practices. While the economic transformations we associate with the early modern world may seem inevitable in hindsight, its course and outcome were unclear to contemporaries, even for commentators who condemned or praised the rise of the market and all it involved.[2] Households were the very nexus of market economies, as sites of production and consumption, of credit extension and debt collection, and, of course, of tax assessment. In these ways, the early modern economy was a profoundly family business for spouses, neighbours, and communities.

For families, the evolution of the market was fraught with uncertainty and risk. While pre-modern families had long experienced precarious circumstances, urban working households were in particularly perilous situations in the sixteenth and seventeenth centuries. New opportunities could reward entrepreneurial initiative, and many artisans began to specialize and subcontract, but new pressures such as fluctuating prices for raw materials, intensified competition, and changing consumer desires, magnified traditional uncertainties tied to crop failure or disease.[3] Litigation over debt increased. Moreover, families like the subjects of this book were the most exposed to rising risk. Nearly all were tenants, their property was almost entirely in movables, and they relied overwhelmingly on making and/or selling goods or services for their livelihoods. Janne Letourneux articulated the increased hazards of such circumstances when she explained, for example, that her household's difficulties in the 1690s came about because she and her husband, whose shop sold silk and linen clothing items, had lost money when fashions changed.[4]

[1] For the financial histories of Cornet and Carcanac before and after their marriage, see ADR 8B729-1–8. For the litigation over the bankruptcy insult, see ADR 8B729-6, 7 October 1707.

[2] I do not mean to suggest that by the early modern period anyone was detached from the market or that medieval people did not use markets. The longstanding debate about whether what happened in the early modern economy constitutes a transition to capitalism or an intensification of market practices, is beyond the scope of this project. For a synthesis of the debate, see Robert Duplessis, *Transitions to Capitalism in Early Modern Europe* (Cambridge, 1997).

[3] For the role of credit, and especially women's role in it, in medieval societies, see William C. Jordan, *Women and Credit in Pre-Industrial and Developing Societies* (Philadelphia, 1993). For artisan innovation in meeting the demands of the market, see James R. Farr, 'On the shop floor: guilds, artisans and the European market economy, 1350–1750', *Journal of Early Modern History*, 1, 1 (February 1997). The other side of the possible opportunity, however, was possible risk. For a summary of these evolving pressures, see Duplessis, *Transitions to Capitalism*, 124–5.

[4] ADLA B6681, 25 August 1692.

Reliance on borrowing, and complex attitudes towards borrowing, were central to the ways in which families participated in, and experienced, economies of markets. The market, as many historians have noted, was a process as well as a place. Early modern working families were engaged in interlinked economies of markets for money and reputation as well as commerce, and borrowing was the common thread between them. Loans underpinned every level of early modern society from state to household.[5] Borrowing was a key financial instrument in working families and in an evolving economy, but access to it, and attitudes towards credit and debt, were shifting. Increasing anxieties about borrowing were articulated in the criminalization of bankruptcy across Europe from the early sixteenth century. Although households had used credit for centuries, dependency on borrowing increased as the economic environment became more uncertain, with both opportunity and risk. That dependency raised all kinds of challenges. How was credit secured? How could people predict when a creditor would accept an uncertain repayment schedule or no repayment, or when the creditor might go to court to obtain an order to have their assets seized and sold? When loans were ubiquitous, what distinguished good borrowing from bad, or credit from debt? When did the customary conventions that had coded borrowing still prevail, and when might new practices create novel expectations?

The loan-centred economies of markets explored here, focusing on household borrowing, intersect with several historiographies. First, much economic history has been devoted to debates about the changing nature of the early modern economy, and the role of institutional credit within it; but the essential uncertainties of the transition for men and women who lived through it, and their roles in shifting practices, remains less clear. Second, the dynamics of borrowing at the level of households and small enterprises remain largely unexplored.[6] Literature

[5] Explorations of the structure of borrowing in public finance for the French state, for example, include Françoise Bayard, *Le Mondes des Financiers au XVIIe Siècle* (Paris, 1988); Daniel Dessert, *Argent, Pouvoir et Société au Grand Siècle* (Paris, 1984), and Mark Potter, *Corps and Clienteles: Public Finance and Political Change in France, 1688–1715* (Aldershot, 2003). For a detailed exploration of the institutional credit market in Paris, see Philip T. Hoffman, Gilles Postel-Vinay, and Jean-Laurent Rosenthal, *Priceless Markets: The Political Economy of Credit in Paris, 1660–1870* (Chicago, 2000). For a succinct summary of some of the varied ways in which credit undergirded early modern urban economies, see Martha Howell, *The Marriage Exchange: Property, Social Place, and Gender in Cities of the Low Countries 1300–1550* (Chicago, 1998), 70. For an extensive and provocative effort to grasp a big-picture view of early modern credit, see Craig Muldrew, *The Economy of Obligation: the Culture of Credit and Social Relations in Early Modern England* (London and New York, 1998).

[6] For the general tendency towards the omission of the lived experiences of the shift to a market economy, see, for example, Duplessis, *Transitions to Capitalism*. For a pioneering effort to explain transformations in the rural economy in France that pays close attention to lived experience and individual decision making (although its argument emphasizes large structural factors as key determinants), see Hoffman, *Growth in a Traditional Society*, esp. 3–80 and 193–205. For a different perspective on the dynamics and consequences of rural debt for peasant households, see Thomas Edward Brennan, 'Peasants and debt in eighteenth-century Champagne', *Journal of Interdisciplinary History*, 37, 2 (Autumn 2006), 175–200. Examples of neglect of borrowing as a

on credit has largely focused on the state or large-scale borrowing of various kinds, and work on household economies has highlighted other issues. Ingenious efforts to reconstruct family budgets, for example, have shown how precarious the finances of early modern families were, or demonstrated the importance of a variety of makeshifts, but usually omit the role that borrowing played in making ends meet during ordinary and extraordinary times. Third, while access to credit has become a primary early modern story, we still know little about day-to-day money management in working families. A kind of tunnel vision has developed that marginalizes questions about repayment. Very simply, to use credit meant to be in debt, and the resolution of debt requires as much interrogation as the patterns of credit creation. In all three regards, the ways in which gender was central to these issues has received little attention.[7]

The management of borrowing as a political economy of daily life shared many dynamics of other aspects intrinsic to early modern family business examined in this book. As the experiences of Carcanac and Cornet suggest, neighbourhood values about meanings of property and particular forms of property were critical in accessing loans as well as in defining credit/debt status in positive or negative ways. A public economy of information was central to those efforts. Those

household tool are widespread, although many historians have shown the shortfall between income and basic needs or increasing wants as consumer culture to hold. See, for example, the otherwise meticulous budget calculations in James R. Farr, *Hands of Honor: Artisans and their World in Dijon, 1550–1650* (Ithaca, 1986), and Richard Gascon, *Grand Commerce et Vie Urbaine au XVI Siècle: Lyon et ses Marchands (Environs de 1520–Environs de 1580)* (Paris, 1971); much of the literature on consumption, including Amanda Vickery, 'Women and the world of goods: a Lancaster consumer and her possessions, 1751–81', in John Brewer and Roy Porter (eds.), *Consumption and the World of Goods* (London and New York, 1997), and Daniel Roche, *A History of Everyday Things: The Birth of Consumption in France, 1600–1800* (Cambridge, 2000), 54–72; and the family economy literature, dating from Olwyn Hufton's seminal article, 'Women and the family economy', *French Historical Studies*, 9, 1 (Spring 1975), to Jan de Vries, 'Between purchasing power and the world of goods: understanding the household economy in early modern Europe', in Porter and Brewer, *Consumption and the World of Goods*.

[7] For insightful discussion of 'the ubiquity of credit relations' and the 'surprisingly little' historical knowledge about how working people managed 'cash flow', see James R. Farr, *Artisans in Europe, 1300–1914* (Cambridge, 2000), 58–60. For pioneering efforts to look at borrowing on this level, see Steven Kaplan, *The Bakers of Paris and the Bread Question, 1700–1775* (Durham, 1996). My thinking about borrowing has been shaped by an emerging new literature that has begun to lay out alternative methodological and empirical approaches. It suggests that the historicization of debt practices requires problematizing debt, identifying the centrality of borrowing as a familial strategy that could involve contention as well as cooperation, and locating credit patterns in social, cultural, and political as well as economic contexts. See, for example, Claire Haru Crowston, 'The Queen and Her "Minister of Fashion": gender, credit, and politics in pre-Revolutionary France', *Gender and History*, 14, 1 (April 2002); Laurence Fontaine, 'Antonio and Shylock: credit and trust in France, *c.*1680–1780', *Economic History Review*, 54, 1 (February 2001); Laurence Fontaine and Jurgen Schlumbohm (eds.), *Household Strategies for Survival, 1600–2000: Fission, Faction and Cooperation* (Cambridge, 2000); Margaret R. Hunt, *The Middling Sort: Commerce, Gender and the Family in England, 1680–1780* (Berkeley and Los Angeles, 1996); Kaplan, *Bakers of Paris*; Beverly Lemire, Ruth Pearson, and Gail Campbell (eds.), *Women and Credit: Researching the Past, Refiguring the Future* (Oxford and New York, 2001); Muldrew, *Economy of Obligation*; Alexandra Shepard, 'Manhood, credit and patriarchy in early modern England', *Past and Present*, 167, 1 (May 2000).

same neighbourhood imperatives were asserted and authorized through the legal system, just as were issues about marriage.[8] The state had a clear interest in economic productivity, and sought to promote commercial activity in a variety of ways, including new legislation, such as the bankruptcy laws, to protect creditors, and requirements that separations be publicized. Nevertheless, the prominence of debt on court dockets was primarily due to individuals who sought legal resolution of their borrowing conflicts through civil litigation. As in other matters, the response that court users anticipated reflected local culture as well as metropolitan opinion. In many ways, the state's involvement and the pattern of judgements resulted from grassroots initiatives rather than top-down disciplinary efforts. In all these regards, women as well as men, along with gender assumptions and rank, critically defined outcomes.

Spouses and neighbours, plaintiffs and defendants, witnesses and judges, all articulated, debated, and wrestled over the expectations and obligations at stake in borrowing, whether in community interactions or in a variety of legal proceedings from investigations into trading failures to the myriad papers that families deposited with the court in that regard, to debt litigation, and to separations suits. When creditors sought repayment of debts, they forced issues about law and property, and about family life in urban communities, into sharp focus. The reliance on borrowing as a mundane reality of household and commercial life became transparent, as did the intense cultural energy devoted to the definition and stabilization of the many subjective aspects of credit/debt practices. Issues such as the appropriate relations between creditors and debtors, the definition of a collectible debt, the importance of economic as well as social order in family life, and the connection between honour/dishonour and credit/debt, were all mapped.

Early modern families were at a nexus of exchange transactions that were at the heart of household and individual survival as well as commercial viability. They moved backwards and forwards across boundaries that were far more porous in pre-modern times than they became from the eighteenth century—between written contracts and oral negotiations, between monetary and in-kind payments, and between formal and informal obligations. The co-existence and interdependence of various kinds of liquidities and various forms of transactions, the role of personal property, the way in which gender structured men's and

[8] For other explorations of legal process debates as critical factors in attitudes towards property, see, for example, the case of gender and credit in nineteenth-century consumption explored in Erika Rappaport, 'A husband and his wife's dresses: consumer credit and the debtor family in England, 1864–1914', in Victoria de Grazia with Ellen Furlough (eds.), *The Sex of Things: Gender and Consumption in Historical Perspective* (Berkeley, 1996); and neighbourhood constructions of property, in Lena Cowen Olin, 'Fictions of the early English probate inventory', in Henry S. Turner (ed.), *The Culture of Capital: Properties, Cities, and Knowledge in Early Modern England* (New York, 2002), 51–84.

women's involvement, and the relationship between family property and creditors' rights, also entered the debates surrounding borrowing-centred economies of markets.

Pierre Carcanac and Catherine Cornet strategized to borrow money as an integral element in their livelihoods, and argued with their creditors and neighbours, in the street and in court, over their credit/debt history and its meanings. This chapter explores how they, like other city residents, sought to negotiate economies of markets. It examines how they discussed borrowing in a wide range of records to reconstruct borrowing practices and to unpack the subjectivities of credit/debt definition.[9] It looks at the legal and economic contexts of the culture of the market, at borrowing as a key instrument in household strategies to make ends meet, and at the way in which gender shaped those strategies. Finally, it interrogates the cultural work that coded some kinds of borrowing as credit that carried high status, and other kinds as debts that suggested dishonour or worse. Urban workers saw borrowing as an essential reality, but, amongst themselves and in legal processes, energetically marked the boundaries of borrowing between credit and debt, between honour and dishonour, and between high status and criminal bankruptcy.

FAMILIES IN THE MARKET, THE MARKET IN FAMILIES: LEGAL MATRIXES

The intertwining of family and market was never more closely knit than in the nexus of credit and debt. The lack of institutional and legal protection that later sheltered families' personal property from commercial insolvency made urban working households extraordinarily vulnerable to unstable market conditions. Unpaid creditors could seize merchandise from the shop, or pots and pans from the hearth, with no distinctions as to source or purpose between family/domestic and market/public.[10] This harsh reality, replayed repeatedly on early modern streets, as Cornet and Carcanac's lives illustrate, was only one of multiple legal issues that were integral to the family business of economies of markets.

Yet relations between creditors and debtors were more complex, legally as well as culturally, than the snapshot of creditors' sales of household items indicates. New laws aimed at protecting creditors were balanced by older practices that protected family property. Working families together, and spouses independently, manoeuvred within, between, and around a multilateral legal

[9] On the importance of exploring early modern property relations and transitions of all kinds, as cultural as well as economic systems, see, for example, the essays in Turner, *Culture of Capital*.

[10] For an eloquent discussion of this dynamic in the English case, see Hunt, *The Middling Sort*, 22–45.

web. Legal constructions profoundly shaped the forms of credit in France, and households' ability to access and manage debt.

French historians, including myself, have highlighted loans in the form of *rentes* in our happy stories about the availability of credit. These notarized legal devices effectively loaned money with interest, although the contracts involved elaborate fictions to circumvent the prohibitions on usury. This fiction had some important consequences, notably that creditors could not demand repayment as long as interest was paid on time. This provision made *rentes* a very low-risk form of debt. For working families, money borrowed in *rentes* presented good opportunities for relatively little risk. They could not be forced to repay the capital. Interest rates were quite low; and for a host of reasons, lenders were often slow to press for repayment, even of interest arrears.

In contrast to the historiographical high visibility of *rentes*, small loans have been largely invisible, partly because they did not generate the copious notarial paper-trail that *rentes* provide, but these far more frequently incurred debts were potentially very risky. They could be called in, and the pressure to repay even quite small sums could easily push urban households over the edge into destitution. Creditors frequently sought permission to move to seize household assets to cover repayment for relatively small amounts, usually of less than 100 *livres*, and often much less.

Moreover, in France, as in most of Europe and with endless variations, legal constructions divided family property into lineage property and community property. The legal division of the property that women brought to marriage, or inherited, entailed an important complication: the husband had absolute discretion (broadly speaking) over what became community property, whereas he managed, but was not supposed to alienate without her permission, or put 'at risk', the portion that was categorized as her lineage property.

The concept of lineage property is difficult to grasp concretely in the context of working families. Lineage property was a legal designation that had nothing to do with the actual form of the property. Any part of a dowry could be designated as lineage property, whether it was land, houses, offices, tools, *rentes* or cash. In working families in the seventeenth century, marriage contracts usually designated more than half the dowry as lineage property.[11] Sometimes, depending on family circumstances, the assets protected as lineage property might be very small, as little as 100 *livres* in some of the litigation. Yet since dowries were critical contributions to domestic economies, the physical character of lineage property was amorphous. Since dowries were almost all cash in working families, in practice both the portion nominated as lineage property, and the rest, was quickly used to pay rent, buy tools, or procure household

[11] Farr, *Hands of Honor*, 145; Julie Hardwick, *The Practice of Patriarchy: Gender and the Politics of Household Authority in Early Modern France* (University Park, PA, 1998), 62–3.

essentials of all kinds. Moreover, any use of the dowry really put it at risk, and yet it was useless to working families if they did not deploy it to meet their needs.

A variety of new laws that sought to address the perceived perils of unpaid debts, and protect the rights of creditors, were passed in the sixteenth and seventeenth centuries. In France in 1536, bankruptcy, defined as intent to defraud creditors rather than honest failure, became a crime punishable by a fine and confinement to pillories, and it was elevated to a capital offence in 1560. The crown's efforts to protect creditors included the only royal legislation that touched on separations in the early modern period. Royal decrees that sought to regulate commerce in 1629, 1647, and 1673 included repeated insistences that separation agreements had no legal force until they had been publicized to safeguard creditors' interests.[12] The rewriting of the Commercial Code in 1673 was intended to unify judicial practice across France, and to require enforcement of payment to creditors.[13]

This legal web affected household borrowing in complex and sometimes contradictory patterns in terms of how money was borrowed, how borrowing was managed, and how creditors might seek to collect. Gender was at the centre of this conundrum. Legally, married women could not borrow money without their husbands' permission, but legal responsibility for the creation of credit and resolution of debt could fall on the whole households in various ways. Husbands often needed their wives or kin to co-sign loans if they were to obtain *rentes*, for example, because wives' lineage property provided the security. Wives often faced bankruptcy investigation alone after husbands fled, until the status of the failures was ruled on, and creditors could seize and sell any kind of household asset to cover unpaid debts. A husband's highest obligation, in terms of debt, was to his wife for her dowry.[14]

Separate property laws likewise demonstrated the complexity of legal process with regard to gender and borrowing. Women could petition to preserve the lineage property portion of their dowries if they could show that those assets were imperilled. Yet in practice, virtually no working household could have been safe from allegations that its everyday money management practices imperilled the critical cash assets that had been legally designated, however nebulously practically, as lineage property. When wives secured separate property they became the first creditors of their household above all other creditors. Their legal

[12] Isambert, *Recueil Général*, **12**, 527, **14**, 95, **16**, 267, **17**, 64, **19**, 102.

[13] For the intent of the 1673 Commercial Code, see Amalia Kessler, 'Enforcing virtue: social norms and self-interest in an eighteenth-century merchant court', *Law and History Review*, 71 (Spring 2004), and Kessler, 'A "question of name": merchant-court jurisdiction and the origins of the Noblesse Commercante', in Mary Jane Parrine (ed.), *A Vast and Useful Art: the Gustave Gimon Collection on French Political Economy* (Stanford, CA, 2004).

[14] These issues are more fully examined later in this chapter.

standing deprived husbands of the control over household property that was a defining characteristic of adult masculinity.

In practice, financial imperatives and customary cultures, as well as legal regulations, framed conventional behaviour for creditors and debtors in ways that shaped borrowing and the control over property in which it was embedded. The number of bankrupts was probably few, but wives who sought separate property were more common, creditors' efforts to use the courts to collect unpaid debts mundane, and borrowing ubiquitous. Literally everyone was involved with the quotidian tasks of raising money and collecting what had been lent, as well as differentiating behaviour that parsed debt practices into categories from bankruptcy to separate property to ongoing credit. Neighbourhood practice and expectation meant that daily practice in markets and in courts framed the borrowing and repayment dynamics that undergirded political economies of daily life in various ways.

CONSTELLATIONS OF CREDIT: MAKING ENDS MEET

Perrine Leguy and Nicolas Provost, like Carcanac and Cornet and many working spouses, did what they could to earn their living however they could. She sold 'supplies of fabric' from a counter in front of a shop, from a bench at the end of an alley, and in other places. Leguy borrowed money, bought inventory, and strategized about making sales. She borrowed money 'forty or fifty times' from Anne Gerard, who was married to a baker, so that she could buy fabric, and she repaid her 'in proportion to what she sold'. Over a period of at least a decade, the couple borrowed 'a number of sums of money' from 'various different merchants', as well as amounts that ranged from a few *livres* to 2,000 *livres* from many neighbours.[15] These kinds of exchange were quotidian features of early modern life, and intrinsic to economies of the market. For spouses in working families, borrowing was a critical element in making a living, whether to fund commerce, or to make up the difference between what their households needed to live and what they earned by borrowing. The creation and resolution of debts were fundamental challenges that families surmounted or to which they succumbed. The management of complex and fragile networks of debt and credit was a crucial element in early modern households and their experiences, repeated hundreds of thousands of times, were central to the macro- as well as micro-economy.

Loans of every size and every variety ran through every part of life, creating a kind of constellation of credit. Money was loaned and borrowed in people's homes, in shops, in the offices of notaries, and in bars. People borrowed

[15] ADLA B5852, (no date or month) 1716.

money from family members, servants, acquaintances, shopkeepers, priests, and strangers. Most people were borrowers as well as lenders. Working families in the seventeenth century faced the kinds of recurring shortfalls that had beset their ancestors and were to plague their descendants, but their options and constraints, as well as the meanings associated with those choices, were much more specific to particular contexts. Early modern French families did not, for instance, have any of the institutional resources, such as banks, friendly societies, or specialized pawnshops, that were important features of strategies for making ends meet in later centuries. Instead they relied on their ability to utilize a wide range of customary and creative debt options. Steven Kaplan has evocatively characterized relations between bakers and their suppliers and customers in eighteenth-century Paris as a 'great chain of credit' without which none could function.[16] Yet borrowing was essential to all aspects of daily life, far beyond shop relations, and was enmeshed in every aspect of the social and spatial universe of early modern working families. This constellation of credit was a key instrument in families' ability to make ends meet.

Recovering the daily money management practices of early modern families has proven very elusive for historians, particularly with regard to the role of borrowing as a crucial financial strategy. In the French case, historians' focus on *rentes* and other kinds of medium or long-term institutional credit has so far left aside the many kinds of small-scale borrowing that households undertook, although these were in all likelihood larger in terms of numbers of transactions, if not in terms of volume of capital. The available evidence has often seemed either too much or too little. Debt litigation was rampant, leaving so many records that the sheer volume can seem overwhelming. Few of the personal records, such as household accounts, that have been useful for later periods survive for working families in the seventeenth century. In fact, historians' efforts to reconstruct the budgets of working families have often (as we have seen) omitted credit, even while highlighting the eternal shortfall between income and outgoings and the many kinds of makeshifts used to meet that dilemma.

Household borrowing was recorded in many forms of varying legal enforceability and, although institutionalized lending was critical for many large-scale transactions (whether through bills of exchange, state loan, or other means), for working families, access to capital more often involved participation in a wide range of small transactions of widely varying legal standing and formality. Marriage provided an important source of capital through the dowries brought by wives, but otherwise borrowing was essential. *Rentes* were notarized contracts for which the lender could not demand repayment. Other loans were also made by a variety of notes, recorded with different levels of formality, called *obligations, cedulas, memoires* or *billets*, and others still simply by verbal arrangement 'by oath' or 'without any act'. Shopkeepers noted credit in record book tabs, and

[16] Kaplan, *The Bakers of Paris*, 377.

other means of tracking debt also existed, such as the wooden sticks (*tailles*) used by bakers to mark notches for each loaf sold.[17] Family members might co-sign, and a variety of household items could be used as security, as pawnable material, or as an alternative to money as a form of exchange.

The sites of borrowing were as varied as the forms. Families could hope to borrow large amounts of money, such as to pay for dowries, or to purchase the tools and inventory that could establish careers, in notaries' offices in the form of *rentes*. Spouses might need to find co-signers, most of whom came from the ranks of kin. The cash raised in this way was always at least several hundred *livres*, and often considerably more. Notaries usually brokered these deals, knowing both the people who wanted to lend money, and those who needed to borrow it.[18]

Shops provided a variety of borrowing, as traders ran tabs that allowed customers to defer payment, or lent money outright. A Nantais locksmith, Jan Papit, for example, made a list, in his will, of debts that his customers owed—some of which were quite small (under 10 *livres*), but others of which were very substantial, amounting to sums in the region of 150 or 200 *livres* 'for keys and locks'.[19] In April 1699, a Lyonnais barber–surgeon gave Pierre Carcanac a note that recorded past debts and anticipated future services. Carcanac, he said, owed 20 *livres* for 'medicine I have provided and for his beard trims until the next feast of St John the Baptist'. In mid-June, Carcanac paid on the note.[20] Traders also sometimes simply lent money. Shopkeepers themselves bought from their supplies on credit.

Bars were also significant sites of varied debt creation. Barkeepers, like shopkeepers, sold on credit, and loaned money outright. When Catherine Cornet ran a bar in Lyon, she gave credit for drinks and for card games, and lent money outright.[21] Customers (nearly all men) also lent each other money. Men lent money 'without notes', or agreed to provide guarantees for other people's loans while they were in bars. Sometimes no doubt, they were under the influence of alcohol, but it was also as part of the culture of masculine sociability where the mutual exchange of money underwrote the drinking, eating, and gambling. These loans were often very informal, with borrowing and lending between strangers as well as acquaintances, and often without any record. Louis Belot, for instance, like many contemporaries, lent money 'to all kinds of people and without getting personal notes' in the bars he frequented.[22] Men also incurred debts when they gambled away more than they had.

Servants and wet nurses provided credit as debts ran through social relations of all kinds. Early modern employers usually paid their servants only at the end of their terms of service, a form of arrears that constituted a kind of forced

[17] For bakers' use of *tailles*, see Kaplan, *Bakers of Paris*, 136–41.

[18] Hardwick, *Practice of Patriarchy*, 34–41.

[19] ADLA 4E2/1429, 2 November 1660.

[20] ADR 8B729-4, 23 April and 16 June 1699.

[21] ADR 8B729-4, undated account book.

[22] ADLA B5838, 30 January 1686.

loan, thereby deferring the costs, but servants could also provide extra sources of finance in other ways. Some servants lent money to their employers. Other servants provided goods for which they were only reimbursed at a later date. The notary Noel Bezic noted in 1587, for instance, that he owed his servant 15 *livres* in pay and for 'a pair of shoes'.[23] Working families frequently deferred paying wet nurses too, effectively eliciting credit as they did with servants, but imperilling the circumstances of their infants even more than the mere practice of wet nursing, with its notoriously high mortality rates. The wet nurse of an infant of the butcher Claude Vacher and his wife, for instance, had letters written that seem strategically ominous. They opened with descriptions of the charming playfulness of their toddler son, and urged the parents to visit him, but closed with the news that since they were more than three months behind with what they owed her, she could no longer take care of him, and 'would have to find another place for him' if they did not pay her immediately.[24]

Families often accrued debts to their landlords as they fell behind with their rent. Most urban working families were tenants, rather than owners of the spaces in which they lived, and rents were payable half-yearly. Many working families moved frequently, and falling behind with the rent was common. Pierre Carcanac and Catherine Cornet, for example, were frequently pursued by their landlords for being in arrears of many months with their rent; they moved almost every year, and their mobility was common to many working families who faced tight and expensive urban housing markets in early modern towns.[25] Cash-strapped families facing choices about what to pay often found it easier to defer the payment of rent than to delay other payments, even if rent arrears ultimately caused families to move or to be evicted. Moreover, while landlords would eventually take legal action to collect their rents, many seem to have tolerated arrears for up to a year.

Men and women pawned household items to raise money, or used household items as collateral. Pawning was far more informally organized, in terms of both location and obligation, than in the nineteenth century, when specialized shops and contractualizing tickets monopolized pawning. It was arranged between individuals rather then being the specialized prerogative of particular traders. A shoemaker, for instance, pawned small pieces of jewellery, as well as pots and

[23] Records of debts often noted monies owed to servants. See, for example, Archives Municipales de Nantes, II131, 30 March 1587; ADLA B6666, 10 May 1650; ADLA 4E2/1195, 14 October 1652. For historians on loans from servants to masters, see, most recently, Giovanna Benadusi, 'Investing the rich of the poor: servant women and their last wills', *American Historical Review*, **109**, 3 (June 2004).

[24] ADR 8B1260-1, no date.

[25] ADR 8B 729-4. For the expensive residential rental market and high rates of mobility, see, for example, Nicolas Lozanic, 'Le logement au Lyon au XVII et XVIIIe siècles, une approche: le bail à loyer', *Cahiers d'Histoire*, 4 (1999), 537–58; and Ollivier Zeller, 'La mobilité residentiale de François Valesque, epicier en gros et echevin de Lyon 1706–1791', *Cahiers d'Histoire*, 4 (1999), 559.

pans, to a neighbour. Many neighbourhood people were willing, on occasion, to lend money if goods of various kinds were given as security. Martine Garreau, to give one example, noted that she owed a Sieur Dronet 83 *livres* for wine that he had sold her, and for which she had given him custody of a 'gold and silver cup'.[26] Any matrix of debt practices was filled with such examples.

Each individual borrowed amounts of money in many different ways on many different occasions. For example, in 1652 Pierre Babin, a notary, owed money to a priest (100 *livres*), a blacksmith (36 *livres*), a petty trader whose name he did not know (6 *livres* 15 *sous*), a baker (three *livres*), and a servant.[27] Some of these debts were recorded in writing while others were completely unrecorded, and they involved collateral and arrears as well as cash. Babin had given the priest,who was a canon in the 'Collegial church', a diamond necklace and a silver cup as security for the 100 *livres* he owed. This exchange may have been common, especially for debts that went beyond a few *livres*, as it was noted repeatedly. Babin owed the baker for 'bread as well as money', and noted that he owed the blacksmith money 'beyond what I owed to him for services'. The money which Babin borrowed from someone whose name he did not know, and who did not live in his neighbourhood but in a district just outside the walls on the other side of the city, may have been the result of a casual encounter. It may perhaps have occurred in a bar, as it was for quite a small sum—enough, perhaps, to buy drinks or gamble. Babin noted that he had not paid his servant since the inventory of property taken after his wife's death. He had also borrowed larger sums (with his wife as co-signer) in the legally contractual form of notarized *rentes*, and almost always using the same notary, Guillaume Garnier, who presumably arranged for loans for him.[28]

Babin's contemporaries showed similar patterns both in the spread of loans and in the distinctions made between them. The notary, Jan Bonnamy, for example, remembered twenty-eight outstanding debts in his 1630 will.[29] The sums owed varied from 4 to 150 *livres*. He differentiated between eleven *cedulas*, six loans for which 'no acts' existed, one loan owed 'by oath', one loan recorded by *memoire*, and a variety of goods and services. He owed two surgeons and a doctor for various 'treatments', 'medications', 'visits', and 'prescriptions', all perhaps incurred during the 'corporal illness' that had caused him to write his will. He had received, but not yet paid for, goods that included a robe, 'merchandise' from a hatmaker, a watch, and a saddle. He owed a widow a small

[26] ADR BP5825, 28 April 1670; ADR BP3984, 4 February 1675; ADLA 4E2/243, 2 April 1646.

[27] ADLA 4E2/1195, 14 October 1652.

[28] For examples of Babin's *rentes*, see ADLA 4E2/1701, 16 September 1643; ADLA 4E2/831, 17 September 1644; ADLA 4E2/833, 6 March 1647; and ADLA 4E2/1194, 21 September 1651.

[29] ADLA 4E2/94, 9 September 1630.

sum 'for expenses'. He borrowed money from the person who sold the saddle to him, and borrowed other money from one person with a *cedula*, and additional sums from that same person 'without any act'.

In addition, of course, most people were lenders as well as borrowers, whether as shopkeepers who owed suppliers, as holders of *rentes*, or in personal capacities. Individual lending of this kind could be of very small scale, and often seemed not to involve any documentation. The list of monies owed in the will of a widow, Martine Garreau, in 1646, offers one glimpse of these kinds of debt. The sums she had lent were usually very small. She noted one loan of 50 *livres* made by *obligation*, but the other seventeen sums were all for less than 14 *livres*, and several were for only 2 or 3 *livres*. A couple of the loans had been made with *cedulas*, but the others were simply noted as 'for money lent', with no reference to any written record.[30]

Whether these kinds of small-scale borrowing transactions, so crucial to household life in terms of production, consumption, and subsistence, carried interest is a fascinating and elusive question. Elaborate means of circumventing early modern prohibitions on usury characterized large and medium-term credit of all kinds, whether in terms of state or mercantile borrowing. Interest was either explicitly included, as in the legal fictions of *rentes*, or bills were discounted so that the repayment fee included interest.[31] However, we know very little about interest on short-term or informal transactions between individuals, between shopkeepers or artisans and customers, or between local suppliers and the traders who bought from them. In the seventeenth century, notations of payment in account books, or details about disputed debts in court cases, did not specify interest, whether because it was not charged, or because it was not acknowledged because of usury, or because it was included in the credit price.

These endlessly varied micro-credit arrangements were critical in every family's efforts to make ends meet and to continue their working lives, and just as important as the much better documented, legally binding, and larger-scale *rentes*. Debt practices of all kinds, repeated hundreds and thousands of times in communities on a daily basis, were key strategies in meeting the challenges of daily life. For working families, complex and fragile networks of debt and credit were fundamental parts of daily life, leaving many households wobbling between opportunity and catastrophe. Gender, reputation, and law configured

[30] ADLA 4E2/243, 25 April 1646.

[31] The history of interest remains to be written. For interest on long- and medium-term institutionalized borrowing, see Hoffman *et al.*, *Priceless Markets*, 1–25. The authors note that they pay little attention to interest rates, as they 'played a relatively minor role in allocating credit'—even on the scale they examine. For an overview of interest in early modern Europe that again emphasizes larger and more formal borrowing, see Thomas Luckett, 'Interest', in Jonathan Dewald (ed.), *Europe, 1450 to 1789: Encyclopedia of the Early Modern World*, 6 vols., 3 (New York, 2004), 280–3.

this constellation of credit in specific ways for specific types of debts at specific moments in the cycle of creating, managing, and resolving debts.

GENDER AND THE DYNAMICS OF DEBT

The experiences of couples such as Catherine Carcanac and Pierre Cornet, or Perrine Leguy and Nicholas Provost, not only illustrate that raising money was a fundamental feature of life for all working households and for both spouses, but that despite women's legal disabilities with regard to debt, married as well as single women borrowed, lent, and collected obligations as a daily and essential matter. Female participation was central not only to an exchange complex involving women, but to debts of all kinds and all sizes, and to all stages of the debt cycle. Gender shaped access to credit/debt continuously, but not in consistent patterns. The gender fault-lines around economies of markets could be unpredictable, and suggest some of the historical specificities that lay behind what at first seem like almost universal practices. Gendered, socio-spatial debt practices highlighted the potentially different meanings and opportunities that different forms of credit offered to men and women. They illustrate that individual gendered constraints and choices shaped debt practices, as well as family strategies. This section explores gender as part of working people's lived experience of borrowing, in legal terms, in the overlapping and diverging elements of men's and women's loan practices, in uses of various forms of exchange, and in retailing. These patterns also suggest that important changes around gender and debt occurred as market relations trumped customary practices more frequently.

Men's and women's borrowing practices had much in common: both engaged in small-scale informal borrowing, men and women borrowed money from each other, and sometimes spouses used this kind of borrowing to meet the common needs of their households (running tabs with shopkeepers, for example). Women's loans were often small, but so were many men's loans. Women's borrowing was often informal in the sense of undocumented, but so was much of men's borrowing. Thus the microcredit label which historians sometimes attach to female borrowing disguises the variations in the size as well as forms of lending for working men and women.

The legal status of spouses with regard to borrowing was in practice less distinctive than an isolated focus on the legal identity of husbands and fathers as household property managers suggests. Even in the best documented cases, the example of *rentes*, while married or minor women could not initiate *rentes* without permission, gender and familial considerations also shaped men's access to *rentes*. Kin rarely used the form of *rentes* to lend money to each other, but married men frequently found that lenders required their wives to co-sign *rentes*, or used their wives' male kin as guarantors. Wealthy widows, who were legally entitled to lend or borrow money in their own right, used *rentes* and other interest-paying lending as valuable investment options.[32]

Moreover, local courts did not uphold the limitations on married women's ability to engage obligations without their husbands' permission. In 1682, for example, Louis Liron, a merchant, went to court to try to collect 80 *livres* he claimed he was owed by Charles Beguillon and Claudine Lambelot. Liron said he had delivered goods to them in August 1679, for which he had agreed a price with Lambelot, and for which she 'who managed their trade' promised to pay by August 1680. Beguillon duly paid all but the last 80 *livres*, which he refused on the grounds that 'it was his trade' and that his wife's note had been 'extorted' from her 'without his involvement or authorization'. Liron argued that Beguillon was guilty of bad faith, because he had paid the balance. The court agreed with Liron that Lambelot's promise was enforceable, and required the spouses to pay the remaining 80 *livres*.[33] In finding for Liron, the judges either concurred that the couple's customary practice was for Lambelot to manage the accounting with the debt and credit obligations that entailed, or that husbands such as Beguillon were liable for wives' obligations, even when explicit authorization had not been given. Either way, the court tacitly acknowledged the reality and enforceability of wives' independent debt creation.

Spouses sometimes borrowed money without the other's knowledge, much less consent, and they were able to do so with small, informal debts far more easily than with the paper-trail loans such as *rentes*. François Boursillon, for instance, borrowed money from several people, and told them that he did not want his wife to know (even though he used jewellery that was probably hers, as surety). He needed the money to pay off gambling debts, which he described as 'matters of honour' although not apparently the kind of honour he expected his wife to sympathize with.[34] Marie Monnier borrowed 96 *livres* from a textile worker, asking him 'not to tell her husband . . . because she wanted to put the money aside for her own use'.[35]

Certainly, loans of this kind were potentially fertile ground for spousal conflict. Wives often complained about husbands who had lent money unwisely. Ellen Ross has argued that in late nineteenth-century London, pawning became a combative wifely activity.[36] It could certainly be a source of tension, and spouses

[32] For the family dynamics of *rentes*, see Hardwick, *Practice of Patriarchy*, 181–91. For the role of 'rich widows' in investing in interesting-bearing capital instruments, see James B. Collins, 'The economic role of women in seventeenth-century France', *French Historical Studies*, **16**, 2 (Autumn 1989), 456–7.

[33] AML FF329, 6 March 1682.

[34] ADLA B5853, 29 November 1719.

[35] ADLA B5843, 31 July 1691.

[36] Work on the history of pawning is very limited. For a valuable discussion of rare seventeenth-century French institutionalized pawning—the institution established in Avignon to counteract usury—see Roche, *Everyday Things*, 209–13. For the eighteenth century, see Beverly Lemire, 'Introduction. Women, credit and the creation of opportunity: a historical overview', and Laurence Fontaine, 'Women's economic spheres and credit', both in Lemire, *Women and Credit*. For later

sometimes recovered items which their husbands or wives had used to raise money when they found out. François Boursillon's wife, for example, paid to retrieve a ring a few days after her husband had used it to borrow 35 *livres*, and Catherine Menager bought back the pewter dishes her husband had pawned the previous day. A merchant gave René Piou money on a dozen oilskins, but alerted Piou's wife, Marie Bernier, who arrived a couple of hours later to get them back.[37] Yet pawning did not appear to be any more of a vehicle for gender antagonism than many debt practices, perhaps because early modern borrowing patterns were far more fluid than those in later periods, and often involved exchanges of goods other than cash.

Although men's and women's debt practices overlapped in these ways, gender did shape borrowing patterns. Men frequently loaned each other money in bars, or ran tabs with the barkeeper, and often used that money to buy drinks or to gamble as they participated in the culture of male sociability. The buying of rounds of drinks was in itself a means of circulating credit, as well as a social expectation. These economic as well as cultural markers of masculinity had no apparent feminine parallel, and while men could argue that they were essential, wives, as we will see, frequently contested such consumption as an unmanageable burden on precarious household finances. Women conversely raised money primarily either for household emergencies, or funded their trading activities in more informal ways than men may typically have done.

Perhaps because wives did not have the legal right to borrow money, and did not have the access to cash injections available to men (dowries, for example, provided men with capital that could be used to underwrite the costs of establishing occupations or for other purposes), they seemed to have relied, in significant part, on a female credit network as a buffer against disaster as well as for opportunity. Wives who did not have food for their families, or who faced the prospect of bailiffs selling their items to cover creditors' notes, borrowed money from other women. Marguerite DelaVergne, the wife of a notary, borrowed money 'for necessities' from Julliene Saupin, who did laundry for her on occasion.[38] A shoemaker's widow saw a bailiff throw a quilt out of the window of the house of her neighbour, Perrine Bureau, for example, and quickly agreed to Bureau's request for money to stop the bailiff leaving with the quilt or any another goods. Another neighbour, a baker's wife, lent Bureau money on two other occasions, once to stop bailiffs again before they removed property, and on another occasion to retrieve goods that had already been distrained.[39]

time-periods, see Ellen Ross, *Love and Toil: Motherhood in Outcast London, 1870–1918* (Oxford, 1993), 81–4, and Hoffman, *Priceless Markets*, 223–4 and 255–6.

[37] ADLA B5853, 29 September 1719; ADLA B5853, 28 February 1720; ADLA B5853, 3 March 1721.

[38] ADLA B5806, 16 January 1626.

[39] ADLA B6675, 7 June 1681.

These incidents are among the many examples that suggest that women's lending to each other provided a last bulwark of defence against desperation.

Female-provided credit also allowed women to pursue commerce, however. Towns were full of female petty-traders, married and single, who (like all commercial actors) needed credit to maintain inventories; and women were very important suppliers to each other of the financial means to access bare-bones inventories that permitted trading. When Catherine Cornet wanted to start trading in small personal decorative items such as ribbons, bows, and lace and silk bonnets in Lyon in the late 1690s, she did not have the necessary capital. Instead, she relied on various kinds of credit to set up her own operation. She rented a room, with a lease guaranteed by her future husband, where two sisters had previously run a shop with similar merchandise, presumably hoping to inherit their clients. She also rented, very cheaply at 50 *sous* a month, another small room to live in, bought two wooden benches to serve as counters on which to display her wares, and bought thirty-four items on seventeen occasions—all from another woman, Mademoiselle Guynard. The rent, the display benches, and the inventory were all obtained on credit.[40] Although few trading wives established themselves as legally independent and able to borrow in their own right (the status of *femme marchande*), married female traders like Cornet were in practice able to secure lines of credit in their neighbourhood in return for regular payments.

In households (not to mention early modern economies generally) that were cash poor, movable property, as well as credit, was an enormously valuable asset not only for its actual worth but because of its versatility. Both men and women used personal property as a means of liquidity and as facilitators of debt exchanges. It could be sold, of course, but also pawned, offered as security, used as payment, or seized by creditors. All kinds of goods were, on occasion, used as means of exchange. The laundrywoman Antoinette Carvet, for example, noted on a piece of paper what she had received from 'Dufour or his wife to make good on what they owe me' in 1692. The couple continued to pay off their debt, which amounted to 211 *livres* 10 *sous*, with many small payments through the summer of 1694. They sometimes paid small amounts of cash, sometimes grain of various kinds, and once a big piece of cheese.[41] In 1650, a widow, Janne Mesnard, recalled some of the ways in which she had paid a variety of debts in that year. She owed Marie Charier for two years of domestic service, and for 60 *livres* she had borrowed from her, and paid her in wine. When the baker's wife came to collect what Mesnard owed her for bread, she took pewter goods.[42] Many men used jewellery—presumably, if not always, their wives' jewellery—to

[40] ADR 8B729-5, 3 April 1700.
[41] ADR 8B696 (no date or month), notes dated 1692 and 1693.
[42] ADLA B6666, 10 May 1650.

raise money. Guillaume Hore, for example, gave a barkeeper, to whom he owed 2 *ecus*, a watch that he promised to retrieve later in lieu of a cash repayment.[43] Pots were also exchangeable. Marie Chee received 25 *livres* from François Bridonneau for a bed, two sheets, half a dozen napkins, and a cooking pot that she sought to recover six months later by paying the same sum for them.[44]

Transportable personal property greased the wheels of all kinds of debt practices for both men and women, but a gender pattern also emerges in the forms and ways in which personal property was used. It suggests, too, some sense of the uncertainties that people faced in navigating an evolving economy in which debt litigation was on the increase and contractual relations were perhaps more likely to be enforced. To illustrate how gender patterns may have created new fault-lines as the economic climate changed, consider the experience of Anne Collaud. At about eight o'clock on a Saturday evening in March 1691, a Nantais landlord arrived with a bailiff and some 'associates' at the door of the house of his tenants Anne Collaud and Allexis Couraud. With Allexis absent, the men forced Anne, 'her baby in a cradle', and a servant out on the street, and locked the door. Anne and her porter husband were a year behind with their rent, and to avoid the seizure of their property she had already offered payment to the landlord in the form of 'a quilt, six sheets, twelve men's shirts, a tablecloth and twelve napkins'. Nevertheless, the landlord proceeded with the seizure, leaving Anne, her baby and servant facing a winter's night on the street.[45] Although many aspects of this episode remain unclear and unknowable, it points towards clashing expectations between Collaud and her landlord. Collaud apparently expected or hoped that the court would side with her on the basis of her observance of customary practices about the timing of evictions and the good intent she had shown in paying, even in kind. The landlord's insistence on payment, in full and in cash, may have reflected an emerging trend towards contractual market relations.

Collaud sought to deploy linens which, along with jewellery and pots and pans, provided the three dominant alternative forms of liquidity to money. These had important common qualities: they were portable, durable, and valuable, and yet were goods (presuming they did not relinquish their last pot) without which households could manage temporarily. Clothes were rarely involved, although they shared the first three of these qualities, and from the mid-eighteenth century became important pawnable items as personal clothing stocks increased.[46] Presumably, as inventories suggest, early modern working families rarely had sufficient clothes to have any to spare before the eighteenth century,

[43] ADLA B5825, 28 April 1670. [44] ADLA B5846, 18 May 1697.

[45] ADLA B6681, 21 March 1691.

[46] Very little is known about pawning before the eighteenth century, but an Avignon pawning fund had very few deposits of clothes in the early seventeenth century, and a rapidly increasing quantity and variety of clothing into the eighteenth century. Roche, *History of Everyday Things*, 209–13.

whereas even families of modest means had a substantial portion of their assets in supplies of linen, as well as owing a few pots and perhaps a couple of pieces of jewellery.

Linens, in particular, played vital roles in securing credit, serving as an alternative means of liquidity that intertwined with hard coinage in a spectrum of financial exchanges, practices, and attitudes. In working families, the value of linens often amounted to a third or more of the household's wealth, and household supplies of sheets, napkins, tablecloths and the like, were surprisingly large. Linen items and money were both usually kept in locked cupboards, and the loss of either was a serious matter. Debt dramas suggest that linen's importance in early modern households lay not only in its asset value as a share of the family wealth, in its status value as a display item or in its use value, but also its exchange value.

Yet the personal property that had an integral role in many debt practices had specifically gendered qualities, and women may have been more likely than men to utilize highly gendered personal property as a means of exchange. The forms of property most often used as means of exchange (linen, pots, and jewellery) were all forms of property that were very closely associated with women, who often took stocks of linen and pans to households as part of their dowries, and received jewellery from their husbands as wedding gifts. Claude Revollet sought to explain to his brother-in-law, the dyer Claude Hacte, why he could not yet repay what he owed. He noted not only that he could not support his five children, who would have been homeless without the kindness of a friend who lent money for rent, but that 'his wife had nothing to pawn, not even her jewellery'.[47] Even this last resort of desperate households had been exhausted.

Although, as we have seen, wives did in practice lend and borrow money independently of their husbands, linen may have circulated more fluidly in a female microcredit network that relied on an appreciation of the value and validity of linen as a means of exchange, as well as on personal knowledge of who might have a quite significant amount of cash to lend. When Catherine Jaunet, a wife with separate property, needed to borrow thirty *livres* in 1677, for example, she asked four local women in turn, offering a variety of linens in return. They all refused, saying that they did not have the money, but recommended another local woman, Janne Teze, who duly agreed to lend Jaunet the money in return for some linen (on the condition that if Jaunet did not repay in six months, she would consider the items hers as if she had bought them). Each of the women knew how much linen, and of what sort (sheets, napkins, and so on) Jaunet had to offer, and could estimate its value.[48] One told her she would ask another, who lived in the same building, who would in turn persuade Teze to lend her the money.

[47] ADR 8B952, 27 July 1699.

[48] ADLA B5834, 9 May 1682. This micro-credit network came to light when five years later Jaunet and Teze ended up in court in a dispute over repayment.

Anne Collaud's dispute with her landlord suggests not only how linen was gendered in its associations, but perhaps hints that men and women viewed its potential liquidity differently. Anne claimed to the court not only that she should not have been evicted after dark because such seizures were supposed to take place between sunrise and sunset, but that the sale of the linen items she had given him would cover the rent owed. She noted, though, that he was 'not content with this', and his subsequent legal actions clearly indicated his dissatisfaction. Their dispute may, of course, have been rooted in unknown grievances, but it raises two possibilities in terms of thinking about how individuals navigated the shifting economies of markets. First, that women were more comfortable than men with using linen as a means of exchange. Second, that the conflict illuminates that shifting expectations in a fluid and evolving market were not always synchronized between individuals. Anne may have known many people who still paid their rent in kind without problem, and perhaps had done so herself. Her landlord, utilizing the increasingly popular action of going to court to resolve the conflict, may have insisted, in contrast, on the cash payment to which their agreement legally entitled him. While he defined her as a delinquent tenant, she thought it at least worthwhile to see if the court would defend her efforts as valid.

Gendered experiences of a different kind are highlighted in shopkeepers' record books. The records of a Lyonnais candlemaker in the middle decades of the seventeenth century, like those of other traders, offer perspectives on early modern borrowing from the point of view of the creditor rather than the debtor. We know remarkably little about shop-keeping practices in the seventeenth century, although much more work has explored the later eighteenth-century practices.[49] Shopkeepers' records indicate, however, that men and women had access to different kinds of opportunity and obligation, and that shopkeepers favoured particular forms of credit. In these ways they illuminate not only the ubiquity of credit but also the complexity of the topography of debt in early modern towns and cities.

Catherine Revol ran a candlemaker's shop in Lyon, with three consecutive husbands, from the late 1630s until at least the late 1660s. Two shop books

[49] We know very little about the specific daily mechanics of early modern purchasing practices, despite the dense literature on workers of all kinds, especially before the eighteenth century. Yet the modest literature all indicates the centrality of credit as key to purchasing in urban and rural areas. See Farr, *Artisans in Europe*, 60–1; Beverly Lemire, *Dress, Culture and Commerce: the English Clothing Trade before the Factory, 1660–1800* (New York, 1997); and for pedlars in rural areas, Margaret Spufford, *The Great Reclothing of Rural England: Petty Chapmen and their Wares in the Seventeenth Century* (London, 1984), and Laurence Fontaine, *History of Pedlars in Europe* (Durham, 1996). For a fascinating exploration focused primarily on elites, see Evelyn Welch, *Shopping in the Renaissance: Consumer Culture in Italy, 1400–1600* (New Haven, 2005). For eighteenth-century shopping practices in France, see, for example, Jennifer Jones, *Sexing La Mode: Gender, Fashion, and Commercial Culture in Old Régime France* (Berg, 2004), and Kaplan, *Bakers of Paris*, esp. 137–51 and 377–423.

survive, covering the years from the mid-1640s to the late 1650s, and offer an extraordinary, albeit complicated, glimpse of retailing in the mid-seventeenth century.[50] The Revol shop (apparently known by Catherine's name after her father, judging by the account books), like other *chandeliers*, sold a far greater variety of goods than just the tallow wax which its name indicated. Customers bought the mainstays of the trade like wax, lard, olive oil, and vinegar, which were apparently always on sale, and a wide variety of other goods on occasion. These included plates, pots, glass bottles, various other containers, soap, pepper, buttons, silk, lace, hairpins, shoes, food items including fruit and meat, and individual sales of a wide variety of goods.

The focus of record-keeping clearly indicates the centrality of credit in early modern shop-keeping, although the system of notation was capricious by modern standards, and the omissions were significant.[51] Catherine and her husbands ran tabs for many customers, although the books did not note cash payments, and so the proportion of cash to credit sales is unclear. Customer tabs provided the main organizational principle, rather than sale by date or type of purchase. Cash payments went straight into apron pockets or boxes, but many, perhaps most, people bought what they wanted on tabs. Shops may have sold more on credit than they did for cash. Janne Letourneux, the wife of a Nantais linen and silk goods trader, whose shop sold items such as stockings and cravats, recalled that in one two-day period in the summer of 1692 her cash sales amounted to 52 *sous* 6 *deniers*, but that she sold nearly six times that amount, 300 *sous*, on credit.[52] The shop books, then, were in the modern sense not so much accounts as debt records.

Revol and her husbands, like other shopkeepers, frequently extended credit in cash, as well as by running tabs, both to customers who added the money loans to their tabs, and to people who did not have tabs. The individual loans were numerous and modest, and usually for very small amounts of not more than a couple of *livres* a time. The loans were in cash, and were unsecured. The records of another Lyonnais shopkeeper, the butcher Claude Vacher, from a century later, show the same pattern, with many small loans in cash.[53] These

[50] ADR 8B1171-1.

[51] Like other Lyonnais account books of petty traders in the pre-1750 period, the Revol books were a chaotic mix of lists of transactions, with individuals mixed with sundry and often apparently randomly noted records of other observations and expenditures. There was no effort whatsoever, among this *milieu*, to practice the double-entry book-keeping that Italian merchants were supposed to have standardized during the Renaissance, although large-scale Lyonnais merchants did keep much more methodical account books along these lines. Account books rarely listed purchases for which cash was paid, so it is impossible to gauge, for example, the proportion of sales made on credit to cash. They did not note purchases of inventory, so the link between what was bought and what was sold cannot be established. Moreover, since, as we saw earlier, credit was extended both on and off the books, many small loans may also have been left out. This chaotic quality in record-keeping seems to have been the early modern norm. See Kaplan, *Bakers of Paris*, 141–2, and Muldrew, *Economy of Obligation*, 63.

[52] ADLA B6681, 25 August 1692.

[53] ADR 8B1260-2.

debt relations, above and beyond the credit for goods, may have been important for shopkeepers to cultivate clients, and for their customers to access liquid resources.[54]

Although rough reckonings that included various forms of payment were common between creditors and debtors, shopkeepers did not seem to engage in pawning, nor accept goods in part payment. This preference suggests that bartering as well as pawning, at least through the mid-eighteenth century in France, largely took place between individuals rather than in shops. The Revol accounts show only one exception, and a familial one at that, when Revol's 'brother' Jean Roche used some wheat as part payment for three pairs of stockings and two handkerchiefs. The butcher Vacher maintained a similar pattern a hundred years later, with only one customer debt marked with a notation about repayment or security in kind, 'on which I received two pairs of shoes'.[55] Shopkeepers' preference for cash relations may have been due to both the difficulty of managing their own inventories, if goods of all kinds were exchanged for their inventory, and because they themselves stocked supplies on credit, and needed cash to settle obligations to their suppliers.

The practice of credit extension was much more clearly noted in the account books than were payment rates. Some tabs were marked as paid, but many more were not. It is impossible to determine whether these absences were the result of casual accounting, which certainly abounded, or whether they reflected long-deferred payment or actual lack of payments. The financial summaries of Nantais shopkeepers certainly suggest that the proportion of bad or uncertain debts was significant (as we will see later), although they were, of course, people whose businesses had failed. Perhaps shopkeepers simply refused to extend tabs for goods or money to customers who did not repay fairly reliably. For example, in May 1647 Revol noted that she had accounted with a Monsieur Copie for 2 *livres* 12 *sous* 7 *deniers* for goods, and 1 *livre* 7 *sous* more for money lent to Madame Copie. The entry was marked 'paid' at the start of June, and Madame Copie borrowed another few *livres* at the end of that month.

The tabs in the Revol books again suggest that access to particular forms of credit was gendered. The tabs for both goods and money were almost exclusively run in men's names, although historians usually associate the purchase of provisions with wives. At the least, men as well as women were customers buying these kinds of supplies. In some cases, shopkeepers may have maintained tabs in men's names because their wives could not legally contract debts without

[54] The second book—kept by Revol's second husband, Pierre Clerc, for five years in the 1650s—had no entries for shop sales or tabs to customers. It mostly consisted of notes of major sales between two other people, of which the purpose or relationship to the Revol shop is unclear, and included occasional entries recording loans that were much larger than the shop book showed. Clerc noted, for instance, on 29 January 1652, 'I lent to Sr Jean Bernard the sum of 120 *livres* which he promised to return to me on the first day that I ask him for it'. The entry was marked 'paid'.

[55] ADR 8B1260-2.

their husbands' permission. The notations in the Revol shop book sometimes indicate this pattern clearly. On 3 June 1647, for instance, an entry noted 'Monsieur Paduc owes three *livres* for money lent to his wife'; and on 24 January 1658, another recorded an 'Account of what Nicolas Courdry owes me for the merchandise his wife has taken 2 *livres* 11 *sous*'. Yet as we have seen, married women frequently borrowed money on their own, and local courts even held them liable for those debts, so the male tabs may have represented customers as men quite accurately.

Wives who worked in shops may have played important roles in regulating the extension of credit in shops, both on and off the books. Perrine Dohu, the wife of a butcher, sold meat at their counter 'without money' and 'on credit'. When Anne Anizon, a widow, wanted to borrow some money, she went into a locksmith's shop and asked the locksmith's wife directly for money. The wife 'took it out of her pocket and counted it', the widow recounted it, and then put it in her apron pocket and left the shop. Despite all that counting, two hours later Anizon returned to complain that she had been shortchanged. As the locksmith's wife made up the difference she added: 'That makes 105 *livres* you owe me, please let me have a receipt.'[56] Evidently the locksmith's wife did not record the debt in her books, as the women were later in court, and the locksmith's wife was forced to rely on three witnesses to attest to the loan's existence.

Accounts attest to the particular kinds of credit customs located in particular sites at particular times (although our very limited knowledge of debt practices among early modern families and shopkeepers still makes comparison difficult). Married women in France in the seventeenth century did not yet have access to the book credit for goods or money that they were to have by the second half of the eighteenth century, or that they may have had in England even by the late seventeenth century, to judge from the accounts of a London haberdasher, John Pope.[57] They were not identified as independent consumers, as they were to be in the eighteenth century, suggesting that seventeenth-century working wives had access to loans in shops primarily in an off-the-books manner. Shops were important sources of small loans, and were largely cash or credit nexuses. Pawning remained largely a matter for individuals in neighbourhoods, even more clearly in France than in England, and varied forms of liquidity that facilitated exchanges on streets and in homes were less frequently used in shops.

Credit practices seem to have shifted in the eighteenth century. Just as court clerks began to articulate the work identity as well as household status of female witnesses in the eighteenth century, shopkeepers' records indicate evolving perceptions and responsibilities too. A hundred years after Revol's death, another

[56] ADLA B5852, 4 June 1718; ADLA B5840, 22 July 1688.

[57] For Paris, see Crowston, 'The Queen and Her "Minister of Fashion"', and for John Pope's haberdashery shop accounts, see Beverly Lemire, 'Introduction. Women, credit and the creation of opportunity: a historical overview', in Lemire, Pearson, and Campbell (eds.), *Women and Credit*, 6–8.

Lyonnais candlemaker, Guillaume Audibert, and his wife Bartheleme, ran tabs for women as well as men, while the butcher Claude Vacher recorded lists of 'what is owed me', in which women were named as the debtors for nearly 70 per cent of the sums.[58] The emergence of new consumer aspirations may have fostered the formal extension of shop credit to women. The debt records of various eighteenth-century Lyonnais hairdressers and needlewomen, for example, indicate that they ran extensive tabs with female clients. For instance, in the 1730s the hairdresser Mademoiselle Lafont recorded tabs for many female customers that often included numerous hair arrangements (often more than twenty counted on her tabs simply with tally marks), as well as decorative accoutrements such as ribbons and lace. Needlewomen in the 1750s and 1760s kept accounts for many female customers.[59] Likewise, elite dressmakers in Paris, by the time of the Revolution, attributed financial responsibility to wives as well as their husbands, although social rank as well as gender identity may have encouraged Parisian merchants to view aristocratic wives as autonomous consumers by that time.[60]

Gender was a component, although not a determinant, of how individuals and families navigated economies of markets. No easy distinction is possible between a male-dominated written formal economy and an informal oral female economy. Much of men's activity was of the face-to-face off-the-books variety, as was women's activity. Men and women were both involved in microcredit networks in ways that largely overlapped, but the frequency with which each sex resorted to particular strategies varied in important ways. Moreover, as contractual market relations increasingly prevailed over customary practices, gender patterns may have become more pronounced.

RESOLVING DEBTS: BETWEEN LIQUIDITY AND LIQUIDATION

Family management of economies of markets included the unravelling of debts, as well as the borrowing of money. Creditors' efforts to collect overdue debts were omnipresent, and debt litigation so commonplace that every household was familiar with the sight of sergeants delivering orders to distrain goods to neighbours, if not to them personally.[61] Complex and fragile credit/debt

[58] ADR 8B627 *et passim*; ADR 8B1260-2. Examples include 15 November 1755 and 3 March 1759.

[59] ADR 8B985; ADR 8B632; ADR 8B1246.

[60] For the gender identity of customers of the leading Parisian fashion merchant Rose Bertin and a couple of more minor shopkeepers in the 1780s, see Crowston, 'The Queen and Her "Minister of Fashion"', 98–104.

[61] And not only in France. Garthine Walker suggests that in early modern England too, 'Although the initial plaint was usually sufficient to achieve settlement, the scale of litigation was so great that by the later sixteenth century almost all households were likely to have experienced or

networks were ubiquitous but precarious financial instruments for urban working families. Access to credit was a two-edged resource that could provide the critical difference in families' abilities to make ends meet, but which could also leave them precariously close to household catastrophes if they could not repay debts when called upon to do so. For working families, debt was often a more mundane danger to their efforts to secure some small measure of stability and success through the combined efforts of both spouses than the dramatic Malthusian disasters of war, disease, or famine that are more visible in historical hindsight. Credit offered expanded liquidity, but debt entailed the threat of liquidation. Creditors could wait, accept payment in kind, seek to establish a schedule for repayment over a period of time, refuse to extend further credit until existing amounts were repaid, write off the debt, or begin to litigate to seek repayment. Debtors faced challenges with enormous implications in trying to assess what a creditor might do, or decide how to respond, especially as litigation over debt increased even while customary practices remained common.

This section explores the challenges and strategies involved in the navigation of the unravelling of the multiple obligations created by families. While some of these were predictable, many were not: if creditors unexpectedly demanded repayment or changed the terms of repayment, or when one household's credit network was endangered by the failure of another. Men's and women's experiences differed in debt resolution as much as in credit creation, and women were at the centre of the process of unravelling debts as they were of borrowing. (Historians have shown that women were less active in debt litigation than were men, but this form of gender marginalization seems to have been specific to court actions.[62]) Spouses' strategies were sometimes cooperative, but circumstances could dictate that one or the other follow individual paths too. Moreover, neighbours were deeply invested in their neighbours' fortunes, and their judgements were critical in providing or withholding help, mediation, and perhaps depositions.[63]

Borrowers knew that different forms of loans posed very differential risks to their households. Debts notarized as legal contracts, in the form of *rentes*, were the most secure for borrowers, even though they were usually the largest debts incurred by a household, because creditors were not allowed to call them in. Many loans, on the other hand, were made informally, and with no written proof. This lack of proof offered many opportunities for conflict, and made enforcement of collection difficult. Pierre Carcanac, for instance, took a secondhand seller, Ollive Guillet, to court to force her to pay him for three white dresses he had

witnessed an arrest, attachment, or distraint of goods for auction.' Garthine Walker, *Crime, Gender and Social Order in Early Modern England* (Cambridge, 2003), 250.

62 See, for example, Muldrew, *Economy of Obligation*, and Cornelia Hughes Dayton, *Women before the Bar: Gender, Law, and Society in Connecticut, 1639–1789* (Chapel Hill, NC, 1995).

63 Many historians have pointed out that a focus on household interests alone assumes a commonality of interests that elides the possible conflicts of interests between household members.

given to her. She said, however, that she had not agreed to buy them, but only accepted them to sell on his behalf.[64]

Rent defaults and relatively modest but documented debts to merchants were far more fraught with peril for families than were other kinds of loan, large or small, because these creditors seem to have been the most likely to choose litigation. The median debt for which creditors named in separations suits had sought permission to seize and sell household assets, was 180 *livres*, and almost all named creditors were described as merchants rather than, for example, retailers of provisions.[65] These were cases in which written records backed the loans, and in which creditors had sufficient to gain to justify legal actions.

Although debt litigation was increasing, customary practices were still common as borrowers and lenders moved between different forms of lending. Guillaume Hore's experiences indicate the variety of patterns, and of creditor responses. In 1668, Hore, a notary, borrowed some money from Perrine Bouyer, a married neighbour. A couple of years later, Bouyer heard that Hore's landlord had moved to obtain a court order to sell some of Hore's household property because he and his wife were in arrears with their rent. Bouyer offered to pay the rent in return for some of their personal goods, and Hore gave her a number of items including 'bed coverings, chests and linen'. After she had had them 'for a long time', and often asked him if he wanted them back, he finally said she would have to keep them to cover the debts he owed her. Hore also borrowed 2 *ecus* from an innkeeper, Guy Charon, and when Charon went to his home to collect his repayment, Hore offered him a watch as security, saying he would definitely get it back. Yet he never did.[66] In these ways, Hore successfully worked a variety of customary credit arrangements until he found a creditor who chose litigation as the strategy of choice for collection.

The challenge of knowing when payment could be postponed, made in part or in kind, or had to be promptly repaid in cash and in full must have been difficult, but families could be taken by surprise when their creditors' choices were not as they assumed, and unexpected calls for payment might easily create financial chaos in a household. Consider the experience of the household of the haberdasher Jean Richard and Françoise Gayot. They had traded with Pierre Marin, another haberdasher, for three years, and always paid 'in exchange of merchandise' rather than in cash. In October 1693, Richard reckoned up accounts with Marin's wife, who recorded their settlement in her 'little book', and they agreed that Richard owed Marin 80 *livres* and 10 *sous*. Richard paid just over 41 *livres* in merchandise, and 'took a note of what he still owed'. A few days later, Marin demanded repayment, but Richard

[64] ADR 8B729-5, 17 October 1703.

[65] The debts collected varied enormously from almost 5,000 *livres* to 31 *livres*. Almost all named creditors were artisans or merchants.

[66] ADLA B5825, 28 April 1670.

said he could not pay because 'he had not had time to have them made and besides he was squeezed'. While Richard gathered the merchandise he could use for payment, he heard that Marin had taken legal action to collect the remaining 39 *livres*. Richard immediately offered payment in merchandise, but Marin refused, insisting on cash. Marin persisted, and obtained a court order to seize and sell their assets. Richard opposed the efforts to collect on the grounds of their past practices; that is, that payment in kind had previously been satisfactory.[67]

This episode highlights the unpredictability of creditor–debtor relations, and illustrates how everyday debt practices could suddenly become perilous. Richard and Gayot objected to Marin's efforts to collect a debt they acknowledged they owed, on several levels—on the speed and insistence he expressed, and on his refusal to continue what had become a customary exchange in kind. It illustrates how suddenly the juggling of loans, on which all households relied, could evolve into a crisis that left bailiffs on the doorstep, or worse. Families could not know when a creditor who had been patient might insist on payment, when a creditor with whom in-kind exchanges had been the norm might suddenly demand cash, or when a creditor might suddenly decide to seek the help of the legal system in collecting.

This unpredictability meant that, for many households, recurring threats from creditors to start legal actions for seizure became part of a debt cycle that might or might not also include sales. Sometimes, creditors probably had little intention of seizing assets but used court orders to pressure for repayment, though on other occasions if debts were not paid, sales went ahead. A debtor of the barrelmaker, Fleury Martin, for example, wrote to him to say that he had received notice that Martin had secured a court order against him (presumably giving permission to seize property prior to sale), and asked that Fleury 'wait until the end of the present month' when, he promised, he would repay the debt.[68] Neighbours of Marguerite Deserreur and Henry Lohier said they had seen sergeants at their home, asking for money, several times. Marguerite Raffin, the wife of a boatyard worker, said she had 'very often' seen sergeants at the home of Perrine Ripocheau and Sebastien Jarnigan 'in order to move to sell their goods'. Anne Roussy, the wife of a 'merchant', claimed that creditors' orders to start sale procedures were a 'daily' occurrence in her household.[69] The sight of legal officials delivering court orders to pay debts must have been common.

The collapse of one household's financial juggling had domino effects for other households to whom it was linked directly by debts or more indirectly by pooled responsibility for taxation. When Claude Greffet's insolvency became clear in

[67] ADR 8B1249-1, 13 September 1694. [68] ADR 8B1033, 19 April 1745.

[69] ADLA B5806, 7 February 1624; ADLA B5833 *bis*, 15 July 1681; ADR BP420, 12 April 1631. There were many such references to the repeated appearance of sergeants with creditors' court orders. See, among many examples, ADLA B5817, 24 July 1658; ADLA B6675, 7 June 1681; ADR BP3984, 18 December 1691.

1619, for instance, the consequences affected the households of his creditors as well as his own. His default promised potential catastrophe not only for his family but for the families of his creditors too. Greffet's debts included 3,900 *livres* owed to Jehan Mirailles, 1,800 *livres* for money borrowed in a *cedula*, and the rest for merchandise. Mirailles was in Turin when his wife, Marie Girel, wrote to tell him the news that Greffet had ceased trading. Girel told her husband that she had not written sooner 'because of the affliction that the miserable state of our affairs has given me'.[70] Girel, made ill with anxiety about the impact of a debtor's illiquidity on her own previously liquid household, articulated the peril that a debtor's difficulties posed to her own household.

Accounts of creditor-initiated sales indicate that neighbourbood embeddedness in borrowing networks could provide help as well as risk, as they suggest that a local culture of trying to protect absolute necessities existed in which female neighbours in particular may have played prominent roles. Everyone knew (as we have seen) that creditors were legally entitled to sell whatever goods they found until debts were covered, and repeated sales, or even threats to sell that led debtors to pawn or sell property to raise case, could soon deplete families' always limited assets. Family members and neighbours could seek to provide some minimal buffer on the losses in a variety of ways. When a sergeant arrived to start the sale of the goods of Anne Hubert and François Fariseur, for example, at least one other creditor had previously seized household assets. Hubert 'begged the court to leave to her at the least some clothing, linen and goods for the use of her and her children'.[71] Although the sergeant said he could not agree without the consent of the creditors, their exchange hints that a culture existed of selling non-necessities first. Certainly, neighbours sometimes bought some goods prior to or during sales to keep them for families.

In these ways and others, women had a variety of prominent roles in the cycle of seizure and sale. Wives in the midst of a creditor squeeze that took the path of legal action, could try diverse strategies to deflect the sale (as we have seen) or, in the end, watch as their goods were auctioned to the value of their debts. Female as well as male neighbours were spectators, and also potential buyers, as court officials sold household property in the street. Women dominated the work of appraising household goods. The female secondhand traders who were so prominent in early modern urban retailing often purchased significant portions of the household goods sold on such occasions, and used them to re-stock their own inventories.[72]

[70] AML FF116, undated letter in Greffet bankruptcy file.

[71] ADLA B5597, 9 June 1716.

[72] The many court records of the sales that followed *saisi* orders clearly indicate these patterns. See, for instance, the sale of the goods of Jean Cottel in 1660 at the request of a butcher. Cottel's belongings were sold in 25 lots—ten of which went to women, and half of that ten to one woman, Louise Roux. ADR BP2926, 19 July 1660. For the scope of the purchases and resales of one secondhand seller, see the papers of Claudine Scarron, a Lyonais *revendeuse*, dating from 1684 to 1723, in ADR 8B1149-1 and 2.

The decision to cease trading was another possible response to creditor pressure, and it also involved gendered consequences. Men's legal standing as the family members responsible for debts made them the primary target of creditors' actions, and if these led to a decision to cease trading men often took flight, at least temporarily. They did so less to avoid their creditors than to wait out of the reach of justice while courts determined whether they were mere failures who should make arrangements with their creditors and get on with their lives, or whether they were to be judged criminal bankrupts who could be severely punished. Wives in these households were often left to deal with creditors, to be interviewed by bailiffs and sundry other officials, and to watch the sales if their husbands were absent.

In a household that ceased trading, a wife played a critical role in efforts to establish that the difficulties were due to legitimate failure rather than felonious bankruptcy. Wives who were not willing to be co-operative partners with their husbands in saving the day could make that clear, either by seeking separate property or by other means. Marie Perrot, for instance, found herself facing acute debt difficulties twice, and responded in two different ways. On the first occasion, in 1685, she defended her husband and household, and successfully came to terms with creditors so that her husband Guillaume Debie was able to return to town and re-establish their trade. Two years later, however, after, as one witness noted, Debie 'continued to engage in debts too easily and without taking the precautions that a trader should both in his commerce and in the obligations he joins', she faced the same situation and made a different choice. When Debie left town again, Perrot moved to seek separate property.[73]

As Debie's case indicates, wives found themselves in double roles in the decision to cease trading: they became the households' primary creditors for the surety of their dowries, and they were pivotal in defending or undoing the financial integrity of their households. The financial summaries which families created when they suspended their commerce reiterated the sense of households as sites of production and consumption, credit extension and debt collection, and domestic and market economies. In these *états*, men provided balance sheets of their financial situations in which wives were listed as the first creditors. For example, Louis Garreau, a silk merchant, presented his 'Summary of the situation of his commercial affairs' to creditors.[74] The first and last expenses he noted were household ones: 'First he owes to his wife for her dowry the sum of 3,000 *livres*' and the final item was an estimate of his household's yearly expenses for board and lodging. In between, Garreau valued his merchandise at 9,000 *livres*, and the personal property (movables such as furniture) and linen in his household at 1,500 *livres*. He said he was owed more then 5,000 *livres* by individuals to whom he had sold merchandise on credit, but did not expect to be able to collect more than 2,000 *livres*. This pattern was repeated in every *état*.

[73] ADLA B5839, 13 January 1687. [74] ADLA B5597.

The notes exchanged between Jehan Mirailles and Marie Girel, after the insolvency of Claude Greffet in 1619, offer a personal perspective that rarely survives, both of the mobilization of spousal efforts to manage risk, and of the complementary yet potentially conflicting stakes that spouses had in debt management. She signed a note 'I remain as ever your obedient wife', but ended a letter 'your wife and assistant'.[75] Her rhetorical slippage between the conventions of obedient wifedom and the realities of spousal collaboration might suggest that her obedience and assistance were tied to his fulfilment of his responsibilities in an understanding that was evident elsewhere among working people, that gendered privileges (his right to her deference, for example) were contingent upon performance. Marie gave her husband detailed instructions, promised to send a 'note' by messenger about the unfolding legal actions (presumably with guidelines for creditors, and so on), and urged him 'to follow it as exactly as you can' and 'to do everything wisely'. She reminded him 'of the obligation that a husband and a father has for his wife'. He had to do what was necessary, or perhaps face her pursuance of a protective path of her own that might be detrimental to his status, such as seeking separate property.

Wives who chose to defend their households' integrity, as well as their own good standing in the event of the cessation of trading, did so strategically, just as they did in other kinds of interactions with the court system. Court officials arrived at their homes to interview them and any household workers about events as they sought to determine what had happened. In these encounters, working wives carefully and skilfully sought to manage the representations of their husbands and households. Wives in failed enterprises, of whatever kind, routinely deployed a rhetoric that portrayed them as innocent bystanders who knew nothing, and certainly never had anything to do with shops or businesses. If the position was absolutely at odds with daily realities, as everyone must have known, it was common and often successful for wives navigating legal shoals in a variety of circumstances.[76] Wives savvily followed tight scripts that directly addressed ways in which prosecutors identified guilt of bankruptcy. A Lyonnais prosecutor noted, for example, that 'nobody can doubt' that Nicolas Boynin was guilty of bankruptcy, because 'his failure is notorious since he is absent, hidden, and has not returned, he has not accorded with his creditors, sold the inventory of his shop on the eve of his departure, diverted his property, money and papers, and made notes and obligations' under another name when his own affairs were in great disarray.[77] Wives therefore countered such suspicions by insisting that while their husbands were absent and they had no knowledge of their business dealings, they were sure neither of them had

[75] AML FF116. Letter and note undated, but in the file for the bankruptcy of Claude Greffet, their debtor, in 1619.

[76] For more on this strategy, see Julie Hardwick, 'Women "working" the law: gender, authority and legal process in early modern France', *Journal of Women's History*, 9, 3 (October 1997).

[77] ADR BP4046, (no date or month) 1636.

'diverted' any of their property, and that all relevant record books and papers were secured.[78]

Wives were not always, of course, successful in avoiding charges of criminal behaviour in their management of the cessation of trading because of debts. A Lyonnais prosecutor, for instance, urged that Janne Vincent be found guilty of bankruptcy, although her husband had died by the time the investigation of their affairs had finished. The prosecutor expressed scepticism about all aspects of her defence: if she only sought to preserve what was hers as she claimed, why did she, with her servants and others, remove furniture, linen, papers, pewter and provisions in the middle of the night, instead of allowing it to be inventoried? This behaviour, he thought, provided evidence of 'her bad faith'. She had also collected and hidden away money repaid by debtors of her husband. 'Adding to that', the prosecutor said that her self-representation had been unsatisfactory, with the 'absurd and stubborn denigrations and complaints of wrong doings of Justice' which she had made in her first response to the enquiry. Finally, the depositions on her behalf came from 'suspicious people' (including people of known bad reputation, such as servants, debtors, and kin), and could not be given much credence. The prosecutor concluded that Vincent had made, removed, and hidden household property to the prejudice of the creditors, and was a responsible party in her (dead) husband's bankruptcy.[79] As in other debt disputes, the court found her responsible, despite the technical legal distancing of wives from debt. Moreover, the prosecutor's emphasis on her demeanour, as well as on her actions, illustrates how wives had to address various issues in managing the legal process.

Charles Besnard and Janne Letourneux ran a silk and linen goods shop in a Nantais parish, and the unravelling of their affairs indicates the centrality of wives' choices and roles, as well as neighbourhood attitudes, in shaping the outcome in such situations. Because of his debts, Besnard left town in early August 1692. Three weeks after his departure, news of his absence reached court officials, and they began to investigate his 'failure and bankruptcy'. They pursued enquiries first with their servant, Gilberde Olliveau, and then with Letourneux. Olliveau claimed total ignorance: she did not know why her master had left, did not know if he had taken money or merchandize with him, and had not helped him 'divert' any cash or property before he left. Letourneux artfully distanced herself from any responsibility, while casting her husband in the best possible light. She used a carefully elusive phrase when she said she had no 'positive knowledge' of her husband's debts. Far from long expecting their failure, as the court official suggested, she insisted that she had no such inkling of any problem, and in fact

[78] For examples of this kind of testimony in Lyon, see AML FF208, 6 September 1654; AML FF211, 20 April 1651; AML FF200, 31 May 1653; and AML FF201, 21 August 1653. The Nantais consular court records do not survive before 1700, but show a similar pattern. See, for example, ADLA B5597, 16 March 1716.

[79] ADR BP4046, (no date or month) 1636.

only learned of it just before Besnard's departure. Asked whether she and her husband had 'diverted' their 'best goods and money to frustrate their legitimate creditors', she responded that they had not done so, and insisted that her husband had not taken anything with him. She indicated that her husband had sent her a letter with a 'note' of what he owed, and that the shop's books were locked in the shop. She admitted that she had kept the shop open for two days after Besnard left, until a lawyer told her that their creditors could 'worry her' if the shop were open, which she therefore locked and had not been in since. Letourneux noted that her husband had left her with only 6 *ecus* in cash, which she had spent immediately to pay their baker and another woman to whom they owed money, so she had been forced to borrow money from her mother for household necessities. The court officials made an inventory of all the possessions in their home as surety against their being removed.

As the investigation continued over the next three months, neighbours and creditors, as well as Letourneux, played crucial roles in shaping the outcome. Four witnesses, all neighbours from their street, including a widow, a female trader, a tailor, and a merchant, confirmed that the shop had been closed since Besnard left, and that it was common knowledge that he had left because of debts. The court ordered Besnard to appear to answer the charge; but he apparently did not, and instead the court let stand, as his reply, the handwritten 'Note of what Charles Besnard owes' which his wife had presented at the start of the investigation. It assessed his debts to twelve creditors at more than 5,000 *livres*. Besnard carefully observed that he had written records, if personal rather than notarized, for all the debts. By mid-November, Letourneux had made an agreement with their creditors, and the court released the household goods to her that had been inventoried for safe keeping in August.[80] Besnard was free to return, designated as a 'failure' but free of the criminal stain of bankruptcy, and they could reopen their shop, or commence whatever activity they could find to earn their living.

Letourneux's shrewd management of the legal process that would assess Besnard's actions as failure or bankruptcy successfully allowed her household to resolve its debt disaster on the best available terms. Her careful shift between insisting that she had no knowledge of their difficulties (an unlikely tale, but one necessary for the preservation of her own standing) and attributing the losses to changes in fashion cast her husband as a prudent but unfortunate trader rather than a perpetrator of criminal fraud. Her use of Besnard's 'note' made the same point, as it demonstrated that he had written records of his debts and had not fecklessly incurred them. Letourneux's story about using all the little cash he gave her to pay down what she owed their baker and another lender also established their good intentions towards creditors. (That strategy probably had a doubly beneficial effect in not only seeking to reassure other creditors, but also in serving

80 ADLA B6681, 25 August 1692, and attached papers.

to extend her credit with the baker and ensure, at least for a while, a continued supply of the staple of early modern diets.)

Wives who were faced with the meltdown of their household assets could make pro-active choices, however, as well as responding to creditor-imposed crises, and neighbourhood opinion must have been critical in determining which options were available. Janne Letourneux's own actions illustrated how wives had more than one option. In the same year that she represented a hard-working, competent husband and household to avoid bankruptcy in one court, she started, in a different court, a case against her husband for separate property, in which her witnesses alleged that he was a drinker, a gambler, and a wife-beater.[81] The neighbours who provided testimony in both cases articulated judgements about borrowing and marital expectations. They confirmed his absence and the fact that his debts were common knowledge, but they did not apparently interpret his absence as evidence of fraud, no doubt being all too familiar with the possibility of disequilibrium with creditors. Yet they did indicate in their testimony that his behaviour failed to meet the standards for spousal obligations. The judgement of neighbours that Besnard's behaviour did not amount to criminality, but did merit the civil penalty of loss of control over his household property, was critical to Letourneux's ability to use the court system in the interest of her family business.

Like Letourneux, wives could handle the debt difficulties that were so rife in early modern families in another way by pursuing separate property. Separations were one possible curb on the liquidation of households that debts threatened, because wives with separate property were entitled to claim their trousseau items (often household essentials) as well as the portion of their dowries designated as lineage property. Creditors did occasionally complain that the ability of wives to seek separate property offered a means of defrauding them, and claimed that by such means spouses were able to protect a portion of their household assets from the rightful claims of people to whom they owed money.

Yet judges and prosecutors in courts of first instance were remarkably sceptical about creditors' infrequent claims of spousal collusion or any other expression of creditor opposition, and did not apparently give them any credence. In practice, creditors rarely entered objections to separation requests. Perhaps they recognized there was little point, as the examples of two Lyonnais cases from the same day indicate. When Gabrielle Fontaine sought separate property from her surgeon husband Etienne Bonnefont, she cited a court order starting legal action to seize their property to cover a debt of 902 *livres* on behalf of the guild of surgeons. The lawyer for the surgeons argued that 'it is not difficult to see that the requested separation is only demanded to defraud the surgeons and the collusion and cooperation between husband and wife is clearly visible'. They sought to be given 'privilege and preference' over her as his creditor, but all to no avail, as Fontaine

[81] ADLA B5843, 18 August 1692.

was granted the separate property she sought. Creditors who bothered to oppose the suits could also do so on grounds of other kinds of weaknesses in wives' cases. Noel Lerat, for example, a creditor for 125 *livres* which he had started legal action to collect, opposed Benoiste Barollier's request for separate property on the grounds that she did not have proof that her dowry of 25 *livres* had actually been paid, so she could not claim to be the household's primary creditor for that amount.[82] Again, though, the court ignored the complaint and granted separate property.

These claims of wifely financial distress and husbandly incompetence or worse, and counter-claims of spousal collusion, require some careful unpacking. As in every type of judicial process, the evidence given was shaped by the legal imperatives of the case, as well as the self-interest of the parties. Although little systematic work has been done on property separations, especially before the eighteenth century, most historians have been inclined to accept the perspectives of jurists and creditors who decried separate property litigation as a matter of spousal collusion.[83] Certainly wives, through self-interest and legal requirement, had reason to emphasize the antagonism associated with their household's dire straits, and to blame their husbands. Creditors who charged collusion, however, were also self-interested, because a wife's successful request for separate property moved them down the list of creditors. Judges too had a stake in particular outcomes, and perhaps favoured wives over creditors in the interests of household stability and in recognition of neighbourhood desire to provide a safety net against the risks and dislocation of market intensification. Jurists may have been influenced by reading of the very few, and arguably highly unusual, cases from courts of first instance that were appealed.[84] With all parties

[82] ADR BP3985, 11 February 1673. The courts also ignored other kinds of creditors' reasons for turning down separate property requests, including, for example, from the same year, ADR BP3985, 17 June 1673 (the creditor said a *saisi* of 31 *livres* was 'too small' to warrant separate property); ADR BP3985, 1 July 1673 (the creditor opposed separate property as unnecessary, because despite a previous *saisi* by another creditor, the household's assets still far exceeded her legal claims); ADR BP3985, 21 February 1673 (a butcher and his wife demanded to be given priority over a wife seeking separate property who cited a *saisi* of 41 *livres*, because they had provided meat to the family on credit).

[83] Historians such as Zoe Schneider and Daryl Hafter have argued that separate property suits were matters of collusion between spouses, although concrete evidence is slim. Schneider, for example, suggests that we can 'surmise' that collusion was involved, but offers jurists' claims, rather than cases, as evidence. Hafter notes that 'many examples reflect situations in which there was antagonism' between spouses, but suggests property separations became 'a regular business technique' to protect households' resources. Again, the evidence for collusion and business technique comes primarily from jurists rather than the evidence of lawsuits. Kaplan's reading of a sampling of separate property suits in eighteenth-century Paris, however, does suggest that spousal conflict was the key. See Zoe Schneider, 'Women before the bench: female litigants in early modern Normandy', *French Historical Studies*, 23, 1 (Winter 2000), 20–1; Daryl Hafter, *Women at Work in Preindustrial France* (University Park, PA, 2007), 76–9 ; Kaplan, *Bakers of Paris*, 328–35.

[84] Piant, *Une Justice Ordinaire*, 277, argues that very few lawsuits from courts of first instance were in fact appealed, and that such appeals usually involved very unusual cases, so conclusions based on readings of such cases tends to distort perceptions of the mundane dynamics of those courts.

invested in particular self-representations, there seems little reason to privilege one view—that of judges and creditors—over the perspectives of wives and judges. Moreover, witnesses, whose self-interest in terms of assessing collusion or conflict was small, consistently emphasized spousal antagonism.

Evidence from suits in courts of first instance, as well as of the lived experience revealed in those cases, strongly suggests that if spouses occasionally surely co-operated to secure property separations, most wives who sought separate property had decided to assert interests independent of their husbands who were often quick to voice opposition. Court officials seem to have accepted this reality too, in their reluctance to admit creditors' claims of fraud. Most wives who chose to pursue separate property wanted to protect their own future interests. These households had few assets before the wives came to court, and wives hoped to preserve basic necessities and future earnings or inheritances rather than existing resources. Separate property as a practical remedy primarily placed future revenues under wives' control.

In this redefinition, the persistent presence of lineage property in women's dowries, even as other economic forces evolved, played an important but complex role as a node where credit and debt, and domestic and market economies, intersected. In France, inalienable lineage property was a powerful legal concept that provided a profoundly rooted claim of ownership, and lineage property was a key basis for married women's property claims. In practice, the legal promise of protection for women's lineage property was countered by the reality of the immediate deployment of what was usually a cash dowry, of which a portion was designated as lineage property, in working families. As soon as couples married, the dowry, lineage portion or not, would be out of cash and into tools, loans, and other daily needs. The practical fungibility of lineage property in the budgets of working families made it more amorphous, by the seventeenth century, than the legal concept envisioned. If the dowry was not at risk in these families, it would have been no use at all. But as many women could demonstrate that their dowries were in peril by this standard, the option of seeking separate property was open to them.

In all these ways, women as well as men were at the centre of the means by which debts unravelled, often unpredictably, in uncertain times. Even the most careful of families could find that misfortune, changes in trading circumstances, or creditors' unexpected decisions, could move their household's grasp on the slippery distinction between essential credit and catastrophic debt. As members of elaborate and varied credit networks that criss-crossed neighbourhoods, spouses must have watched in consternation as a neighbour's difficulties imperilled their own liquidity. While husbands were the legal managers of household property, whether assets or debts, wives received court orders that allowed creditors to start the steps leading to sales, watched sales of their goods, helped neighbours whose goods were being sold, bought distrained goods to sell on their own behalf, defended their households in investigations that threatened to add criminal penalties to financial difficulties, and resolved to separate their interests from those of their spouses through the pursuit of separate property.

MAKING SENSE OF A PRECARIOUS ECONOMY

Early modern men's and women's explanations of how households ran into difficulties suggests how they thought the economy worked, and offer a window into why particular marital attributes were valorized in a precarious economy. Petitioners rarely acknowledged structural factors in explaining their financial difficulties. Although the complexities of everyday debt management (as we have seen) underlay many families' difficulties, spouses rarely cited inability to collect money owed as the reason for their difficulties. Instead, spouses and witnesses explained difficulties primarily in terms of personal shortcomings, whether financial or moral.[85] All kinds of behaviour could be held up for criticism in this way, from dallying with prostitutes to 'spending money on flowers'.[86] Men were criticized for their lack of attention and devotion to working at their trades. They wasted their time, energy and resources, and their households could not afford it. Husbands were blamed for shortcomings in basic competence as craftsmen and traders.

These narratives vastly oversimplified, individualized, and gendered the process of financial difficulty. The personalization of failure may be predictable. Even today, people have difficulty identifying the structural rather than individual factors that shape their situations. No doubt a few of these husbands were feckless losers. Moreover, a focus on individual shortcomings in many ways met the requirements of the legal process. When petitions identified husbands as responsible, and household difficulties as their individual burden, women were distanced from responsibility for debts and losses, as if they were helpless bystanders and victims of their husbands' commerce and cupidity. (Of course, when separate property suits succeeded, these same wives assumed the competence to manage whatever household property remained, and the court often charged them specifically with using revenues from it to support their families.)

Yet these narratives of failure illuminate what early modern working families identified as problematic, and explain why hard work was valorized as a key spousal attribute and the antidote to risk. Spouses often disagreed about how resources such as time and money were to be assigned, and over other strategies. Andrée Hamlin complained to her husband, Mathieu Petit, that they would be better off if he worked in his craft rather than dabbling in trade. Janne Dote

[85] Other kinds of explanation were rare. Occasionally, wives cited ill health (for example, ADR BP419, 17 December 1630) or bad luck (for example, ADR BP420, 6 May 1631).

[86] ADLA B6155, 24 January 1682; ADLA B5838, 30 January 1686.

criticized Pierre Chevallier for 'not doing business like her first husband'. Anne Anizon quarrelled with Pierre Lejage over the use of their money, which she argued should be used to support their children.[87] Husbands could argue their side too, and emphasize wives' own actions as the sources of difficulty. Nicolas Lemercier contested Anne Bridon's petition on the grounds that she was responsible for what he referred to as their financial 'disorder' because she had pressured him into buying the house that was their major obligation.[88]

Such discussions of why households were in danger of falling between the cracks explicitly resonated with key features of economies of markets. Money, trade, and reputation were all at stake in this language of household difficulty, yet hints of the roles of over-extended borrowing and the uncertainties of a market economy were also evidence. Wives and neighbours complained about men who spent money 'at the wrong moment' (a phrase that, from the 1680s, became a favourite) or 'uselessly'. They suggested that men had 'no capacity for bargaining' or were simply poor judges who bought at high prices and sold at low prices.[89] The hard work and sound judgement that were valorized as spousal qualities must have seemed to provide an indispensable antidote to the risks and opportunities presented by the new market.

A CULTURE OF BORROWING: NEIGHBOURS AND COURTS NEGOTIATE CREDIT AND DEBT

By modern standards, Perrine Leguy and Nicolas Provost seemed like bad risks for lenders, and yet their neighbours repeatedly lent her (if not him) money in sums large and small over many years. The couple's precarious finances were well known to their neighbours. Acquaintances knew the couple had 'quite a difficulty living'. They were 'often very pressed to repay', and had to sell household goods too 'to avoid the costs and legal actions' that creditors threatened. They characterized Prevost as a 'debauched, argumentative and usually drunk' man who did nothing except eat, drink, and often beat his wife. In contrast they praised Leguy, who 'alone conducted trade'. She worked hard and made 'great efforts for her family', but received only 'a bad return from her husband'. A neighbour noted that although Leguy had often borrowed money from neighbours to buy merchandise and circumvent legal action from creditors, she always repaid her lenders, and 'took a lot of care and worked hard to support her family and

[87] ADLA B5837, 23 October 1685; ADLA B5833 *bis*, 28 July 1682; ADLA B5840, 22 July 1688.

[88] ADLA B6145, 27 July 1665.

[89] See, for example, ADLA B5838, 5 September 1686; ADLA B6155, 21 October 1686; ADLA B 5615, 31 August 1647; ADLA B5846, 18 July 1697; ADLA B5836, 29 May 1684; and ADLA B5837, 6 October 1685.

maintain the little credit she had'. A servant described how carefully Leguy sought to look 'well supplied', for instance, by cutting up pieces of material so that the merchandise would seem more ample, and she would 'conserve her credit'.[90]

The ongoing ability of the Leguy–Provost household to access loans highlights key aspects of the culture of borrowing in early modern urban communities. If families relied on mobilizing and managing a constellation of credit in which gender shaped strategies to make ends meet, fundamental issues remain. Who would lend money to whom, and on what terms? What were the expectations about repayment? When borrowing was ubiquitous, what separated good credit and high status from bad debt and possible bankruptcy? As the experiences of Leguy and Provost suggest, the fact of loans which were ubiquitous seemed less significant than the actions of borrowers and the meanings attached to those actions. A high level of borrowing could easily be seen as a positive, an indicator of high credit and status, so owing money in itself was not the problem. As in other matters, neighbourhood judgements were articulated and authorized in multiple settings on the street and in legal proceedings.

Residents of early modern cities negotiated the meanings of lending in and out of court. Their discussions engaged the expectations that underlay loans, how these expectations shaped who could borrow money, and why lenders were motivated to extend credit or to call in debts. Local values about borrowing were articulated in letters and in a variety of legal proceedings (criminal proceedings for bankruptcy, separations cases, or litigation over unpaid debts), and many varieties of lending practices and behaviour were discussed. As all creditors and debtors were familiar with the potentially perilous threats that household debts could present, the languages of lending illuminate some of the conventions that shaped creditor–debtor relations of all kinds, commercial and domestic. Although the French monarchy, like many of its peers, relied on borrowing on a vast scale, the legal management of issues about credit, like separations, remained largely a matter of court practice in a dynamic that emphasized how central litigation remained in shaping French society and economy. Generally, then, local litigation communities determined how borrowing would be handled. This section explores the assumptions embedded in discussions of borrowing, how these assumptions shaped decisions about lending, expectations about repayment, determinations of wrongdoing in lending that amounted to justifications for bankruptcy or separate property, and patterns of legal actions.

The historiography that has addressed the dynamics of early modern debt has emphasized a variety of issues. Historians have emphasized that factors such as reputation, social obligation, mutual aid, dependency, rank and Christian morality shaped relations between borrower and lender and assumptions about credit. Natalie Davis argued that the extensive petty indebtedness in France

[90] ADLA B5852, (no date or month) 1716.

should be located within the context of gift exchange.[91] A lively debate about the relationship between gender and credit has emerged. Seeking to complicate the traditional perspective that men's reputation was tied to credit and women's to sexual morality, historians argue that credit was a gender-related rather than gender-specific phenomenon, and that economic as well as sexual standing shaped women's reputations.[92]

Yet multiple potential fault-lines existed in the constellation of credit in the seventeenth century, leaving creditors and debtors to navigate between many possible borrowing scenarios. If many debts were not repaid for long periods of time, suggesting that some lenders saw their transactions as part of a broader circulation of power, services, and support, high and rising levels of debt litigation indicate that mutual aid and social obligation had limited resonance. If early modern conventions extended gifting and its associated reciprocities into much more extensive circles than today, households also accounted very closely for matters that might now be handled as a more general matter of familial obligation. Guardians of minor children were expected to account scrupulously for the money they handled, for example, and families calculated equal shares of inheritance down to the last penny.[93] If loans were everywhere, their many forms carried diverse implications. The most basic division, for example, was between *rentes* and other forms of credit. Notaries brokered most *rentes* for which lender and borrower might never meet, and they publicly recorded legally binding contracts of the transactions. Moreover, since creditors could not legally ask for *rentes* to be repaid, borrowers controlled the timing of repayment (although lenders could always sell the debts on to release their capital, and a lively resale market in *rentes* existed). Loans as *rentes* offered transactions that were more relatively impersonal and narrowly economic than most debt relations. The many other, much more frequently used, kinds of debt mobilized quite different dynamics. They were much more loosely structured, often lacked written documentation, and were usually made on a one-to-one basis. Kin, who virtually never lent money to each other in the form of *rentes* (although their willingness to co-sign was often a crucial factor in securing them), often borrowed and lent money informally.[94] Most important of all, creditors could expect repayment.

Contemporary articulations, whether lexicographical or legal, highlighted this fluidity, and indicate the variety of meanings that could be attached to the

[91] For the historiographical debate about credit, see, for example, Hoffman, *Growth in a Traditional Society*, esp. 69–80; Farr, *Hands of Honor*; Kessler, 'Enforcing Virtue'; Fontaine, 'Antonio and Shylock'; Muldrew, *Economy of Obligation*; Natalie Zemon Davis, *The Gift in Sixteenth-Century France* (Madison, 2000), 54–5.

[92] For the debate about gender and credit, see Gowing, *Domestic Dangers*, 128–33; Crowston, 'The Queen and Her "Minister of Fashion"'; Scott Taylor, 'Credit, debt, and honour in Castile, 1600–1650', *Journal of Early Modern History*, 7 (2003), 8–27; Sheppard, 'Manhood, Credit and Patriarchy', esp. 90–106.

[93] See Hardwick, *Practice of Patriarchy*, 143–58.

[94] For patterns in *rentes*, see Hardwick, *Practice of Patriarchy*, 181–91.

practices of borrowing. The very definition of credit in the seventeenth century, as Laurence Fontaine has recently noted, seems 'complex and puzzling' by modern standards, as symbolized by the seventeenth-century French lexicographer Antoine Furetière's definition of credit as variously meaning credibility, respect, reputation, money-lending, or something which was pointless.[95] A legal distinction was introduced in France, like England, in the 1530s between simple insolvency, classified as a 'failure' (*faillité*), and the felony of bankruptcy, defined as the intentional defrauding of creditors. The behaviour of the debtor, rather than the fact of unpaid debts, was the critical differentiation.[96]

Seventeenth-century discussions of what situated a borrower as a bankrupt rather than a good debtor amplified the focus on the actions rather than on the obligation. Jean Domat, in a famous seventeenth-century commentary on French civil law, carefully elucidated the qualities of a bankrupt as distinct from a person who simply could not meet his debts. 'A fraudulent bankruptcy is a kind of theft', he said, and 'fraudulent bankrupts are to be prosecuted and punished in an extraordinary Manner'. He defined the fraudulence as a person who 'carried off his effects or that he has set up pretended Creditors, or that he has declared himself to be indebted more than he really was to true Creditors'.[97] Moreover, responsibility for the actions that constituted bankruptcy rather than failure was not limited to the person who was the legal party to the debt. Other associates, especially wives, were also vulnerable to prosecution, for as a Lyonnais royal prosecutor explained: 'Bankruptcy is a crime for which not only he who commits it is punished, but those who have disguised and encouraged his withdrawal and those who have undertaken to remove his effects in whatever way which is to the prejudice and fraud of the true and legitimate creditors.'[98]

The language of lending suggests that creditors and debtors alike saw borrowing as a secular matter. The daily discourse about loans in early modern French cities was strikingly secular in every forum from bankruptcy proceedings to personal letters. As in the case of discussions about marriage, the structure of legal proceedings was certainly important in shaping a secular tone. Yet the similarities in non-legal sources such as letters as well as court documents suggest that a secular orientation with regard to borrowing was broadly rooted in neighbourhoods as well as constantly reinforced in court cases. Working people, whether in depositions or letters, framed discussions of debt in secular terms, an important rupture with the religious discourse that framed much of the

[95] Fontaine, 'Antonio and Shylock', 39–40.

[96] Bankruptcy legislation was introduced in France in 1536, and was reiterated several times before the distinctions between failure and bankruptcy were confirmed in the Commercial Code of 1673. See Isambert, *Recueil General*, **12**, 527, and **19**, 104–5. For a brief overview of early Anglo-American developments, see Bruce Mann, *Republic of Debtors: Bankruptcy in the Age of American Independence* (Cambridge, 2003), esp. 46–7.

[97] Jean Domat, *Civil Law in its Natural Order together with the Public Law*, translated by William Strahan (London, 1737), vol. 2, 644.

[98] ADR BP4046, (no date or month) 1636.

angst-ridden early modern prescriptive literature about debt or the competitive piety that Craig Muldrew has argued characterized the language of credit in early modern England.[99]

As early modern men and women made distinctions between the mundane juggling of debts, the mismanagement separate property legally required, honest failure, and bankruptcy, they identified indicators of good credit that included publicity and hard work and of bad debt that included secrecy and fraud. Categorizations of bankruptcy and separate property involved similar judgements about wrongdoing of various kinds that went beyond the ubiquitous, perhaps seemingly almost inevitable, difficulty in meeting one's debts. Husbands whose wives sought separate property, like suspected bankrupts, were alleged to have diverted assets, and/or ran their affairs into the ground through commercial shortcomings. A legal rhetoric of fraudulence of creditors included separate property as well as bankruptcy. As we have seen, the only royal legislation to regulate separate property was part of the broad early modern efforts to protect commerce and creditors that also produced bankruptcy laws. In both cases, *mal mesnagement* (literally bad management, or bad husbandry) was at stake.

Wives and creditors, as well as husbands and debtors, used similar language to differentiate between good credit and bad: they focused on transparency or deceit, and hard work or debauchery. Debtors provided information about their affairs to defend themselves because privacy could be taken as *de facto* proof of intent to defraud. Wives who sought separate property alleged, as we have seen, that their husbands' debauchery imperilled their households, or that they were lazy, and often away from their workplaces. When Antoine Trouillet, a Lyonnais silk merchant, was charged with bankruptcy, his defence very explicitly engaged these issues. He demonstrated his constancy in his claims that he always kept his shop open and was a 'perpetual presence' there. He insisted that he was not given to extravagance or 'any other debaucheries'. No reason existed, he said, to doubt his 'honour'. Trouillet denied that any personal fault caused his problems: he claimed that his difficulties were due to those who had 'deceived' him, and to his creditors who had seized and sold his goods 'at a poor price', leaving him penniless and without the means to pay all his debts. Jean Revollet, a merchant still trying to keep his head above water and avoid bankruptcy, despite a rising tide of debts, explained his situation in similar terms: he had lost his credit through no fault of his own, and without any debauchery on his part. His honour remained intact.[100] Trouillet and Revollet articulated similar assessments to defend their credit against allegations of debt, although they defended their behaviour in different contexts: Trouillet in a court case, and Revollet in family letters.

[99] James Q. Whitman, 'The moral menace of Roman law and the making of commerce: some Dutch evidence', *Yale Law Journal* (May 1996), 1871. I thank Jay Westbrook for this reference. Muldrew, *Economy of Obligation.*

[100] AML FF115, 13 June 1619: ADR 8B952, 17 August 1690.

Would-be borrowers and lenders relied on an economy of information, as made clear by the assumptions, articulated in the languages of lending, which shaped decisions about to whom lenders would extend credit. Access to micro-credit depended in significant measure on participation in neighborhood networks in which lenders were sufficiently familiar with potential borrowers to assess the publicity, intention, and effort with which they met the financial challenges that all households faced. In making these measures, gender seems to have been a relatively minor distinction.[101]

Familiarity was a key attribute. For example, Genevieve Maignard, the wife of a stockingmaker, refused to lend money to an apprentice who offered her two diamonds as surety, because 'she did not know who they belonged to'. She later lent the money to his employer François Boursillon, a music teacher, when Boursillon visited her to say that the diamonds were his property. Jan Bonnier asked a widow who earned her living as a secondhand seller to buy some linen because he needed to raise money to pay his rent. She 'had some difficulty in buying from him because she did not know him', so she asked around, and acquaintances told her that he was a petty trader and that 'she could buy securely from him'.[102]

Familiarity was important because it led to certainty despite the informal nature of most micro-credit, not necessarily about repayment but about legality. The daughter of an innkeeper refused to lend Boursillion money on the basis of jewellery offered, 'because he should not be engaging his wife's jewellery' (part of her personal property). A reseller who took clothes from Pierre Carcanac, to sell on consignment, discovered they were 'contraband' (and therefore handed them in to the *greffe* and informed the silk-workers' guild), and subsequently refused to sell anything else for Carcanac.[103]

The differential neighbourhood assessments of Leguy and Prevost are instructive in illuminating how an economy of information allowed neighbours to assess the couple's creditworthiness. Neighbours saw Prevost as a lazy, quarrelsome drunkard, and he was therefore a bad credit risk. Leguy, in contrast, was viewed favourably as a borrower. She worked hard, practised her trade skilfully, and repaid loans regularly if not quickly, even if she borrowed from Peter to pay Paul. Moreover, to maintain independent access to loan, Leguy assiduously cultivated her own credit by her openness about the difficulties her household had with creditors, and her very visible efforts to make ends meet. She publicly demonstrated creditworthiness and successfully earned borrowing privileges, while Prevost publicly displayed indications that he might be a bad debtor, and spoilt his credit. For neighbours, the existence of many loans, and even trouble

[101] In these ways, what historians have often called 'reputation' as a key determiner of access to credit, had very specific components.

[102] ADLA B5853, 29 November 1719; ADLA B5851, 6 April 1713.

[103] ADLA B5853, 29 November 1719; ADR 8B729-5, 17 October 1703.

with creditors in a community where debt was ubiquitous, was not an indicator of bad credit. The behaviour of the spouses in managing the economies of markets was critical. Leguy's labour and transparency secured her ongoing access to loans, while Provost's slothfulness undermined his credibility. The spouses' experiences suggest not only that credit was contingent rather than something neighbourly expectations would automatically deliver, but that credit was in practice a spousal as much as a household matter, whatever the legal disability of married women in this regard.

The assumptions about good borrowers and bad debtors were also embedded in expectations about repayment. While some loans were no doubt initiated as, or converted into, gifts or charity, in the main eventually both parties had to be willing to close the circle, although creditors who sought to collect, as well as borrowers who faced repayment, were expected to observe customary courtesies. While lenders' expectations about repayment were certainly more amorphous than modern credit terms allow, the ubiquity of debt did not mean that repayment was optional.[104] Certainly the issue of the timing of repayments could be contentious, but the fact that repayment was usually expected seems clear. Debtors as well as creditors accepted that even the most informal loans were ultimately liable to be repaid. Perrine Meneurier, a widow, for example, said that 'in his job as a mover' her husband was 'very often in a position of lending money and borrowing it', and that 'since his death many people had brought money to her that they owed to her husband without her knowledge'.[105] Borrowers and lenders could distinguish between discretionary repayments and the discretion to repay.

Conventions about lender patience and borrower commitment to regular, if partial, payments framed expectations about honourable repayment practices. Borrowers and lenders employed a rhetoric of patience to frame appropriate relations between creditors and debtors, as letters between parties clearly indicate. Borrowers urged lenders to give them time to pay, and lenders urged borrowers to pay because they had been given ample time. As Escalle Lainée wrote to a pursemaker who owed her more than 200 *livres*, 'You see that I have been very patient waiting for you and given the time that I have asked for it, it is only fair that you must pay me.'[106] The dyer Claude Hacte wrote to a debtor in 1693. He said he wanted to 'refresh your memory' and invoke 'your conscience about what you have owed for so long'. Hacte's brother, another of his long-time debtors, reiterated similar themes: 'I could never accuse you of surprise' in demanding repayment, the brother wrote, 'because I have been in your debt for so long'. He sought to stabilize his position as a good borrower by explaining that his failure to respond was not based on any intent to deny what he owed, but because of his

[104] Hoffman argues that the expectation of repayment of loans was also clear in rural economies; see Hoffman, *Growth in Traditional Society*, 74.

[105] ADLA B6170 (no date).

[106] ADR 8B1109, 12 February 1765.

'embarrassment' that he was unable to pay what he owed.[107] A good borrower willingly acknowledged and reacknowledged what was owed, even if repayment was delayed, and a worthy lender accepted the realities of slow repayment.

Creditors and debtors identified observation of the customary conventions about repayment as matters of honour, and their neglect as dishonour or evidence of evil intent. Claude Hacte became frustrated with a debtor whose failure to respond to letters he took as a sign of ill intent: 'I would never have believed' that 'a man of honour like you' could deny accountability in this way. Debtors sometimes saw creditors who used legal means to press them as motivated by factors other than financial. Antoine Trouillot argued that his creditors brought 'slanderous lawsuits' designed 'to ruin his honourable reputation', and that because of the costs of these malicious court actions he could not pay all he owed. Françoise Gayot said that the 'rigour' of a creditor who obtained a court order, to cover a debt she acknowledged that she and her husband owed, was motivated by his desire to 'ruin' her. Christophe DelaRome blamed the 'precipitous' demands of his creditors for his difficulties, rather than his own actions.[108]

Community judgement also mediated relations between creditor and debtor. For instance, Jan Gaudien, a butcher, complained that when Jan Lesperier, a porter, failed to repay him for five loans for very considerable amounts, which he had promised to pay 'a very long time ago', he had secured a court order to have a sergeant make a seizure of Lesperier's property. But when the sergeant arrived, 'several' neighbours assaulted him and prevented him from doing so. The creditors of Pierre Chesneau explained to the court that after he alarmed his relatives by leaving town he asked them for three months' grace to allow him time to come to terms with them. Instead, after they agreed, he made no effort to settle with them and had instead used the time to abscond with his property. If the neighbours and kin of these debtors thought customary practice required more patience for repayment, Chesneau's creditors carefully noted, as had Gaudien, their own observance of the customary conventions about patience when they claimed that Chesneau had left 'without being pursued or harassed by any of them'.[109]

Either party failed, on occasion, to observe customary conventions for a number of reasons. Sometimes, debtors simply could not repay. As in all kinds of litigation, the court system could be used to settle other grievances, and certainly disputes between the households that went unstated in the court records may have played a role in creditor decisions to litigate.[110] Creditors may have pressed new emphases on narrowly contractual relations, or decided that they had observed

[107] ADR 8B952, letters dated (no day) August 1693 and 4 May 1701.

[108] ADR 8B952, (no day) August 1693; AML FF115, 12 June 1619; ADR 8B1249-1, 13 September 1694; ADR BP3985, 17 June 1673.

[109] ADLA B6671, 30 April 1669; ADLA B6668, 19 March 1656.

[110] A recent study of court actions in late medieval Marseille, for example, has argued that plaintiffs and defendants used court actions as a marketplace for 'emotional transactions'. See

the customary patience honourably and that it was time for debtors to honour their responsibility to pay. This moment was subject to constant negotiation, and could be fraught. Pierre Jousseaux asked his neighbour, Jacques Challans, a tailor, to repay money he had lent him. Challans said he did not have the money, and Jousseaux observed that 'it was some time since he had promised to pay him.' Challans accused him of being a crook, and attacked him so that he fell to the floor, 'saying he would give him the money when it seemed good to him'.[111]

Despite the potential for disagreement over the terms of repayment, the goal of repayment was a central feature of the culture of borrowing in this milieu. Uncollectable debts were certainly facts of a trading life, and tradesmen who ceased trading often listed 'bad debts' as worth as much as 40 per cent of their ledgers. Shopkeepers and traders of all kinds, from petty pedlars to high-end purveyors to elites, could not stay in business without extending credit. Early modern selling was a very competitive business, and urban economies were still relatively cash-starved, making credit a key way to attract new customers and to retain existing customers.[112] With this imperative, many traders seem to have been willing to extend credit to customers who paid in part in cash as well as running tabs, and who paid their tabs regularly, even if not completely. Many customers realized (as we have seen) that on the whole, small payments encouraged shopkeepers to maintain their credit line. Catherine Cornet and Pierre Carcanac, for instance, bought various food supplies from a local market stall holder, including some fish, some artichokes, some eggs, some cherries, some cheese and some *fromage blanc* for just over 9 *livres*, of which they paid a little more than 7 *livres*, leaving just under 2 *livres* on credit. Many of their other food receipts showed a similar pattern.[113] Rather like paying the minimum rather than the full balance on a credit card bill, many accounts show that borrowers sometimes paid something towards their overall debt every now and then, and the prospects for the full amounts ever being cleared are difficult to estimate.

In the same way, creditors who dealt with families whose businesses had failed often accepted repayment schedules that would recover only about 50 per cent of what they were owed. In both cases, creditors faced difficult choices; that is, to accept partial repayment as a cost of business, or to lose customers or debts completely. As one failed pursemaker bluntly pointed out to her creditors, if they did not accept a repayment schedule which would allow her to restart her trade, they could not hope to be repaid any of what they were owed.[114]

Daniel Lord Smail, *The Consumption of Justice: Emotion, Publicity, and Legal Culture in Marseille, 1284–1463* (Ithaca, NY, 2003).

111 ADLA B6671, 11 January 1667.

112 For the use of credit as essential across the range of selling environments, from pedlars to bakers to couture in the eighteenth century, see Fontaine, *History of Pedlars*; Kaplan, *Bakers of Paris*; Crowston, 'The Queen and Her "Minister of Fashion"'.

113 ADR 8B729-4, receipts all unsigned and undated.

114 ADR 8B1109, 10 August 1762.

Lenders' expectations about repayment were reflected in the variety of strategies which they used to to try to ensure that they could recoup their money, long before they reached the stage of litigating over debt. Creditors required many kinds of obligations from *rentes* to loans made without any record for a handful of *livres* to be secured with guarantees of various kinds, either personal or property. Even the most apparently spontaneous and charitable lending was often underpinned with efforts to guarantee personal security. Marguerite Chiron, for instance, lent money to the widow Roze Chartier, her neighbour, so that Chartier could buy her own personal clothing during a creditor-initiated sale. Altruism might seem to have guided her actions. Yet subsequently, Chiron took 'a big part' of Chartier's clothing to her house, apparently as security for the money being reimbursed. The sequence was repeated 'several other times'.[115] Chiron was, in fact, careful to protect her own financial position while participating in the effort to keep Chartier's household afloat.

The moment at which creditors might choose to switch to legal means to secure repayment was infinitely variable, and was probably motivated by many factors. Whether creditors ceased to be patient because they wanted immediate repayment, because they felt that they had waited appropriately patiently, or because they were settling some other score, the turn to use legal means to collect what they were owed marked a pivotal shift in relations, and one which rising rates of debt litigation suggest creditors moved to with increasing frequency over the early modern period.[116]

The perceived threats that dubious debt practices posed to civil society were sometimes articulated in heated rhetoric in bankruptcy and separate property cases. A royal prosecutor recommended that the merchant Antoine Trouillet, found guilty of bankruptcy, be executed so that the 'gangrene' could be cut out, and asserted that no other remedy would 'purge the body and the state . . . and dissolve the bilious humours that trouble the harmony of commerce on which the civil society of men rests'. Only execution, the prosecutor said, would allow 'the flow and exercise of commerce', and remove 'the malignancy of a fever that quickly brings losses'. Pierre Marin, a creditor of Françoise Gayot and Jean Richard, opposed the granting of separate property to Gayot, and said that if Gayot's effort to obtain separate property on the basis of 'very modest sum', for which he sought repayment, was successful, 'we will see legitimate creditors facing the loss of what they are owed every day'.[117]

The criminalization of bankruptcy throughout early modern Europe, from the early sixteenth century, provided some of the clearest indications of rising anxiety about the potentially disruptive effects of debt. This legislation was rooted in a

115 ADLA B5594, 4 November 1709.

116 Historians of early modern England have debated whether increased litigation generally, and debt litigation in particular, was correlated to an overall increase in economic activity, or to increasing willingness to use the courts. For this debate, see Muldrew, *Economy of Obligation*.

117 AML FF115, 13 June 1619; ADR 8B1249-1, 13 September 1694.

widespread perception that 'the declaration of bankruptcy was the single most scandalous phenomenon of commercial society'.[118] The pan-European rhetoric of bankruptcy emphasized intentional fraud with damage to creditors, and called for punishments that publicly shamed those found guilty, whether of the crime of bankruptcy, or of inability to pay creditors, rooted in honest failure.[119]

Certainly, people found guilty of bankruptcy as a criminal offence in French cities could face severe punishments. The Lyon *cour de conservation*, for example, investigated whether debtors should be charged with criminal bankruptcy, or whether their difficulties should be classified as simple 'failures' which allowed them to settle with the creditors and carry on with commercial affairs. The court could severely shame and punish those whom it designated as bankrupts. In 1619, for example, the royal prosecutor recommended that the merchant, Antoine Trouillot, first be tortured to reveal where his assets might be, and then, carrying a sign with the words 'FRAUDULENT BANKRUPT', proceed to Lyon's main square, where he was to be hanged and strangled, after which his body would be left in place for twenty-four hours. The four men found guilty of abetting him were to accompany him to the execution, also wearing signs—in their case declaring themselves to be 'BANKRUPT'S ACCOMPLICE', and then to pay fines before being banished from the city. Sentences for bankruptcy were less draconian in other cases, but the shaming theme, common in prescription across much of Europe, remained as an element of bankruptcy sentences.[120]

However, despite these occasional severities, judges who assessed reasons for trading failures were usually reluctant to recognize the fraud that would allow the full rigour of penalties or creditors' claims to play out, and so punishments such as that meted out to Trouillot seem to have been highly unusual. Just as local judges and prosecutors gave little credence to creditors' occasional claims of spousal collusion or to expression of creditor opposition in separation suits, they were extremely reluctant to find the intent to defraud in creditors' behaviour that was the essence of bankruptcy. Findings of simple failure dominated the courts'

[118] Whitman, 'The Moral Menace', 1871.

[119] On the development of a legal distinction between intent to defraud and unavoidable insolvency, see Whitman, 'Moral Menace', 1875–6. There has been very little empirical work on early modern bankruptcy, and it concentrates almost exclusively on the bankruptcies of wealthy merchants in terms of business history. See Thomas Max Safley, 'Bankruptcy: family and finance in early modern Augsburg', *Journal of European Economic History*, **29**, 1 (200), 53–75, and Kaplan, *Bakers of Paris*, 380–404.

[120] AML FF115, 12 June 1619. A female accomplice of Trouillot was found guilty too, but was sentenced differently. The court noted that as her husband was not guilty, and banishment for her 'would be a penalty that would cause a kind of divorce in their marriage', she was sentenced to pay a fine three times larger than her male peers, and to stay in prison until it was paid, though she was permitted to remain a resident of Lyon. The shaming element seems more persistent than the execution when debt failures were categorized as felonious bankruptcies. In 1654, for instance, a royal prosecutor recommended that Antoine Martigny be sentenced to process, declaring his intent to commit fraud and to ask God, the King, and justice for pardon for his actions, but was not, apparently, sentenced to execution. AML FF208, 1654 (no date or month).

records. Moreover, there is no evidence that adjudications of simple failure were accompanied by shaming rituals of any kind. Indeed, as Pierre Carcanac's riposte to his critics indicates, simple failure does not seem to have been shameful. Such failures must have been common, and difficulty with debts was absolutely mundane.

Judges' willingness to grant separate property and their reluctance to find behaviour that justified bankruptcy were linked in judicial practice by the disinclination to identify actions as fraudulent. Separate property could not be granted if spouses colluded to defraud creditors, and bankruptcy required evidence of intent to defraud creditors. When judges allowed separate property, and adjudicated failure over bankruptcy, they limited the ability of creditors to collect what they were owed in favour of protecting households.[121] Local management of disequilibrium between debtors and creditors in Nantes and Lyon suggests,whether from the perspective of courts or of lenders and borrowers, that everyday practice in neighborhoods and courts took a nuanced attitude that was rooted in the reality of pervasive and elaborate debt networks.

Moreover, for creditors who opposed separate property requests, or were owed money by borrowers being assessed for bankruptcy or failure, the legal process played an important role besides judicial remedy in this political economy of daily life as it did others, especially with regard to the mobilization of publicity and the maintenance of a reliable economy of information. Litigation communities functioned to discuss, dispute, and resolve neighbourhood values about appropriate and inappropriate borrowing practice, as in domestic violence or many other matters. Wives or creditors could rely on going to court to publicize their grievances and offer a reprimand to unsatisfactory borrowers. Their efforts were defensive in the sense of protecting their rights, but offensive in terms of public assault on the reputations of their antagonists. In all court proceedings involving debt, publicity was, in fact, a key, whether to discipline debtors and husbands or to protect creditors and wives. Creditors who initiated legal proceedings immediately publicized their debtors' financial precariousness, not only to the court, but to neighbours, friends, and commercial contacts who watched as bailiffs arrived to serve notice of the order to seize assets, and who saw the subsequent sales if the proceedings continued. Wives who went to court exposed their difficulties when they told their own stories, and summoned witnesses to corroborate their accounts. Publicity characterized the penalties for bankruptcy and separations. News of separations was announced by court sergeants in market squares and outside Sunday masses. People who were found guilty of bankruptcy were sentenced (as we have seen) to punishments in which

[121] We know very little in detail about debt actions across France. However, this pattern of protecting debtors (and their households) over creditors may have been true of other kinds of debt actions in courts across France. See, for instance, the discussion of the Parisian consular court's uneven enforcement of creditors' rights in the eighteenth century, in Kessler, 'Enforcing virtue'.

public shaming rituals were integral. Even people assessed as failures found their difficulties widely known, with their trading suspended by the court until they came to terms with creditors in public meetings.

To be called a bankrupt was a serious insult in communities where neighbourhood regulation of the distinction between good credit and bad debt depended on an economy of information built on familiarity and transparency. Pierre Carcanac's willingness to take his critics to court over their name-calling indicates the vulnerability of men whose wives had litigated to secure separate property, in terms of association with serious wrongdoing. Legally they were not bankrupts, as bankruptcy implied fraud and was thus a felony, but culturally their wives' success in securing separate property did mean that they publicly lost the legal monopoly over property management that was a key privilege of married manhood, and reinforced the public associations of incompetence and wrongdoing that were closely associated with bankrupts too. When Carcanac sought to defend his name against these implications with his assertion that Cornet took over the café with his permission, he sought to reiterate not only his own honour and reputation, but demonstrated that he too recognized the links between credit, law, and gender which enmeshed property and status.

Yet the languages and practices of lending indicate how women, as well as men, cultivated credit and were burdened with debt. As we saw in Chapter 3, communities were, in fact, concerned about married men's sexual reputation as well as women's, and were also concerned about female financial capacity as well as male. Just as men occasionally complained to the courts about being insulted as bankrupts, women also found such slurs damaging. For example, in 1664, Catherine Philipeau, the wife of a linen merchant, complained that a stockingmaker who came into their shop insulted her by saying 'she had been a bankrupt', along with 'other wounds to her honour', whereas in fact she claimed she was always 'a good trader' and 'lived honourably without any reproach'.[122] As with Perrine Leguy, occasional articulations of positive assessments of female capacity for borrowing also survive. For example, Jan Vrignaud, a surgeon, noted that when he and René Daguin married, she promised to bring him her 'property, credit, and goods', and to give him disposition over her 'credit' and property.[123] Even the use of a sexual slur might imply financial disorder rather than a specific challenge to chastity.[124] During the same hostile dispute in which Carcanac's critics called him a bankrupt, they called Cornet 'a bitch and a whore' in connection with her running their bar while having separate property. Carcanac's rebuttal suggests that he read their attack as a matter of economic

[122] ADLA B6670, 15 November 1664. For complaints to courts that insults of bankrupt damaged 'honour and good reputation', see, for example, ADLA B6668, 27 April 1657, and ADLA B6671, 2 April 1668.

[123] ADLA B6671, 11 April 1668.

[124] For this broader use of sexual slurs to reference financial disorders in early modern England, in what Laura Gowing calls an 'economy of whoredom', see Gowing, *Domestic Dangers*, 90–4.

rather than sexual honour, as he defended her reputation on the basis that she started to sell drinks to support their family rather than articulate a defence of her sexual virtue.

The languages of lending suggest that a culture of social responsibility emerged in which older habits of Christian charity and neighbourliness, embodied in practices of mutual obligation and gifting, fused often uneasily, and always uncertainly, with newer realities, especially the financial pressure of an evolving economy, and the rising willingness to see the state through the court system as a possible resource for disputes between borrowers and lenders. Repayment was not discretionary, although the timing of repayments was a focus of tensions between customary practices that had given debtors' considerable discretion and emerging imperatives towards full timely repayment. For Leguy and Provost's neighbours, their own interests, as well as the transparency or lack thereof with which Leguy and Provost managed their affairs, and the distinction between his flaws and her good intentions, all shaped access to the market for money as a critical element of the economies of markets whose management required much effort from all households.

CONSTELLATIONS OF CREDIT, BLACK HOLES OF DEBT

Pierre Carcanac and Catherine Cornet juggled debts and creditor pressure in and out of court for years, but when Carcanac felt that an allegation that he was a 'bankrupt' impugned his honour, he expected, or at least hoped, to redeem his reputation in court, even though his trade had been classified as a legal failure and his wife had secured separate property. His response picked apart the distinctions that contextualized the facts of debts, even unpaid debts, in many different ways. Did his adversaries mean he was legally a bankrupt, or did they deploy a perhaps increasingly common usage that applied the term to describe all debtors? Carcanac, at least, was still deeply sensitive to the pejorative implications of the term, and keen to mark his debt difficulties as 'only' those of failure and loss of control over marital property. Perhaps Carcanac's disgruntled customers used the term 'bankrupt' because they believed he defrauded them of their rightful winnings in gambling games. The imperatives of the economies of markets in working communities required Cornet as well as Carcanac to work proactively to create, manage, and resolve their borrowing, without which their household, like the households of all working families, could not survive.

Borrowing was at the heart of early modern political economies of daily life, freighted with cultural and political as well as economic meanings, and of the family business in which households, neighbourhoods and the state were invested. The creation, management, and resolution of borrowing were at the intersections between property and gender, between domestic and market economies, and between litigation and liquidity. While working households have long relied on loans, notable continuities over long periods are evident in the makeshift approach of such families, and the social embeddedness of credit relations is now accepted. Men and women in early modern urban households mobilized contextually specific practices that not only responded to the economy, but shaped the way the larger economy developed.

We know an enormous amount about household production and consumption in the early modern economy, but the centrality and complexity of borrowing as a crucial household and indispensable commercial instrument compels us to take the processes of credit extension and debt collection just as seriously. Management of debt was a fundamental charge of early modern household life. As men and women juggled loans, their borrowing integrated specie and personal property, as well as legalized contractual debts and informally arranged obligations. Working families' debt practices involved an exchange matrix rather than a kind of formal contractual economy beneath which an informal neighbourhood black market functioned or a male economy versus a female economy.

Seventeenth-century families used borrowing in various ways, sometimes to lever their participation in the expanding economic opportunities that the intensification of market practices offered (for example, by purchasing supplies to make goods that were newly in fashion) and at other times defensively to secure the survival of their households, often against the buffeting and uncertainty increased by the same intensification of market practices. No doubt the same household at different moments might entrepreneurially borrow money to take advantage of new practices and potential profits, or to purchase the emerging range of consumer goods, and defensively borrow money to ward off bailiffs or secure necessities. Similarly, the same lender might take one borrower to court while leaving another to pay over an extended and indeterminate time-frame when he or she could, and borrowers likewise might move between contractual and customary practices. Then as now, market economies offered pitfalls as well as opportunities, and borrowing was dictated, as it is still, by a variety of factors, whether familiarity, kinship, social responsibility or desire for profit, and provided on a wide variety of terms.[125] The uncertainty and risks of a changing economy are clear, however, as is the ubiquity of borrowing as an inescapable

[125] For a thoughtful assessment of recent historiographical positions about the relationship of borrowing to market change—that is, was it a sign of exploitation and desperation or of rational investment in an expanding economy?—see Brennan, 'Peasants and debt in eighteenth-century Champagne', 175–9 and 196–200. Analysing the impact of peasant debt, Brennan notes the need for seeing that the involvement in, and impact of, borrowing varied. Although he argues that wealthier peasants were more involved in rational taking on of debt for investment, whereas the poorer used debt to manage poverty, the distinctions were not always aligned in predictable ways with the opportunity or exploitation elements of economic shifts. See Hoffman's argument that peasants used borrowing more entrepreneurially than elite landlords. Hoffman, *Growth in a Traditional Society*.

and essential instrument of daily life. The fine line between the opportunities offered by the constellation of credit and the dangers posed by black holes of debt was one that all working households had to navigate.

The borrowing that was critical to household economies of markets indicates how political economies of gender shaped personal and commercial financial patterns. Women and men both used multiple aspects of this exchange complex, but the different positioning of men and women in many aspects of debt practices meant that gender coloured these familial economies in kaleidoscopic ways. When men ceased trading and summarized their affairs, they listed bad debts which they expected not to be able to collect, along with more promising ones. But their first entries were their wives' dowries, while their last were assessments of their households' yearly expenses. Women—married, single, or widowed—as well as men were at the centre of the creation, management, and resolution of debts, even if studies of debt litigation specifically seem to indicate that women were much less active. In all these ways, women as well as men were at the centre of the means by which debts were unravelled, often unexpectedly and unpredictably, as well as created. They received court orders that allowed creditors to begin the steps leading to sales, they watched sales of their goods, they helped neighbours whose goods were being sold, they bought distrained goods to sell on their own behalf, and they managed the legal challenges that arose.

Men and women faced different consequences as the requirements of the market-place and the imperatives of gender converged. To be successful heads of household (as opposed to being guilty of bad householding) meant to manage the overlaid challenges of domestic and market economies successfully. Husbands who fell between the cracks of the requisite calculations found that lawsuits could remove their control over household property. They were almost literally unmanned when they lost one of the defining privileges of adult men in early modern society. Wives with separate property might find themselves with very little property, but they were publicly and rhetorically repositioned, not only as the legal managers of their property, but as the first creditors of their households, and as the designated providers for their family.

In the process of creating, resolving, and managing debts, men and women, creditors and debtors, and judges and plaintiffs refined and redefined their relationships to each other, to their households, to the economy, and to the state. Borrowing practices demonstrated that gender, and concepts of lineage property, as well as commercial forces, complicated relationships between spouses, between debtor and creditor, and between household and state authority. Debtors and creditors, enmeshed in a lived experience of the economic vagaries of the seventeenth century, defined lending in terms of a complex culture of social responsibility. Individuals and families were enmeshed with economies of markets, whether as borrowers or lenders. For lenders, considered loans to hard-working transparent neighbours were a form of social investment that was essential to the maintenance of both parties' financial stability. Lenders recognized the integral relationship between their own security and that of their debtors. If other households failed, they would not have customers, tenants or people to borrow from when they needed to. They would have fewer households among whom to divide the parish-allocated taxes. The failure of one household could, and did, ripple dislocation into other households, and so lenders protected their own security by considered investment in neighbours' households. Their discussions about borrowing, however, were not framed in terms of mutuality or gifting or Christian morality, but focused resolutely on the secular and the self as the nodes of reputation. As in the case of the secular discussions of marriage, the legal imperatives of court cases were in part responsible for this emphasis on secular repayment over the motives of charity or morality or gifting which may have shaped some borrowing. Nevertheless, the huge volume of debt cases and the community discussions around them made this discourse an important alternative to other ways of talking about, and thinking about, how the economy could and should work. In the economies of markets, self-protection and security were integral elements of a culture of social responsibility that framed expectations about repayment and assessments of lending risks.

The dialogues of litigation communities about the economies of the market demonstrated that local judicial practice, as well as neighbourhood judgement, recognized the reality that women as well as men undertook the critical task of borrowing to keep families' needs, and that household stability was of paramount concern. Relations between creditors and debtors were fluid and in transition. As is often the case, the new national legislation, which sought to enhance the operations of the market through protection for creditors, indicates more about the difficulty creditors could have in making claims than about their triumph. Women's ability to seek separate property to protect lineage property trumped the 'legitimate' claims of creditors. Ironically, because the law interpreted debt as a man's affair, indebtedness could provide the basis for married women to secure separate property. Customary practices that allowed payment in kind or in part, and the emerging insistences on payment in full and in cash, were mediated by the persistence of the legal category of lineage property, as well as by the emergence of new market forms. In thousands of repetitions of separate property suits, household preservation based on claims to lineage property trumped market relations in the form of the legitimate claims of creditors. The interests of households over creditors were similarly preserved in the preference for judgements of failures over bankruptcy. Among the many factors that shaped the development of capitalism in early modern France (a much debated historiographical subject), the ways in which families held property, and in which courts valued property of particular kinds, were critical.

The family business, in which the risks of marital status, of going to law, and of borrowing were calculated and negotiated, in and out of court as part of the political economies of daily life, was also enmeshed in economies of violence. Household liquidity was so fragile that it could be worth fighting over. Working people constantly calculated a fine line between success and failure: at work, about how much to buy, and when, and for how much; at home, in their decisions about how to borrow money, when to borrow it and from whom, and who to lend it to; and at play, in rounds of drinking and gambling. Spouses found the margins between security, peril, and catastrophe to be narrow, and easily eroded by longstanding features of early modern life, whether misfortune or the complexities of navigating essential debts. For spouses, neighbours, and courts, the use of force was a resource that, like borrowing, was ubiquitous but could be coded as appropriate or abusive.

5

Economies of Violence: Battery, Neighbourhood Values, and Legal Remedies

Family battery took many forms in early modern society. Evidence of every variety of domestic violence survives, at least in traces, in the archives. A husband called his wife 'atrocious and scandalous names' while he kicked and punched her all over her body until blood ran. A wife slapped, kicked, and scratched her husband, locked him out, and poured a urine-filled chamber pot over him. Surgeons visited a beaten toddler with multiple bruises, open wounds, and mangled limbs. A man beat his mother-in-law. A son abused his siblings, threatened his father, and even hired men to beat him up.[1]

This chapter explores economies of family violence to examine how and why individuals and communities defined the use of force between family members. Despite clichés about the early modern period's acceptance of wife-beating, attitudes towards domestic violence were complex. Certainly, men's aggression towards their wives was naturalized to a degree, and women's violence against their husbands demonized.[2] But in practice, women as well as men, in households, communities and courts, negotiated parameters that defined appropriate and inappropriate use of force in families. What issues defined behaviour as abusive rather than 'corrective'? What catalysts triggered wife-beating? What resources were available to battered wives? How did the experiences of working families differ from those of elite families? How did husbands' and children's experiences of battery compare with those of wives?

Early modern domestic violence raises critical questions about two broader historiographical debates. First, the dense literature that now exists on many aspects of gender and family has explored how law, religion, economics, and social rank, as well as demographic structures, influenced household relations in the early modern period. The intersections between religious, legal, and cultural

[1] ADLA B6670, (no day or month) 1666; ADLA B5843, 19 July 1691 and 31 July 1691; ADR 4506, 27 May 1633; ADLA B5819, 15 December 1663; ADR BP2845, 17 March 1661.

[2] Frances Dolan, *Dangerous Familiars: Representations of Domestic Crime in England, 1550–1700* (Ithaca, NY, 1994); Joy Wiltenburg, *Disorderly Women and Female Power in the Street Literature of Early Modern England and Germany* (Charlottesville, VA, 1992).

prescription, and daily life, have been important foci.[3] Yet although household battery was a fundamental feature of gender and family life, it has received relatively little attention, especially for continental Europe in the period before 1750. We know almost nothing at all about forms of family violence besides wife-beating, whether in terms of the use of force by family members besides husbands, or on family members besides wives.[4] Historians of childhood have considered abuse in the context of education and foundling institutions, but paid very little attention to the use of force within the family.[5]

A comparison of regional studies of husbands' violence against their wives, usually based on very few cases, offers only a fragmentary picture with a mixed, if suggestive, bag of indicators. Even on basic issues such as what kinds of help battered wives could seek or expect, patterns are unclear: were church courts more sympathetic than secular courts, or did secular jurisdiction offer new and positive recourses through application of longstanding guild practices or innovations such as local police?[6] The extent to which battered wives could rely on help from

[3] Two useful syntheses of this now vast literature that include valuable bibliographies are Merry Wiesner, *Women and Gender in Early Modern Europe* (second edn., Cambridge, 2000), and Olwen Hufton, *The Prospect Before Her: A History of Women in Western Europe, 1500–1800* (New York, 1996).

[4] An almost singular exception is a study of police complaints about family violence in eighteenth-century Paris which shows that wives' complaints against husbands, although by far the single largest category, made up only just under half of the total. See Alan Williams, 'Patterns of conflict in eighteenth-century Parisian families', *Journal of Family History*, **18**, 1 (1993), 39–52.

[5] Here and throughout this chapter, my thinking on the question of the use of force on children owes much to the generous suggestions and expertise of Prof Christopher Corley, for which I am very grateful. Historians of early modern childhood have addressed abuse almost exclusively in the context of education or child abandonment (with the subsequent experiences of children in hospitals and orphanages), rather than in families and households. Prescriptive literature dominates the source base for assessments of this kind. These perspectives are shared by the founding works in family history and by recent synthetic interpretations. See, for example, Phillipe Ariès, *Centuries of Childhood: A Social History of Family Life* (New York, 1962); David Hunt, *Parents and Children in History: The Psychology of Family Life in Early Modern France* (New York, 1970); and Lloyd Demause, *History of Childhood* (New York, 1974). For recent work, see, for instance, Hugh Cunningham, *Children and Childhood in Western Civilization since 1500* (New York, 1995); and Colin Heywood, *A History of Childhood* (Malden, MA, 2001). I leave aside here the sexual abuse of children, which has received little attention, and the various forms of non-familial violence that may also have occurred in households. Many servants had coercive sexual relations with men in the families for whom they worked, but while these illicit pregnancies had to be publicly declared in theory, the men involved did not seem to suffer any real penalty. Servants were subject to the discipline of heads of household, as wives and children were, but prosecutions for abuse of servants did not appear in court records before the middle of the eighteenth century. For servants, see Laura Gowing, 'The haunting of Susan Lay: servants and mistresses in seventeenth-century England', *Gender and History*, **14**, 2 (2002). For sexual abuse of children, see Ulrinka Rublack, *The Crimes of Women in Early Modern Germany* (Oxford, 1999), 231–54, and Martin Ingram, 'Child sexual abuse in early modern England', in Michael J. Braddick and John Walker (eds.), *Negotiating Power in Early Modern Society: Order, Hierarchy, and Subordination in Britain and Ireland* (Cambridge, 2000).

[6] For brief synthetic overviews, see Roderick Phillips, *Putting Asunder: A History of Divorce in Western Society* (Cambridge, 1988), esp. 323–44 (dominated by Anglo-America), and Julius Ruff, *Violence in Early Modern Europe* (Cambridge, 2001), 131–40. On the issue of church court versus secular jurisdiction, the success of women in Cambrai and Venice seems in stark contrast to the very

extra-legal sources remains uncertain. While historians concur that domestic violence was widespread, one prominent synthesis argues that wives could expect little help from neighbours, church, or state, and another study has concluded that by the 1790s battered wives could expect female but not male neighbours to provide help.[7] Historians of early modern Britain have identified several possible approaches to domestic battery, as they have located it as part of a broader culture of violence or of contests over household economy and domestic power.[8] The historicization of domestic violence illuminates key issues across time and space, and, for example, allows us to interrogate the often cited but underexamined link between alcohol use and domestic violence.[9]

Second, battery within the family took place not only in the context of household dynamics, but within a broader and evolving context in which attitudes towards violence, a popular culture of peacekeeping, and senses of 'public' and 'personal' were enmeshed. A rich literature has explored how states

low rates of success in secular courts in Rouen. (I note that this low success rate in French secular courts is misleading, because women used separate property requests, as well as suits for separation of person and property, as remedies for domestic violence.) However, a German study suggests that in reformed Protestant cities in the sixteenth century, municipal courts built on medieval guild tradition to discipline abusive husbands, while a Parisian study suggests that the emergence of local police in the eighteenth century provided embattled wives with a new valuable recourse. See Alain Lottin, 'Vie et mort du couple: difficultés conjugales et divorces dans le nord de la France aux XVIIe et XVIIIe siécles', *XVIIe Siècle Revue*, **102–103** (1974), 59–78; Roderick Phillips, *Family Breakdown in Late Eighteenth-Century France: Divorces in Rouen, 1792–1803* (Oxford, 1980), 108–24 and 185; Joanne M. Ferraro, 'The power to decide: battered wives in early modern Venice', *Renaissance Quarterly*, **48**, 3 (1995), 492–512; Lyndal Roper, *The Holy Household: Women and Morals in Reformation Augsburg* (London, 1989), 185–94; Williams, 'Patterns of Conflict in Eighteenth-Century Parisian Families'.

7 Ruff, *Violence in Early Modern Europe*, 131–40; and Phillips, *Family Breakdown*, 185.

8 See Susan Amussen, 'Punishment, discipline, and power: the social meanings of violence in early modern England', *Journal of British Studies*, **34**, 1 (1995), 1–34, and '"Being Stirred to Much Unquietness": violence and domestic violence in early modern England', *Journal of Women's History*, **6**, 2 (1994), 70–89; Laura Gowing, *Domestic Dangers: Women, Words, and Sex in Early Modern London* (Oxford, 1996), 206–29; Margaret Hunt, 'Wife beating, domesticity, and women's independence in eighteenth-century London', *Gender and History*, **4**, 1 (1992), 10–33; Leah Leneman, '"A Tyrant and Tormentor": violence against wives in eighteenth- and early nineteenth-century Scotland,' *Continuity and Change*, **12**, 1 (1997), 31–54.

9 Much more work has been carried out for the modern period, primarily for Britain, in terms of the genesis of conflicts and the evolution of responses and resources. See in particular, Anna Clark, *The Struggle for the Breeches: Gender and the Making of the British Working Class* (Berkeley and Los Angeles, 1995), esp. 63–87 and 259–63; Linda Gordon, *Heroes of Their Own Lives: The Politics and History of Family Violence, Boston, 1880–1960* (New York, 1988); Ellen Ross, '"Fierce Questions and Taunts": married life in working-class London, 1870–1914', *Feminist Studies*, **8** (1982), 575–602; Ross, *Love and Toil: Motherhood in Outcast London, 1870–1919* (Oxford, 1993), 84–7; Nancy Tomes, 'A "Torrent of Abuse": crimes of violence between working-class men and women in London, 1840–1875', *Journal of Social History*, **11** (1978), 328–45; Martin J. Wiener, *Men of Blood: Violence, Manliness and Criminal Justice in Victorian England* (Cambridge, 2004). For France, see Eliza Ferguson, 'Reciprocity and retribution: negotiating gender and power in fin-de-siècle Paris', *Journal of Family History*, **30**, 3 (2005), 287–303. Christine Daniels and Michael V. Kennedy (eds.), *Over the Threshold: Intimate Violence in Early America* (New York and London, 1999), includes examinations of a variety of forms of family violence, mostly after 1750.

and communities regulated various kinds of uses of force, whether shouting matches or physical assaults, by a variety of means. Neighbours and family members were important arbitrators of acceptable behaviour, and often observed and intervened. Many historians have argued that the nature of violence, and attitudes towards violence, changed over the early modern centuries, as physical assault may have become less common, perhaps to be replaced by more use of slander, and certainly by more prosecution of property crime.[10] Whether these changes were due to a 'civilizing process', to the disciplining efforts of states and reformed Catholic and Protestant churches, or to campaigns for manners, many forms of violence became increasingly unacceptable, while many aspects of household life became (at least rhetorically) more private. Where and how family violence might fit into these paradigms is, again, elusive, with no consensus even on fundamental questions such as whether it increased or decreased over time.[11]

Early modern domestic violence is interrogated here through discussions of family battery in more than 250 cases. This volume of evidence contrasts with most work on early modern family battery which has usually relied on very few instances. Certainly, these cases frame domestic violence in very particular ways. They foreground spousal battery, which was a matter for judicial remedy, and elide other kinds of household violence in which courts had virtually no interest. Incidents where women were the aggressors, or during which other household members (such as children) were beaten, were revealed rarely or only indirectly. Unquestionably, most victims of family violence did not resort to court, so the lawsuits do not indicate the statistical extent of domestic battery. The abusive behaviour recounted in some cases was certainly extraordinary, even by early modern standards, and went far beyond the casual violence that was so common. Rose Lin, for example, reported that her husband, Jean Aubert, tied her up, often without food, and compelled her to travel with him over hundreds of miles.[12] As in all court records, there may have been rhetorical strategizing and narrative tropes. Some wives who sought separations of property

[10] For an overview of the literature on many forms of violence, see Ruff, *Violence in Early Modern Europe*. Ruff primarily uses the concept of a 'civilizing society' pioneered by Norbert Elias—in which early modern people increasingly came to reject violence—to explain declines in violence. Important interpretations of neighbourhood management of violence include James R. Farr, *Hands of Honor: Artisans and Their World in Dijon, 1550–1650* (Ithaca, NY, 1986), esp. 150–95, and David Garrioch, *Neighbourhood and Community in Paris, 1740–1790* (Cambridge, 1986), esp. 31–55. For perspectives on the emergence of the concept of privacy, see the *History of Private Life* series, esp. the fourth volume, Roger Charter (ed.), *History of Private Life: Passions of the Renaissance* (Cambridge, MA, 1989).

[11] On the lack of consensus, see, for instance, the opposing conclusions of Ruff (*Violence in Early Modern Europe*), who argues that domestic violence declined from the mid-eighteenth century as violence became more unacceptable and victims and neighbours were more willing to complain, and historians such as Clark (*Struggle for the Breeches*) or Ross ('Fierce Questions and Taunts'), who argue for increases in domestic violence accompanied by the increasing reluctance of neighbours or family to intervene.

[12] ADR BP4045, 9 April 1720.

and person may have exaggerated violence to demonstrate that their lives were endangered.[13] In this regard the testimonies of witnesses are vital, as they had fewer motives to exaggerate than did wives, as is evidence from property separation cases in which neither wives nor witnesses had legal standards to meet in their discussions of battery. Yet these qualities shape rather than undermine the compelling and credible evidence of the early modern practice and experience of domestic violence, about which almost no evidence survives in any other form.

Early modern spouses and their neighbours debated the parameters of the use of force in domestic life at home, in the street, and in court, just as they negotiated expectations about marriage and about borrowing, as well as many other matters. The mobilization of an economy of information was critical in the dynamics of domestic violence, and the emphases on transparency and publicity that safeguarded good credit, even in the case of unpaid loans, were as important in assessments of the use of force within families. Decisions about using the judicial system as an individual resource, or as a site for the authorization of neighbourhood opinion, were also key in the management of family violence. If transitions to a market economy involved more use of courts to demarcate appropriate relations between debtors and creditors, emerging concerns about privacy may have caused victims and observers of family violence to be less inclined to seek a judicial remedy.

This chapter interrogates the economies of family violence as time, place, and rank- and gender-specific.[14] Attitudes towards and experiences of the uses of force, as well as material, cultural, and legal familial issues, shaped expressions of family violence, the choices victims made, and neighbourhood responses. These factors shaped how contemporaries assessed use of familial force as appropriate or abusive, and how family members, their communities, and the state dealt with domestic violence. It examines both husbands' abuse of wives and other forms of family violence. Key themes in all forms of family violence included a community discourse about when the use of force was appropriate, a willingness to use publicity or lack thereof, and a judgement by neighbours about when and how intervention might be warranted. Yet while striking similarities existed among all forms of family violence, participants and neighbours responded differently, depending on the identity and status of the victim of battery.

[13] For a rich discussion of how sixteenth-century petitioners, including some women, presented themselves in seeking pardons from death penalty sentences for homicides, see Natalie Zemon Davis, *Fiction in the Archives: Pardon Tales and Their Tellers in Sixteenth-Century France* (Palo Alto, CA, 1987). For narrative tropes in litigation, more broadly, see Gowing, *Domestic Dangers*, esp. 232–62.

[14] In this usage I mean 'economies of violence' to be more strategic and multivalent than the usage given in the book with a similar phrase, Malcolm Greenshields, *An Economy of Violence in Early Modern France* (University Park, PA, 1994).

THE BOUNDARIES OF VIOLENCE: FAMILY DISCIPLINE AND FAMILY BATTERY

Early modern attitudes to violence and gendered authority shaped interpretations of use of force within the family. Individual and community negotiation over the use of force within families took place in a context in which law and custom in France, as in other western countries, indubitably gave men the right to discipline their wives, and parents the right to discipline their children.[15] Yet the legitimacy of this prerogative was tied to what communities defined as appropriate use. In this matter as in others, the legal and cultural privileges that husbands and fathers enjoyed as heads of households were extensive but not unlimited.[16] Participants' and observers' discussions of actual incidents of family battery unpacked the criteria that differentiated culturally accepted use of force, often framed as discipline, from abusive treatment. Their markers included the conduct of the person using the force, as well as the behaviour of the victims, the household status of the parties involved, and the social rank of the family.

Identifying the boundaries of acceptable violence in early modern France can seem like trying to hit an ever-moving target. Contemporary authorities categorized some types of violence (such as capital punishment) as legitimate, and others (such as riots and brawls) as illegitimate.[17] Communities themselves assessed some expressions of violence as being within the boundaries of usual practice, and others as transgressions of those boundaries. Individuals too made similar judgements. Although much of this evaluation took place outside of court proceedings and is difficult to recover, the contingency of acceptable or unacceptable behaviour is clear, as is the negotiation between individuals and within communities over a dividing line that was written in sand rather than concrete. The status of the parties, the circumstances in which the use of force took place, the previous histories of those involved, and perhaps local expectations, all shaped the process of making judgements. A punch could have different meanings, for instance, depending variously on where the incident took place (in public or private, in a household, bar, or street), on who was involved,

[15] For a brief overview of the legal history of men's entitlement to use force against their wives, see Phillips, *Putting Asunder*, 323–32.

[16] Charivaris, for example, were ritual expressions of community disapproval of wife-beating husbands who were seen to have gone too far. Natalie Zemon Davis, *Society and Culture in Early Modern France: Eight Essays* (Palo Alto, CA, 1975).

[17] For a valuable discussion of various forms of early modern violence, see Amussen, 'Punishment, discipline, and power'. For the role of violence in elite French culture, see Stuart Carroll, *Blood and Violence in Early Modern France* (Oxford, 2006).

on whether it was spontaneous or premeditated, on whether it was the first dispute or the latest in a long line, and so on.[18]

No early modern state was concerned about family violence as a criminal matter and, given the legal right of men to discipline their wives, the French legal system had little interest in spousal violence short of homicide as a matter for criminal prosecution; but the civil remedy of separation did provide a means for the recognition of spousal violence as a focus of official concern and an appropriate subject for judicial attention.[19] In this formulation, however, it was wives' property status that provided the basis for remedy, leaving other family members with little protection. Moreover, as a civil matter, violence became an official concern only when a spouse or community member brought it to the court's attention and provided verification as witnesses of a violation.

The existence of a debate about the use of force within families is clearest when it concerned men's use of force on their wives. Early modern urban communities in France engaged in lively and ongoing grassroots negotiation about what constituted appropriate levels of spousal force.[20] As one Lyonnais royal prosecutor explained, while laws acknowledged the authority of husbands to pursue 'light correction', in no case did this authority extend to 'violence'. Yet he continued to articulate an understanding that the line between light correction and violence was relative rather than absolute, as he noted that judgements should be made on the 'circumstances of each case'.[21]

Expectations about married life framed debates about what constituted domestic 'violence'. Court officials, lawyers, and spouses contrasted the conflict-ridden

[18] For an insightful discussion of how contextual variables shaped the meanings of violence and insults, see Catherine Ditte, 'La mise en scène dans la plainte: sa stratégie sociale. L'exemple de l'honneur populaire', *Droit et Cultures*, 19 (1990), 23–48. For other examples of the historiographic effort to reconstruct the boundaries of acceptable or transgressive violence, almost all for the eighteenth century, see the essays in the special forum 'Porter Plainte: stratégies villageoises et institutions judiciares en Ile-de-France (XVIIe–XVIII siècles)', *Droit et Cultures*, 19 (1990), 7–138, and Alfred Soman, 'Le temoinage maquille: encore un aspect de l'infra-justice a l'epoque moderne', in Yves-Marie Bercé and Yves Castan (eds.), *Les Archives du Délit: Empreinte de Société* (Toulouse, 1990).

[19] I have not found any criminal prosecutions for spousal violence short of murder under any category in sampling criminal records in either Nantes or Lyon. Similarly, no criminal complaints of spousal violence are extant in a recent exhaustive study of the records of a court of first instance in Vaucouleurs. See Hervé Piant, *Une Justice Ordinaire: Justice Civille et Criminelle dans la Prévôté de Vaucouleurs sous l'Ancien Régime* (Rennes, 2006), 164. For figures on criminal prosecutions of familial homicides, see Ruff, *Violence in Early Modern Europe*, 138.

[20] An extensive print debate about husbands' discretionary use of violence of the kind that took place in England did not apparently occur in France. Nevertheless, most French authors of literary texts in the sixteenth and seventeenth centuries did condemn wife-beating: Constance Jordan, *Renaissance Feminism: Literary Texts and Political Models* (Ithaca, NY, 1990), 191. For the print debate in early modern England, see Amussen, '"Being Stirred to Much Unquietness"', and Hunt, 'Wife beating'.

[21] ADR BP5985, folder 1653, 30 January 1653.

marriages in question with prescriptive deferential but complementary partnerships. In 1654 a Lyonnais royal prosecutor noted: 'The woman has not been formed from the foot of the man, but from one of his sides in order to show that she is a companion, not a slave.'[22] Wives rhapsodized about ideal marriages in which women dutifully respected their husbands in word and deed, and spouses lived in peace and showed one another 'courtesy'. Meanwhile they characterized their actual experiences as the 'victims' of 'tyrants'—as in the case of Anne Simond, who said of her bookseller husband that she was 'in effect his victim instead of his wife'.[23]

Wives, husbands, and witnesses all conceded too that husbands were entitled to some measure of discipline over their wives; it was the terms and the degree of that force that was contested. Husbands who countered allegations of excessive force represented physical contact as part of the routine disputes of married life, and justified their actions as conjugal prerogative.[24] Jacques Lyon said that he and Marguerite Barry had argued 'as spouses do' and he had given her some 'slaps' on those occasions, but her battery claims were 'without foundation'. François Romain rebuffed Anne Marie Delafont's allegations of violence, saying that he had never hit her 'except for two or three little slaps as a means of correction'. André Maury described his blows to his wife, Anne Faure, as 'some light and moderate correction', noting that husbands enjoyed 'this right and authority by human and divine law'. He asserted that women could complain only when husbands behaved with 'atrocious and extraordinary cruelty'. One husband simply asserted that 'none could live in peace' with his wife.[25] Husbands' assertions framed their use of force as commonplace examples of what historians have identified as the right to 'moderate correction'.[26]

Witnesses and wives distinguished between situations in which the husbands used forms of force that were broadly accepted, or had cause from those in which they beat their wives 'excessively' or 'without apparent legitimate reason'.[27] Jeanne Chevallier accepted the 'authority and power of the husband', but claimed that her own spouse, Pierre Thiolelar, had 'abused' that role and 'exercised continual tyranny over her'.[28]

[22] ADR BP3985, 10 February 1654.

[23] For the persistence of very similar rhetoric in late eighteenth-century separation suits, see Jeffrey Merrick, 'Domestic politics: divorce and despotism in late eighteenth-century France', in Carla H. Hay and Sydney Congers (eds.), *The Past as Prologue: Essays to Celebrate the Twenty-Fifth Anniversary of ASECS* (London, 1995), 373–86.

[24] Other husbands simply denied their wives' complaints completely, or responded defensively to the legal standard by asserting that their behaviour had not imperiled wives' lives.

[25] ADR BP3985, 17 August 1656; ADR BP4045, 31 August 1720; ADR BP4045, 18 June 1691.

[26] See, for instance, Phillips, *Family Breakdown in Late Eighteenth-Century France*, 120.

[27] ADR BP3985, 5 February 1649.

[28] ADR BP3985, 21 December 1641; BP4045, 19 January 1690.

Wives defended their 'innocence', noting carefully that they were blameless, as neither their words nor actions called for discipline. In fact, their self-representations highlighted their efforts to endure, and even to reform, their husbands' behaviour. Marguerite Cottin described how she had always done her utmost 'to support her household' through her work as a nurse, while her scalemaker husband 'did hardly anything', but that nevertheless she had given him some of her earnings and 'always behaved well and without making any reproach'. Catherine Puy complained of her husband's 'entirely wild life', as well as of the blows and venereal diseases he gave her, but claimed to have endured for years 'in the hope that by her patience she would soothe his ferocious temperament and that with age he would pull back from his profligacy'.[29] The goal of such rhetoric was to demonstrate that no cause for discipline existed.

Husbands, wives, neighbours, and courts all concurred that women's inappropriate speech could be cause for conjugal discipline, even if they did not always agree on what constituted 'inappropriate'. As people differentiated between punishment and violence, they often linked women's speech and men's actions. A baker, Jullien Feriant, highlighted the most frequent interpretation in assessing relations between his neighbours, Louis Thebaudeau, a shoemaker, and Marie Monnier. Thebaudeau had beaten her, he confirmed, but Monnier called her husband names such as 'rogue', and moved to slap and kick him, which 'obliged him to hit her and to push her away from him.'[30] Wives were careful to emphasize that their speech had been appropriately deferential. Anne Dufournil described, for instance, how 'her forbearance, her entreaties, her groans, and her tears' had all failed to stop her husband's violence. Charlotte Bonnefoy claimed that she had always given her husband 'all the obedience, respect, and duty that an honourable woman owes her husband.'[31]

Husbands, meanwhile, frequently focused on their wives' speech as just cause for beatings. André Debourg said that he had hit Gabrielle Fayet only twice: once when she had 'provoked' him during a dispute about money (presumably with what she said), and once when she had insulted him with 'outrageous words.'[32] Wives' verbal challenges to their husbands' authority included other situations: men asked their wives for money, and the wives turned them down; wives refused to provide guarantees for loans; wives took their husbands to task for habits they did not like; a husband complained that his wife gave him 'endless criticism' or that they were 'quarrelling because she remonstrated with him about his drinking and gambling.'[33] In men's narratives, beatings often followed these speech challenges.

[29] ADR BP4045, 30 June 1690; ADR BP4045, 2 October 1691.
[30] ADLA B5843, 8 August 1691.
[31] ADR BP4045, 3 November 1700; ADLA B5815, (no date) 1647.
[32] ADR BP4045, 11 April 1691.
[33] ADLA B5815, 16 September 1647; ADLA B5813, 13 May 1645.

Witnesses could be reluctant to characterize beatings as excessive when women were thought to have spoken inappropriately. A shoemaker carefully observed, for example, that he had often seen Marye Thomas and her clockmaker husband Pierre Grebannal quarrel, but that he had seen Grebannal hit his wife only once, when she was speaking 'injuriously'—which is to say that she insulted him.[34] Even when women's speech was not posited as justification, it could limit husbands' culpability as abusers. A scribe, Jean Letellier, who helped Anne Vallois on several occasions with injuries that included a black eye and bleeding mouth, characterized her husband as 'a violent man', but observed, too, that he had heard Vallois call her husband 'a bugger and a knave'.[35] No challenge to a husband's authority in his household was more widely recognized as fraught with peril than a chastising wife.

This focus on female speech indicates how communities authorized different patterns of men's violence at different moments. Women's verbal challenges were particularly likely to be classified as 'provocations' that required punishment in the early modern period, because they evoked widely diffused stereotypes about female capacity to undermine social and political order with natural unruliness and loose tongues.[36] Implicitly at least, claims like these acknowledged that less submissive speech might draw a forceful response to which legitimate objection was difficult in the cultural environment of the day.

Participants and observers who defined conjugal discipline simultaneously parsed what constituted 'excessive' spousal battery in terms that assessed not only whether cause existed, but how men chose to exercise force. Men's use of force against their spouses was regarded as inappropriate if their wives' behaviour did not justify it, or when husbands were innately violent or drunk, when the wives were pregnant, when an implement was used, when women's suffering led them to seek shelter or help from neighbours or kin, or when the violence was repeated and ongoing.

Contemporaries identified some men as 'vicious' or naturally violent, but did not consider that temperament excused battery. François Dyver, a street porter, described his fellow porter Jan Priou as a man who is 'susceptible to wine... quarrelsome in company and is violent and often quarrels with those he hangs out with and when he is drunk beats those around him'. Charlotte Bonnefoy asserted that 'all the cruelties, excesses, injuries, and outrages' she had

[34] ADLA B5830, 17 October 1677. [35] ADLA B5834, 13 April 1682.

[36] See, for instance, David Underdown, 'The taming of the scold: the enforcement of patriarchal authority in early modern England', in Anthony Fletcher and John Stevenson (eds.), *Order and Disorder in Early Modern England* (Cambridge, 1985), 116–36. Evidence from elsewhere also suggests that for early modern women, inappropriate speech was a catalyst for domestic violence; see, for instance, Roper, *Holy Household*, 189. For early modern concern to discipline speech broadly, and women's speech in particular, see Gowing, *Domestic Dangers*, and Jane Kamensky, *Governing the Tongue: The Politics of Speech in Early New England* (New York, 1997).

suffered came from 'the evil temperament and from the libertine and unregulated life' of her surgeon–husband Jan Delagarde.[37]

Husbands who were drunk when they beat their wives were also judged to have exceeded their authority. A woodworker who was a 'close neighbour' of Jean Parizot noted one version of a common sequence: 'When he comes home drunk, he beats and mistreats his wife without any subject.'[38] In this equation, an inebriated husband's use of force was deemed inappropriate because it was irrational, lacking both cause and self-restraint.

Men undermined their right to assert their household authority if they beat their wives frequently or used verbal abuse. Witnesses distinguished carefully between singular, occasional, or routine acts of battery in finely sliced comments on how often violence occurred. The tailor–neighbour of Jan Jagueneau and Anne Vallois recounted that 'in the last five or six weeks' he had heard 'Jagueneau cursing and his wife crying out on three occasions and he had twice accused Jagueneau of abusing his wife'.[39] Witnesses noted that wives were beaten 'daily', or 'whenever he comes home drunk', or that 'not more than a week' went by without beatings. Witnesses also commented on men who swore (especially blaspheming) and insulted their wives, either during beatings or on other occasions. For observers, such obvious lack of self-discipline revealed more about men's own shortcomings than about the wives' need for discipline.

Husbands were liable to be categorized as disrupting a social order which they were supposed to maintain when domestic incidents spilled outside households. Violence often ended when wives ran outside to neighbours or family, or when husbands forcibly put women out, leaving them to spend nights outside or requiring neighbours to shelter them. The locksmith who described Jean Robert, who 'came home late and at all hours of the night and on entering his home argued with his wife, beat her, and dragged her into the street kicking her and locking her out so that she was forced to go into her neighbours', reiterated the commonly articulated sentiment that a defining element of battery was disturbance of surrounding households.[40] Neighbours commented repeatedly not only that they had seen husbands batter wives, but that wives, as a neighbour of the tailor Ollivier Raoul noted, 'had to stay with neighbours to avoid more beating'.[41]

Witnesses made little comment about husbands' slapping or even kicking, but the use of almost any implement drew careful elaboration. Husbands used whatever was available for their battery, from domestic supplies (one husband poured boiling water from a hearth pot onto his wife's legs) to occupational tools (a wigmaker stuffed a wig into his wife's mouth).[42] Most often, the

[37] ADLA B5802, 10 May 1617, and ADLA B5815, (no date) 1647.
[38] ADLA B5817, 29 November 1657.
[39] ADLA B5834, 13 April 1682.
[40] ADLA B5834, 10 September 1682.
[41] ADLA B5814, 13 May 1626.
[42] ADLA B5841, 17 June 1689; ADLA B5825, 22 May 1670.

implements were iron rods (probably hearth tools) or knives. Although many early modern households might have owned firearms, domestic violence very rarely involved guns.

Onlookers used the visual evidence of women's physical appearance to assess husbands' actions. Bodies—especially women's bodies—were rich symbolic signifiers for inscriptions of order or disorder.[43] Husbands, wives, and witnesses were all careful observers and practitioners of body language of all kinds. While witnesses, not surprisingly, interpreted bleeding wounds, black eyes, or body bruises as telltale signs of battery, disruptions of pregnancy, clothes, and hair were also judged as mistreatment rather than discipline. A married woman's honour and reputation could hardly be more seriously impugned than by the uncovering of her hair.[44] Witnesses therefore commented critically if a wife 'seemed dishevelled and her headdress was torn'.[45] A mundane use of force was likely to be defined as extraordinary if the victim was pregnant. Battered wives and their neighbours clearly condemned a husband who beat his wife 'even though she was pregnant' or 'without considering that she was pregnant'.[46] Although early modern communities were committed to the punitive supervision of disorderly women of all sorts, married mothers were valued and protected.

Women and men recognized the significance of body language, and both could seek to use it. Nicolas Guischard, for example, started to argue with his wife, Marguerite Cousturier, outside their candlemaking shop after she complained about her mother-in-law. As a crowd gathered to watch, Guischard started to slap Cousturier, who was spinning on the steps, and took her inside. When Cousturier cried out, one bystander went in and saw Guischard and his mother 'pull her cap off' and slap her face. Cousturier then came out 'all capless and dishevelled' but apparently without other marks of mistreatment. Cousturier recovered her distaff from the gutter, where her husband had thrown it, and resumed her spinning.[47] To onlookers, Cousturier's self-discipline, commitment to a quintessentially valuable and honourable wifely labour, and apparent silence after the initial dispute, contrasted starkly with Guischard's resort to a gesture that was widely identified with scurrilous sexual implications. Her appearance and actions identified him as the source of disorder, and rendered his use of force illegitimate.

[43] See, for example, James R. Farr, 'The pure and disciplined body: hierarchy, morality, and symbolism in France during the Catholic Reformation', *Journal of Interdisciplinary History*, 21, 3 (1991), 391–414, and Peter Stallybrass, 'Patriarchal territories: the body enclosed', in Margaret W. Ferguson, Maureen Quilligan, and Nancy J. Vickers (eds.), *Rewriting the Renaissance: The Discourses of Sexual Difference in Early Modern Europe* (Chicago, 1986), 123–42.

[44] For early modern associations between free-flowing hair and prostitution, see, for example Farr, 'The pure and disciplined body'.

[45] ADLA B5834, 13 April 1682.

[46] See, for instance, ADR BP3985, 7 September 1665; ADR BP3985, 20 September 1673.

[47] ADLA B5839, 6 and 9 December 1687.

The attitudes that men and women such as tailors, porters, servants, and secondhand sellers expressed about husbands' use of force indicate that while the use of force in the form of casual slaps or kicks in response to particular shortcomings was an intrinsic element of many early modern marriages, men's privileges with regard to the use of violence were strictly defined. They were contingent on men's ability to order their own behaviour in how and when they used force, as well as judgements about whether the actions of the wives (as well as presumably children, servants, or apprentices, although little of their treatment found its way into court records) merited correction. When husbands failed to respect conventions about when or how the use of force was appropriate, they found they were no longer regarded as household heads exercising their right to discipline but, like Mathieu Tarze, who 'beat his wife to the scandal of his neighbours', as saboteurs of household life.[48] In these ways, urban communities defined quite specifically what the conjugal right to correction meant in working families, and continuously reiterated expectations about legitimate masculine prerogative.

The debates about boundaries of violence in other varieties of familial situations, whether due to differences in social rank or to the status of the perpetrator and victim, emphasize the contingency of the line between discipline and violence. Extant discussions are much more fragmentary than for wife-beating, because they rarely surfaced in court proceedings. Yet these do suggest both the pervasiveness of a sense of distinctions being made and the varying measures by which such distinctions might be made.

Jurists openly acknowledged that social status provided a variable marker in differentiating between discipline and abuse, suggesting that they at least categorized urban working families' behaviour separately from the behaviour of elites. The prominent legal commentator Claude-Joseph Ferrière noted that for women to seek a separation of person and property for 'cruelty and mistreatment', such abuse 'must be considerable and repeated . . . Thus the threats made by the husband to his wife are not sufficient cause.' He went on, however, to make an important distinction in which rank was critical: 'Serious threats accompanied by atrocious public slanders directed to a person of high status can touch the Judges and provide grounds for a separation; because between persons of quality public slanders are as wounding as the cruelty and mistreatment between common people.'[49]

[48] ADLA B5834, 20 April 1682.

[49] Ferrière, *Dictionnaire de Droit et de Practique*, 2, 863. Jurists often made these kinds of distinctions; for instance, that a slap or punch was sufficient evidence for separation in high-status families, whereas it was not—at least unless often repeated among ordinary people—or that insults, which ordinary people had been accustomed to since childhood and to which they were hardened, were a grave matter among elites accustomed to high standards of civility. See Lottin, 'Vie et mort du couple', 76.

Local court officials shared a similar set of assumptions about rank as a variable when they assessed what was conjugal authority and what was abuse. In domestic disputes, social standing could in principle determine whether the case would proceed as a civil action. Husbands sometimes made requests to clarify the civil status of their wives' suits, and, as a royal prosecutor explained in one case, they were 'civilized because of the status of the parties'.[50] A prosecutor who reviewed a case between an artisan and his spouse, for example, argued that incidents of domestic violence in working households rarely met the standards of life-threatening violence, as they were usually only 'superficial disputes . . . often the result of the husband's debauchery and the wife's impudence in insulting him when he is drunk and incapable of reason'.[51]

While these discussions suggest that in theory at least, the meaning of a specific level of husbandly force varied according to social rank elites, the debates about the battery of husbands or children indicate a similar contingency. No cultural vocabulary existed which framed appropriate circumstances for a wife to discipline her husband. Indeed, popular culture references highlighted wifely violence in the form of murder as the highest form of outrage (classified in England—although not in France—as petty treason in a remarkably literal equation of state and conjugal authority), or as the focus of community mockery of the husband through rough music of various kinds rather than aid.[52]

Child abuse in the form of violence is nearly invisible in early modern court records, and subsequently in the historiography of family or childhood.[53] From this distance it is impossible to assess how often men who beat their wives also beat their children, and neither can the extent of the battery of children be determined. Although children were unavoidably often spectators of family violence when their fathers beat their mothers, and sometimes intervened to get help in those cases, their own circumstances remain elusive. Violence against children could be the subject of criminal prosecution, but it is striking that virtually all such prosecution was directed at the abuse of children by people outside the family. Criminal records show the prosecution of masters for abusing apprentices, for example, or for people hiring out young girls for sex.[54] In such cases, prosecution was probably due to damage to the honour of the child's family, rather than being motivated by concern for the child. Prosecutions for incest may have been the primary exception to this pattern, but they were very

[50] ADR BP4046, 12 June 1640. Other requests from husbands to clarify the civil nature of the suits include ADR BP3984, 22 September 1682; ADR BP4045, 22 February 1691; ADR BP4045, 16 June 1691.

[51] ADR BP3985, 10 February 1654. See also Lottin, 'Vie et mort du couple', 75–7.

[52] Davis, *Society and Culture*; Dolan, *Dangerous Familiars*.

[53] An omission epitomized by a recent excellent collection edited by Jean-Pierre Bardet, *Lorsque l'Enfant Grandit: entre Dependence et Autonomie* (Paris, 2003).

[54] Information about the patterns of court cases involving children drawn from Christopher Corley's work, in progress, *The King's Families: Parenting and Adolescence in Early Modern France*.

rare.[55] Neither civil nor criminal courts, in fact, seem to have engaged with the regulation of violence inside the household or family (words that were early modern synonyms), except in the case of wife-beating. Yet various forms of violence within households must have been a common occurrence.

Certainly, early modern standards for good parenting were quite different from modern standards, but much remains unknown about the most basic elements of early modern parenting practices besides the use of force. A dispute between Leonarde Regnaud and Pierre Coquet, a gold-leaf worker, in the 1670s, offers an unusually direct illumination of divergences in expectations about appropriate infant care. Regnaud criticized Coquet's bad husbandry for reasons that included his failure to hire a wet nurse after the birth of their last child. He explained his failure not in terms of the welfare of the child (which certainly was better served in terms of mortality rates by being nursed by the mother), but as a simple financial matter: they could not afford to pay a wet nurse, due to money difficulties for which he blamed her.[56] Whatever the truth, it is striking to modern observers that Regnaud framed her husband's failure to put their newborn out to a wet nurse as proof of shortcomings, when modern historians have often interpreted the popularity of wet nursing as a sign of early modern parenting inadequacies.

Specifically early modern expectations about appropriate parenting must have shaped attitudes toward use of force on children. Early modern parents, especially fathers, indisputably had the right to discipline their children. Obedience was regarded as the first obligation of children to parents, as many prescriptive political commentators from the sixteenth and seventeenth century emphasized as they linked orderly families to political stability. Clearly, parents had significant discretion, and examples of parenting discipline that are astonishing to modern observers are plentiful. The diary of a royal doctor who was the attendant to Louis XIII as a child, recorded repeated, severe beatings of the prince from the age of 2 to secure princely obedience. The Burgermeister father of Anna Buschler chained her to a dining table for six months in response to her disputatiousness and perceived immorality in a German town in the 1520s. Children could also be subjected to extraordinary force outside domestic settings. Philippe Ariès' classic study of the history of childhood emphasizes the brutality of corporal punishment in early modern schools, at least through the seventeenth century.[57]

Whether rank shaped expressions of violence against children as it did with wives is not clear. Much of the prescriptive evidence speaks, of course, to expectations in elite families, as does the extraordinary treatment of the future king, Louis XIII, and to a significant extent the experiences of schoolboys. The theatrical discipline to which the heir to the French throne was subjected does

[55] Rublack, *The Crimes of Women*, 231–54. [56] ADR BP3984, 19 August 1677.

[57] Hunt, *Parents and Children*, 145–52; Steven Ozment, *The Burgermeister's Daughter*, 115–16; Ariès, *Centuries of Childhood*, 241–86.

suggest some resonances with a broader performance of noble violence that may resemble some of the experiences of elite women (as we will see).

Legal commentators' observations and the discussions of guides for early modern parents about the nature of acceptable violence towards children clearly indicate that a boundary between discipline and abuse existed with the treatment of children as it did with wives. Early modern jurists who commented on the rights of parents over children liked to contrast the 'humanity' of contemporary French practices, leavened by Christian morality, with the absolute authority exercised by the Romans over their children.[58] A jurist writing on questions about the guardianship of children noted simply: 'The father and mother also have the right of correct but they are not permitted to use too great a severity.'[59]

Similarly, fragmentary evidence points to the existence of a working community discourse of discipline versus battery in assessing the treatment of children that resonated with their discussion about husbands' use of force on wives. Like husbands who rationalized their treatment of their wives, parents could frame their treatment of children as a matter of necessary discipline rather than abuse. Pierre Coquet, for instance, defended the 'blows' he had given to his teenage daughters as necessary responses to their bad behaviour and disobedience. They were, he claimed, 'always doing contrary to what I ask them', and he emphasized that he had shown 'extraordinary forbearance and patience'. A mason said he had often seen a mother beat her children 'under pretext of maternal correction'.[60] This kind of language closely resembled the justifications involved in wife-beating.

While parents clearly had broad prerogatives with respect to the use of force under the rubric of correction, the parameters of battery are much more difficult to locate, and perhaps legitimized far more extensive force within parental purview than that allowed to husbands. Whereas the use of husbands' force on wives was a clearly enunciated early modern problematic, the use of violence on children was another matter. No judicial remedy existed for abuse of children within the family that fell short of murder. Elaborate accounts of spousal battery in separation cases, including witness testimony, rarely mentioned children at all, much less violence against children. While this omission may partly be explained by the legal imperative of separation cases in which the abuse of children played no role, witnesses often introduced material that was not pertinent (as we have seen), as did wives who sought separate property but presented evidence

[58] See, for example, François Perrier and Guillaume Raviot, *Arrests Notables du Parlement de Dijon, Recueillis par M. Francçois Perrier Substitut de Mr. le Procureur Général, Avec des Observations sur chaque Question par Guillaume Raviot Ecuyer, Avocat au Parlement, et Conseil des Etats de Bourgogne*, 1 (Dijon, 1735), i–ii; and Jean Bouhier, *Les Coutumes du Duche de Bourgogne*, 1 (Dijon, 1742), 294–307.

[59] Jean Meslé, *Traité des Minoritez des Tutelles et des Curatelles et des Droits des Enfans Mineurs et Majeurs* (Paris, 1713), 14–16.

[60] ADR BPP3984, 19 August 1677; ADLA B6184, 15 January 1743.

primarily of domestic violence. From many angles, parental prerogative about the legitimate use of force on children seems to have been extensive.

The behaviour of perpetrator and victim, the rank of the families, the status within the household of the parties, and the behaviour at issue, were all elements in an elaborate matrix of distinction between discipline and battery. These same elements were part of a calculus that underlay other aspects of family abuse, as the catalysts for violence, the behaviour of the victims, and the resources and remedies available, were similarly contingent on multiple variables. Lived experiences of family violence suggest that the prescriptive fluidity of boundaries between discipline and excess carried over into practices of household battery too.

CATALYSTS FOR VIOLENCE

Contemporary studies of family violence have emphasized the need to go beyond broad cultural patterns to identify specific risk factors.[61] Unlike present-day abusive marriages in which violence usually starts very quickly, no chronological pattern is apparent in early modern families, where the use of force in a way that might be categorized as abusive began at many different points in marriages.[62] If women's speech was a common early modern spark for conflict, alcohol, money, and sex—common factors in domestic violence in many cultural and chronological contexts—were at the forefront of many incidents of spousal violence too, but space, time, and rank-specific qualities coded their place in household battery.

The differing senses husbands and wives could have of the costs and benefits of male sociability provided ground for conflict. Historically, husbands and wives have often had conflicting spending goals, but their contrasting perspectives

[61] See, for instance, Jane Jasinski and Linda Williams (eds.), *Partner Violence: A Comprehensive Review of 20 Years of Research* (Thousand Oaks, CA, 1998), 21, which lists 'risk markers' as substance abuse (especially alcohol); socio-economic factors (especially unemployment or part-time work only); income (especially poverty); status incompatibilities (as when a wife works, or works more than her partner).

[62] The timeframe for the use of violence varied widely. Some wives claimed that battery started within days; others that they had been married for long periods before abuse began. A baker's wife, for example, described how her husband had beaten her 'on many occasions so outrageously' since their marriage only three months earlier. In contrast, Marguerite Barry, the wife of a builder, said of her husband of fourteen years that 'for some years they lived on good terms', so much so that 'they had nine children of whom four remain'. Yet about four years earlier 'and without anyone knowing why', he developed 'such an animosity' for her that he beat her 'perpetually' and often chased her from their home, so that she had to sleep elsewhere. ADR BP3985, 19 April 1661; ADR BP3985, 17 August 1656. Modern studies suggest that a quick commencement of marital violence is tied not only to general cultural patterns, but to the fact that some men may have had a psychological proclivity to act aggressively, and to the generational cycle of children witnessing abuse (or worse, being beaten) and then becoming abusers. It seems that similar preconditions must have existed in early modern marriages, but distinctive factors (such as the willingness to accept the use of force in some circumstances) may shape both the use of violence and wives' perceptions of it.

in early modern cities were rooted in specific constraints and opportunities. Moreover, in working families, incidents of domestic violence were often linked to men's drinking. A boatyard worker said his neighbour Sebastien Jarnigan 'gets drunk easily and when he is drunk beats and abuses his wife and children'. Anne Perrichon's neighbour neatly summed up her husband's routine: 'When he drinks, which is usually every day, he beats her.'[63] Yet this succinct equation compressed a gendered political economy that was always potentially explosive, in which household needs were often at odds with broader cultural, legal, and economic imperatives.

Married men were enmeshed in what we have seen was a complex repertoire of practices of masculinity, a matrix that could pull them in two directions: household responsibilities, and a culture of manhood that encouraged participation in extra-household activities in militia, parish, and bar. Men were expected to work diligently to support their families. This emphasis echoed long-established guild commitments to household order, as well as the new Protestant and Catholic moralities that emerged in the sixteenth century.[64] Yet being a man also involved participation in the extra-household life of the neighbourhood in a variety of ways, from serving as witnesses to drinking in bars. These patterns of masculine sociability had benefits such as access to credit and job information, as well as real material costs in time and money for any working household, and could jeopardize household viability or spousal co-operation if men did not calibrate their sociability carefully or if pressure from other sources was especially acute.

For working men in early modern French cities, bar-place rituals of drinking, gambling, and money-lending were essential components of the sociability and economics of gender identity. Men (but very rarely women) gathered in bars, where they ate, shared rounds of drinks, borrowed and lent money, exchanged news and perhaps traded job contacts. Whereas men tended to see bar life as essential, for women it was always expensive and sometimes ruinous. Violence often started when husbands wanted bar money, and wives sought to resist on the grounds that they needed that money for daily necessities, or had no money to give. Françoise Gorgette, the wife of the notary Jean Cassard, complained that her husband constantly took money and merchandize that was in the house 'for the support of his household and family', to spend in bars, where he drank, gambled, and lent money to strangers without obtaining guarantees. When 'she wanted to remonstrate with him about his wasting money, he abused her with words and blows'.[65]

[63] ADLA B5806, 7 February 1624; ADR BP3985, 7 April 1672.

[64] See, for instance, Lyndal Roper, *The Holy Household: Women and Morals in Reformation Augsburg* (Oxford, 1989), and Merry Wiesner, '*Wanderwogel* and women: journeymen's concepts of masculinity in early modern Germany', in her *Gender, Church and Society in Early Modern Germany* (New York, 1988).

[65] ADLA B6150, 17 January 1675.

Tensions over legal access to household property also fuelled the conflict that could lead to domestic violence, and the legal concept of lineage property contributed to often high spousal tension over the management of household economies, especially with regard to the securing of credit. Men who wanted to borrow money often needed their wives to co-sign to use the lineage property as security, and men who borrowed or lent money indiscriminately imperilled their wives' lineage property. Husbands often responded, with frustration and battery, to the limits on their control over the allocation of a household's resources. Wives complained over and over again that their husbands had beaten them to force them to co-sign loans. Women's powerful if indirect role in determining the use of lineage property combined with the daily realities of working families to cause tensions that often ended in domestic violence.[66]

The publicly articulated construction of sparks for domestic violence, however, varied with rank: while access to credit and bar culture framed narratives in working families, female sexuality dominated in the few cases started by women of high status. Spouses in these families articulated wifely sexuality as a core topic of contention, but they inevitably disagreed about whether any actual wrongdoing had taken place, and whether husbands' actions constituted discipline or battery. Working men's references to wives' sexuality rarely extended beyond their favourite spousal insult: 'whore', a gendered but generic slander that had gained broad connotations about failures of all kinds.[67] Elite men, however, whether wealthy merchants or nobles, fixed on specifics of their wives' alleged sexual behaviour. One nobleman, for example, demeaned his wife as 'a bitch in heat' who wanted to have sex with their gardeners or servants, while another assailed his wife as a 'brothel madam' and alleged that her friendship with a young man was adulterous. Marie Renaud, wife of a wealthy merchant, complained that his jealousy made him suspicious even if she visited her parents or attended mass; he refused to let her go to mass at all when they were in the country, as he alleged that she looked at the priest 'with lascivious eyes'.[68]

A matrix of interwoven concerns about lineage and legitimacy provided at least a rhetorical authorization for elite battery. Although inheritance issues were

[66] Such tensions may have been particularly acute in the households of widows who remarried, especially if they remarried younger men. The widow Anne Marie Delafont said that her new husband Francois Romain, a journeyman hatmaker, had 'deceived her' by claiming to be his own master, when in fact 'he was only a simple worker', beat her daily, and although 'he had not brought any property to her house', had spent 400 of her *livres* in the months of their marriage. She claimed that Romain threatened every day to beat her if she did not give him her money. ADR BP4045, 31 August 1720. Anecdotal evidence at least suggests that in these marriages, where issues about gender and power with regard to control over money were most blatant, domestic violence was especially likely. Other examples include ADR BP3984, 18 November 1679; ADR BP4045, 16 June 1691; ADR BP4045, 3 November 1700.

[67] For the various meanings of whore in early modern England, see, for example, Gowing, *Domestic Dangers*, esp. 79–105.

[68] ADLA B5842, 31 May 1690; ADLA B5840, 2 December 1688; ADR BP4045, 21 October 1685.

pressing for wealthy and working households alike, the imperatives of domestic economies differed. Elite husbands usually had significant property of their own that they could mortgage as security for loans, in addition to resources that kept the household viable and insulated it from the costs of their socializing. Financial irresponsibility seemed less threatening than ungirded female sexuality.

For families of higher status, allegations of female sexuality may have provided a prism through which conflicts over other matters played out. Wives' worth was inscribed in their bodies, which conveyed heirs and assets that were both vital to patrimonial success. Wifely chastity safeguarded family fortunes as well as reputations. For men who were barristers, successful merchants, or nobles, actual or imagined wifely promiscuity threatened to undermine economic, social, and political prospects.

These patterns suggest that in early modern households, perceived threats to the political economy of families provided the critical catalysts for domestic violence. Not surprisingly, the risk of violence heightened when the economies of masculinity seemed imperilled. Yet patriarchal imperatives seem to have been invoked selectively, because these economies were configured differently, depending on status. While all husbands were concerned about marital fidelity, the authority of men of high status was inextricably tied to their ability to control women's sexuality.[69] For working men, the ability to fund a particular culture of sociability that was an essential element of their identity was inexorably linked to access to their wives' labour and lineage property. In either case, factors specific to early modern household economies, to French law, and to urban life, emerged as primary catalysts for violence.

RESOURCES AND RESPONSES

The specificity in the context and content of domestic violence was echoed in the resources available to battered women. In the seventeenth century, spousal violence was a public rather than personal matter for wives, neighbours, and officials of the state. The material circumstances of urban working families, and a culture of violence and peacefulness that regulated many kinds of neighbourhood conflict, shaped both wives' resources and neighbourhood responses. The state, through its court system, also offered the possibility of specific and limited, but nonetheless valuable, help.

In a striking contrast to modern patterns, early modern working women employed a repertoire of publicizing actions as a central part of their strategy to secure help. They spoke freely of their injuries and of their husbands' culpability in a variety of forums. Many accounts echoed that of a baker's daughter who

[69] James R. Farr, *Authority and Sexuality in Early Modern Burgundy* (Oxford, 1994).

recalled how she had heard on 'seven or eight occasions' her neighbour Marie Bellier call, 'Come, my husband's beating me.'[70] Battered women were quick to display physical evidence to verify their verbal accounts. Louise Ferraud showed 'bruises in different places on her body that she said her husband had given her' to the wife of a bargeman in an oft-repeated interaction between battered wives and their peers in the community.[71] Women who went to court moved the level of publicity beyond the neighbourhood. They not only gave a public account, but also initiated a series of repeated tellings of the stories of their abuse, as witnesses provided depositions that reiterated various aspects of the incidents.

Moreover, cultural practice and practical logistics meant that early modern urban people were inevitably close observers of each others' lives. The contingent meanings of domestic violence in early modern communities may have allowed women to look to their peers for support more quickly than modern women, whose highly privatized and romanticized conceptions of marriage often make them slow to publicize abuse. It may have been easier for a woman to challenge the treatment she received when men's use of force on their spouses was routine, and the debate was about the extent rather than the mere fact of violence.

Most families lived in multi-family buildings with shared stairways, balconies, latrines, wells, and yards, and women must have known that simply calling out would quickly attract attention and help. Many neighbours recalled that they had heard screams from wives living nearby, and had gone with other neighbours to see what was happening. Marie Brossard's account of the violence between Louis Brellet and his wife Jacquette Yvon highlights the porous nature of household boundaries. Brossard, a widow, said she and her mother were eating supper when they heard screams. The noise 'obliged her to look through a little staircase window which opened into the kitchen of Brellet and his wife', and she saw him hitting his wife 'excessively like you would hit a cow'. While Yvon begged her husband to stop, Brossard shouted at him that he was wrong to beat his wife like that. Meanwhile Brossard's mother ran downstairs to the courtyard, where several neighbours had gathered. A servant who worked for Brellet and Yvon opened their door, shouted for help, and allowed Yvon to run to find refuge at a neighbour's house.[72] In these circumstances, domestic violence could not possibly be shrouded in the secrecy and isolation that characterized much twentieth-century battery.

These material realities facilitated an awareness of battery, and forged a critical link between publicity and accountability that working women were quick to exploit. Husbands acknowledged as much when they locked their doors, leaving worried neighbours or family outside demanding to see what was going on. Other husbands tried to inoculate themselves from oversight by choosing their moments. Magdelaine Ganiet claimed that her husband 'always tried to abuse

[70] ADLA B5838, 8 March 1686.
[71] ADLA B6154, 2 December 1684.
[72] ADLA B5833, 31 July 1680.

her when they were alone'.[73] Another woman said of her husband that 'to remove her means of complaint,' he took her to a ramshackle, isolated hovel on their rural smallholding, where 'far from her whole neighbourhood he could without fear, without respect, and without consideration' treat her cruelly.[74]

In cities, women could turn to many people for help: kin, servants, neighbours, or even casual acquaintances or passers-by. Louise Desvignes' experiences show how several levels of community oversight, aid, and intervention operated for battered women. In fifteen years or so of recurring domestic violence, neighbours, family members, a doctor, a marquise, 'several ladies of high rank', and her parish priest, all proffered various kinds of help and mediation.[75]

Close neighbours, both male and female, provided aid of all kinds: they responded to cries for help, took in women who were fleeing abuse or the threat of it, provided medical treatment for injuries, and sought to ameliorate fallout from domestic conflicts in large and small ways. A barkeeper, Jacques Robereau, described a common scenario: he had heard and seen the wigmaker Jacques Leschallier beat his wife Anne Bourguillon 'since their marriage . . . in such a manner that men and women neighbours many times were obliged to run to help Bourguillon and to reprimand Leschailliers for mistreating his wife.'[76] Jeanne Renaud often heard disturbances in the home of the candlemaker and his wife, and on one occasion the clamour was so loud that she and another neighbour went to 'make peace'. Jeanne recalled, too, how she had watched him push his wife out of their door, and later eject a child who started to cry and call for his mother. When the child fell down in the road 'in a dirty place', Jeanne picked him up and took him to his grandmother's house.[77]

Kin provided refuge, mediation, and direct intervention. Help came from fathers and brothers as well as mothers and sisters, from in-laws as well as birth families, and from children. Many abused women returned to their parents, sometimes staying for days or even weeks, to avoid or recover from beatings. When the father of Françoise Bridon arrived in her silk-merchant husband's boutique as his son-in-law hit her in the stomach, he quickly stopped the abuse, and shouted 'You are very disreputable to beat my daughter like this in my presence and in front of everyone.' Bridon left with her father. During an earlier incident, her brothers had similarly intervened. A woman's in-laws, as well as her own kin, could come to her help, as when a neighbour called the father of the butcher Claude Gaillard to come to the aid of his daughter-in-law during a domestic violent incident; it was Gaillard's father who 'made his son open the door and took his daughter-in-law away to safety'. Moreover, the few women who successfully secured separations of persons and property sometimes went back to live with their parents. Family members also served as go-betweens, seeking

[73] ADR BP4045, 2 June 1720. [74] ADR BP3985, 21 December 1641.
[75] ADR BP3984, 22 September 1682 and 9 January 1683.
[76] ADLA B5825, 22 May 1670. [77] ADLA B5837, 20 December 1685.

to help wives by extracting commitments to better behaviour from husbands. Jeanne Terrasse recalled how the 'persuasion of both their kin', along with her husband's promise to treat her better in the future, had led her to withdraw an earlier court complaint. Even children could summon aid if their mothers' cries did not. Anne Vallois' son, from her first marriage, ran upstairs to tell a neighbour that his stepfather 'was beating his mother' and to beg the neighbour 'to go down to their rooms to try to make the peace'.[78]

Some parents tried to mobilize a kind of community watch over husbands. The mother of Phillipe Chauveau, for instance, not only called for help when her son beat his spouse, Françoise Gaultier, but on another occasion visited the couple's neighbour and asked her, 'in case there was any disturbance', to go to their residence and 'make the peace'. The neighbour noted that when she later heard such a disturbance, she duly intervened and 'remonstrated' with Chauveau.[79] Just as kin co-signed loans, gave advice as to who should be guardians for minor children, or provided a thousand other material and emotional supports for each other, they supervised the relations between spouses.[80]

The single female servants who were ubiquitous in early modern households could be crucial allies for wives. They often intervened during the conflict itself. A female servant remembered how she had stopped Jean Mellet hitting Jeanne Richard with an iron rod. Another recalled how she had saved her employer from drowning after her husband put her into a water-filled barrel.[81] Equally importantly, they often provided eye-witness testimony for wives' court cases.

In all such cases, observers of domestic violence seem to have shown little reluctance to intervene, and had low tolerance for wife battery when they identified the level of force as problematic. They quickly assessed incidents in terms of possible cause and manner of force. Whether as kin or neighbours, men and women seem to have been equally likely to lend aid. Although men might have been expected to be more sympathetic to husbands than wives in cases of domestic violence, it is impossible to discern any such difference in their actions.[82] For men and women, men's privileges seem to have rested on the appropriate handling of them.

In fact, many aspects of wives' strategies and neighbours' responses were part of a much broader set of practices by which communities customarily sought to maintain civil relations and curb violent conflict. Participants in many

[78] ADLA B5849, 20 June 1707; ADR BP4045, 23 May 1699; ADR BP3985, 26 May 1671; ADLA B5834, 13 April 1682.

[79] ADLA B5831, 5 February 1678.

[80] For the myriad interactions between kin in seventeenth-century urban communities, see Hardwick, *The Practice of Patriarchy: Gender and the Politics of Household Authority in Early Modern France* (University Park, PA, 1998), *passim*.

[81] ADLA B5814, 22 April 1651, and B5815, 21 January 1647.

[82] In contrast, based on a study of Rouen in the 1780s, Phillips, *Putting Asunder*, 337–8, suggests that gender differences existed in response patterns, with men being more reluctant than women.

disputes took their complaints to the public theatre of the street—not only because of the material limitations of their homes, but to elicit the observation, judgement and possible intervention of their neighbours. Onlookers not only passed unfavourable judgement on those seen to be in the wrong, but enhanced their own standing by upholding standards for appropriate behaviour that were widely held.[83]

Wives in working families were very savvy about mobilizing the customary culture of conflict management, as well as markers of battery rather than discipline, to seek help with their difficulties. When they shouted out or ran outside, ensuring the disturbance of neighbours, or when they lifted up their clothes to show bruises, they made their treatment a matter for public assessment and intervention. Not only could they expect help in the immediate crisis, but the men and women whose interventions were sought could endorse or downgrade the reputations of the spouses and at the same time affirm their own standing as arbitrators. Both wives and witnesses engaged the expectations about peaceful coexistence when they spoke of how spouses had desired to 'live in peace' or were 'always quarrelling'. The work of reputation was critical in early modern communities, because it was valuable not only as a matter of honour, but in many other ways such as in securing access to credit or being given entry into occupations.

Battered wives could also turn to local clergy and convents for help. Parish clergy provided mediation between spouses, and saw intervention in domestic conflict as a pastoral responsibility. Pierre Barat noted that his wife had 'several times' tried to convince him to visit their parish priest to discuss his treatment of her. When Jeanne Reillat's husband began to beat her almost every day within days of their marriage, she 'had the priest of her parish talk to him' to persuade him to treat her better. The priest of a Nantais parish was walking past the home of a couple for whom he had 'done what he could' to persuade them to live together in peace, when he heard a disturbance. He went into the house, and the wife claimed that she had been beaten in an argument about money. The priest 'remonstrated' with both of them, but they would not listen, so he left! The authority of the church could be more mobilized even more overtly, as when a husband was persuaded to 'reiterate his promises' not to beat his wife any more in his parish church in front of a priest.[84]

Convents often functioned as early modern versions of safe houses for battered women.[85] Sometimes they provided the security that neighbours could not—as

[83] For these patterns of neighbourhood management of conflict, see, for instance, Farr, *Hands of Honor*, 150–95, and Garrioch, *Neighbourhood and Community in Paris*, 31–55.

[84] ADR BP3984, 13 May 1682; ADR BP4045, 21 June 1700; ADR BP4045, folder 1709–1710, 23 October 1710; ADR BP3984, folder 1682, 9 January 1683.

[85] This function of convents complicates our notion of the roles they played for women: they might also be used as places where families could detain errant wives or daughters, or as sites where women could pursue alternatives to marriage. See Sarah Hanley, 'Engendering the

in the case of Anne Simon, a bookseller's wife. After one incident of battery she went to stay with another bookseller and his wife, but as her husband came there seeking to beat her again, she 'was constrained to go to a Religious house to find security'.[86] Wives, especially those who had petitioned for separations of person, might also withdraw to convents to escape irate husbands while court cases were in progress. Finally, women who had secured separations of person sometimes chose to retire to local convents.[87]

Sometimes, high-status neighbourhood women seem to have become community specialists in domestic violence. A 'marquise' visited a battered wife whom she 'heard about', and then sent porters with a sedan chair to take the victim to recuperate in her house. Jeanne Greillat, a haberdasher's wife, visited a doctor's wife 'as the person in whom she had the most confidence', and asked her 'to offer reprimands' to her husband for his beatings. Marie Thomas complained to 'Ladame Leduc', who lived nearby, 'of the blows and mistreatment her husband gave her', and 'showed her body', which seemed 'very much abused with black and bloody blows'. This same woman had a year earlier sheltered Thereze Massoneau, who 'withdrew to la femme Leduc's because of the battery her husband was giving her.'[88]

Nevertheless, neither neighbours, family, nor clergy were necessarily infinitely sympathetic to battered wives. Broad expectations that women had to endure their situations accompanied limited tolerance for conjugal violence and the willingness to help abused women. When Marguerite Delavergne asked her brother-in-law to help her secure a separation, he reminded her that she had chosen to marry and so had to bear whatever her husband handed her.[89] Battered wives were expected to try 'prayers' as well as 'caresses and gentleness' to ameliorate their situations.[90] Suzanne Fauchet, the wife of a cardmaker, recalled that she had 'devoted all her efforts, all her prayers, and even had recourse to those of the church' to try to change her husband's behaviour.[91]

state: family formation and state building in early modern France', *French Historical Studies*, **16**, 1 (1989), 4–27, and 'Family and state in early modern France: the marital law compact', in Marilyn J. Boxer and Jean H. Quataert (eds.), *Connecting Spheres: Women in the Western World, 1500 to the Present* (Oxford, 2000), 61–72; and Elizabeth Rapley, *Les Dévotes: Women and Church in Seventeenth-Century France* (Montreal, 1993).

[86] ADR BP4045, 19 January 1690.

[87] Marianne Bernard, for instance, the wife of a scalemaker, asked to go to a convent outside of town 'because it will be cheaper and he is only a worker'. Claude-Joseph Ferrière, *Dictionnaire de Droit et de Practique*, 2 (second edn., Paris, 1740), 862; ADR BP3985, 25 September 1673; ADR BP4045, folder 1709–1710, 2 July 1710. Other examples of women using convents as safe houses during various moments in domestic violence cases include ADR BP3984, 18 October 1674; ADR BP4045, folder 1691, 23 May 1699.

[88] ADR BP3984, folder 1682, 9 January 1683; ADR BP3984, 20 August 1680; ADLA B5829, 19 March 1676; ADLA B5830, 17 October 1677.

[89] ADLA B5806, 16 January 1626.

[90] ADR BP4045, folder 1709–10, 21 December 1710.

[91] ADR BP3984, folder 1676, 12 April 1674.

Neighbours, however ready to aid battered wives, might also grow impatient when a household's domestic violence frequently spilled over into their own lives. Neighbours repeatedly stopped Phillipe Chauveau beating his wife Françoise Gaultier, for example, and sheltered her in the safety of their homes. Yet, after several such incidents, they 'threatened to make them move because of the disturbances they were causing'. A group complained to a judge that a case of battery in their neighbourhood was causing 'extreme inconvenience and public scandal' because the wife repeatedly sought refuge with them.[92]

Charlotte Bachot's efforts to obtain help illustrate both the kinds of aid that battered women could seek, and the impact of assessments about the validity of the use of force. She visited a lawyer, telling him 'there was trouble' between her and her husband and stepchildren, and the lawyer said he would go to their home. He told her husband Albert Nicollon that he had come 'to see if there was not any way of re-establishing peace between them'. The spouses said they had talked to a friar whom the lawyer went to see. The latter told him that 'he had learnt from their neighbourhood that Bachot had indeed taken some clothes and personal property from their household'. Her husband and stepchildren repeated this complaint, and for lawyer and friar, her actions may have endorsed the legitimacy of Bachot's beatings. Finally, Bachot initiated a court complaint.[93]

The support of witnesses provided a critical link between community and state. The endorsement of witnesses endorsed the behaviour as inappropriate by local standards, and framed it as the appropriate subject for judicial remedy. That is, violence of this kind became the concern of the state through private concerns. In this way, family business became the focus of state activity, not only as the result of the (often rhetorical) ambition of the government, but through the practical desires of members of local communities.

Women who went to court may not always have wanted separate households, but instead wanted to pressure their husbands to stop the battery. They could play several cards in a complex legal strategy. Courts provided some prospects of legal remedy, but they also offered yet another level of publicity and a valuable negotiating lever. Wives and their witnesses mobilized the court of public opinion as they recounted tales of battery for the judiciary. Some battered women were in and out of courts with repeated complaints in an indication that they could use the legal option as a useful negotiating strategy as well as, or rather than, as a path to a legal remedy. Jeanne Chevallier noted how she had withdrawn a petition for separation of property and person when her husband promised to treat her 'maritally', and when he recommenced his abuse she reminded him 'that she would be constrained to take up her court complaint again' if he did not stop. Magdelaine Leotard recalled that her husband's beating had led her,

[92] ADLA B5831, 5 February 1678; ADR BP3985, 11 January 1649.

[93] ADLA B5833, 23 September 1680. The outcome of her court case is unknown, as only the *enquête* survives.

'with the advice of her family', to make a complaint to the court 'that she had left unexecuted in the hope that her husband would correct his ways over time'.[94] Many women mentioned having withdrawn one or more earlier petitions because spouses had made similar promises.

Yet all battered wives faced a similar reality: the community and the courts shared a reluctance to see women leave their husbands permanently because of battery. Judges' preferences for separate property, rather than separations of property and person, as responses to the grievances of battered wives indicate that they acknowledged the need to curb excessive violence, but sought to do so in a context of preference to keep households together, for both economic and ideological reasons. Women who headed separate households might easily find themselves in precarious economic circumstances, potentially creating a public burden. Moreover, as a Lyon royal prosecutor explained when he recommended that a claim for separation of person and property be denied and separate property alone granted, a favourable decision would have the 'pernicious consequence' of indirectly introducing divorce, 'which Christianity forbids'. He went on to recommend, however, that the husband be 'enjoined to treat his wife maritally on threat of separation of person or even of exemplary punishment'.[95] Judges often included such warnings, even in separate property proceedings. Over and over again, neighbours like Thereze Massoneau's told both how they had helped a battered woman and then sought to bring husband and wife together again. When Jeanne Terrasse made her fifth complaint to the court in 1673, she observed that she had withdrawn each earlier petition when her husband 'had used people of high rank who persuaded her to return to him on the basis of the promises he made to treat her better in the future'.[96] When judges denied requests for separations of person and property, they frequently required husbands to treat their wives 'maritally and humanely' in the future. Domestic violence often included many repetitions of a predictable sequence: battery, short-term informal separations after a woman had fled, efforts by family, friends, or others to ameliorate the conflict and return the wife to her husband, one of more appeals to the courts (or at least threats to do so), and reconciliation of some kind.

THE MANY FORMS OF FAMILY VIOLENCE

If we compare the dynamics of family violence when husbands beat wives in urban working families to the patterns of the use of force in elite families, or to incidents when children or husbands were the victims of battery, the variables

[94] ADR BP3985, 21 December 1641; ADR BP4045, 18 January 1720.

[95] ADR BP3985, folder 1653, 7 July 1652.

[96] ADLA B5829, 4 January 1676; ADR BP3985, 20 June 1673.

as well as the common experiences are striking. While other expressions of family violence are much less well documented than wife-beating, the attitudes and actions of family members, observers, and the legal system offer suggestive indicators of how fluid and situational attitudes towards violence were, in early modern society, within the household as well as without. Social rank and the household status of the beater and beaten were critical in shaping the responses to, and resources of, other victims of family violence besides wives. The community assessment and oversight that was critical in managing wife-beating was evident in other forms of family violence, as in all expressions of extra-household violence too. However, when wives of high rank were beaten, when women used violence, or when husbands or children were the subjects of the use of force, the victims and observers responded differently than in the battery of working women.

Elite wives appeared in only a small number of court cases of this kind, but their experiences provide a basis for some speculation about the impact of rank and of emerging rhetorics of privacy on the long history of domestic violence. Such women may have found themselves with fewer resources, because socially specific factors affected women's ability to mobilize help and men's willingness to use force. Wives of high status seemed very reluctant to publicize their conjugal difficulties for a variety of reasons. Perhaps they went to court only in the most extreme circumstances rather than being able to make good on the promise of a lower legal standard. Generally, they may have preferred to pursue personal rather than judicial remedies, probably for a variety of reasons tied to different household dynamics as well as greater sensitivity to the significance of familial as well as personal reputation.[97]

Although jurists repeatedly suggested that legally a lower standard of husbandly force was sufficient to be defined as abuse in high status families, on the rare occasions when elite wives went to court they alleged that their husbands had used violence that was brutal by any standards, and they often responded in ways different from their peers in working families. Anne Raoul, for instance, claimed that her husband's abuse included an instance when he beat her 'with all his might for more than a quarter of an hour until he couldn't anymore leaving her all bloody . . . and all the while shouting names like bitch and whore'. Marie Renaud, the wife and daughter of wealthy merchants, claimed that her husband beat her, tried to strangle her, and knelt on her stomach even though she was pregnant. Izabelle Coquet's husband was a judge and royal prosecutor in a jurisdiction adjacent to Lyon. In her account, he kicked her in a street until

[97] Elite reluctance to use the civil remedy of separations for spousal violence may have been widespread. A recent study of the culture of violence in the French nobility provides little evidence of domestic violence in court cases, short of spousal murder, and in a local court in Vaucouleurs, in eastern France, no elite women asked for separations of property and person on the basis of violence, even though local elites were active in the court in other kinds of cases. Carroll, *Blood and Violence*, 235–40, and Piant, *Une Justice Ordinaire*, 163.

she ran into a house, where he beat her around the head and shoulders with a stick so severely that, as she put it, she 'has not and will not ever fully recover'. Subsequently, she said, he tried to choke her on her sickbed, and refused to let either doctors or priests visit her.[98]

The households of French elites varied enormously, from the urban townhouses of professionals such as barristers to the chateaux of the French nobility; but all were much more spatially expansive than working households. Yet women of high status were not physically isolated in the ways that, for example, twentieth-century suburban wives were, because kin, visitors, and household staff constantly surrounded them. Any of these people might provide help. When Françoise Martel, for instance, arrived home one day with a niece, her noble husband greeted them with 'Ah here are our whores', pushed her against the wall and, according to her, tried to strangle her; her niece and a servant 'threw themselves' at him to end the assault.[99]

Nevertheless, the public of wives of high status differed from the public to whom working wives appealed, and did not always provide the same responses. Elite wives may neither have sought nor received the support that urban working women requested and secured. The numerous servants who worked in wealthy households may have been less reliable sources of help than those in working families. Hierarchies were more rigid and loyalties more complex in households with many servants of both sexes than where wives worked alongside lone female servants. Elite husbands as well as wives found servants willing to give evidence in their favour.[100] Even where servants were sympathetic to wives' plight when they testified, they sometimes seemed slower to intervene during battery than their peers in working households. Dame Anne Raoul's husband, Louis Delaroche, for example, repeatedly assaulted her in full view of their staff. Two former servants testified that they had seen him slap and kick her, lock her in a small room with only bread and water for weeks, and rape her in a vineyard in front of 'fifteen or sixteen' peasants. Yet the servants not only did not help her as the abuse happened, but one of them, on his employer's orders, even tied her to bed-posts and held her skirts up during the subsequent beating.[101] No doubt Raoul's husband's quasi-theatrical displays of household disciplining reiterated his authority over servants as well as spouse in ways that may well have coerced them into being bystanders through fear that he might be quick to beat them

98 ADLA B5842, 31 May 1690; ADR BP4045, 21 October 1685; ADR BP3985, 5 November 1668.

99 ADLA B5840, 2 October 1688.

100 For servants' conflicting testimonies that supported claims of both spouses, see, for instance, ADR BP3984, (no day) August 1683; ADLA B5837, 28 June 1685.

101 ADLA B5842. 31 May 1690. Servants' accounts of these episodes could be graphic. In the vineyard, for instance, a servant recalled that Delaroche asked his wife 'if she wanted to get fucked by these country buggers and said he wanted to fuck her in front of them'. She declined, citing 'modesty'; they argued, and 'calling her names, he pushed her to the ground', and 'in the presence of the witness and fifteen or sixteen peasants had sex with her'.

too. For whatever reasons, servants do not seem to have been as constant allies for wives of high status as for working women.

Women of high rank, whether wives or observers, seemed hesitant to speak out about domestic violence, perhaps because they were more concerned about the damage that allegations of spousal violence might do to a family's reputation than were working women. Elite wives expressed reservations of this kind repeatedly across several decades, from Bonnaventure Domet, who in 1649 said she had endured her husband's violence for more than a decade 'to avoid scandal and the shame and ruin of their children', to Magdelaine Leotard, whose petition in 1720 began with the claim that it was only with 'great regret that she was forced to have recourse to justice'.[102] This recurring language of concern about a potential negative impact on familial honour, even as a trope, was absent from the petitions of working wives.

Female observers of high rank seemed equally tentative about publicizing husbands' violence, or sometimes even acknowledging it. When Françoise Martel accused her noble husband of battery, for instance, two of her female peers presented very cautious testimony. One said simply that she did not know anything except that she had once seen Martel with a black eye that Martel attributed to her husband. Another said only that when Martel cried out for help one night, she had gone twice to investigate but did not see anything amiss. She admitted that the next day she saw Martel's face all bruised, but maintained that she had no other relevant knowledge. Anne Therese Sebouez saw Louis Delaroche slap Anne Raoul's face while they were all in his carriage on their way to visit a friend who was about to leave town. She commented to him only that 'if he did that in fun, it was too hard and if he meant to hurt her he had succeeded'.[103] These restrained responses contrasted with the quickness to intervene, judge, and reprimand that characterized witness accounts of the disputes of working families.

While working women depended on publicity to counter their batterers, and showed little concern for the costs to their husband's or family's reputation, elite women may have been more keenly invested in the maintenance of the honour and reputation of spouses and family, even at significant personal cost. They may have preferred to pursue private remedies, such as agreements mediated by kin and signed in personal papers rather than legal records, or to take refuge in convents. Wives in elite ranks may also have been influenced more quickly by broader changes, such as an increasing distaste for the use of violence and

[102] ADLA B6665, 13 July 1649; ADR BP4045, 18 January 1720. Many variations on this theme were made. See, for instance, Anne Raoul, who claimed 'she had not wanted to complain for fear of scandal', while Catherine Arthaud said she had been reluctant to 'complain to Justice' about being beaten by her husband, a *chevallier* and *tresorier de France*, out of 'the consideration that she had always had for his family'. ADLA B5842, 31 May 1690; ADR BP3984, 11 June 1683.

[103] ADLA B5840, 2 December 1688.

emerging concepts of privacy, both of which may have made women more concerned about acknowledging their husbands' abuse to the outside world.[104]

Contemporary studies of spousal abuse have shown that many other kinds of family violence often accompany wife-beating, and that women as well as men sometimes use force against family members. Although the construction of force as authorized or illegitimate that shaped wife-beating in early modern society also framed various other expressions of family violence, the dynamics of child abuse or husbands who were beaten differed from wife-beating in significant ways. Women as well as men were agents as well as subjects of the many varieties of intrafamilial conflict.[105] Other victims were much less proactive than working wives in seeking publicity or using the courts, and neighbours' attitudes towards the use of force and about intervention depended in significant part on the familial identity of the victim.

Complicated inheritance rules, the presence of lineage as well as community property in spousal assets, and the broad expectation that kin could oversee household property management all made for a potentially combustible relationship between in-laws, and intrafamilial conflict along these lines was not uncommon. Husbands frequently complained that their wives' parents encouraged or helped daughters to remove property of various kinds. Arguments of this kind were often heated, and frequently escalated to threats, or actual use of force. For instance, François Boursillon, a music teacher, threatened to push his mother-in-law into the fire during an argument of this kind, and René Peigne, a barrelmaker, threatened to kill his father-in-law during a long dispute over the payment of a dowry. Marguerite Cousturier's mother-in-law pulled her hair and removed her hat during a dispute. Adrienne Monnier and Guyonne Lecourt had a dispute with their sister-in-law Renée Leblee that followed a classic escalation: they called her a whore who had two or three bastards, ripped her cap off and tore it in two, hit her, and threw mud on her face. Charlotte Bachot beat her stepdaughters with a cane, and they in turn abused her in a variety of other ways, such as making her sleep outside.[106] The repertoire of insults and threats, the resort to gestures such as uncovering the hair, with a derogatory meaning which was clear, and the use of force was similar to wife battery, although the use of sticks or other tools of abuse seems to have been less common.

[104] A recent study of violence in the French nobility suggests, based on other forms of force, that elite attitudes to violence changed in the later seventeenth century. See Carroll, *Blood and Violence*, esp. 306–29.

[105] For discussions of women's capacity for violence, see Kristen B. Neuschel, 'Noblewomen and war in sixteenth-century France', in Michael Wolfe (ed.), *Changing Identities in Early Modern France* (Durham, NC, 1996), 124–44; Frances Dolan, 'Household chastisements: gender, authority, and domestic violence', in Patricia Fumerton and Simon Hunt (eds.), *Renaissance Culture and the Everyday* (Philadelphia, 1999), 204–25; Catarina Lis and Hugo Soly, *Disordered Lives: Eighteenth-Century Families and their Unruly Relatives* (Cambridge, 1996), 85–91.

[106] ADLA B5852, 27 August 1718; ADLA B5853, 29 November 1719; ADLA B5833, 23 November 1680.

Women's use of force against their husbands was a recurring motif in family conflict. The relative visibility of this form of household violence, compared to child or elder abuse, is due in part to the fact that sometimes husbands who opposed their wives' claims, and witnesses too, raised the issue of women's own behaviour as a context for their husband's actions (as we have seen). Yet wives' use of violence is more than a quirk of the source material, as other indications also suggest that wives' resort to force, while much less common than husbands', was not uncommon. Husbands who alleged battery by their wives constituted a fifth of family violence complaints to the police in eighteenth-century Paris.[107] Some early modern wives were ready to use violence either in self-defence or as a form of contention.

Sometimes wives hit their husbands as part of spousal conflicts where the dynamics seemed very similar to those when the situation was reversed. When Janne Belot sought a separation of person and property from Jan Duval in 1678, Duval responded that he had 'more reason to complain than she did', and deposed five witnesses who said they had seen her drink with other women, then swear at her husband and beat him, so that he often had to leave their home to avoid her abuse. A swordmaker recalled going home with François Angebaud, a potmaker, 'to have some drinks'. Catherine Menager, Angebaud's wife, greeted them by telling them to leave because there was nothing to drink, and shoved her husband with her hands, leading the swordmaker to take Angebaud home with him for the night 'to avoid talk'.[108]

The ubiquitous use of mundane violence as a part of many early modern marriages provided a context for wives as well as husbands. Cecile Burot and René Provost came to court, for example, with a long history of high levels of verbal and physical conflict between them. Elizabeth Bonet, a young woman who had lived for a year in a room above theirs, simply said that they 'were always in conflict and mistreating each other with blows'. She recalled an evening when she heard a noise from their rooms before Provost ran downstairs, and said that his wife had abused him. The next day, Burot admitted, without any apparent remorse or sense of shame, that she had 'hit her husband over the head with a pot, and that she had thrown a foot warmer at his head that she truly believed might hurt him a lot'. She had done so 'because he called her bad names'. On another occasion, Burot shown Bonet bruises she claimed were the result of Provost's hitting her with a candlestick. When Bonet asked Provost about it, he said that surely enough he had hit her, but only with a punch, and because she would not let him get into bed with her.[109] Many other witnesses for both spouses recalled similar episodes.

107 Williams, 'Patterns of conflict', 45.
108 ADLA B6674, 5 February 1678; ADLA B6853, 28 February 1720.
109 ADLA B5855, 8 July 1729.

Some of the women who struck their husbands were probably battered wives whose actions were at least, in part, self-defence (although the predominance of this pattern may be exaggerated by the nature of court cases for separations which were brought by women who used spousal violence as one form of proof). For example, in 1714 Renée Leblee sought separation of person and property from her husband Étienne Monnier, a used-clothes seller. Some of her witnesses noted that while she had shown them various bruises and wounds that Monnier gave her, he too had been the victim of physical aggression. Rose Taron, the wife of another used-clothes seller, noted, for instance, that Leblee had on several occasions sent a girl to fetch her to show her injuries. When she met Monnier in a bakery and 'reproached him for his mistreatment', he replied 'yes it's true that I hit her but you don't know why because she threatened my life'. He showed her and the other women in the shop his shirt, and they saw that it was 'all bloody'. Taron continued that the next day she had seen a surgeon visit Monnier to treat him for his injuries. Perhaps because her husband's injuries were well known, Leblee deposed an unusually high number of witnesses (twelve), many of whom attested to the repeated beatings she had experienced, and one of whom, a priest, even said flatly that 'it is public knowledge that Monnier caused the death of his first two wives'.[110] The cycles of violence in such households are easier to imagine than reconstruct.

Observers assessed and responded to wives' use of force differently than to husbands' in at least two key ways. While they carefully registered rationales for assessing husbands' use of force as justified or abusive, they never suggested that women's violence might be legitimate. They did not perceive wives to have any culturally or legally authorized rights to discipline their husbands, or even to defend themselves. Moreover, although observers of all kinds intervened in disputes when men abused their wives, they seemed very hesitant to step in when men were the subjects of violence.

Spectators who were slow to come to husbands' aid may have taken their cues from husbands themselves, who seem to have been more reluctant to seek aid than their wives. Men rarely utilized the repertoire of publicizing strategies which their wives deployed, nor did they use the courts to seek relief. Men could not use separations as a legal remedy for domestic violence as their wives could, but they did not seem to use the courts at all to respond to spousal violence. While men in the Netherlands in the late eighteenth century used custody orders to have violent wives committed, urban men in France in the seventeenth and early eighteenth century at least chose to represent their disgruntlement in such petitions as rooted in their wives' immorality, not their own treatment at her hands.[111] When masculinity was defined in part by men's ability to maintain an orderly household, a man who could not even control his wife was perhaps more

[110] ADLA B5851, 2 August 1714.

[111] For patterns in the Netherlands, see Lis and Soly, *Disordered Lives*, 85–91.

likely to find himself the subject of derision than sympathy, and might have been reluctant to take his domestic strife to the community.

The use of violence on children, albeit scantly documented, again indicates patterns that both overlapped and diverged from other forms of family violence. The material culture of early modern life that made neighbours unavoidably aware of wife-beating also kept them abreast of the use of force against children. Two neighbours of Marie Dargent and André Gabory, for instance, noted that they not only lived next door, but that the divisions between their homes were so flimsy, with holes in the walls, that they could easily see as well as hear what was going on. Gabory himself said that 'the cries of these poor unhappy children' when their mother abused them 'made all the neighbours weep'.[112]

Boundaries between appropriate and inappropriate use of force existed in practice with regard to children, as they did for wives, but they were drawn differently. Community tolerance for the use of parental force on children may have been higher than for husbands' beating of wives, and on the rare occasions when judicial intervention was sought, the issue of the authority of the person who used the force to do so, rather than the question of the level of force, seems to have been the primary question. When evidence of child battery did enter court dockets, the issue was usually who had the right to discipline children rather than the treatment of the child *per se*. In 1666, for example, Perrine Rouard and her husband, a shoemaker, petitioned the court in 1666 for redress against Madame Legendre, the wife of a cakemaker. Rouard complained about the damage to her reputation inflicted by Legendre's insults. The source of the women's dispute, however, was Legendre's treatment of her 2-year-old child, whom she had chased down the street, shouting and hitting. When Rouard told her that she was wrong to treat such a young child in such a manner, and and added that if she had a child she would not treat her like that, the women began a shouting match. Janne Duboys' complaint against Madame Lehoux resulted from a similar pattern. Duboys complained that Lehoux had thrown herself on her, torn off her cap, and beaten her in the aftermath of a dispute about the treatment of a child. Their dispute suggests another boundary of informal management of the treatment of children rather than judicial resolution. Duboys's neighbours alerted her that someone was beating her 'ten or eleven'-year-old son in the market-place near the house. She ran over to find Lehoux, a secondhand seller, hitting her son. Lehoux said she did it because the boy had beaten her son. Duboys claimed to have responded that 'it wasn't up to her to chastise him and she [Leroux] ought to have brought her complaint to' Dubois as the boy's mother.[113] This sense of parental obligation and right to the discipline of children being up to parents was occasionally articulated in other disputes too.[114]

112 ADLA B6184, 12 and 15 January 1743.

113 ADLA B6670, 19 June 1666; ADLA B6664, 9 November 1647.

114 ADLA B6682, 9 September 1695.

The dynamics of child or husband abuse shared important features with abuse of husbands that differed from wife-beating in terms of the willingness to publicize difficulties, and of the option of institutional remedy. Children, even more clearly than husbands, did not themselves seek to remedy their distress with the strategies used by battered women, whether to engage in the forms of publicity or to go to court. Legal remedy was elusive. When older children, at least teenagers or older, did occasionally complain to the courts, they usually did not make the mistreatment itself the subject of their requests, but used it to justify particular courses of action. In Lyon in the 1670s, for example, Blaize and Eleonor Coquet (sisters in their early twenties) had stayed in a convent for a couple of months due to their father's battery, but could not afford to stay there any longer. They asked to be allowed to live with their mother, due to their father's battery, even though their parents were not legally separated. The court agreed. Two other children in their twenties both complained that their fathers used violence to make them sign contracts of various kinds against their wishes, and asked the court to record their opposition to whatever documents they might subsequently sign in their fathers' presence.[115] However, even adult children's efforts to use the courts to manage parental abuse were very rare.

A comparison of the different legal opportunities available to the various victims of household battery suggests that three key factors shaped the availability of remedies for family violence: property, publicity, and extended kin. The early modern legal system had a broad commitment to the protection of property, and battered wives were able to use the property of their labour and lineage claims as an avenue to seek legal redress. Adult children who did occasionally seek to find a legal remedy for their abuse used property issues as their wedge. Minor children had no property claim on which to stake a judicial case. Moreover, wives themselves initiated cases. both literally when they went to court, and more broadly in their efforts to create a context of local knowledge by publicizing their difficulties. Children could not initiate cases alone, and had nobody who could do so on their behalf. The neighbours who were aware of household abuse, and might seek to regulate some manifestations of it, certainly did not usually initiate legal proceedings on behalf of any family battery victim. A wife's possession of a legal claim to safeguard her dowry, and extended kin who continued to have a lineage property interest in her property, provided her with the possibility of seeking a legal form of protection. Children lacked these assets, as well as the sensibility about the imperative for publicity. Parents who might go to court to seek redress if an outsider abused one of their children because of the damage to the family's honour, found they had more leeway to abuse their own children. Like children, although for different reasons, elite women and husbands usually did not engage in the campaigns of publicity about their difficulties, of which going to court was one element.

[115] ADR BP3984, 30 March 1674; ADR BP1643, 30 April 1700; ADR BP1643, 29 July 1705.

The few instances of family violence evident in high-status households hint that rank was vitally important. Although elite women faced a lower prescriptive legal standard than working women for their husbands' actions to be classified as 'abuse', some were still battered, and in practice they may have had fewer resources.[116] Their concern for the preservation of family reputation may have trumped their willingness to use the strategies of publicity. Moreover, while all early modern women faced the stereotype of female wantonness, they were not regarded as equally likely to be promiscuous, and their sexuality was not equally charged. If widows and single women were well-known likely targets for allegations of sexual misconduct, elite men's preoccupation with wifely sexuality might suggest that their spouses had to meet narrower definitions of chaste living and appropriate interactions with men than other married women.[117]

The parallels and differences between wife-beating and other forms of family violence are illuminating. While a neighbourhood negotiation about legitimate use of force included wives and children, responses to, and resources for, family violence varied quite widely, depending on the status of the victim. The experiences of battered elite women, husbands, and children suggest that their responses and resources varied significantly from their contemporaries in urban working communities, although we need to know much more about the attitudes to, and patterns of, the many forms of family violence to draw firm conclusions. They do make clear, however, the imperative need to recognize the contingencies that shaped experiences of early modern family violence.

FAMILY VIOLENCE, NEIGHBOURHOOD VALUES, AND LEGAL REMEDIES

Whether household battery was more or less widespread in early modern French cities than at other times in other places is difficult to gauge, and any useful quantifiable measure is probably impossible.[118] The historical resilience

[116] Susan Amussen suggests that in early modern England 'women most vulnerable to domestic violence were those cut off from the community—usually women of gentry status.' Amussen, 'Being Stirred to Much Unquietness', 81. Elite women were not cut off, but their distinctive circumstances do suggest, as I argue here, that the experiences and resources of elite wives who were battered, differed from those of women of lower status.

[117] Elite women's particular forms of vulnerability may have persisted into the twentieth century. Laws introduced to protect wives from men's violence in England from 1870, for instance, framed domestic battery as a working-class phenomenon. For the class bias of legislation to police domestic violence, see Ross, *Love and Toil*, 86.

[118] It seems impossible to establish any usable quantitative sense of the pervasiveness of battery at any historical moment. The debate over whether domestic violence increased or decreased over the long term is filled with pitfalls. While we may tend to assume that domestic violence has become less common (at least in the casual use of mundane force that early modern communities broadly

of family violence is stunning, and requires historians to acknowledge that continuities matter in the histories of violence, of women, of children, and of gender dynamics in families.[119] Yet early modern discussions of family violence illustrate not only the specific conditions of domestic battery in particular circumstances, but point to the changes in authorizations and justifications as well as experiences of battery, responses and resources. In early modern urban communities, family violence was interwoven with the fabric of the economies of daily life that included marital status, law, borrowing and violence as well as rank and gender. The politics and culture of family violence were embedded in material, legal, economic, sexual, and cultural factors. Litigation communities were active in the management of force, as they were of debt or marital expectations, and in that community assessment an economy of information played an important role.

Although early modern law broadly legitimized men's use of force for household discipline and provided a means of social discipline for women in a variety of ways, the particularities of legal systems could channel conflict, and shaped battered wives' resources. French women's legal rights to property fuelled conflicts in specific forms. Husbands who needed wives' consent to the alienation of resources designated as their lineage property, faced obstacles to their management of households that were not present where no such restrictions encumbered men's right to manage household property, such as in England or colonial British America. Consequently, loans were a volatile matter in domestic relations and in family violence, whereas other issues took centre stage elsewhere.[120] In France itself, the Revolutionary abolition of lineage property left nineteenth-century husbands without any such difficulty. Although divorce was illegal in early modern France, wives and judges used the possibility of separations of either kind as a means to reprimand husbands whose behaviour was abusive. The publicity, process, and potential consequences probably offered more valuable resources than other legal regimes in which the potential for divorce existed in principle but was rarely accessible in practice, as in England, or was available for causes such as adultery or desertion but not for battery, as in early New England colonies.

tolerated), contemporary experts in intimate violence note that even with zero tolerance legislation, wives and neighbours in many communities in practice remain reluctant to define a wide range of abusive behaviour as 'violence', and force often has to be repeated and extensive before intervention is sought. I thank Jeana Lungwitz for this point.

[119] For a forceful statement about the power of continuity in gendered patterns in another realm, women's work, see Judith Bennett, *Ale, Beer, and Brewsters: Women's Work in a Changing World, 1300–1600* (Oxford, 1996), esp. 6–8 and 152–7.

[120] Studies of battery in Britain for the early modern era and nineteenth century, for example, all show a variety of financial issues to have been at stake in domestic violence, but none of these focused specifically on loans, as so often in the French case. See Amussen, 'Being Stirred to Much Unquietness'; Clark, *Struggle for the Breeches*; Hunt, 'Wife beating, domesticity, and women's independence in eighteenth-century London'; Leneman, 'A tyrant and tormentor'; Ross, 'Fierce questions and taunts'; and Tomes, 'A torrent of abuse'.

Regional differences in early modern legal regimes may have had little impact on the incidence of battery, but they powerfully shaped wives' resources.[121]

Expectations about male sociability, female speech, and household economies shaped practices of domestic violence in early modern families. Husbands and wives who both worked and both contributed to building resources, negotiated, argued, and came to blows over the allocation of resources in terms of cash, credit, and consumption. Early modern women in working families were strikingly quick to publicize their battery, to blame their husbands, and to seek the intervention of neighbours and family, who were in turn ready and willing to provide help and judgement. Although we think of early modern Europe as a violent place, early modern urban communities problematized the use of force, and were quick to endorse appropriate and inappropriate resorts to violence. Peers carefully coded men's violence against women, and the reputations of men considered to be batterers rather than discipliners were damaged. Battered women did not blame themselves in the manner characteristic of later periods, and were able to utilize the cultural and logistical imperatives that drove public oversight of marriages and of conflict to mobilize warnings, intervention, aid, reprimand, and mediation. A woman who was unjustly beaten merited relief, and her spouse needed discipline. The strategies of women and communities in managing domestic battery were in all these ways also part of a broader culture of violence management rooted in neighbourhoods.

The dynamics of family violence played out as part of processes that were central to many aspects of the family business whose political economies of daily life were matters of concern for households, communities, and the state. Litigation communities discussed, contested, and negotiated the parameters of family violence in and out of court, as they did many other matters. The circulation of information was as critical in community assessment as it was in the handling of credit extension or debt collection. The willingness of victims to participate in this economy of information, and their skill in shaping the representations of their situation within it, were critical, whether in domestic violence or debt. Similarly, the victims of family violence made choices about whether to go to court or to seek some other means of relief. The specifics of the legal and cultural construction of property, and the attitudes of communities and judges to protecting it, were pivotal. The critical significance of the community in making matters subjects for judicial, and thus state, supervision was highlighted in the handling of family violence as a civil and property rather than criminal matter.

[121] For example, early modern Venetian women could apparently use cases for separations of person and property (still heard in church courts in Italy) to protect themselves against battery while women in colonial Connecticut could not obtain divorces on the grounds of cruelty, however serious, until the mid-eighteenth century. Ferrero, 'The Power to Decide'; Cornelia Hughes Dayton, *Women before the Bar: Gender, Law, and Society in Connecticut, 1639–1789* (Chapel Hill, NC, 1995), 105–56.

The family business in which states, communities, and working families were enmeshed in the long seventeenth century engaged with working out meanings and practices which were in transition in the early modern world, but perhaps families of high status in the seventeenth and early eighteenth centuries may have been at the leading edge of changing attitudes to violence and domestic life, and to uses of the legal system. As the use of violence became increasingly unacceptable and even embarrassing, and expectations about the privacy of family life became sharper, domestic battery became something to be hidden or ignored. Elite wives who were beaten were reluctant to let anyone know, because violent behaviour was increasingly frowned upon. By the middle decades of the eighteenth century, both the persistence of dynamics crystallized in previous decades and the emergence of new, strikingly different patterns highlighted the complex topography of the long history of the relationship between families, states, and economy.

Epilogue: Family Business on the Cusp of the Modern World

In 1743, André Gabory, a dyer, asked the Nantes provost to commit his wife, Marie Dargent, to stop her abuse of their children. Gabory and Dargent had 'eight or nine children', the oldest of whom was about eleven, as well as his two children from a previous marriage. Witnesses graphically alleged many varieties of cruelty. Dargent forbade the children to come near the fire in winter, with the result that at least one of them had frostbite. She beat them with 'instruments' that included wet and dry ropes as well as rods, so the children were covered with multiple bruises and wounds, and had 'blood running down their bodies'. She pushed one daughter onto the fire irons so that she was burned over a considerable part of her body. Another was locked naked in a room for a beating that left 150 bruises on her body. Dargent brutalized her younger as well as older children: a 23-month-old was black and blue 'from head to toe and back and front'. Gabory described their family life as a 'perpetual war' due to his wife's 'barbarity', and noted that he sometimes left the house for days at a time to avoid his wife's wrath. He blamed her for the 'ruin' of his trade.[1]

Neighbours observed, reprimanded, helped, and finally joined with Gabory to urge the court to put Dargent in the city's poorhouse to save the children from her 'cruelty'. When they found one of the children naked outside in the middle of the night, they took her to an aunt's house. One neighbour, who recalled that Marie Dargent's 'favourite occupation' was to beat the children severely, 'sometimes remonstrated with her that she was not right to abuse them so seriously'. Another said that she too 'had remonstrated' with Dargent, telling her 'she was wrong to treat [the children] in such a manner'. On several occasions, the children's cries led 'a group of neighbours' to gather 'at the door' of Gabory's shop, although they feared to enter in case they too were subjected to similar treatment. She was thought of, they claimed, in 'all the neighbourhood as a mad woman who must be shut up'. The court agreed to commit Dargent.[2]

1 ADLA B6184, 12 and 15 January 1743.

2 She was sent to the Sanitat—a nominal hospital that also served as a poorhouse, a place of confinement for prostitutes, and an asylum.

Gabory's complaint on behalf of his children is the only extant petition dated before 1750 for either Nantes or Lyon when an individual turned to the courts with the explicitly articulated goal of seeking a remedy for violence against children. This was a request that did not fit into any usual judicial category, and as such it hints at changing constructions of 'family business' as well as ongoing challenges. While we cannot know how typical or atypical any one case may be, the dynamics of the Gabory–Dargent case, like other disputes that came to court in the middle decades of the eighteenth century, suggest some of the ways in which economies of daily life continued to share key qualities with those evident in the long seventeenth century that this book has explored, and point to the emergence of new trends that would become ever more powerful in subsequent decades. If family business remained critical for the state, communities, and individual household members as the early modern world gave way to the modern, expectations evolved for spouses and their neighbours as well as states about how families could and should appropriately secure stability, productivity, and morality. While households still struggled to make ends meet and to regulate relations between family members, new emotional grids for domestic life developed, litigation rates declined in favour of new ways of managing household difficulties, the meanings and practices that underlay borrowing were redefined, and attitudes to violence were revised. In the Gordian knot of family business, shifts in the political economies of daily life were enmeshed and intertwined.

In the short and long term, powerful continuities characterized the political economies of daily life as the family, economy and state triad continued to be inextricably linked. Marriage remained a process and a risk, and marital status a negotiable resource, as the experience of the Dargent–Gabory household showed. The political potential of economies of litigation remained clear. The courts were still as much an option for local communities as they had been in the seventeenth century. Indeed, three of the women who testified in the case not only expressed their concern and frustration, but suggested to the court the remedy of the poorhouse. With their recommendation of a solution, these female witnesses went far beyond speaking to the facts of the case. Surely neighbours, and perhaps Gabory, had discussed what should happen out of court, and they may have known he had asked for this remedy or even urged him to do so. Their initiative in articulating this case to the court suggests a strong sense that husband, family, and neighbours hoped the court would recognize and enforce the opinion of the community that Dargent should be removed from her children. The ghastly circumstances of the Garbory–Dargent children indicate that communities in this matter, as in others, still considered going to court as a tool that could be mobilized to authorize and enforce neighbourhood judgements, even if no specific institutional legal remedy existed.

Local legal cultures like these, embedded in litigation communities of the kind that had powerfully shaped judgements in city courts of first instance in the seventeenth and eighteenth centuries, continued to sway legal decision-making. Whether in nineteenth-century domestic violence suits or twentieth century bankruptcy cases, the perspectives of the community remained important shapers of legal practice.[3] Although litigation rates *per* se dropped in the eighteenth century, law courts continued to be critical sites for interplay between state and community.

For state and subjects, and then state and citizens, the legal process remained an important site of political, economic, and cultural production in which family business was central. The valencies of domestic life for political patterns continued to be potent. The emphases of wives' petitions remained remarkably consistent until the Revolution: a stable litany of complaints about financial and physical abuse, with embroiderings about inappropriate sexuality and occasional use of more explicitly political language.[4] These continuities suggest that a deeply rooted local discourse about domestic politics provided an easily available language to justify political opposition of all kinds. From the 1760s, in both court cases and print culture, attacks on the royal family and other elite families used the themes of gender disorder, sexual immorality, and financial wrongdoing to symbolize all that was wrong with the Ancien Régime. These themes were not, in fact, novelties as much as more widely publicized articulations of concerns that working families had long negotiated in their own local litigation.[5]

The compelling political Revolutionary discourse about the alleged threats that the royal family in particular, and noble families at large, posed to political stability, economic productivity, and cultural morality indicates the long life of family business, but the experience of negotiating familial authority provided

[3] For these more recent examples of the impact of local legal cultures, see, for instance, Eliza Ferguson, 'Judicial authority and popular justice: crimes of passion in fin-de-siècle Paris', *Journal of Social History*, **40**, 2 (2006); Teresa A. Sullivan, Elizabeth Warren, and Jay Lawrence Westbrook, *As We Forgive our Debtors: Bankruptcy and Consumer Credit in America* (Oxford, 1989); and Teresa A. Sullivan, Elizabeth Warren, and Jay Lawrence Westbrook, *The Fragile Middle Class: America in Debt* (New Haven, 2001).

[4] For the very similar patterns in Parisian wives' complaints (albeit to police rather than courts) in 1775 to those voiced in Lyon and Nantes a century earlier, see Jeffrey Merrick, 'Domestic conflicts and political culture in late eighteenth-century France', in Suzanne Desan and Jeffrey Merrick (eds.), *Family, Gender, and Law in Early Modern France* (University Park, PA, 2009).

[5] For the importance of lawsuits that framed political critiques in domestic terms in the political culture of the decades before the Revolution, see, for example, Sarah Maza, *Private Lives and Public Affairs: The Causes Célèbres of Prerevolutionary France* (Berkeley, CA, 1993). I would suggest that the novelty was in the much broader publicity about these kinds of cases rather than in their politics. For the Revolution itself as a family affair, see Suzanne Desan, *The Family on Trial in Revolutionary France* (Berkeley, 2004), as well as Lynn Hunt, *The Family Romance of the French Revolution* (Berkeley, 1992).

For an illustration that these critiques of the royal household were economic as well as political, see Claire Crowston, 'The queen and "Her Minister of Fashion": gender, credit, and politics in pre-Revolutionary France', *Gender and History*, **14**, 1 (2002).

more than a family discourse of politics in terms of state formation. Working people's lived experiences of the state were more fluid and heterogeneous than the monolithic and expansive reach of royal legislation and rhetoric imagined. The state had a capacity for initiative, but the community also had the ability and willingness to invite in the state, in early modern terms, largely through use of its courts and later through multiplying bureaucracies, to help manage personal situations. The character of that intersection depended, in the seventeenth century and in subsequent centuries, in large part on whether working families saw the court system working in ways that met their perceptions of what was appropriate.

Moreover, the challenges of daily life for working families were persistent. Violence survived as a feature of spousal relations, even as attitudes towards the use of force changed. Although the statistical rate of domestic violence is impossible to assess reliably, historians have argued that the nineteenth century saw higher rather than lower rates of domestic violence. For elite families, the eschewal of violence became a marker of status, and later legislation would frame domestic abuse as a working-class phenomenon; but this same prescriptive rejection of intimate violence may have made elite women even less likely to make any abuse public or to go to court. It is less clear whether working-class families even regarded all use of violence between spouses as wrong, and they may have continued to differentiate between legitimate force and abuse.[6]

The relationship between gender, family, and economy remained critical. Amy Erickson observed that whereas historians have considered at length how economic matters have shaped gender, the question of how gender has shaped economic patterns is just as significant.[7] Similarly, families shaped the transition to the market as well as being the subjects of it, and continued to be agents and objects of the changing economy. Borrowing remained a fundamental household instrument throughout the following centuries, as well as a critical element of commercial activity. In fact, the expansion of consumption, and the extension of shop credit to women, allowed the continual renegotiation of patterns apparent in the seventeenth century. Although informal credit practices were institutionalized in the nineteenth century, and consumption became feminized, courts favoured bolstering husbands' authority (and protecting family property) over creditors' right. In the nineteenth century, families shaped the development of production

6 For the class basis of domestic violence legislation in the nineteenth century, see Ellen Ross, *Love and Toil: Motherhood in Outcast London*, 86. For an important study of intimate violence in late nineteenth-century Paris that refigures many historiographical assumptions based on work on England, see Eliza Ferguson, 'Reciprocity and retribution: negotiating gender and power in fin-de-siècle Paris', *Journal of Family History*, **30**, 3 (2005), 287–303. As more detailed work is done, the need to consider variations within and across national and chronological timeframes becomes more apparent.

7 Amy Erickson, 'Coverture and capitalism', *History Workshop Journal*, **59**, 1 (Spring, 2005) 1–16.

in critical ways.[8] Issues about gender and family remained key to the structuring of the economy long into the history of capitalism.

Yet a series of overlapping and intertwined shifts in the political economies of daily life reframed lived experience in some important ways. A significant adaption in the economies of marriage became evident by the mid-eighteenth century. A new language of marriage began to appear. Whereas seventeenth-century wives had acknowledged a gender hierarchy in which they owed obedience and respect, even while they emphasized the obligations of their husbands, as the mid-eighteenth century approached, some wives began to employ a rhetoric that reframed marriage as a matter between equals, based on affection. When Marie Bree told her husband that she 'wanted to have her turn as master' she envisioned spousal roles in terms different from those of her peers in previous generations. The transitory nature of this change was evident in the varying responses of observers of their conversation. A widow who overheard it while in their shop noted the comments without any elaboration. A lawyer who was there at the same time described her assertion as 'very unrespectful'. The judge who denied her request for separation of person and property told her to give her husband 'honour and reverence'; that is, he reiterated the customary language of marriage.[9] Likewise, whereas wives and witnesses had previously articulated the material factors in spousal choice quite openly, discussions of marriage began to condemn marriage for 'interest' (by which they meant property) as bad, and marriage for 'affection' as good. In a sign that the shift was not strictly gender specific, a husband in a contentious case supported his claim to be the wronged spouse by calling numerous witnesses who confirmed that his wife had said on many occasions that she had married him for his property rather than for affection.[10] Litigation communities shifted from a linguistic code that openly acknowledged labour and property as central in marriage, to one that valorized companionship based on mutual affection.[11] Moreover, while seventeenth-century jurists had

[8] The best work on borrowing from the eighteenth century onward is for England. Erika Rappaport, '"A Husband and His Wife's Dresses": consumer credit and the debtor family in England, 1864–1914', in Victoria de Grazia with Ellen Furlough (eds.), *The Sex of Things: Gender and Consumption in Historical Perspective* (Berkeley, CA, 1996), *passim*. On ubiquitous borrowing patterns and their implications in the later eighteenth and nineteenth centuries in England, see Margot Finn, *The Character of Credit: Personal Debt in English Culture, 1740–1914* (Cambridge, 2003). For examples of how gender and family issues shaped economic development in the nineteenth century, see Tessie Liu, *The Weaver's Knot: The Contradictions of Class Struggle and Family Solidarity in Western France, 1750–1914* (Ithaca, 1994), and Tamara Hareven, *Family Time and Industrial Time: the Relationship between the Family and Work in an Industrial New England Community* (Cambridge, 1982).

[9] This is the earliest reference I have found to this kind of language. Another witness decribed a variation of the same claim: she wanted 'to be the master as well as him'; ADLA B6172, 11 March 1717.

[10] See, for instance, the testimony of witnesses in ADLA B5855, 7, 8 July 1729.

[11] For the connotation of 'amitié' as mutual affection between peers, see the various eighteenth-century lexicographical definitions cited by the ARTFL project: http://colet.uchicago.edu/cgi-bin/dico1look.pl?strippedhw=amitie

decried 'divorce' as against God's will but spouses and their witnesses never used the phrase, women and their neighbours began to use 'divorce' as a popular synonym for rupture in the following century.[12] If seventeenth-century spouses understood that the terms of even hierarchical marriage could be renegotiated if either spouse failed to meet their obligations, eighteenth-century working people began to reframe marital relations in ways that emphasized equality and the possibility of dissolution rather than renegotiation. While this new emotional grid resonated with the much discussed rise of companionate marriage, there is no evidence that mere emulation of elites caused this shift.[13] Rather, working families' notions of marriage evolved as one integral element of a multifaceted shift in the political economies of daily life.[14]

Changing patterns of separations were part of a new economy of marital status. Although lack of research makes it impossible to establish whether the numbers of petitions for separate property changed absolutely in the eighteenth century, it is clear that cases for separation of person and property both declined in number and became more difficult for wives to win. In Nantes, separate property requests outnumbered those for separations of property and person by 4 to 1 between 1650 and 1699, but by more than 10 to 1 between 1700 and 1750 (see Table 1.1). Elsewhere in France, separations of person and property seem to have become not only rarely requested, but even more difficult to secure over the course of the eighteenth century. Property separations outnumbered separations of person and property by the huge margin of more than 40 to 1 in Paris in the mid- to late eighteenth century. By the 1780s, only 10 per cent of requests for such actions in the northern city of Rouen were successful. Only where separations remained under the authority of church courts did wives have a high rate of success in pursuing these kinds of action.[15] These instances seem, however, to have been entirely exceptional.

[12] The first reference I have found to this use of divorce is by a female witness in 1716; ADLA B5852, 23 June 1716.

[13] A vast literature exists on the history of marriage and the rise of 'companionate marriage'. For a starting point, see Martha Howell, 'The properties of marriage in late medieval Europe: commercial wealth and the creation of modern marriage', in Isabel Davis, Miriam Muller, and Sarah Rees-Jones (eds.), *Love, Marriage, and Family Ties in the Later Middle Ages* (Turnhout, 2003), 17–61.

[14] Thus I would argue that the shift in expectations about marriage occurred for different reasons in different social groups, rather than trying to locate a common cause for the rise of companionate marriage, or relying on a trickledown explanation that has underlaid much European work on the family. In contrast, historians of nineteenth-century American families have argued, for example, that New York working-class families and former slaves in the South each adopted patterns that looked like middle-class domesticity, but each for their own reasons. This multi-track model seems more persuasive. For classics statements, see Christine Stansell, *City of Women: Sex and Class in New York, 1789–1860* (New York, 1986), and Jacqueline Jones, *Labor of Love, Labor of Sorrow: Black Women, Work and Family from Slavery to the Present* (New York, 1985).

[15] For Paris, samples of three different years show that separations of person and property outnumbered property separations by a huge margin of 218 to 7. Giacomo Francini, 'Divorce and separations in eighteenth-century France: an outline for a social history of law', *The History of the Family*, 2, 1 (1997); Phillips, *Family Breakdown in Late Eighteenth-Century France: Divorces in Rouen, 1792–1803* (New York, 1980). For success in church courts, see Lottin,

Moreover, wives not only sought separations much less frequently by the mid-eighteenth century, but the few women who did so were members of far more affluent families than the working households who dominated this type of litigation in the seventeenth century. Dowries of wives who sought separations of either kind in the 1730s and 1740s were on average more than triple the size of those of their predecessors in the previous century. Going to court to resolve marriage difficulties became a much less common resort, and one that was the privilege of families who were firmly above the line of economic and political security.[16]

The new pattern of separations was intertwined with changes in economies of justice as well as marital status, as the declining numbers of separations were part of a broader downward trend in litigation. Litigation as a popular phenomenon declined in the eighteenth century in France and across Europe, for reasons that are not yet well understood. New broad concerns about civility may have been one causal factor. Other forms of dispute resolution emerged, such as police forces. Perhaps the rising use of arbitrary extrajudicial royal orders, as well as the paralysis of the judicial system that resulted from royal reform efforts in the 1770s, also may have played roles. Rising court costs may also have imposed new barriers too in the eighteenth century.[17] Whatever the cause, the decreasing resort to litigation broke the monopolies of courts and of civil litigation were broken as a key means for state to interact with families and for families to mobilize the authority of state.

New resonances about what strong families involved may have made working family members less likely to go to court. If marriage was about affection rather than property (whether in the form of labour or material), then going to court for separate property was no longer an appropriate remedy for marital woes of various kinds. A new remedy would be needed, more appropriate to the breakdown of a marriage between equals due to a shortfall of affection, however expressed. It was furnished, at least temporarily, during the French Revolution, when legislation permitted no-fault divorce by mutual consent, or unilateral divorce for a wide

'Vie et mort du couple', and Joanne Ferraro, *Marriage Wars in Late Renaissance Venice* (New York, 2001).

[16] Likewise, cases for separations of property and person in the famous eighteenth-century Des Essart published collection of celebrated court cases were all for bourgeois women. See Tracy Rizzo, *A Certain Emancipation of Women* (Selinsgrove, PA, 2004), 67.

[17] For possible explanations of the decline of litigation due to the replacement of litigation by complaints to the new police, or by the use of *lettres de cachet*, see, for example, Alan Williams, 'Patterns of conflict in eighteenth-century Parisian families', *Journal of Family History*, **18**, 1 (1993), and Arlette Farge and Michel Foucault, *Le Désordre des Familles: Lettres de Cachet des Archives de la Bastille* (Paris, 1982). On possible explanations for eighteenth-century changes in litigation practices in England, see Robert Shoemaker, 'The decline of insult in London, 1660–1800', *Past and Present*, **169**, 1 (2000), 97–131, and David Lemmings, 'Women's property, popular cultures, and the consistory court of London in the eighteenth century', in Nancy E. Wright, Margaret W. Ferguson, and A. R. Buck (eds.), *Women, Property and the Letters of the Law in Early Modern England* (Toronto, 2004).

variety of causes.[18] New concerns about privacy may have made working women, as elite women had been since earlier decades, reluctant to resort to the publicity of court cases to handle their difficulties. Although it is as yet unclear how widely strategies such as securing a royal *lettre de cachet* were used outside of Paris in the old régime, this means indubitably resolved family crises outside the public eye. A Revolutionary innovation in marital litigation practice starkly illustrated the broad sense in which the public and political implications of this dynamic changed. Revolutionary legislation not only replaced separations with divorce, but provided a new process as well as a new cause for dissolution of marriage: the no-fault divorce for incompatibility, which required no witnesses.[19] The rush of divorces in the 1790s mobilized the brief opportunity for marital renegotiation with minimal public washing of marital dirty laundry.

As individuals, communities, and the state began to think of families in new terms, ideas about solutions to family crises began to fragment. Whereas reconciliation was a broadly sought-after goal for communities and states in the long seventeenth century, the appeal of André Gabory and his female neighbours to the local court, which stood in for the state in their world to break up the household, signified a new direction. The imperatives of states to keep families together, whatever the internal dysfunction, would remain powerful in the following centuries, but the possibility of breaking up households came ever more clearly into play from several sides. Proponents of divorce and bureaucracies charged with investigating neglected children, among others, raised the possibility of the disbanding of households as the desirable outcome for 'problem' families.

If Gabory's passing reference to the 'ruin' of his trade as a result of his wife's behaviour serves as a reminder that material issues remained critical in the construction of stable families, the legal and cultural parameters that framed economies of markets in general, and borrowing in particular, shifted. The ongoing expansion of the market economy was accompanied by a collapse in the distinctions between honourable failure and fraudulent bankrupt, in popular as well as lexicographical usage. Even by 1694, the first edition of the *Dictionary of the French Académie* offered a broad definition of a bankrupt as 'someone who does not pay his debts', as well as a specific legal definition of someone whose non-payment entailed a criminal fraud. It gave the meaning 'to put a bankrupt to the pillory' as its first usage of 'pillory', suggesting a shift in punishment away from the application of a capital penalty. A despairing debtor, Claude Revollet, wrote to his brother, Claude Hacte, in Lyon in the 1690s—admittedly a very difficult decade economically, even in the context of a difficult century—that there were 'many bankrupts in the neighbourhood'.[20] His usage, like the Académie's

[18] For the Revolutionary discourse and practice of divorce, see Desan, *The Family on Trial*, 93–140.

[19] Desan, *The Family on Trial.*

[20] ADR 8B952, 27 July 1699.

definition, suggests failure to pay debts rather than criminal fraud. By the 1780s, French lexicography identified a bankrupt primarily as someone who did not pay debts, for whatever reason. It noted that the term was also an insult, while 'failure' was the polite term for non-payment of debt. By the early nineteenth century, law followed this linguistic collapse when the 1808 Commercial Code allowed for 'bankruptcy' in two categories: a 'simple bankruptcy' (failure to pay creditors) and a 'fraudulent bankruptcy' (the result of bad faith).[21]

Moreover, the emphasis on affection and children over labour and property increasingly reworked the economies of markets in the remaking of familial politics. Although Gabory mentioned that he stayed away from his work for days to avoid his wife's violence, and indicated that customers stayed away too to avoid her, he and his witnesses overwhelmingly emphasized the children's peril rather than the threat to the household's livelihood. The new emotional grid for family life foregrounded affection, or lack thereof, rather than unreliable labour as the critical evidence for marital crisis, and raised children's welfare to a new primacy. Violence against children was virtually invisible in court cases in the seventeenth century (as we have seen), and even wives with extraordinary stories of their own victimization rarely mentioned the plight of their children. On the rare occasions when they did so, they made glancing mention of the financial plight rather than the threat to physical wellbeing that the behaviour of husbands and fathers posed.

The emotive language used to describe the children's situations suggests that the hand-in-hand rise of affection and children as the defining elements of marriage worked to hide the economies of markets while accentuating sentiment. The rich language of suffering and sensitivity to pain in this case is strikingly different from seventeenth-century descriptions of family violence which were much more matter of fact. Historians have charted the rise of an 'emotional revolution' in the eighteenth century. Although contemporaries often regarded the capacity for sensibility as a preserve of elites, and historians have sometimes located the shifting emotional patterns as a bourgeois phenomenon, the eighteenth-century recasting of human experience in terms of empathy for suffering as a key to virtue circulated widely in all kinds of cultural forms, popular as well as elite, and oral as well as in print.[22] If neighbours who helped manage household and community disputes in the seventeenth century drew status from their

[21] See the evolving definitions of 'banqueroute' in French dictionaries from 1694 through the 1870s, at http://colet.uchicago.edu/cgi-bin/dico1look.pl?strippedhw=banqueroute

[22] The emergence of sensibility in the West from the mid-eighteenth century has been a rich topic in recent historiography. The phrase 'emotional revolution' is from William Reddy's interrogation of the possibility of a history of emotions which includes the most helpful discussion of the spread of sensibility in eighteenth-century France. See William M. Reddy, *The Navigation of Feeling: A Framework For the History of Emotions* (Cambridge, 2001) *passim*, but esp. 141–72. For the assumptions then and now about the class basis of sentimentalism, see Reddy as well as Rizzo, *Certain Emancipation*, and Desan, *Family on Trial*, esp. 69–89. Sensibility was an international phenomenon, and the work on Anglo-America is especially rich. See, in particular,

policing of the parameters of economies of violence and markets, observers of violence in the eighteenth century increased their own virtue (and status) with their ability to empathize with, and be horrified by, the suffering that they witnessed.[23]

Other shifts in economies of violence also took place. Strikingly, female but not male neighbours came to the aid of Dargent's children, even though observers of both sexes clearly identified the mother's treatment of her children as excessive. A gendered response to the use of force against children seems apparent. While women tried to help the children in various ways, male spectators of all kinds expressed horror but seemed reluctant to step in. Even their father seems to have been largely passive over many years. He apparently made little proactive effort on their behalf (and continued to conceive more children) until he finally went to court. He did, however, repeatedly summon a surgeon, Simon Besson, to treat the children, both at home and when they were with relatives. Besson recalled the extensive injuries he had seen on various visits, yet he took no action—not even reprimands as far as he noted—other than to treat the injuries.

In this first extant appearance of child abuse as the central feature of a petition to the local courts, the focus is firmly on women, as perpetrators and problem solvers. Not only was the language of suffering far more graphic than in earlier domestic violence cases, but the emphasis changed too. Whereas seventeenth-century witnesses characterized abusive husbands as having naturally 'violent temperaments', or tied their behaviour to drunkenness, these mid-eighteenth neighbours condemned Dargent for her 'cruelty' and 'barbarity'. Madness, they thought, must lie behind such maternal treatment. Perhaps child discipline may have been long considered a maternal responsibility.[24] Among elites, new concepts of childhood and aversions to physical punishment were part of the culture of sensibility. Yet for working families as well as states, the new family positioned women as the guardians of morality and as the culprits when virtue failed. A mother who battered her children was shockingly unnatural, and it fell to the charge of her female neighbours to help the poor children, reprimand the mother, and finally petition the court to remove her from the household.

The feminization of the handling of the crisis of the Dargent children may have gone hand in hand with broader changes in community responses to family violence. Whereas neighbours were quick to intervene if they thought wives

G. J. Barker-Benfield, *The Culture of Sensibility: Sex and Society in Eighteenth-Century England* (Chicago, 1992).

[23] For a provocative reading of the new dynamics of spectatorship in cultures of sensibility, see Karen Halttunen, 'Humanitarianism and the pornography of pain in Anglo-American culture', *American Historical Review*, **100**, 2 (1995), 303–34.

[24] There is virtually no evidence concerning this question. The beatings of Louis XIII were to be administered by a governess rather than his father, but that case is so exceptional as to require extreme caution about any extrapolation. David Hunt, *Parents and Children in History: The Psychology of Family Life in Early Modern France* (New York, 1970).

were being abused in the seventeenth century, by the mid-eighteenth century observers declined to step into a dispute which they interpreted as domestic, and male neighbours became increasingly unwilling to go to the aid of battered wives. Domestic violence shifted from a matter for public debate and regulation to the periphery of public life. By the second half of the eighteenth century, as more people began to adopt a logic of privatization, discomfort with public discussion of spousal battery may have begun to become more common.[25] Residents of working neighbourhoods in French cities were still ready to intervene in many kinds of violent conflict, but made distinctions—not made by their ancestors—about violence between spouses being a special category. When they saw a man assault a woman, they looked the other way if they thought he was her husband, or waited for family to intervene rather than offer personal help.[26]

Economies of violence evolved with the expectations about appropriate family life. As men became designated as breadwinners who assigned their wives specific sums for housekeeping, and retained spending money for their own use, and women (although they often in practice continued to contribute to the family economy in many ways) found their roles as wives and mothers given highest ideological priority, family violence continued unchecked but with new legitimizations. Thus while early modern abusive husbands articulated their actions as responses to their wives' failure to speak respectfully, men subsequently identified women's failures to perform domestic tasks as primary catalysts for their anger.[27] The use of violence against children—hardly problematized if it occurred within the family in the seventeenth century, when neighbourhoods and state concurred on wide discretion for household discipline—emerged as a serious issue in which mothers bore responsibility, whether for the abuse or for failing to stop it.[28] Meanwhile, battered wives lost the discourse of correction as a tool for self-defence in the romance of marriage for love

[25] Margaret Hunt has argued, from a sample of about ten cases, that key changes in attitudes in working families happened as early as the 1690s in England, but I find no indications of such a shift in France by that point. Margaret Hunt, 'Wifebeating, domesticity, and women's independence in eighteenth-century London', *Gender and History*, 4, 1 (1992).

[26] For Paris, see David Garrioch, *Neighbourhood and Community in Paris, 1740–1790* (Cambridge, 1986), esp. 5 (for refusal to help if a husband was presumed to be the batterer) and 80 (for neighbours deferring to kin in regulating domestic disputes); Roderick Phillips, *Putting Asunder: A History of Divorce in Western Society* (New York, 1988), 337–8, argues that male neighbours were unwilling to intervene in Rouen in the 1790s.

[27] For the development of breadwinning and housekeeping identities in working families as key structures in conflicts between spouses, and the centrality of failure to perform domestic tasks as the major rhetorical focus: Anne Clark, *The Struggle for the Breeches: Gender and the Making of the British Working Class* (Berkeley, CA, 1995), Ellen Ross, '"Fierce Questions and Taunts": married life in working-class London, 1870–1914', *Feminist Studies*, 8, 3 (1982), and Nancy Tomes, 'A "Torrent of Abuse": crimes of violence between working-class men and women in London, 1840–1875', *Journal of Social History*, 11, 3 (1978).

[28] For the focus on mothers as the investment of states in child welfare grew, see, for instance, Sylvia Schafer, 'Between paternal right and the dangerous mother: reading parental responsibility in

which permitted little acknowledgement of family violence. Domestic violence gradually became a criminal rather than civil legal matter, with legislation passed, for instance, in England in 1870, but not until the twentieth century in France. In practice, however, any legal recourse became very difficult, as both wives and their peers clearly increasingly blamed women for the treatment meted out by their husbands. The enhanced association of women with the maternal morality that accompanied a modern emotional familial regime, based on sensibility and companionship, also emphasized women's responsibility for family problems.

In all these regards, the relationship of litigation to economies of information shifted. The option of going to court, and the strategy of using the publicity that it entailed, was an important resource for the management of the political economies of daily life in the seventeenth century. Yet as new concerns about privacy arose, going to court in the eighteenth century became a potentially dangerous way of exposing oneself and one's family to public and political scrutiny. The publicity that had been key to resource management in the previous century became something to be avoided as the line between personal and public was demarcated more clearly as a concept, especially in terms of family matters.

The long history of family business highlights the centrality of the lived experiences of working families in comprehending major political, economic, and cultural transitions. Whether for Louis Thebaudeau and Marie Monnier and their peers in the seventeenth century, the community of André Gabory and Marie Dargent in the mid-eighteenth century, or their modern descendants, the perils as well as promises of family business for spouses, neighbourhoods, and states have persisted even while the political economies of daily life have often been reframed. Spouses often found that the experience of marriage continued to be fraught with more uncertainty and risk than was indicated by the promise of affectionate equality. Precarious market relations and ubiquitous borrowing remained critical challenges. Violence, too, often survived as a marker of inequality in families. Legal process continued to be a powerful site of cultural production, as well as a means of subject/citizen negotiation or contestation. Then as now, families were essential as both agents and objects in the rise of the market and the process of state formation—phenomena in seventeenth-century Europe that, as we now know, were critical to the making of the modern world.

nineteenth-century French civil justice', *Journal of Family History*, **23**, 2 (1998), 173–89, and Ellen Ross, *Love and Toil*.

Bibliography

PRIMARY MATERIAL

The research for this book took place in local archives, primarily in Lyon and Nantes. I also briefly sampled court records for Macon held in the *Archives Départementales de Saône et Loire*. For maximum utility for readers with potential research interests in these archives, I provide the following brief notes to the main collections in which I worked, although I consulted many others which proved less relevant, as well as the specific references to all material used in the notes.

In Lyon I made extensive use of collections in the *Archives Départementales du Rhône* and the *Archives Municipales de Lyon*. Two big series of records proved particularly rich. The extensive court records of the Lyon *sénéchaussée* are catalogued as series BP in the Departmental Archives, for which a typescript inventory exists. The vast and almost unexplored records of the *Cour de Conservation* are divided into two: the boxes of family papers deposited as part of the legal investigations into debt are catalogued as series 8B in the departmental archives (a typescript inventory exists), and the court documents themselves are catalogued as series FF in the municipal archives (a typescript inventory is available of more than 700 boxes in this series).

In Nantes I examined all surviving records of the Nantais provost's court for the seventeenth and early eighteenth centuries, and the earliest surviving records of the city's consular court, which exist only for the eighteenth century, all of which are held in the *Archives Départementales de Loire–Atlantique*. These provost's court records—which have been divided into depositions, sentences, and so-called 'police' records (actually public disorder complaints)–are catalogued as series B. The consular court records are also catalogued as part of series B.

PRINTED PRIMARY MATERIAL

Coustumes Générales des Pays et Duché de Bretagne. Second edition. Rennes, 1680.

Coutûme Générale des Pays et Duché de Bourgogne avec le Commentaire de Monsieur Taisand. Dijon, 1698.

Bouhier, Jean. *Les Coutumes du Duche de Bourgogne*. Arnaud Jean-Baptiste Augé, Dijon, 1742.

Diderot, Dénis (ed.). *Encyclopédie ou Dictionnaire Raisonné des Sciences, des Arts et des Métiers*. 35 vols. First published 1765; reprinted by Fromann, Stuttgart, 1967.

Domat, Jean. *Civil Law in its Natural Order together with the Public Law*. Translated by William Strahan. 2 vols. Printed for D. Midwinter, London, 1737.

Favre, Antoine. *Abregé de la Practique Judiciare et Civile*. Geneva, 1627.

Ferrière, Claude Joseph de. *La Science Parfaite des Notaires ou le Parfait Notaire*. Paris, 1682; revised edition, Paris, 1741.

—— *Dictionnaire de Droit et de Practique*. Second edition, 2 vols. Au Palais, chez Brunet fils, à l'Envie, Paris, 1740.

Isambert, François. *Recueil Général des Anciennes lois Françaises depuis l'an 420 jusqu'à la Révolution.* Paris, 1829–33.

Laye, Francois. *La Nouvelle Practique Civile, Criminelle et Beneficiale ou Le Nouveau Practice Francois.* Paris, 1694.

Meslé, Jean. *Traité des Minoritez des Tutelles et des Curatelles et des Droits des Enfans Mineurs et Majeurs.* Jacques Le Febvre, Paris, 1713.

Perrier, François and Raviot, Guillaume. *Arrests Notables du Parlement de Dijon, Recueillis par M. Francçois Perrier Substitut de Mr. le Procureur Général, avec des Observations sur Chaque Question par Guillaume Raviot Ecuyer, Avocat au Parlement, et Conseil des Etats de Bourgogne.* Chez Arnauld Jean Baptiste Augé, Dijon, 1735.

Pothier, Robert Joseph. *Oeuvres Complètes de Pothier.* Depelafol, Paris, 1835.

Rochette, Claude LeBrun de la. *Les Procès Civil et Criminel Contenants la Methodique Liaison du Droict, et de la Practique Judiciare Civile & Criminelle.* Lyon, 1628.

Tagereau, Vincent. *Le Vray et Novveav Practicien François.* Dernière edition. Lavrent Metton, Lyon, 1666.

SELECT SECONDARY MATERIAL

(Forum), 'Porter Plainte: stratégies villageoises et institutions judiciares en Ile-de-France (XVIIe–XVIII siècles).' *Droit et Cultures,* **19** (1990), 7–138.

Amussen, Susan. '"Being Stirred to Much Unquietness": violence and domestic violence in early modern England.' *Journal of Women's History,* **6**, 2 (Summer 1994), 70–89.

—— 'Punishment, discipline, and power: the social meanings of violence in early modern England.' *Journal of British Studies,* **34**, 1 (January 1995), 1–34.

Andrews, Richard Mowery. *Law, Magistracy, and Crime in Old Régime Paris, 1735–1789.* Cambridge University Press, New York, 1994.

Ariès, Philippe. *Centuries of Childhood: A Social History of Family Life.* Translated by Robert Baldick. Knopf, New York, 1962.

—— *L'Homme devant la Mort.* 2 vols. Éditions du Seuil, Paris, 1977.

Astarita, Tommaso. *Village Justice: Community, Family, and Popular Culture in Early Modern Italy.* Johns Hopkins University Press, Baltimore, 1999.

Bardet, Jean-Pierre, Luc, Jean-Noël, *et al. Lorsque l'Enfant Grandit: Entre Dépendence et Autonomie.* Presses de l'Université de Paris-Sorbonne, Paris, 2003.

Barker-Benfield, G. J. *The Culture of Sensibility: Sex and Society in Eighteenth-Century England.* University of Chicago Press, Chicago, 1992.

Bayard, Françoise. 'Témoins et témoignages aux XVIIe et XVIIIe siècles. Le cas Lyonnais', in *Les Témoins devant la Justice. Une Histoire des Statuts et des Comportements,* edited by Benoît Garnot. Presse Universitaires de Rennes, 2003.

—— *Le Mondes des Financiers au XVIIe Siècle.* Flammarion, Paris, 1988.

—— *Vivre à Lyon sous l'Ancien Régime.* Perrin, Paris, 1997.

Beik, William. *Absolutism and Society in Seventeenth-Century France: State Power and Provincial Aristocracy in Languedoc.* Cambridge University Press, Cambridge, 1985.

Bell, David. *Lawyers and Citizens: the Making of a Political Elite in Old Régime France.* Oxford University Press, Oxford, 1994.

Bély, Lucien. *Dictionnaire de l'Ancien Régime: Royaume de France XVIe–XVIIIe Siècle.* Presses Universitaires de France, Paris, 1996.

Benadusi, Giovanna. 'Investing the rich of the poor: servant women and their last wills.' *American Historical Review*, **109**, 3 (June 2004), 805–26.
Benedict, Phillip. 'More than market and manufactory: the cities of early modern France.' *French Historical Studies*, **20**, 3 (Summer 1997), 511–38.
Bennett, Judith. *Ale, Beer, and Brewsters in England: Women's Work in a Changing World, 1300–1600*. Oxford University Press, New York, 1996.
Bossy, John (ed.). *Disputes and Settlements: Law and Human Relations in the West*. Cambridge University Press, Cambridge, 1983.
Bourdieu, Pierre. *Outline of a Theory of Practice*. Cambridge University Press, Cambridge, 1977.
Breen, Michael. *Law, City, and King: Legal Culture, Municipal Politics, and State Formation in Early Modern Dijon*. University of Rochester Press, Rochester, NY, 2007.
Brooks, C. W. *Pettyfoggers and Vipers of the Commonwealth: The 'Lower Branch' of the Legal Profession in Early Modern England*. Cambridge University Press, Cambridge, 1986.
Brunelle, Gayle. 'Policing the monopolizing women of early modern Nantes.' *Journal of Women's History*, **19**, 2 (Summer 2007), 10–35.
Burns, Kathryn J. 'Notaries, truth and consequences.' *American Historical Review*, **100**, 2 (April 2005), 350–79.
Carey, John. *Judicial Reform in France before the Revolution of 1789*. Harvard University Press, Cambridge, MA, 1981.
Carroll, Stuart. *Blood and Violence in Early Modern France*. Oxford University Press, Oxford, 2006.
Castan, Nicole. 'Summary Justice', in *Deviants and the Abandoned in French Society: Selections from the Annales: Economies, Sociétés, Civilisations*, edited by Robert Forster and Orest Ranum. Translated by Elborg Forster and Patricia Ranum. Johns Hopkins University Press, Baltimore, 1978.
—— *Justice et Répression en Languedoc à l'Époque des Lumières*. Flammarion, Paris, 1980.
Castan, Yves. *Honnêteté et Relations Sociales en Languedoc (1715–1780)*. Plon, Paris, 1974.
Certeau, Michel de. *The Practice of Everyday Life*. University of California Press, Berkeley, CA, 1984.
Charter, Roger (ed.). *Passions of the Renaissance:A History of Private Life*. Vol. 3, edited by Philippe Ariès. Cambridge, MA, 1989.
Chittolini, Giorgio. 'The "Private", the "Public", the "State".' *Journal of Modern History*, **67**, supplement (1995), S34–61.
Clark, Anna. *The Struggle for the Breeches: Gender and the Making of the British Working Class*. University of California Press, Berkeley, 1995.
Cohen, Anthony. *The Symbolic Construction of Community*. E. Horwood, Chichester, 1985; reprinted by Routledge, New York, 1993.
Cohen, Thomas, and Cohen, Elizabeth. *Words and Deeds in Renaissance Rome: Trials before the Papal Magistrates*. University of Toronto Press, Toronto, 1993.
Collins, James B. 'The economic role of women in seventeenth-century France.' *French Historical Studies*, **16**, 2 (Autumn 1989), 436–70.
—— *Classes, Estates, and Orders in Early Modern Brittany*. Cambridge University Press, Cambridge, 1994.

Corley, Christopher. '*Justice Gracieuse*: municipal magistrates and the state in early modern Dijon.' Paper presented at the Annual Meeting of the Society for French Historical Studies, Scottsdale, March 2000.

Croix, Alain. *La Bretagne aux 16e et 17e Siècles: la Vie, la Mort, la Foi*. Maloine, Paris, 1981.

——*Nantes et le Pays Nantais au XVIe Siècle: Etude Démographique*. S.E.V.P.E.N., Paris, 1974.

Crowston, Clare Haru. *Fabricating Women: The Seamstresses of Old Régime France 1675–1791*. Duke University Press, Durham, NC, 2001.

——'The Queen and Her "Minister of Fashion": gender, credit, and politics in pre-Revolutionary France.' *Gender and History*, **14**, 1 (2002), 92–116.

Cunningham, Hugh. *Children and Childhood in Western Society since 1500*. Longman, New York, 1995.

Daniels, Christine, and Kennedy, Michael V. (eds.). *Over the Threshold: Intimate Violence in Early America*. Routledge, New York, 1999.

Davis, Natalie Zemon. *Fiction in the Archives: Pardon Tales and Their Tellers in Sixteenth-Century France*. Stanford University Press, Stanford, CA, 1987.

——*Society and Culture in Early Modern France: Eight Essays*. Stanford University Press, Stanford, CA, 1975.

—— *The Gift in Sixteenth-Century France*. University of Wisconsin Press, Madison, WI, 2000.

—— *The Return of Martin Guerre*. Harvard University Press, Cambridge, MA, 1983.

Dayton, Cornelia Hughes. 'Rethinking agency, recovering voices.' *American Historical Review*, **109**, 3 (June 2004), 827–43.

——*Women Before the Bar: Gender, Law and Society in Connecticut, 1639–1789*. University of North Carolina Press, Chapel Hill, NC, 1995.

Debordes-Lissillour, Séverine. *Les Sénéchaussées Royales de Bretagne: La Monarchie d'Ancien Régime et ses Juridictions Ordinaires (1532–1790)*. Presses Universitaires de Rennes, 2006.

DeMause, Lloyd (ed.). *History of Childhood*. Harper & Row, New York, 1974.

Desan, Suzanne. *The Family on Trial in Revolutionary France*. University of California Press, Berkeley, 2004.

Dessert, Daniel. *Argent, Pouvoir et Société au Grand Siècle*. Fayard, Paris, 1984.

Dessertine, Dominique. *Divorcer à Lyon sous la Révolution et l'Empire*. Presses Universitaires de Lyon, 1981.

Dewald, Jonathan. Review of John Hurt, *Louis XIV and the Parlements: The Assertion of Royal Authority*. Manchester University Press, New York, 2002; in *H-France*, **2**, 81 (August 2002).

Dickinson, John A. 'L'activité judiciare d'après la procédure civile: le bailliage de Falaise 1668–1790.' *Revue d'Histoire Économique et Sociale*, **54**, 2 (1976), 163–4.

Ditte, Catherine. 'La mise en scène dans la plainte: sa stratégie sociale. L'exemple de l'honneur populaire.' *Droit et Cultures*, **19** (1990), 23–48.

Dolan, Frances. 'Household chastisements: gender, authority, and "domestic violence",' in *Renaissance Culture and the Everyday*, edited by Patricia Fumerton and Simon Hunt. University of Pennsylvania Press, Philadelphia, 1999.

Dolan, Frances. *Dangerous Familiars: Representations of Domestic Crime in England, 1550–1700*. Cornell University Press, Ithaca, NY, 1994.

Duplessis, Robert. *Transitions to Capitalism in Early Modern Europe*. Cambridge University Press, Cambridge, 1997.

Erickson, Amy Louise. 'Coverture and capitalism.' *History Workshop Journal*, **59**, 1 (Spring 2005), 1–16.

Farge, Arlette, and Foucault, Michel, *Le Désordre des Familles: Lettres de Cachet des Archives de la Bastille au XVIIIe Siècle*. Gallimard, Paris, 1982.

Farr, James R. 'On the Shop Floor: Guilds, Artisans, and the European Market Economy, 1350–1750.' *Journal of Early Modern History*, **1**, 1 (February 1997), 24–54.

——'The pure and disciplined body: hierarchy, morality, and symbolism in France during the Catholic Reformation.' *Journal of Interdisciplinary History*, **21**, 3 (Winter 1991), 391–414.

——*A Tale of Two Murders: Passion and Power in Seventeenth-Century France*. Duke University Press, Durham, NC, 2005.

——*Artisans in Europe, 1300–1914*. Cambridge University Press, Cambridge, 2000.

——*Authority and Sexuality in Early Modern Burgundy, 1550–1730*. Oxford University Press, New York, 1995.

——*Hands of Honor: Artisans and Their World in Dijon, 1550–1650*. Cornell University Press, Ithaca, NY, 1988.

Ferguson, Eliza Earle. 'Judicial authority and popular justice: crimes of passion in fin-de-siècle Paris.' *Journal of Social History*, **40**, 2 (Winter 2006), 293–316.

——'Reciprocity and retribution: negotiating gender and power in fin-de-siècle Paris.' *Journal of Family History*, **30**, 3 (July 2005), 287–303.

Ferraro, Joanne M. 'The power to decide: battered wives in early modern Venice.' *Renaissance Quarterly*, **48**, 3 (Autumn 1995), 492–512.

——*Marriage Wars in Late Renaissance Venice*. Oxford University Press, New York, 2001.

Finn, Margot. *The Character of Credit: Personal Debt in English Culture, 1740–1914*. Cambridge University Press, Cambridge, 2003.

Fontaine, Laurence. 'Antonio and Shylock: credit and trust in France, *c.*1680–*c.*1780.' *The Economic History Review*, New Series, **54**, 1 (February 2001), 39–57.

——'Women's economic spheres and credit in pre-industrial Europe', in *Women and Credit: Researching the Past, Refiguring the Future*, edited by Beverly Lemire *et al.* Berg, New York, 2001.

——*History of Pedlars in Europe*. Duke University Press, Durham, NC, 1996.

——and Schlumbohm, Jürgen (eds.). *Household Strategies for Survival 1600–2000: Fission, Faction and Cooperation*. Cambridge University Press, New York, 2000.

Forster, Robert. *The House of Saulx-Tavannes: Versailles and Burgundy, 1700–1830*. Johns Hopkins University Press, Baltimore, 1971.

Foyster, Elizabeth A. *Manhood in Early Modern England: Honour, Sex and Marriage*. Longman, London, 1999.

Francini, Giacomo. 'Divorce and separations in eighteenth-century France: an outline for a social history of law.' *The History of the Family*, **2**, 1 (1997), 99–113.

Garden, Maurice. *Lyon et les Lyonnais au XVIIIe Siècle*. Les Belles Lettres, Paris, 1970.

Garnot, Benoît (ed.). *Les Témoins devant la Justice. Une Histoire des Statuts et des Comportements*. Presse Universitaires de Rennes, Rennes, 2003.

Garrioch, David. *Neighbourhood and Community in Paris, 1740–1790*. Cambridge University Press, Cambridge, 1986.

Gascon, Richard. *Grand Commerce et Vie Urbaine au XVIe Siècle: Lyon et ses Marchands (Environs de 1520–Environs de 1580)*. S.E.V.P.E.N., Paris, 1971.

Gaskill, Malcolm. *Crime and Mentalities in Early Modern England*. Cambridge University Press, New York, 2000.

Gatrell, V. A. C., Lenman, Bruce, and Parker, Geoffrey (eds.). 'Introduction', in *Crime and the Law: The Social History of Crime in Western Europe since 1500*. Europa, London, 1982.

Gibson, Wendy. *Women in Seventeenth Century France*. Palgrave Macmillan, London, 1989.

Gordon, Linda. *Heroes of Their Own Lives: The Politics and History of Family Violence, Boston, 1880–1960*. Viking, New York, 1988.

Goubert, Pierre. 'Les officiers royaux des presidiaux, bailliages et elections.' *Dix-Septième Siècle* (1959).

Gowing, Laura. *Domestic Dangers: Women, Words, and Sex in Early Modern London*. Oxford University Press, New York, 1996.

—— 'Language, power and the law: women's slander litigation in early modern London', in *Women, Crime and the Courts in Early Modern England*, edited by Jennifer Kermode and Garthine Walker. University of North Carolina Press, Chapel Hill, NC, 1994.

—— 'The haunting of Susan Lay: servants and mistresses in seventeenth-century England.' *Gender and History*, **14**, 2 (August 2002), 183–201.

Greenshields, Malcolm. *An Economy of Violence in Early Modern France: Crime and Justice in the Haute Auvergne, 1587–1664*. Pennsylvania State University Press, University Park, PA, 1994.

Gresset, Maurice. *Gens de Justice à Besançon: De la Conquête par Louis XIV à la Révolution Française (1674–1789)*. 2 vols. Bibliothèque Nationale, Paris, 1978.

Hafter, Daryl. *Women at Work in Preindustrial France*. Pennsylvania State University Press, University Park, PA, 2007.

Haltunnen, Karen, 'Humanitarianism and the pornography of pain in Anglo-American culture.' *American Historical Review*, **100**, 2 (April 1995), 303–34.

Hanley, Sarah. 'Engendering the state: family formation and state building in early modern France.' *French Historical Studies*, **16**, 1 (Spring 1989), 4–27.

—— 'Family and state in early modern France: the marital law compact', in *Connecting Spheres: Women in the Western World, 1500 to the Present*, edited by Marilyn J. Boxer and Jean H. Quataert. Second edition. Oxford University Press, New York, 2000.

—— 'Family and state in early modern France: the marriage pact', in *Connecting Spheres: Women in the Western World, 1500 to the Present*, edited by Marilyn J. Boxer and Jean H. Quataert. Oxford University Press, New York, 1987.

—— 'The family, the state, and the law in seventeenth- and eighteenth-century France: the political ideology of male right versus an early theory of natural rights.' *Journal of Modern History*, **78**, 2 (June 2006), 289–332.

Hanley, Sarah. '"The Jurisprudence of the Arrêts": marital union, civil society, and state formation in France, 1550–1650.' *Law and History Review*, **21**, 1 (Spring 2003), 1–40.

——'The monarchic state in early modern France: marital régime government and male right', in *Politics, Ideology, and the Law in Early Modern Europe: Essays in Honor of J. H. M. Salmon*, edited by Adrianna E. Bakos. University of Rochester Press, Rochester, NY, 1994.

——'Social sites of political practice in France: lawsuits, civil rights, and the separation of powers in domestic and state government, 1500–1800.' *American Historical Review*, **102**, 1 (February 1997), 27–52.

Hardwick, Julie. *The Practice of Patriarchy: Gender and the Politics of Household Authority in Early Modern France*. Pennsylvania State University Press, University Park, PA, 1998.

——'Widowhood and patriarchy in seventeenth-century France.' *Journal of Social History*, **26**, 1 (September 1992), 133–48.

——'Women "working" the law: gender, authority and legal process in early modern France.' *Journal of Women's History*, **9**, 3 (October 1997), 28–49.

Hareven, Tamara. *Family Time and Industrial Time: The Relationship Between the Family and Work in a New England Industrial Community*. Cambridge University Press, New York, 1982.

Heywood, Colin. *A History of Childhood: Children and Childhood in the West from Medieval to Modern Times*. Blackwell, Malden, MA, 2001.

Hindle, Steve. *The State and Social Change in Early Modern England, c. 1550–1640*. Macmillan, Basingstoke, 2001.

Hoffman, Phillip. *Growth in a Traditional Society: The French Countryside, 1450–1815*. Princeton University Press, Princeton, NJ, 1996.

Hoffmann, Phillip, Postel-Vinay, Gilles, and Rosenthal, Jean-Laurent. *Priceless Markets: The Political Economy of Credit in Paris, 1660–1870*. University of Chicago Press, Chicago, 2000.

Holmes, Clive. 'Women: witnesses and witches.' *Past and Present*, **140**, 1 (August 1993), 45–78.

Howell, Martha. *The Marriage Exchange: Property, Social Place, and Gender in Cities of the Low Countries 1300–1550*. University of Chicago Press, Chicago, 1998.

——'The properties of marriage in late medieval Europe: commercial wealth and the creation of modern marriage', in *Love, Marriage, and Family Ties in the Later Middle Ages*, edited by Isabel Davis, Miriam Muller, and Sarah Rees-Jones. Brelpols, Turnhout, Belgium, 2003.

Hufton, Olwen. *The Prospect Before Her: A History of Women in Western Europe, 1500–1800*. Alfred Knopf, New York, 1996.

——'Women and the family economy in eighteenth-century France.' *French Historical Studies*, **9**, 1 (Spring 1975), 1–22.

Hunt, David. *Parents and Children in History: The Psychology of Family Life in Early Modern France*. Basic Books, New York, 1970.

Hunt, Lynn. *The Family Romance of the French Revolution*. University of California Press, Berkeley, CA, 1992.

Hunt, Margaret R. *The Middling Sort: Commerce, Gender and the Family in England, 1680–1780.* University of California Press, Berkeley, CA, 1996.

—— 'Wife beating, domesticity, and women's independence in eighteenth-century London.' *Gender and History*, **4**, 1 (March 1992), 10–33.

Ingram, Martin. 'Child sexual abuse in early modern England', in *Negotiating Power in Early Modern Society: Order, Hierarchy, and Subordination in Britain and Ireland*, edited by Michael J. Braddick and John Walker. Cambridge University Press, New York, 2001.

—— *Church Courts, Sex, and Marriage in England, 1570–1640.* Cambridge University Press, New York, 1987.

Jasinski, Jana, and Williams, Linda (eds.). *Partner Violence: A Comprehensive Review of 20 Years of Research.* Sage Publications, Thousand Oaks, CA, 1998.

Jones, Jennifer. *Sexing La Mode: Gender, Fashion, and Commercial Culture in Old Régime France.* Berg, New York, 2004.

Jordan, Constance. *Renaissance Feminism: Literary Texts and Political Models.* Cornell University Press, Ithaca, NY, 1990.

Jordan, William C. *Women and Credit in Pre-Industrial and Developing Societies.* University of Pennsylvania Press, Philadelphia, 1993.

Kagan, Richard. *Lawsuits and Litigants in Castile, 1500–1700.* University of North Carolina Press, Chapel Hill, NC, 1981.

Kaiser, Colin. 'The deflation in the volume of litigation at Paris in the eighteenth century and the waning of the old judicial order.' *European Studies Review*, **10**, 3 (July 1980), 309–36.

Kamensky, Jane. *Governing the Tongue: The Politics of Speech in Early New England.* Oxford University Press, New York, 1997.

Kaplan, Steven Laurence. *The Bakers of Paris and the Bread Question, 1700–1775.* Duke University Press, Durham, NC, 1996.

Karlsen, Carol. *The Devil in the Shape of a Woman: Witchcraft in Colonial New England.* Norton, New York, 1987.

Kessler, Amalia. *A Revolution in Commerce: The Parisian Merchant Court and the Rise of Commercial Society in Eighteenth-Century France.* Yale University Press, New Haven, CT, 2007.

—— 'A "Question of Name": merchant-court jurisdiction and the origins of the noblesse commercante', in *A Vast and Useful Art: the Gustave Gimon Collection on French Political Economy*, edited by Mary Jane Parrine. Stanford University Libraries, Stanford, CA, 2004.

—— 'Enforcing virtue: social norms and self-interest in an eighteenth-century merchant court.' *Law and History Review*, **22**, 1 (Spring 2004), 71–118.

Lanza, Janine. *From Wives to Widows in Early Modern Paris: Gender, Economy and the Law.* Ashgate, Aldershot, 2007.

Lelièvre, Jacques. *La Pratique des Contracts de Mariage chez les Notaires au Châtelet de Paris de 1789 à 1804.* Éditions Cujas, Paris, 1959.

Lemire, Beverly. *Dress, Culture and Commerce: The English Clothing Trade before the Factory, 1660–1800.* St. Martin's Press, New York, 1997.

—— Pearson, Ruth, and Campbell, Gail (eds.). *Women and Credit: Researching the Past, Refiguring the Future.* Berg, New York, 2001.

Lemmings, David. 'Women's property, popular cultures, and the consistory court of London in the eighteenth century', in *Women, Property and the Letters of the Law in*

Early Modern England, edited by Nancy E. Wright, Margaret W. Ferguson and A. R. Buck. University of Toronto Press, 2004.

Leneman, Leah. '"A Tyrant and Tormentor": violence against wives in eighteenth- and early nineteenth-century Scotland.' *Continuity and Change*, **12**, 1 (May 1997), 31–54.

Lenman, Bruce, and Parker, Geoffrey. 'State, community and criminal law', in *Crime and the Law: The Social History of Crime in Western Europe since 1500*, edited by V. A. C. Gatrell, Bruce Lenman, and Geoffrey Parker. Europa, London, 1982.

Levi, Giovanni. *Inheriting Power: The Story of an Exorcist*. Translated by Lydia G. Cochrane. University of Chicago Press, 1988.

Lis, Catharina, and Soly, Hugo. *Disordered Lives: Eighteenth-Century Families and their Unruly Relatives*. Blackwell, Cambridge, MA, 1996.

Liu, Tessie. *The Weaver's Knot: The Contradictions of Class Struggle and Family Solidarity in Western France, 1750–1914*. Cornell University Press, Ithaca, NY, 1994.

Loats, Carol. 'Gender, guilds, and work identity: perspectives from sixteenth-century Paris.' *French Historical Studies*, **20**, 1 (Winter 1997), 15–30.

Lottin, Alain. 'Vie et mort du couple: difficultés conjugales et divorces dans le Nord de la France aux XVIIe et XVIIIe siècles.' *Dix-Septième Siècle* **102–103** (1974), 59–78.

—— *et al. La Désunion du couple sous l'Ancien Régime: L'exemple du Nord*. Éditions Universitaires, Paris, 1975.

Lozanic, Nicolas. 'Le logement à Lyon au XVII et XVIIIe siècles, une approche: le bail à loyer.' *Cahiers d'Histoire*, **4** (1999), 537–58.

Mann, Bruce. *Republic of Debtors: Bankruptcy in the Age of American Independence*. Harvard University Press, Cambridge, MA, 2003.

Margolf, Diane. *Religion and Royal Justice in Early Modern France: The Paris Chambre de l'Edit, 1598–1665*. Truman State University Press, Kirksville, MO, 2003.

Marion, Marcel. *Dictionnaire des Institutions de la France aux XVIIe et XVIIIe Siècles*. Burt Franklin, New York, 1968. First published by Éditions A. & J. Picard, Paris, 1923.

Marsh, Christopher. '"Common Prayer" in England, 1560–1640: the view from the pew.' *Past and Present*, **171**, 1 (May 2001), 66–94.

Maza, Sarah. *Private Lives and Public Affairs: The Causes Célèbres of Prerevolutionary France*. University of California Press, Berkeley, CA, 1993.

Merrick, Jeffrey. 'Domestic conflicts and political culture in late eighteenth-century France', in *Family, Gender, and Law in Early Modern France*, edited by Suzanne Desan and Jeffrey Merrick. Pennsylvania State University, University Park, PA, 2009.

—— 'Domestic politics: divorce and despotism in late eighteenth-century France', in *The Past as Prologue: Essays to Celebrate the Twenty-Fifth Anniversary of ASECS*, edited by Carla H. Hay with Syndy M. Conger. AMS Press for the American Society for Eighteenth-Century Studies, New York, 1995.

—— 'Fathers and kings: patriarchalism and absolutism in eighteenth-century French politics.' *Studies on Voltaire and the Eighteenth Century*, **308** (1993).

—— 'Masculinity and effeminacy in the *Mémoires Secrets*', in *The Mémoires Secrets and the Culture of Publicity in Eighteenth-Century France*, edited by Jeremy Popkin and Bernadette Fort. Voltaire Foundation, Oxford, 1998.

—— 'The Cardinal and the Queen: sexual and political disorders in the Mazarinades.' *French Historical Studies*, **18**, 3 (Spring 1994), 667–99.

Moogk, Peter. *La Nouvelle France: The Making of French Canada: A Cultural History*. Michigan State University Press, East Lansing, MI, 2000.

Muir, Edward, and Ruggiero, Guido (eds.). 'Introduction: The crime of history', in *History From Crime*. Translated by Corrada Biazzo Curry, Margaret A. Gallucci, and Mary M. Gallucci. Johns Hopkins University Press, Baltimore, 1994.

Muldrew, Craig. *The Economy of Obligation: The Culture of Credit and Social Relations in Early Modern England*. Macmillan, Basingstoke, 1998.

Munger, Frank. 'Afterword: Studying litigation and social change.' *Law and Society Review*, 242 (1990), 595–615.

—— 'Law, change, and litigation: a critical examination of an empirical research tradition.' *Law and Society Review*, **22**, 1 (1988), 57–102.

Neuschel, Kristen B. 'Noblewomen and war in sixteenth-century France', in *Changing Identities in Early Modern France*, edited by Michael Wolfe. Duke University Press, Durham, NC, 1996.

Ogilvie, Sheilagh. *A Bitter Living: Women, Markets, and Social Capital in Early Modern Germany*. Oxford University Press, New York, 2003.

Olin, Lena Cowen. 'Fictions of the early English probate inventory', in *The Culture of Capital: Property, Cities, and Knowledge in Early Modern England*, edited by Henry S. Turner. Routledge, New York, 2002.

Ozment, Steven. *The Bürgermeister's Daughter: Scandal in a Sixteenth-Century German Town*. St. Martin's Press, New York, 1996.

Pardailhé-Galabrun, Annick. *La Naissance de l'Intime: 3,000 Foyers Parisiens, XVIIe–XVIIIe Siècles*. Presses Universitaires de France, Paris, 1988.

Parsons, Jotham. 'Governing sixteenth-century France: the monetary reforms of 1577.' *French Historical Studies*, **26**, 1 (Winter 2003), 1–30.

Peirce, Leslie. *Morality Tales: Law and Gender in the Ottoman Court of Aintab*. University of California Press, Berkeley, CA, 2003.

Phillips, Roderick. *Family Breakdown in Late Eighteenth-Century France: Divorces in Rouen, 1792–1803*. Oxford University Press, New York, 1980.

—— *Putting Asunder: A History of Divorce in Western Society*. Cambridge University Press, New York, 1988.

Piant, Hervé. 'Le prix de la vérité: témoignage, argent, et vérité dans la justice française d'Ancien Régime. Une analyse de la "taxe" des témoins', in *Les Témoins devant la Justice. Une Histoire des Statuts et des Comportements*, edited by Benoît Garnot. Presse Universitaires de Rennes, 2003.

—— *Une Justice Ordinaire: Justice Civille et Criminelle dans la Prévôté de Vaucouleurs sous l'Ancien Régime*. Presses Universitaires de Rennes, 2006.

Plessix-Buisset, Christiane. *Le Criminel devant ses Juges en Bretagne aux 16e et 17e Siècles*. Maloine, Paris, 1988.

Potter, Mark. *Corps and Clienteles: Public Finance and Political Change in France, 1688–1715*. Ashgate, Aldershot, 2003.

Rapley, Elizabeth. *Les Dévotes: Women and Church in Seventeenth-Century France*. McGill-Queen's University Press, Montreal, 1993.

Rappaport, Erika. '"A Husband and His Wife's Dresses": consumer credit and the debtor family in England, 1864–1914', in *The Sex of Things: Gender and Consumption in Historical Perspective*, edited by Victoria de Grazia with Ellen Furlough. University of California Press, Berkeley, CA, 1996.

Reddy, William M. *The Navigation of Feeling: A Framework for the History of Emotions*. Cambridge University Press, New York, 2001.

Reinhardt, Steven G. *Justice in the Sarladais, 1770–1790.* Louisiana State University Press, Baton Rouge, LA, 1991.

Rizzo, Tracey. *A Certain Emancipation of Women: Gender, Citizenship, and the Causes Célèbres of Eighteenth-Century France.* Susquehana University Press, Selinsgrove, PA, 2004.

Roche, Daniel. *A History of Everyday Things: The Birth of Consumption in France, 1600–1800.* Cambridge University Press, New York, 2000.

Roper, Lyndal. *The Holy Household: Women and Morals in Reformation Augsburg.* Oxford University Press, New York, 1989.

Ross, Ellen. '"Fierce Questions and Taunts": married life in working-class London, 1870–1914.' *Feminist Studies*, **8**, 3 (Autumn 1982), 575–602.

—— *Love and Toil: Motherhood in Outcast London, 1870–1919.* Oxford University Press, New York, 1993.

Rublack, Ulinka, *The Crimes of Women in Early Modern Germany.* Clarendon Press, Oxford, 1999.

Ruff, Julius. *Crime, Justice and Public Order in Old Régime France: The Sénéchaussées of Liborne and Bazas, 1696–1789.* Croom Helm, London, 1984.

—— *Violence in Early Modern Europe.* Cambridge University Press, New York, 2001.

Sabean, David. *Power in the Blood.* Cambridge University Press, New York, 1984.

Safley, Thomas Max. 'Bankruptcy: family and finance in early modern Augsburg.' *Journal of European Economic History*, **29**, 1 (2000), 53–75.

—— *Let No Man Put Asunder: The Control of Marriage in the German Southwest: A Comparative Study, 1550–1600.* Sixteenth Century Journal Publishers, Northeast Missouri State University, Kirksville, MO, 1984.

Salmon, Marylynn. *Women and the Law of Property in Early America.* University of North Carolina Press, Chapel Hill, NC, 1986.

Sandage, Scott A. *Born Losers: A History of Failure in America.* Harvard University Press, Cambridge, MA, 2005.

Sawyer, Jeffrey K. 'Judicial corruption and legal reform in early seventeenth-century France.' *Law and History Review*, **6**, 1 (Spring 1988), 95–117.

Schafer, Sylvia. 'Between paternal right and the dangerous mother: reading parental responsibility in nineteenth-century French civil justice.' *Journal of Family History*, **23**, 2 (April 1998), 173–89.

Schnapper, Bernard. 'Testes Inhabiles: les témoins reprochables dans l'ancien droit penal.' *Tijdschrift voor Rechtsgeschiedenis*, **33**, 4 (1965), 575–616.

Schneider, Zoe A. 'The Village and the State: Justice and the Local Courts in Normandy, 1670–1740.' 3 vols., Ph.D. thesis, Georgetown University, 1997.

—— 'Women before the bench: female litigants in early modern Normandy.' *French Historical Studies*, **23**, 1 (Winter 2000), 1–32.

Shepard, Alexandra. 'Manhood, credit and patriarchy in early modern England.' *Past and Present*, **167**, 1 (May 2000), 75–106.

—— and Withington, Phil (eds.). 'Introduction: Communities in early modern England', in *Communities in Early Modern England: Networks, Place, Rhetoric.* Manchester University Press, New York, 2000.

Shoemaker, Robert B. 'The decline of insult in London, 1660–1800.' *Past and Present*, **169**, 1 (November 2000), 97–131.

Silverman, Lisa. *Tortured Subjects: Pain, Truth, and the Body in Early Modern France.* University of Chicago Press, 2001.

Smail, Daniel Lord. 'Telling tales in Angevin courts.' *French Historical Studies*, **20**, 2 (Spring 1997), 183–215.

—— *The Consumption of Justice: Emotion, Publicity and Legal Culture in Marseille, 1264–1423.* Cornell University Press, Ithaca, NY, 2003.

Soman, Alfred. 'Le témoinage maquille: encore un aspect de l'infra-justice a l'époque moderne', in *Les Archives du Délit: Empreinte de Société*, edited by Yves-Marie Bercé and Yves Castan. Éditions Universitaires du Sud, Toulouse, 1990.

Spufford, Margaret. *The Great Reclothing of Rural England: Petty Chapmen and their Wares in the Seventeenth Century.* Hambledon Press, London, 1984.

Stallybrass, Peter. 'Patriarchal territories: the body enclosed', in *Rewriting the Renaissance: The Discourses of Sexual Difference in Early Modern Europe*, edited by Margaret W. Ferguson, Maureen Quilligan, and Nancy J. Vickers. University of Chicago Press, 1986.

Stansell, Christine. *City of Women: Sex and Class in New York, 1790–1860.* Knopf, New York, 1987.

Staves, Susan. *Married Women's Separate Property in England, 1660–1833.* Harvard University Press, Cambridge, MA, 1990.

Stone, Lawrence. *Family, Sex and Marriage in England 1500–1800.* Harper & Row, New York, 1977.

—— *Road to Divorce: England, 1530–1987.* Oxford University Press, New York, 1990.

Strasser, Ulrike. *State of Virginity: Gender, Religion, and Politics in an Early Modern Catholic State.* University of Michigan, Ann Arbor, MI, 2004.

Stretton, Timothy. *Women Waging the Law in Elizabethan England.* Cambridge University Press, New York, 1998.

Sullivan, Teresa A., Warren, Elizabeth, and Westbrook, Jay Lawrence. *As We Forgive Our Debtors: Bankruptcy and Consumer Credit in America.* Oxford University Press, New York, 1989.

—— *The Fragile Middle Class: Americans in Debt.* Yale University Press, New Haven, CT, 2001.

Taylor, Scott. 'Credit, debt, and honour in Castile, 1600–1650.' *Journal of Early Modern History*, 7, 1/2 (2003), 8–27.

Tomes, Nancy. 'A "Torrent of Abuse": crimes of violence between working-class men and women in London, 1840–1875.' *Journal of Social History*, **11**, 3 (Spring 1978), 328–45.

Traer, James. *Marriage and the Family in Eighteenth-Century France.* Cornell University Press, Ithaca, NY, 1980.

Underdown, David. 'The taming of the scold: the enforcement of patriarchal authority in early modern England', in *Order and Disorder in Early Modern England*, edited by Anthony Fletcher and John Stevenson. Cambridge University Press, New York, 1985.

Vickery, Amanda. 'Women and the world of goods: a Lancashire consumer and her possessions, 1751–81', in *Consumption and the World of Goods*, edited by John Brewer and Roy Porter. Routledge, New York, 1994.

Vries, Jan de. 'Between purchasing power and the world of goods: understanding the household economy in early modern Europe', in *Consumption and the World of Goods*, edited by John Brewer and Roy Porter. Routledge, New York, 1994.

Walker, Garthine. *Crime, Gender and Social Order in Early Modern England*. Cambridge University Press, New York, 2003.

Watt, Jeffrey. *The Making of Modern Marriage: Matrimonial Control and the Rise of Sentiment in Neuchâtel, 1550–1800*. Cornell University Press, Ithaca, NY, 1992.

Weatherill, Lorna. *Consumer Behaviour and Material Culture in Britain, 1660–1760*. Routledge, London, 1988.

Welch, Evelyn. *Shopping in the Renaissance: Consumer Cultures in Italy, 1400–1600*. Yale University Press, New Haven, CT, 2005.

Whitman, James Q. 'The moral menace of Roman law and the making of commerce: some Dutch evidence.' *Yale Law Journal*, **105**, 7 (May 1996), 1841–89.

Wiener, Martin J. *Men of Blood: Violence, Manliness and Criminal Justice in Victorian England*. Cambridge University Press, New York, 2004.

Wiesner, Merry. '*Wandervogels* and women: journeymen's concepts of masculinity in early modern Germany.' *Journal of Social History*, **24**, 4 (Summer 1991), 767–82.

—— '*Wanderwogels* and women: journeymen's concepts of masculinity in early modern Germany', in *Gender, Church and State in Early Modern Germany: Essays*. Longman, New York, 1998.

—— *Women and Gender in Early Modern Europe*. Second edition. Cambridge University Press, 2000.

Williams, Alan. 'Patterns of conflict in eighteenth-century Parisian families.' *Journal of Family History*, **18**, 1 (1993), 39–52.

Wiltenburg, Joy. *Disorderly Women and Female Power in the Street Literature of Early Modern England and Germany*. University Press of Virginia, Charlottesville, VA, 1992.

Winiarski, Douglas L. '"Pale Blewish Lights" and a dead man's groan: tales of the supernatural from eighteenth-century Plymouth, Massachusetts.' *William and Mary Quarterly*, Third Series, **55**, 4 (October 1998), 497–530.

Wollschläger, Christian. 'Civil litigation and modernization: the work of the municipal courts of Bremen, Germany, in five centuries, 1549–1984.' *Law and Society Review*, **24**, 2 (1990), 261–82.

Zeller, Olivier. 'La mobilité résidentielle de François Valesque, épicier en gros et échevin de Lyon 1706–1791.' *Cahiers d'Histoire*, 4 (1999).

Zysberg, André. 'Galley rowers in the eighteenth century', in *Deviants and the Abandoned in French Society: Selections from the Annales: Economies, Sociétés, Civilisations*, edited by Robert Forster and Orest Ranum. Translated by Elborg Forster and Patricia Ranum. Johns Hopkins University Press, Baltimore, 1978.

ONLINE MATERIAL

Dictionnaires d'autrefois: French dictionaries of the seventeenth, eighteenth, nineteenth and twentieth centuries. Eighteenth-century lexicographical definitions cited by the ARTFL project: http://colet.uchicago.edu/cgi-bin/dico1look.pl?strippedhw=amitie

Oxford English Dictionary: http://dictionary.oed.com.

Index